Robert Smythe Hichens

The Slave

A Romance

Robert Smythe Hichens

The Slave
A Romance

ISBN/EAN: 9783744673860

Printed in Europe, USA, Canada, Australia, Japan

Cover: Foto ©Thomas Meinert / pixelio.de

More available books at **www.hansebooks.com**

The Slave

A Romance

By

Robert Hichens

Author of "Flames," "The Green Carnation," etc.

London
William Heinemann
1899

This Edition enjoys copyright in all countries signatory to the Berne Treaty, and is not to be imported into the United States of America.

The Slave

CHAPTER I

On a morning in May two men were strolling in the new sunshine of London along Piccadilly. One was elderly and brown, with a skin resembling parchment, keen and piercing eyes, a wizened figure that had been always small and that now began to shrink, and hair and beard flecked with white. The other was a tall and straight boy of about twenty-three, with fine features, large blue eyes, and very thick and smooth hair, dark brown in colour and growing low on his forehead. The boy was very well dressed in the height of the fashion, and had something of the conventional, and yet elaborate aspect of the true dandy. The elderly man, on the other hand, had a baggy appearance. His suit had come from a good tailor, but it had apparently suffered an irretrievable collapse on first perceiving its wearer, and, unable to recover, it now hung about his figure dejectedly, and gave itself to the breeze or to the dust in a manner so abandoned as almost to suggest impropriety. It were impossible to find in all London two men whose aspects more plainly hinted that they were unsuitable companions. If their mere modes of dress showed a strong difference between them, this was emphasised by the expressions, wary and unwavering, of their eyes, by their strangely dissimilar gaits, even by their hands and by the manner in which they held their walking-canes. The elderly man grasped his firmly with thin and crooked fingers, and struck it sharply upon the pavement as he shuffled onwards. The young man held his lightly, almost frivolously, in the way of a hundred other young men who passed them by, going to clubs or to the Park. Many of these young men nodded to him gaily. Some glanced at his companion, but no one seemed to know him.

"I realise to-day for the first time how long I have been away," said the elderly man, whose name was Sir Reuben Allabruth. "Piccadilly contains a world of strangers. Even you—you, Aubrey," he hesitated obviously before uttering the last word, "are a stranger. You were a schoolboy when I started on my travels. Now you're what a girl calls a pretty boy—a young man with a straight nose and an air. Your mother's prouder of you now than she was even when you were at Eton, but I——."

He paused and sighed, and his sigh was ugly.

"You liked me better as a schoolboy?" said the young man in a conventional voice.

Sir Reuben glanced at him sideways.

"I knew you better," he answered. "I've been away too long. Even my few real friends seem like strangers."

"Except mother, surely?" said the young man.

"Ah! But your mother's unique, Aubrey," Sir Reuben answered, with a flash of feeling that had in it a touch of the grotesque.

"Of course. I know that," Aubrey said, with the slight impatience of one compelled to receive a truism.

He took off his hat to a dowager in purple, who made havoc of the beauty of the gentle morning in a barouche with bright yellow wheels. She smiled at him with the elephantine indulgence of a stout woman for a slim youth.

"That—surely that isn't Lady Helen Marchmont?" said Sir Reuben, looking after her.

"Yes. You knew her, didn't you?"

"She dined with me whenever I asked her. But that was eight years ago. She didn't recognise me. I suppose I have altered more than she has."

"Well, you know you're much whiter than you were," said Aubrey calmly, in the cool and unemotional voice of youth.

"Of course. Any other change?"

"You look a bit tired out," the young man answered frankly.

"Those hot climates, I suppose."

Sir Reuben glanced at him sharply, as if to surprise a sneer. He failed to surprise one, and then, remembering his companion's boy-nature, wondered at his own expectation and at the forgetfulness which had caused it.

"The hot climates!" he answered. "Yes, I suppose so. But your mother didn't seem to notice much change in my appearance."

"Oh, mother never notices anything of that kind," Aubrey said.

And again Sir Reuben was startled by his lack of memory.

"Ah, no! I remember," he said. "But if I had not altered, she might have remarked it."

"Yes. How hot the sun is!"

"It seems very cold to me," said Sir Reuben.

They did not seem to have very much to say to each other, and yet it was easy to note that they were, or had been, upon very familiar terms. The youth was perfectly at his ease. It was Sir Reuben who was a little anxious-minded, staccato, and apologetic at first. Yet, as they walked, with each step he took he appeared to be regaining an equanimity that was really natural to him. London is like an odd and difficult game to the man who has not played it for a number of years; but, if he has ever played it well, he soon remembers his old cunning, and faces the complexities of the game with an assured vivacity. By the time the walkers drew near to Bond Street Sir Reuben was happier. He had greeted two acquaintances, who had instantly recognised him. Perhaps this recognition gave him courage, or perhaps old custom breathed into him certainty and relief. He grew brighter, raised his head, and walked with lighter steps.

"I shall soon feel at home," he said.

"You—in town! I should think so," Aubrey answered.

"And yet," said Sir Reuben, "not as you are—never as you are."

He looked his companion over sharply.

"London fits you like a glove, like a glove from Vennings."

Aubrey smiled.

"It isn't Vennings for gloves now," he said.

"No?"

"Richards and Clayfield's the place now."

"I'll go there and get some gloves. Where?"

"Bond Street—the right as you go towards Oxford Street."

"Thank you! Yes, Aubrey, London fits you now, as Eton did when I went away."

The youth smiled rather cynically.

"You think so?"

"Every one must."

"Perhaps—every one in London. If we don't seem to fit our environment I think we are fools."

They turned into Bond Street.

"You would be at home anywhere?" asked Sir Reuben.

"I hope I should seem to be," Aubrey answered.

He spoke in a voice that was exactly like the voices of a thousand perfectly bred young men. Its intonations are the common property of a certain world. Sir Reuben had spent more years in London than all the years of Aubrey Herrick's life without catching one of them. It is true that he had not desired to catch them, and now he heard them come from the youth at his side with a sensation of disappointment. So her son, too, must be poured into the mould, must be cast, as it were, and turned out a statuette like all the other statuettes. Dolls of women, statuettes of men,—he saw them on every side of him. He had expected to see them, had known that he must see them. Yet the contempt of one of an alien race rose in him as he watched their antics and heard their voices—similar as the voices of two Punches, though certainly more melodious.

The Prince drove by. He was in a brougham. He caught sight of Aubrey and nodded.

"I wonder when he will be dining with me again," Sir Reuben thought.

Bond Street was full of women going to their dressmakers. Many of them were walking and carried purses in their hands. They had an air of preoccupation, and moved slowly with their faces turned towards the windows of the shops. They were often silent. Those who talked spoke of hats and bonnets, of opera wraps, of the dominating colour—the momentary queen of the hues of the world—of the most becoming tint for the hair, of the latest powder, of the latest essence, of the prettiest flower for a table decoration, of the proper height of diamond combs, of the charm— or the reverse—of a throat seen on either side of a tight collar of pearls in the evening, of the utility of earrings in lighting up a dark face, of the absurdity of a modiste who permitted her oldest clients to appear old. Their gowns rustled gently as they walked, and paused, with elvish consideration, before the acres of plate glass. One dropped her purse. Sir Reuben picked it up and gave it to her. She thanked him with a pretty stare, turned to her companion and spoke, with a pale animation, of feather boas, and of a coat which she had seen made of the breasts of seabirds. Two women drove by in a victoria. They were both celebrities, were both very thin, with white faces, dust-coloured hair, and moony smiles. Their long hands lay in their laps, and they talked, in soft and childish voices, of the last new play, condemning it. Seeing Aubrey, they shed their artificial moonlight upon him, and moved on behind their prancing horses.

"Will-power makes them so thin," Aubrey said to Sir Reuben.

"They look half-starved," he replied.

"Oh no; they have no idea of starving themselves. Who has in London?"

He spoke with such a calm simplicity that Sir Reuben did not pause to wonder if he were a cynic. They were now a little way down Bond Street, moving slowly through the crawling women whose eyes were turned to the windows. Laces fluttered against them. Flashing silks beset them as the leaves of the trees beset a man who passes through a forest. The air was full of the soft murmur of feminine voices and of the music of lightly falling feet.

Sir Reuben woke gradually to a curious consciousness of excitement. It was more than seven years since he had heard the rustle of a London crowd of smart women, and he had forgotten its subtle enchantment until now. His large dark eyes began to glow. A smile hovered on his flexible lips. He grasped his cane more tightly, and felt almost like a boy at a fair. Presently he glanced towards Aubrey, and met the calm and reserved gaze of his steady blue eyes. He was totally unconcerned, and Sir Reuben grew red in the secret consciousness of his own boyish elevation. He thought, "Nowadays it is only the old who can have sensations," and yet he wished that he were young. Then, answering Aubrey's calm gaze, he said—

"It seems quite strange to me to see so many Englishwomen again, after the eternal veils of the East, and to see them just as they were eight years ago."

"Looking into shops?"

"Exactly! They will be looking into shops on the morning of the Judgment Day. How easy it is to foresee the life and to foretell the future of many women."

"Do you think so?"

"Don't you? Now, for instance——"

He paused and glanced around. Then he touched his companion's arm and whispered—

"Look there!"

As they walked down the street they had come near to a famous jewel-shop. The crowd had thinned a little here, and they were able to see some short distance before them. Aubrey's eyes followed the gaze of Sir Reuben. It was fixed upon a girl who was standing very still before the jewel-shop. She was dressed with simplicity in black and grey, and wore a small hat which showed her face and hair distinctly. In figure she was tall and thin, like a thousand English girls; but, seen near, she was unlike them all. The live pallor of her face is sometimes seen in Italy, but in that country it is generally framed in dark hair. Her hair was very light and sparkling, as if it had been daintily frosted with some golden powder. Her features were small and aristocratic, and her eyes were very long and grey and full of glittering fire. The head was small and perfectly poised, the mouth at the same time cold and eager. She was a beauty, and a beauty of an uncommon type, fresh without being rosy, calm without being blurred and dull. Nevertheless it was her pose rather than her appearance that had riveted the eyes of Sir Reuben. In Bond Street that pose was peculiar, because it suggested a deep unconsciousness of place. It was surely the still bodily expression of a most absolute interest of the soul. Such an interest of the soul is remarkable in solitude, but it is far more remarkable in a crowd. This girl was evidently for the moment alone, so far as she was aware. She paid no heed to anything except to the shop-window before which she was standing. Her white face was strangely intent. Her long grey eyes were fixed, almost as are fixed the open eyes of one who dreams. By her side, unnoticed and obviously a little bored, waited a small and wispy woman in black, whose meek attitude was almost pathetic, and whose neat gown could have belonged to no one but a lady's-maid. The girl was gazing at some jewels. Behind the plate-glass of the shop there was a gentle slope of pale amber velvet, over which a number of small and shaded electric lights shed a strong white radiance. Stretched upon this velvet slope were diamonds—a chain, earrings, bracelets, a watch, a pendant, a narrow crown. They sparkled fiercely and glowed with a brilliance that was angry. The amber velvet was their humble foil. As they shone out to the street they were like contemptuous living things, indifferent in their glory as a woman who has her foot on the world. And the depths of their silver fire seemed illimitable. In these depths the absorbed girl drowned herself with a grave eagerness that was like the eagerness of sensuality. Her lips parted. Her eyes began to shine. Her small nostrils widened. And then suddenly there floated into her face a sort of mist of romance, of the romance of jewelled things in which lives light and changing radiance. She had been intent. She became imaginative. She had been watching—a soul in her eyes. She seemed now to be thinking—a soul in her heart. The loveliness of dreaming ran over her and the magic of desire. She developed softly into a still marvel of expression under the piercing influence of the angry jewels, which glittered at her, and at the indifferent crowd that flowed by her, with the impudence of accomplished courtesans.

As Sir Reuben touched his arm Aubrey's serenity was broken. When he saw the girl before the window he started slightly and flushed like a boy. But in an instant he had recovered himself, and Sir Reuben was unaware of the little cloud of emotion that had floated over him. Still touching his arm, Sir Reuben murmured in his ear—

"For instance, the future of that girl—can't you read it?"

"No," Aubrey said with a cold abruptness.

"It will be a future of jewels, a diamond future."

"I don't agree with you," Aubrey answered quickly, and with a flash of anger that startled his companion. "You are utterly wrong—mistaken."

As he spoke he moved forward till he stood by the girl before the diamonds. He raised his hat and addressed some words to her.

She turned slowly, withdrawing her eyes from the jewels as if the action were a renunciation which hurt her physically. It seemed that she was indeed a dreamer who could only return from dreamland with pain. But when she saw Aubrey, her lips curved upwards in a smile and she held out her hand.

"Aren't those diamonds pretty?" she said lightly.
"Beautiful! Do you want them?"
This was said for Sir Reuben.
"I suppose all women want pretty things, now and then, for a moment; and men too."

A gleam of coquetry had come into her eyes.
"Sometimes men want pretty things for longer than that," Aubrey said, lowering his voice.
"Do they?" she answered. "I thought they got tired of—things sooner than women. My mother always says so. Isn't she right? Don't answer. You aren't certain. I must be going. Poor Marie is longing to sit down."

It was her maid's normal condition of mind. She loved repose. But now, in broken English, she proclaimed a respectful preference for constant motion. Her young mistress smiled on her rhetoric indulgently, touched Aubrey's hand and moved away. Apparently she had not seen Sir Reuben, who, leaning on his stick, was waiting a few paces off. Her slim and graceful figure, attended by the trotting maid, was quickly lost in the crowd.

"So you know the diamond star-gazer?" said Sir Reuben as Aubrey joined him.
"Everybody knows Lady Caryll Knox," Aubrey answered curtly.
"Who is she?"
"Lord St. Ormyn's daughter."
"St. Ormyn's daughter! She'll get no jewels from him."

They turned into a club of which Aubrey was a member. The long smoking-room on the ground floor was almost deserted at this hour of the morning. They sat down and Sir Reuben lit a cigar. He had realised London now and regained his normal ugly self-possession.

"She is the daughter who was at school in France when I went away," he continued. "People used to say that St. Ormyn was educating her to be a governess, because he'd been hit so hard by the death duties."

Aubrey said nothing. Apparently the conversation did not please him. He looked at his varnished boots meditatively.

"Is St. Ormyn as poor as ever?" Sir Reuben asked.
"Poorer."
"I should have thought that was impossible. But Lady Caryll won't be a governess."

"No?"

Sir Reuben looked at his young companion.

"No. She has made up her mind what her life is to be."

"Really!" Aubrey said, lighting a cigarette slowly.

"Yes. How sensible that is! To succeed one must be a specialist, and one must make up one's mind, when young, what is to be one's *métier*. It is quite useless to be versatile in these crowded days. If you do two things well, you are considered an amateur; if three, a fribble. But if you do only one well, you may be a success. Imagine a doctor who was known as a first-rate doctor and as a first-rate painter. Who would give him a pulse to feel? who would buy his pictures? The shadow of medicine would blight his artistic career; the shadow of art would blight his professional triumph. Successful people are one-sided. Lady Caryll is one-sided; she sees distinctly the vista of her life to come."

"You think so?" Aubrey said, crossing his long legs with deliberation and speaking with a slightly frosty slowness.

"I am sure of it."

"And what is it, then?"

"A vista of jewels."

Aubrey shook his head slightly, but did not speak. Sir Reuben repeated—

"A vista of jewels such as Aladdin may have seen when he descended into the enchanted cavern. Imagination is rare in Englishwomen, but Lady Caryll has it. As she looked at those diamonds she saw her jewelled life, the life that she desires, that she will have. She saw her days of diamonds, of blood-red rubies, of sapphires like the sky at night, of emeralds from the mines of Muzo or from the mountains of Sahara, of orange and crimson vermilions from the East, and spotted turquoises from Persia."

As he spoke it was easy to see that foreign blood ran in his veins; his dark eyes glowed; he was in the magic cavern with Aladdin, and for him each jewel was alive and scented with strange odours of the land from which it came; he smelt the balmy spices of Ceylon, emitted with the resinous brightness of the jargoon; perfumes of India came to him with the sapphire, and with the live sparks of the grey green variolite the wild scents of the Alps; and the atmosphere of Persia, heavy with a sickliness of roses, hung about the cool turquoise. For the moment he was Oriental utterly, and drew into his high curved nostrils the breath of all the jewels of the world. Yet on the edge of rhapsody he paused, remembering that he was in London and with an English youth.

"Did you watch Lady Caryll's face when she was looking at those diamonds?" he said.

"Yes," said Aubrey.

"Don't you think she cares for jewels?"

"As she cares for all beauty. Lady Caryll loves what is beautiful. Those diamonds are beautiful; therefore she looked at them, merely for that reason."

"And lost herself in their fire? No, Aubrey; she was sunk in a lovely dream of light and colour, perhaps, but she was facing her career also. She was thinking of her future as a boy does when he decides on his profession. She means to possess jewels, as the boy means to possess—what? The Victoria Cross, perhaps, if he is going to be a soldier, or a house in Cavendish Square if he is going to be a doctor. And why not? She is like a diamond herself, with that wonderful live white complexion, that sparkling hair, and those glittering grey eyes."

"You have only seen her once, and you don't understand her at all," said Aubrey.

He spoke quietly, but his lips tightened, and he let his eyelids drop lest Sir Reuben should see the expression in his eyes.

"I have only seen her once, but I have seen many women," Sir Reuben replied.

This time Aubrey showed a real impatience.

"I hate that judging of sexes in a crowd," he said, "the women all on one side, the men all on the other. In a crowd of a hundred women there are a hundred individualities."

"And the same little core—the eternal woman—in the heart of each? Would you say that Lady Caryll has it?"

"I say that Lady Caryll is not like ordinary girls."

"I agree with you. I saw that when I looked at her in Bond Street. She has a character far more strange and decisive than most girls."

"Strange—yes, she is that."

"Strange as a jewel. And what, after all, is stranger than a jewel? Really shallow, and yet with apparently endless depths; sparkling as no living thing can sparkle, and yet dead; a coloured torch to which no man has set the light. Yes, Lady Caryll is like a jewel, and you know, Aubrey, I understand jewels."

Sir Reuben had started in life as a diamond merchant.

"Jewels haven't hearts."

"You think all women have?"

"I suppose so. I don't know. Some women don't seem to have any, in London."

"And in the country—in country-houses?"

"Oh, they're very much the same, only a bit noisier. Lady Caryll is never noisy."

Sir Reuben smiled at this sudden return to their first subject.

"No, I don't imagine her that," he said.

He was watching his companion with a curious grotesque sympathy. Almost everything Sir Reuben did had a touch of the grotesque, almost a hint of deformity in it. Yet he was obviously a man accustomed to society, a man of considerable cultivation. He was grim, and yet pathetic; for he seemed like a man who has found everything, and who yet cannot entirely cease from seeking. Perhaps he was seeking something now, but if so, his young companion had no intention of rewarding him with a discovery. But Aubrey sometimes rewarded without intention, in the guileless fashion of youth, which thinks itself so clever, so subtle.

"Is this her first season?" Sir Reuben asked.

"Yes."

"Is she enjoying it?"

"I think so. She's not like some girls. She doesn't mind being poor. Some day she'll be rich, perhaps. Her great-uncle, Lord Verrender, is going to leave her his money. But he's good for twenty or thirty years yet. Lady Caryll doesn't care about money."

"St. Ormyn used to care."

"Oh, he cares still."

"And is still directing companies?"

"I fancy most of them have gone smash now. At present he's incessantly in the courts, giving evidence about people who have been ruined, and doing sums all wrong in the box."

"Rather trying in hot weather. And Lady St. Ormyn?"

"Oh, she's all right. She doesn't care much about being a chaperon, but she'll get used to it."

"Does she still wear pink bonnets?"

"Oh yes."

"She always was a faithful woman, except in matters of religion. I wonder if she'll be jealous of the jewels?"

He spoke musingly.

"What jewels?" Aubrey asked.

"Her daughter's."

"You talk as if she possessed them already."

"I only look forward a little into her bright future."

"Do you claim to be a prophet?"

"No; only a fair judge of character."

Aubrey was drawing on his gloves. He fidgeted with the buttons of one, as he replied, always in the conventional voice of young London—

"Not quite a fair one in this case, Sir Reuben."

Sir Reuben made no reply.

"Shall I prove that to you?" said Aubrey.

"How could you?"

"By introducing you to Lady Caryll. When you know her you'll——"

"Know I've made a mistake?"

Aubrey nodded.

"If I think I have, I'll acknowledge it."

"All right! Come into the Park this afternoon between four and five. She and her mother are certain to be there."

"Lunch with me in Park Lane first."

Aubrey hesitated.

"I'm awfully sorry," he said. "But I can't lunch. I must look in at my tailor's, and at one or two places. And I breakfasted very late."

"Call for me, then."

"I will—about four."

They were at the door of the club now. Bond Street hummed round them. They came to the shop into which Lady Caryll had looked. Sir Reuben stopped Aubrey before it, and they faced the sparkle of the diamonds.

"Look at them," Sir Reuben said, smiling. "What do you see down there in the fire of the stones?"

"Nothing."

"Not a face? Not the face of Lady Caryll, the human diamond?"

"Well, I must be off to my tailor," the youth said quickly. He crossed the street and disappeared in the direction of Hanover Square.

Sir Reuben remained for two or three minutes before the shop-window. He was, as he had said, a very good judge of jewels.

CHAPTER II

AUBREY did not go to his tailor, nor did he lunch. After he had parted from Sir Reuben he made a détour by way of Hanover Square, and presently reached his rooms in Jermyn Street. There he threw himself into an arm-chair and smoked rather violently until it was time to start for Park Lane. And while he smoked he thought about jewels.

He was the third son of Lord Rangecliffe, a peer who was as poor as a church-mouse, although he never went to church. He and St. Ormyn were both very well known in London for their poverty, but they were poor in totally different ways. Lord Rangecliffe was tall, difficult in conversation, conventional in manner, and indecisive in mind. He desired to be rich, but he did not mean to be rich. To mean anything was extremely trying to him. He had never even meant to be a good husband. Nevertheless, he had a strong sense of decorum, and it had been said of him that he lived under the rose. He did little for his four sons—he had no daughters. When he found that he possessed a family he was a good deal surprised, but he kept his astonishment to himself. Later he gave his boys small allowances, and advised them to "do something." In pursuance of this paternal ideal, John, the eldest, went into the Life Guards, and Vane, the second, went to Ceylon with vague intentions of tea-planting. Aubrey was at present supposed to be engaged in looking out for something—rather in the manner of Sister Anne. The youngest boy, Herbert, was at Eton, following the agreeable profession of a "wet bob."

As to Lord St. Ormyn, he loved to present the striking spectacle of a brave man struggling gaily with adversity. He was precisely five feet two inches high, with a very rosy face and a blond beard sprinkled with grey. A mercurial expression beamed in his rascally brown eyes, and his active brain was incessantly at work divining fresh means of ruining himself and others; for his love of being perpetually with his kind had, so far, prevented him from even "going smash," as he called it, alone. There were always various well-meaning people who lost their money with him; elderly country vicars with small livings and large ideas, spinster ladies who wanted fifteen per cent. for their money, youthful sprigs of the aristocracy who didn't know the ropes, suburban widows and rich Americans recently arrived in London. All this varied crowd of people agreed in one thing—they all liked St. Ormyn. He made it his business to know personally as many of those he was going to ruin as possible. At the meetings of the various companies with which he was connected he often took the chair, but he was very seldom in it; as he said, there were so many hands to shake, so many shoulders to pat. St. Ormyn always patted men on the back directly he knew them. The action, as performed by him, established an extraordinary confidence between patter and patted, which endured at least until the last new company went into liquidation, and often for a much longer period. He really was very genial, and always called himself a rascal—the most ingenious method of persuading society that you are a thoroughly good, honest fellow. And then his sacrifices in the great cause of ruining and being ruined were enormous. He had even been known to lunch with one of the suburban widows at her semi-detached residence in Hornsey Rise and to drink to the health of their mutual financial operations in a glass of Australian burgundy. His hostess shortly afterwards found herself obliged to take refuge in a small boarding-house, and to complicate her life with the multifarious occupations of a daily nursery governess. but she always spoke of St. Ormyn with sentimental pride, and the lunch at Hornsey was one of her few precious memories.

Lady St. Ormyn, now for the first time a chaperon, had a certain amount of money of her own, which she wisely kept to herself, long experience of St. Ormyn having bred in her a profound distrust of all men who smilingly said they were ruffians and couldn't help it. She was violently musical, but behaved, as a rule, in a most unmusical manner. A would-be wit had once described her as a polka played by a brass band. The image was not inapt. Very tall, with snow-white hair and vivacious eyes, she was usually dressed in light colours, and was excessively fond of marrons glacés, and pink bonnets. She was never alone, and either had a lunch-party in her own house or went to one in somebody else's every day of the week when she was in London. On Sundays she generally took down a party to a summer-house in a pretty garden which she possessed not far from London. On these occasions there was music in the afternoon, followed by dinner and games on the lawn in the evening. The Good Friday strains from "Parsifal" served as an excellent introduction to Kitchen Lancers and bicycle races, in which many of the most celebrated operatic artists of the day were glad to take part. Indeed, Lady St. Ormyn's Sundays were as famous as Lord St.

Ormyn's bankruptcies, and were very nearly as cheerful. Lady St. Ormyn went to the opera whenever Wagner was given. She had travelled to Bayreuth five times, and spoke of Wotan so familiarly that many uninstructed persons supposed him to be her grandfather, or an uncle from whom she had expectations. She loved a tenor more than most women love a soldier, and had once given a dinner at which no less than five notorious baritones were present. Lady Caryll was her only child.

It was half-past three when Aubrey took up his hat and gloves and strolled out towards Sir Reuben's house in Park Lane. The day was hot, and all the world seemed to be out enjoying the sunshine. Piccadilly was thronged with that peculiarly heterogeneous multitude which lives upon its narrow pavement during the fashionable two months and a half of the year. A great violinist hurried past towards St. James's Hall, his long hair, curving inwards at the neck, spread voluminously abroad to claim attention. Provincial ladies in buff-colour, and laden with strings of parcels, sprang eagerly towards the bun-shops. A thin clergyman stared pathetically at a corner window in which eyeglasses were displayed in vacuous crowds. Some damsels in very large hats made their smiling way towards the Burlington Arcade, and received with simplicity the open-mouthed attention of a large and guileless youth who had come up for the day from Surrey to buy seeds. Two young actresses, very much overdressed, bustled past on their journey to a charitable entertainment at St. George's Hall. They were always performing for nothing, in the vain hope of obtaining recognition and a regular engagement. In fact, they were trying to enter the army through the militia. As they walked they discussed agents and the impotence of the leading ladies of London. A little boy in a sailor suit was being conveyed by his anxious mother to a fashionable dentist in George Street. His round face was very pale as the fatal corner of Old Bond Street was gained, but he struggled bravely with his emotions, and endeavoured to fix his mind on the eventual peace of Gunter's, and the rosy charms of the strawberry ice which was to greet him when the Rubicon was crossed. Numberless young men strolled forward in the sun, and numberless young maidens wondered about them in hansom cabs. Motor cars hissed like angry snakes, and omnibuses jerked along the kerbs, paused, and moved, and paused again.

But Aubrey paid no heed to the turmoil, and had no thought for the thoughts of the pedestrians in Piccadilly. He stared at the little sailor who was going to the dentist, but did not see the round white face, and the large youth who had come up from Surrey to buy seeds jostled him without receiving the delicate attention of a cold remonstrance. Aubrey was indeed singularly abstracted. He was thinking over the conversation of the morning. It was a peculiarity of Sir Reuben that, although he was elderly, plain, and slightly grotesque, he had a singular faculty of impressing himself upon those with whom he was brought into contact. This faculty had contributed not a little to his success in life. It was said by unkind people that he had, on one occasion, succeeded to such an extent in impressing himself upon the Government of a certain foreign country that he had managed to swindle it out of about five hundred thousand pounds over some railways. Whether this were true or false, Sir Reuben was undoubtedly supposed to be very rich, and had undoubtedly at one time been a power in London. He was by birth Oriental, his father having been an Egyptian Pasha and his mother a French dancer. He was born in Cairo, educated on the Continent, and started in life as a jewel merchant, following this sparkling profession at first in Egypt, afterwards in London, where he was given a title because he was rich enough to be exceedingly useful to various people who shall be nameless. He had married a pretty Creole, who had died eight years before. Since her death he had lived abroad, spending long periods in the East, in India, Persia, Egypt, and Morocco, in which places he was vaguely supposed by the world to have "interests." He had now returned to London, much aged and considerably altered in appearance.

Aubrey Herrick was his godson.

This fact arose out of a very strong and remarkable friendship which existed between Aubrey's mother, Lady Rangecliffe, and Sir Reuben. Lady Rangecliffe was a woman who was almost sensationally unselfish. She never thought about herself even when she was alone. She had originally endeavoured to live in her husband. As he had tacitly declined to permit such a loving liberty, she withdrew from him sensitively to her boys so soon as they were born, and spent her life in disorderly attempts to make them happier than any boys ought to be. For Lady Rangecliffe was rather untidy and surprising in her manner of life. It was her nature to be so. It was her temperament to lunch at one o'clock on Thursday and at three on the following Friday, to get up one morning at six and another at twelve, and to be deliriously unpunctual at all times and seasons. She was pictorial and imaginative, a harp with a great deal of wind entangled in its strings. And she was apt, from her absurdly high conception of the nobility of average human nature, to be abruptly confidential with comparative strangers. From this trait in her character had arisen her friendship with Sir Reuben. Her only brother, Lord Henry Grale, fell into a serious monetary scrape. He was much younger than she was, almost a boy, and came to her for assistance, which she was absolutely unable to give. On the evening of the day of his visit she dined out in much tribulation, and happened to sit next to Sir Reuben at dinner. She did not know him very well, but that made no difference. Before the third course she had become confidential. Sympathy always caused her nature to expand with emotional abruptness. Sir Reuben was politely sympathetic. Lady Rangecliffe's nature expanded. Before dinner was over Sir Reuben had promised to use his large financial experience in aid of Lord Henry. He kept his word to such good effect that the young fellow was quickly set upon his feet again. Lady Rangecliffe's gratitude knew no bounds. Had Sir Reuben saved her neck from the block she could not have felt more grateful to him. She desired to show publicly her depth of feeling. Aubrey was her opportunity. He was born soon afterwards, and had to be christened. Lady Rangecliffe asked Sir Reuben to be one of his godfathers. In this manner she made the Egyptian one of the family, and he accepted the situation with a curious sensation of pleasure. He learnt to adore Lady Rangecliffe. She had none of the coldness of many of the patrician women of England. She did not confuse the idea of dignity with the idea of swallowing a poker. Some Irish blood ran in her veins. Perhaps it saved her from the ironmongery of the British matron. When Lady Allabruth died, Lady Rangecliffe was to some extent Sir Reuben's confidante, and knew something of his sorrow. And now, on his return to England after his long absence, he naturally came first to see his godson and the godson's mother. He found the mother unaltered. But the godson was no longer a lively boy, but a young man, dandified in appearance, conventional in manner, and reserved in speech. Sir Reuben was disappointed at the transformation. Yet he told himself that he ought to have expected it. London has an extraordinary knack of turning agreeable boys into disagreeable young men. Aubrey was not disagreeable. But Sir Reuben had thought him decidedly inhuman until this morning in Bond Street. The incidents of the street and of the club seemed to let in a little light upon his young stiffness and rather grim propriety of conduct. As Sir Reuben sat in the smoking-room of his big house in Park Lane he thought them over, with a mingling sense of satisfaction and of dissatisfaction.

And Aubrey thought them over in the street and in Hamilton Place. He remembered every word Sir Reuben had said. He weighed every word in his mind. And he arrived at the house in Park Lane terribly preoccupied.

He was shown at once into the smoking-room, which was decorated in Eastern fashion. Sir Reuben was seated on a divan, looking remarkably old and Oriental. Men of his appearance may be seen any day in the bazaars of Cairo and Constantinople. But long residence in England had robbed him of much of their dramatic manner. He had acquired some of the outward phlegm of the Western, so different from the unutterable repose, often shattered by sharp passion, of the Eastern. In the decorations of his enormous house, however, something of his mind was shown. Strong colours abounded—fierce reds and blues, and yellow as glaring as that so often seen on the walls of low Moorish cafés. The room in which he was sitting was filled with a faint smell of incense and of orange flowers. On a low table covered with lacquer-work was a porcelain cup, which had contained Turkish coffee, on a stand of silver. Sir Reuben invited Aubrey to have some coffee, but he refused.

"We ought to be starting," he said. "Lady St. Ormyn is never in the Park after five. She always goes to parties."

"Very well," said Sir Reuben.

He rang for his hat and gloves. They were brought by an Arab servant who had been in his service for years. His house was opposite to the gates of the Park. They had merely to cross the road to gain the gay crowd which was promenading under the trees, and sitting on the little green chairs to talk scandal comfortably. Sir Reuben drew on his gloves. They were lavender kid, and fitted his thin hands very tightly. His frock-coat was buttoned, and his white satin tie was passed through a broad gold ring, in which was set a gigantic ruby. He walked on wearily in his patent leather boots, glancing at the crowd, and rolling his enormous black eyes hither and thither. Several people greeted him with effusion, expressing delight at his return.

"I was very tired of the yacht," he said, "and I wanted to feel cold again."

"But this is the hottest day we have had this year," said a scarlet elderly lady in black grenadine and a green bonnet covered with ivy.

"It is almost the coldest I have had," he replied.

Aubrey was searching the crowd with his eyes. He seemed to see every one except Lady St. Ormyn and her daughter. There was the vacuous old Scotchman who ran from one smart wedding to another, who bicycled and golfed, and did everything he hated that could possibly lead to the making of a new acquaintance in the smart world. When it was the fashion to have the gout, he had it and went to Carlsbad. When heart failure became the vogue, he was to be seen at Nauheim, as ill as the oldest Royal Duke. He pretended to have discovered Marienbad, but was a failure there because its most distinguished patron always conversed in French, and he had never been able to learn any language except Scotch. Now he was conveying a heavy baroness and her plain daughter to their monstrous family barouche which waited against the rails. There were the Australians who had bought the most exclusive set in town for a round sum, and now aired their Colonial accent and their knowledge of sheep and kangaroos in the drawing-rooms of Mayfair and of Belgravia. There was the money-lender who was the intimate of princes, and the lovely girl who was the most successful tout of a celebrated modiste. There was the titled young man who ran an insurance office, and his old Eton and Christchurch friend who pushed a second-rate wine merchant's business for a consideration. There was the gay gentleman who managed parties and started clubs, chattering to the venerable fragment who wore white garden hats and owned a theatre. There was the Honourable Mrs. Grenwich with her pencil and notebook, picking up a meagre living by getting ready her weekly article on the fashionable world for that refined papei "The Smart Woman." There was the last new beauty, aged eighteen, a girl who six weeks ago had been the most charming and simple creature imaginable, but who was now a mass of affectation, a tricky egoist without a thought that was not concentrated upon herself. There was the lady who had been almost sweet-looking until her picture, by Redding, the great portrait-painter, had been the success of the year at the Royal Academy. There was the agreeable clergyman who ran his church with music-hall singers for the warbling of anthems, and comic actors for the reading of lessons. There was Mrs. Campbell, who sang so exquisitely that Calvé had told her—so she said—that she was too good for the wear and tear of an opera-house. There, in fact, was half the world. But where were Lady St. Ormyn and Lady Caryll?

"Perhaps they are at a concert," said Aubrey. "There are about twenty-five this afternoon. Lady St. Ormyn is fond of concerts."

"I saw in the *Times* that Barré has a recital of his own works at St. James's Hall to-day."

"Ah! then she is there. She adores Barré—at least his music. He is the man who hates Brahms and loves dining out. He has composed himself into society. I think he's awfully dull, but then —ah! there they are! The carriage is just stopping."

The faintest little quiver of excitement shook in his calm young voice for a moment. Sir Reuben heard it. He had sharp ears.

A victoria drew up at the rails. It had bright scarlet wheels, men in black and scarlet liveries, and black horses. In it were seated Lady Caryll and a woman with white hair and rather bright

THE SLAVE 19

eyes, who was dressed in pink and green, and who wore a pink bonnet covered with roses. Perched on a tiny stool opposite to them was a little man with a pointed black beard, who was very smartly dressed, and who wore a large buttonhole.

"They've got Bredelli with them," said Aubrey. "What a bore!"

"Does he still sing?" asked Sir Reuben.

"Yes, as a great favour. He's frightfully rich—from his songs. He composes four a year, one in each season—spring, summer, and so on. He's married now to a woman with a heap of money. They're getting out. Shall we join them?"

"If you like."

They moved forward across the grass, but before they reached Lady St. Ormyn she was joined by an immensely stout elderly man of decrepit appearance, who wore a long and straggling beard, and looked perpetually as if he were on the point of bursting into a flood of tears. This was Mr. Gerry Fane, the friend of kings, the dullest and most sought after man in London. Aubrey's brow grew cloudy at the sight of his approach.

"There's old Fane with them now," he said.

"Still on the verge of tears!" said Sir Reuben. "After all, things don't alter much in eight years."

"Bores don't," said Aubrey, almost crossly.

At this moment Lady St. Ormyn caught sight of him, and nodded. She and her party were strolling towards some chairs under a tree. She was talking eagerly to Bredelli, while Lady Caryll followed silently with Mr. Fane, who seldom thought it necessary to make the effort of saying anything.

"That song about the nun and the lily and Pierrot in a tall hat was delicious," she was saying. "Nobody but a Frenchman could have—ah! Mr. Herrick, why weren't you at Barré's concert? We stayed half an hour, and were delighted. Your friend? Certainly—Sir Reuben Allabruth! I think we've seen each other often at a distance, haven't we, and you know my husband in the City, don't you?"

"Yes, Lady St. Ormyn."

"But you've been staying at Ramsgate, or somewhere, for your health, haven't you, lately?"

"Not at Ramsgate. Persia."

"Oh, Persia was it? Of course! I hope the air did you good? Barré has written an exquisite song about Persian flowers. Are there flowers in Persia? It doesn't matter. The song is beautiful. There are flowers! I must tell Barré. He'll be gratified. He likes to be exact. Do you know my daughter, Sir Reuben? Let me—Sir Reuben Allabruth—Lady Caryll Knox."

The introduction had taken place without Aubrey's help. Sir Reuben remembered being glad of that afterwards.

Lady St. Ormyn sat down under a tree. Her face was flushed with music, and she continued to talk rapidly to Sir Reuben, Mr. Fane, and Bredelli, while Lady Caryll and Aubrey took two chairs a little in the background.

" Barré likes Wagner this season," Lady St. Ormyn said to Bredelli. " It's such a mercy, because it was his only drawback, his hatred, you know, of Wotan. Really, it was almost personal."

" Mine is entirely personal," Bredelli said in French—he had not lived in England long enough to learn its language, having only taken up his residence in London twenty-three years before— " I hate Wotan as if he were my brother."

" Oh, of course, relations are a bore," said Lady St. Ormyn, " as a general rule ; but I think Wotan would have been charming —what do you say, Mr. Fane ? "

But Mr. Fane was sunk in a melancholy reverie.

" Nothing, of course," murmured Lady St. Ormyn. " You like music, Sir Reuben ? "

" It is one of my greatest pleasures."

" That's right ; then you are one of us. Are you engaged next Sunday ? "

" No."

" Come down and spend the day with me at Epsom. I've got a garden there. Barré is coming and some of the people from the opera, and two or three others. I'll ask Mr. Herrick. We shall have music all the time, at least nearly—Are you coming, Bredelli ? "

" I am very sorry, but I have a ' command ' for Sunday afternoon."

" You always have a ' command.' Really, it is quite dangerous to have such a large royal family. One may be obliged to—You are only just back from Persia, Sir Reuben ? "

" I have only been in England four days."

" Then probably you haven't read *Le Sentier Defendu*. It's been out three days. I read it the day before yesterday. You must get it. The author is a great friend of mine, a young Frenchman. He may be at Epsom on Sunday, though he hates music. He's only a boy, and his books are entirely psychological. I prefer that. I hate incident ; don't you ? What we do is nothing. What we feel and think is—Bredelli, I don't agree with you at all about that picture of Legeuve's, ' L'Eau de Vie.' I saw it at Harrington's this morning on my way to lunch with the Larches—Fraulein Marie Brindt was there, not a bit tired after Ortrud—and I thought it magnificent, a marvellous elucidation of drunkenness."

"I do not care for tipsy tableaux," murmured Bredelli, who had an elaborate air of graceful preoccupation.

"Oh, there is an enormous amount of interest in being tip—I mean in seeing other people tipsy. Isn't there, Sir Reuben?"

"No doubt," said Sir Reuben gravely.

"From the philosophic point of view, I mean, of course, the allegory of absinthe, as it were. Do you see, Bredelli? Mr. Fane, don't you agree with me?"

"I thought it was eau de vie," said Bredelli, arranging his button-hole, while Mr. Fane murmured something about "never mix your drinks" that nobody attended to.

"Absinthe or eau de vie, it's all the same to the painter."

"The painter! Oh, possibly," said Bredelli.

"He cares only for the degradation, which is so wonderful as a subject. Talking of degradation, have you seen Kitty Cremlin this season? I never saw such an alteration, and all from morphine. She's all over little marks. One might suppose her a sempstress if one didn't know. Of course you remember Guilbert in 'Morphinée'? Well, really she's like that, only of course without Guilbert's genius. That's what I always say—the true realism is reality beautifully exaggerated. It's the touch of exaggeration that gives perfection. I——"

But at this point Bredelli, with a certain hardy impudence that was supposed to be one of his great attractions, interrupted Lady St. Ormyn by drawing her attention to a cinnamon-coloured lady who was passing at the moment, and who wore a silk gown the colour of a ripe orange, while on her head reposed a sealskin toque trimmed with a remarkably well-developed stuffed fox.

"The touch of exaggeration that gives perfection," he said softly.

"Oh, but Mrs. Luffa Parkinson is always—no, Bredelli, that's not fair, a woman who goes to a dressmaker in Amsterdam for her—no, no. Sir Reuben, you know what I mean, don't you? In all the arts, in music, painting, sculpture—even in dancing, isn't it the touch of—by the way, have you seen Réné Mackintosh dance? Oh, of course, you've been in Persia! Well, last night at the——"

Meanwhile Lady Caryll and Aubrey were talking in low voices. Although Lady Caryll had been to Barré's concert with her mother she was not flushed with music. Pierrot in a tall hat had not excited her. In her white gown and black hat she looked cool and clear and sparkling as frost. It was a physical peculiarity of hers never to get hot, even in the most crowded ball-room, and it was a peculiarity that some men found remarkably attractive. Perhaps Aubrey was one of them. He looked at her now as if he were.

"You know who that is," he said, as they sat down, indicating

Sir Reuben, who, with his hands crossed on the top of his stick, and his body inclined forward, was listening to Lady St. Ormyn's numerous philosophies of life. "My godfather."

"Sir Reuben is your godfather!" said Lady Caryll, shutting her white parasol gently.

"Why not?"

"I don't know why he shouldn't be as well as any one else. I was not thinking of him. I was only trying to realise that you were somebody's godson."

"Is it difficult?"

"Yes," she said, looking at him steadily with her long grey eyes, "I think it is—very."

"And why?" he asked, smiling at her with something of the grave indulgence that paternally inclined people show towards children who are not their children.

"A godson sounds like something innocent, simple, out of the world. It suggests a monastery and a life dedicated to some high aim."

"I see now why it seems rather absurd for me to be one."

"You aren't very simple, are you, Mr. Herrick?"

"Perhaps not."

"And do you honestly wish to be simple?"

"I can scarcely imagine what it would be like," he said seriously and quite truthfully.

He had wondered about this very thing many times since he had left Eton, studied for the Foreign Office, and dropped it for an ordinary London life. Certainly he was not very simple. And he knew it. But there were moments when he had faint and nebulous fancies that to be simple in character, in desires, in aim, in habit of life, was to be nearly beautiful. He found, as a rule, little that seemed to him beautiful in complexity. Yet it was his destiny, so far, to live in the midst of a peculiarly complex world, in a peculiarly complex period of social and civilised life. And it is difficult to grasp thoroughly with the imagination any destiny completely unlike one's own.

"Can you, Lady Caryll?" he added, after a moment of silence.

"I don't know. Yes, I believe I can. I believe I'm rather simple myself, in fact," she added.

She had a very calm unimpassioned voice, that could be bright if she wished it to be bright, but that seldom or never vibrated with any deep feeling, although Aubrey sometimes thought it did.

"You—you say you are simple?" he said.

He looked at her, and thought of Sir Reuben's remark that Lady Caryll was sure to be successful in her aim, because she was one-sided. To be complex was to be many-sided. Was she now unconsciously telling him that Sir Reuben had spoken the truth about her?

"I shouldn't be surprised if I am," she said, touching the blades of grass at her feet lightly with the point of her parasol. "I am not like mother, always excited about something or other, a song, or a picture, or a man. Am I?"

"No, you're not at all like your mother," he said, looking at Lady St. Ormyn, who was holding forth violently in French to Bredelli at the moment, and whose hot voice could be heard saying, "Je n'ai jamais entendu une chose aussi bizarre!"

"But I am not at all sure that you are simple, nevertheless," he went on. "I can't tell. I wish I could. Do you honestly like to be quiet?"

"I don't mind being alone, if that is what you mean."

"Well, but Lady Caryll, when are you alone?"

"Oh, now of course not. But before I came out."

"You were at school in France. You were with other girls."

"Yes. It's true I have not often been alone. But I shouldn't mind it. I know that quite well. To be alone with a gratified desire must be delightful."

She said the last unexpected sentence rather thoughtfully.

"With a gratified desire?" said Aubrey quickly.

"Well, who would wish to be alone with a sorrow?"

"No, of course not. But tell me—do you know what it is to have a great desire?"

"You are very curious."

"Am I? Yes, perhaps, about you. I should like to understand you, Lady Caryll. Are you going to let me understand you?"

"Have I the power of letting you? Has any woman the power to let herself be completely understood by a man?"

"Surely—if she chooses."

"I fancy it depends on the man more than on the woman."

"If that is so, I shall learn to understand you," Aubrey said gravely. "But help me a little now by telling me whether you have a great desire, and if so, what it is."

Lady Caryll did not answer for a moment. As she sat silent on the little green chair, looking away from her companion, there was a smile on her face. She seemed to be musing, and to forget that she ought to reply. Aubrey watched her with a keen, and almost boyish, curiosity. And Sir Reuben, although he seemed to be listening intently to the eternal animation of Lady St. Ormyn, watched her too, and wondered of what pleasant things she was thinking under the shade of the trees.

"You won't answer?" Aubrey said, after a long pause.

The smile died from Lady Caryll's face, like a light that fades and leaves that on which it rested cold and altered.

"I don't know that I can," she said. "Perhaps I have not made up my mind what I want most, what is my greatest desire."

"Isn't it the desire that all women have?" he said very low.

"You think me so very ordinary as that? Must I follow the crowd—all these women?"

She glanced round rather disdainfully. As far as the eye could see, there were women; women old and young, and no age at all; women with grey faces and wrinkled eyelids; women whose cheeks were tinted, mauve or rose-coloured, or dead white like the wall of a foreign house; women with red hair, and powdered hair, and gold hair, and black hair; women with monstrous hats and gay gowns; women smiling, chattering, frowning, looking joyous or tired, or wicked, or ill, or sensitive; women attentive, indifferent, exuberant, enervated, or merely patient—patient of this noisy and persuasive world of London.

Aubrey's face flushed to his forehead.

"Don't misunderstand me," he said hastily. "I did not mean that you are like other women."

"But what did you mean then?"

"That—that there is something in all women that asks for the same gift."

"What is that?"

"Why—a heart."

"Oh, I see."

Her voice, in that reply, sounded very young. There was no tremor in it. And Aubrey thought, "How innocent she is; she doesn't understand what I mean."

Whether she understood or not, Lady Caryll did not give him an opportunity of explaining himself. She looked at the group gathered round her flushed and exigent mother, and remarked, "Is your godfather very old?"

"Over sixty, I should think," said Aubrey, recalled from a distance.

"That is very old."

"To us—yes."

"He has guessed that we are speaking of him. I think he is clever."

Sir Reuben was, in fact, looking steadily at them, and now he smiled at Lady Caryll, and moved slightly backward from Lady St. Ornyn's reminiscences of baritones and of French poets.

"He is clever," added Lady Caryll. "But he smiles like an old money-lender. He could look very fantastic if he were alone."

Before Aubrey had time to make any remark, Sir Reuben joined them.

"Lady St. Ormyn is going in a moment, Lady Caryll," he said.

"She always is," she answered. "She and I make more exits and entrances in a day than an actress does in a month."

"And the comedy amuses you?"

"Sometimes. But I don't know that my amusement will last. Do you like baritones, Sir Reuben?"

He smiled. So did Aubrey.

"I haven't seen many lately," Sir Reuben said. "The last I talked with was an old man with a lantern and a djelabe, who frequented minarets."

"He never comes to Epsom."

"But your mother has kindly asked me to come on Sunday."

"I hope you like music."

"It is one of my greatest pleasures."

"In a shrubbery?"

"Anywhere—if it is good."

"I don't know whether it will be good on Sunday, but it will be in a shrubbery. That is mother's and Monsieur Barré's last idea—to hide the players among plants. You will come to Epsom too, Mr. Herrick?"

"If I'm invited."

"I invite you."

"I will come," he said, trying, successfully, not to look too pleased.

At this moment there was a bustle. Lady St. Ormyn was en route, overturning chairs with the skirt of her gown.

"Caryll!" she cried. "We must go to Lady Harriet's now, or we shall not hear John Dobb's imitations."

"Very well, mother."

"Bredelli, are you coming?"

"No," said the little Italian with sang froid. "John Dobb is for the English, not for me."

"Oh, well, you call me English? Good Heavens!"

"Are you not English, miladi?"

"It is absurd to think about nationality in our world. Don't you agree with me, Sir Reuben?"

Sir Reuben had not time.

"Art has no nationality," continued Lady St. Ormyn, moving towards her carriage, and upsetting another green chair. "Art——"

"But people have," interrupted Bredelli impudently. "You are English, miladi, I am Italian. You like John Dobb. I find him horrible. To me he is like a plum-pudding."

"Now, Bredelli, you have spent Christmas with me, and you know perfectly well that I never have Turkey or——"

She stepped into the carriage, followed by Lady Caryll.

"Don't forget, Sir Reuben—Sunday at four, and you must stay to dinner, and you too, Mr. Herrick. Barré's last quartette will be played in the shrubbery"—Sir Reuben glanced at Lady Caryll with his smile of an old money-lender—"It is on Herr Kranz's account. He is so ugly that it is better not to see him, but he plays the 'cello like a—— Won't he be delicious, Bredelli, among the rhododendrons? Oh, but you can't come! What a pity! Mr. Fane, you can easily get away in time for your dinner with the Prince; so mind, I shall—100 Belgrave Square! After dinner, Sir Reuben, bicycle races by torchlight, French songs from Araki, the Syrian with the red hair, you know! and so on. We shall drive back to town on the coach. Au revoir! Au revoir! We shall be at the opera to-n—— Well, Caryll, what do you think of Sir Reuben?"

"That was a marvellous ruby in his tie, mother. Did you notice it?"

CHAPTER III

SIR REUBEN AUBREY, Mr. Fane, and Bredelli stood in a row by the rails and raised their hats as the black and red carriage drove away. As he replaced his hat upon his elaborately dressed hair, Bredelli remarked, vaguely to the world in general, " Milady came to me to learn singing. That is twelve years ago. But how can she sing when she talks for ever like that, the voice always in the upper register! It is the Queen of the Night talking."

Nobody made any response, unless a heavy, inarticulate sound from Mr. Fane could be considered in the light of a rejoinder. And the Italian moved away, strutting like a bird that has been overfed on grain. He adored his appearance, worshipped his talent, and had been in love with his whole ego since he was a dirty baby playing in a gutter of Naples fifty-five years before. Now he sang little things to Grand Duchesses as a personal favour, and was called "Bredelli" by the whole world. Impudence increased upon him. But that only made him the more popular. For London women love the impudence of fat little foreigners who can sing and who are famous. If Bredelli was disliked, it was always by men, and men were nothing to him. "Give me the women and I have the world," was his motto. Providence had given him the women. So now he lived in Portland Place, and had evening parties to which princesses sometimes came. And he had quite forgotten the gutters of Naples.

After the departure of Bredelli, Mr. Fane looked piteously at Sir Reuben and Aubrey, pulled his immense beard with his enormous hand, said " Club—bye!" in a voice like a muffled drum, and drifted helplessly away towards Achilles.

" He still dines out every night, I suppose ?" said Sir Reuben.

" Every night," said Aubrey. "He's off now to the Marlborough. And you ?"

He looked at Sir Reuben a little uncomfortably, and his young figure was very stiff and English in its attitude of grim attention and consciousness.

" I am going to see your mother."

" Oh, I'll walk with you as far as the house."

They went on in silence. The Rangecliffes lived in Eaton

Square in a large and poorly furnished mansion. They had three men in the hall and threadbare stair-carpets. This was Lord Rangecliffe's idea of keeping up his position. As to Lady Rangecliffe, she had no ideas at all on such a subject. She was very kind to the three men in the hall, and the stair carpets did not enter into her life. Inanimate minutiæ were nothing to her.

In Grosvenor Place Aubrey said, in his cold and conventional voice—

"You found Lady St. Ormyn amusing?"

"Do you mean Lady Caryll?" said Sir Reuben, not without malice.

"Oh, she does not go in for that sort of thing."

"Yet in the end she might prove more amusing than her mother."

"D'you think so?"

"I ought not to think anything till I know her, eh, Aubrey?"

"I daresay you are accustomed to form judgments quickly," said the young man, with a very poor attempt at that deference to age which London youth has so utterly lost the knack of.

"Perhaps I ought not to do so in this case. I may have jumped too soon to my Bond Street conclusion."

They were now at the corner of Eaton Square. They shook hands and parted. Sir Reuben walked thoughtfully to No. 300, and faced the three men in the hall. Lady Rangecliffe was at home to him. He was shown upstairs to her boudoir, and found her in a black stuff gown, sitting in a sea of elderly picture papers, with a bottle of gum in one hand and an *Ally Sloper's Half-Holiday* in the other.

"Please bring tea, Charles," she said to the man who had opened the door. "I am only making a screen, Sir Reuben, for my old women in Whitechapel. Charles, please take those *Lady's Pictorials* off that settee, and put the *Ally Sloper's Half Holidays* on that couch by the window. Thank you; that's it. They like Ally Sloper," she explained to Sir Reuben. "They think him distinguished in appearance, poor old souls."

"So do I," said Sir Reuben, examining that gentleman as displayed at an angle of perhaps forty-five degrees on Lady Rangecliffe's work of art. "Isn't he a little crooked?"

"Is he? I didn't notice it."

She put down the gum in an arm-chair and came to sit down by her visitor.

Lady Rangecliffe was a tall, thin woman of about fifty-one, with broad shoulders, long arms, and jet black hair. She had rather blunt features, a nose that turned slightly up, big, dark, short-sighted eyes, and a generous mouth. As a girl she had been very athletic, and she still rode exceedingly well, and could drive a four-in-hand better than any woman in England. She was slightly deaf in addition to being short-sighted, and partly perhaps in consequence of these defects she liked to sit very close to those with whom she conversed, and had a habit of staring at them very hard while she was talking to them. Her manner was habitually eager and responsive. As a child she had been troubled with a touch of St. Vitus's Dance. It had gone, leaving behind it a characteristic quick movement of the head sideways when she was interested or excited. She was often both. Now, coming very close to Sir Reuben, she sat touching him and said—

"Well, now you've seen Aubrey?"

"I have just left him at the corner."

"Isn't he handsome? He is handsomer than Vane; but then Vane is just like me, poor old boy."

This was said with an accent of convinced and simple regret. And she added quickly—

"Did Aubrey talk much to you?"

"Not very much."

"He's tremendously reserved."

Here tea was brought in. Lady Rangecliffe hastily helped Sir Reuben to some milk and sugar, gave him his cup, and then continued—

"Tremendously—especially with me. That's what mothers have to bear—the reserve of the sons they love, and who love them. Aubrey loves me very much, but he would tell his inmost thoughts and all he does to any one rather than to me. The tea? Oh, didn't I? I beg your pardon. Yes, I'll have some in a minute, too. Those old women in Whitechapel tell me everything, but Aubrey nothing. But of course I know old women are perfectly miserable except when they're telling you how miserable they are. They're happy then. I wish one's sons could be like—no, I don't—no, I don't. Do have something to eat, will you?"

Sir Reuben assented, and said—

"But do you think Aubrey's miserable?"

"Perhaps he is rather. But the terrible thing is that I want him to be very—at least not that. But he'll have to be, unless he's to be more wretched still. Now I'll have some tea, now I've told you."

She helped herself to tea rapidly, and added—

"I tell you this because you're his godfather, Sir Reuben, and besides, you're a man of the world."

"I am afraid you must tell me a little more, if I am to know anything," Sir Reuben said, smiling blandly at Lady Rangecliffe's rather crude idea of a full explanation. She sat a little nearer to him, and approached her large and short-sighted eyes close to his lined and sunburnt face.

"Don't you understand?"

"No."

"Why, it's simply this, that the more Aubrey doesn't tell me he's in love with her the more I know it. After all, mothers have that advantage—of knowing perfectly what their boys won't tell them for anything, I mean. Of course I wouldn't let Aubrey understand that for the world, and he'll never find it out. Boys think themselves so wise. I do love boys for that. Girls only think themselves shrewd, but boys think themselves wise. Isn't that the difference?"

"Ah! And women and men?"

"Oh, we're old and uninteresting, so it doesn't much matter what we think of ourselves."

Sir Reuben could not wince at such hasty sincerity. Indeed, although Lady Rangecliffe was wanting in tact, she never lacked the truest delicacy.

"But Lady Caryll is only a child," she now exclaimed abruptly. "And then she is really clever, that's so unfortunate. So is Aubrey, of course. But a girl always gets the best of it."

"Lady Caryll Knox?" interrupted Sir Reuben at this juncture.

"Yes, exactly. Isn't it a pity? And Aubrey is terribly imaginative—like me in that way."

"Is he?"

Sir Reuben put down his cup, and tried not to knock Lady Rangecliffe's head with his own; his plan of action being to keep his head perfectly still while they conversed, and to allow hers the complete monopoly of movement. By this means a collision was successfully avoided.

"Is Aubrey imaginative?"

"I'm sure he is, and very poetical. He is a dreamer, too—so totally unlike other London men. I'm glad of that in most ways, but it makes such a matter as this very painful."

"Do you mean that he's in love with Lady Caryll, and that you don't approve of her?"

Lady Rangecliffe looked rather aghast.

"Oh, I wouldn't say that. In many ways I do approve of her. She's beautiful, and perfectly well bred, of course—not like her— I mean not like some poor girls who've been rather foolishly brought up. But she would not make Aubrey happy. She hasn't his depth of human feeling. It isn't her fault. She can't help it. But Aubrey needs love, almost like a woman. It isn't only that he wants it. He needs it. Some men don't."

She thought of her husband at this moment.

"I don't know the new Aubrey, the grown-up Aubrey, yet," Sir Reuben said slowly. "I don't know him at all."

"Scarcely anybody does. That's owing to his reserve. However, I'm his mother, and I know him, dear old boy, in spite of all his little precautions. That can't be helped, and so long as he isn't aware of it, I don't think it matters, as I said before. I fancy he'll propose to Lady Caryll quite soon now. That's why I'm in such trouble."

She looked as anxious as a kind dog that has missed an expected caress.

"I should not be surprised if he did," Sir Reuben said.

"Wouldn't you? Why not?" cried Lady Rangecliffe with some irrelevance.

"I was with them both to-day."

"Were you? Where?"

"In Bond Street this morning. In the Park this afternoon."

"Ah! Now what do you think of her?"

"I think her both beautiful and interesting."

"Beautiful! Yes; isn't she? Ah! I remember now—you worship beauty. Still? You love a pretty face still?"

She looked at him so steadily that his large eyes began to wink, as eyes wink in fierce sunshine.

"Why not?" said Sir Reuben, with a trace of hurried discomfort.

"It ought to mean so much," Lady Rangecliffe said doubtfully.

"It does mean much," answered Sir Reuben, and there came into his eyes a dramatic expression that transformed him. "Physical beauty turns the world round. And why not? It means much, but not always much that is good. Why should we ask that of it?"

"Is it real beauty unless there is some high-mindedness in it?"

"Certainly," he said. "Goodness is not for sale, but beauty is —here, in London, as well as in Zanzibar. And it is worth buying —well worth buying—though the price is often high."

He looked very ugly while he spoke, but Lady Rangecliffe was so short-sighted that she was seldom able to see anything ugly.

"I am so glad Aubrey has no money," she remarked. "He'll never be able to buy beauty of that kind."

"Ah, you are very different from all of us!" Sir Reuben exclaimed, with a flash of worship for this elderly woman who had no beauty. "I wonder if Aubrey is like you."

"A little bit here and there, but he's not so odd, and that's a great mercy for him. I don't know. And so you've seen Lady

Caryll and Aubrey together. Do you think he's going to propose to her? But it doesn't matter really whether you do or not, because I'm quite sure he is."

"Are you quite sure she will accept him?" said Sir Reuben quietly.

"I'm never sure about women," said Lady Rangecliffe. "When you know a horse, you know what it will do on any occasion, whether it will shy or jib, or be as quiet as a lamb. It's very much the same with a man when you know him. Aubrey's very attractive," she concluded with a jerk. "And Lady Caryll's very young. What will they live on?"

Sir Reuben had been well accustomed to the Irish proceedings of his friend's mind eight years ago. Now, however, they almost confused him. Lady Rangecliffe's appearance was most distressed.

"But it's not that," she continued, with much vivacity of sorrow. "Money is nothing. We've got none, and half our friends have less. It is the difference in temperament. Sir Reuben, you're his godfather and you're a man."

Again he endeavoured to conceal a smile.

"Can't you suggest—don't say it, suggest it—to Aubrey that Lady Caryll will be unhappy with a pauper?"

"Ah, you do understand Lady Caryll a little!"

"Oh, women always understand each other a little. It's the very human people who can be happy in poverty. Lady Caryll is very beautiful, but there's something—I say it to you only because you're Aubrey's godfather and you ought to know—something—well, decidedly inhuman about her. She's a dear girl, I'm sure, and she can't help it, but Aubrey would find it out and be miserable. What are you going to do?"

Sir Reuben happened to be stretching out his hand with his teacup in it.

"I only want to put my cup down," he said.

"No, but about Aubrey."

"You wish me to do something definite."

"Ask him to dine."

"Yes; that is definite so far. And then?"

"Then act as you think best. Mothers can only influence their sons by living. Talking is very little good, because boys always think that women, and especially mothers, don't understand the world. With you it is different. You've been in Persia."

"That's true."

"Well, don't smile. Even that is something—with a boy who hasn't, don't you see? That's the thing with a boy. Of course, if Aubrey had been in Persia too!"

"Ah!"

"Aubrey's impressionable and might be influenced. Though really I don't suppose he can," she concluded, with an abrupt access of sincere hopelessness.

"You don't think Lady Caryll could be influenced?" said Sir Reuben.

He spoke very quietly, but his black eyes shone with a light that seemed kindled by malice, or at least by mischief.

"I'm sure not by me," said Lady Rangecliffe with hearty conviction.

"No. But by me?"

Lady Rangecliffe stared into his face at excessively close quarters. It was sufficiently obvious that she was mentally calculating his physical charms. The sum of them was not great, and her expressive though plain features quickly betokened that she was aware of it. The dawning query in her eyes faded ere even it came to a sunrise, and she shook her head.

"No," she said. "Oh no."

"I shall meet her again on Sunday, with Aubrey."

"At one of those Epsom parties of Lady St. Ormyn's? I wish people wouldn't entertain so much on Sundays. It's the servants I think of, but I know every one laughs at me. I'm certain our poor men get very tired of that hall, so I always send them out on Sunday. Are you going on the coach?"

"No; but we may come back on it."

An earnest expression came into her face.

"Don't let Lady St. Ormyn drive you," she cried with great animation. "She's the most good-natured woman in the world, and capital at music or anything of that sort, but she'd ruin the mouth of any horse, and then she catches all the corners."

"I'll come home in my carriage," said Sir Reuben with conviction.

"Do. Her roans were first-rate goers when she first had them, but now——"

And Lady Rangecliffe launched forth into a thrilling dissertation on horse-flesh which lasted till Sir Reuben rose to go.

"Must you? But you've never told me what you mean to do on Sunday?"

"I mean to drive home behind my own cobs."

"No, no—about Aubrey and Lady Caryll—take care of the *Ally Slopers!* What do you think?"

"I think," said Sir Reuben, who had his hand on the door, "that if Aubrey does propose, Lady Caryll will refuse him."

He was now three or four yards away from Lady Rangecliffe, and she saw him as a faint blur of darkness. She could not observe

c

that his mouth was twisted into a smile like an old goblin's smile, and that his brown fingers twitched round the stick they held. She could only hear his rather grating voice as it spoke with a curious confidence.

"Do you really?" she cried. "Poor old boy! He'll be terribly miserable—not like other men, who forget a thing like that in two minutes. I fancy she likes him very much."

"I'm sure she does."

"Well, then?"

"I'm equally sure that she'll refuse to marry him."

He turned and shuffled out of the room.

Lady Rangecliffe took up the gum-bottle out of the armchair very thoughtfully.

CHAPTER IV

ON the Saturday before Lady St. Ormyn's party at Epsom there was a great sale of jewels at Murphy's in King Street. Sir Reuben Allabruth went to it. Among the jewels offered to the public there was an enormous emerald which had at one time belonged to that astounding courtesan, Catherine the Great of Russia. It was engraved with three figures representing the soul being carried away by pleasures. The bidding for this jewel lay between Sir Reuben and two dealers of world-wide notoriety, and Sir Reuben secured it at a fabulous price. The people in the rooms held their breath when it came into his possession, and some of the women present looked at him with an expression that was like a silent solicitation. For this emerald was one of the finest in the world.

"Who's the woman?" murmured one young man to another.

"Haven't an idea. But I don't envy her," answered his companion, with a glance at Sir Reuben's brown and wizened face and incoherent, elderly figure.

The dealers were in a flutter. They had seldom to contend against such triumphant rivalry. One of them was in a towering passion. He muttered curses to a solicitous understrapper, who agreed with him in muffled whispers and grew very warm in the process. The heat in the rooms was, in fact, excessive, but Sir Reuben made his way out into the street looking perfectly cool and unaware of the excitement he had created. On the pavement he met a well-known stockbroker with whom he had had many business dealings. The stockbroker congratulated him on his success, and could not refrain from adding—

"I had no idea you collected jewels, Allabruth. I suppose you saw many splendid stones in India and Persia?"

"Yes, but I did not buy any."

"You waited till you were back in London among enormous prices?" said the stockbroker, with obvious surprise.

"The competition amuses me," said Sir Reuben carelessly, as he got into his brougham.

As he drove away a friend joined the stockbroker.

"Has Allabruth told you who that jewel is for?" he asked.

"No. Has anybody an idea?"

"Not a soul. He's only just back from the East. Perhaps he's brought a harem with him. The extraordinary thing is that when Lady Allabruth died he sold all her jewels. Now he's starting again in his old age."

"I wish he'd invite me to Park Lane and show me his house," said the stockbroker. "Perhaps she's black and will wear the emerald in her nose."

"More likely she's a chorus girl, without an *h* in her composition, playing in some musical comedy," said the other.

Sir Reuben was well aware of the excitement he had created, but he was entirely indifferent to it. Nevertheless as he passed through the crowded streets, shut in by the padded green walls of his carriage, he was conscious of a strange thrill of anticipation that flickered up suddenly in his heart, and made him feel that there was youth in him yet, the power to enjoy and even to exult. This man was a Christian. His father had been converted to Christianity by his mother. For the ex-dancer had become ecstatically devout when she found herself unexpectedly received into the haven of matrimony. In his middle life he had been much in the best English society. He was now fatigued and elderly. He had worked hard. He had suffered. Yet his inherited nature had remained unaltered. This nature was Oriental. Beneath his frock-coat beat a curious heart, a heart that could be cruel, jealous, uncivilised, and fiercely dramatic in its passions. And this heart was now full of a lust of desire, an ardour of pursuit, not wholly unlike the ardour of some animals that do not dwell in kennels. Since the death of Lady Allabruth Sir Reuben had not felt so young as he felt to-day.

His dark eyes glowed as he leaned back in the carriage, and watched the vanishing pictures presented to him by the streets : a girl mounting carefully into a barouche preceded by an enormous mother; two self-conscious young men in a motor car that hissed at the contemptuous drivers of the hansoms; a roaring blind man hammering with his stick to make the world give way before his triumphant infirmity; a group of old ladies perched anxiously upon the kerb to see their sovereign pass; an elderly minister giving his daily dole to a conservative crossing-sweeper; a flushed man in a tall hat ensconcing himself carefully in a brougham that was embowered in samples of silks. He saw pictures of a modern world, of a world led by the iron hand of civilisation to the inmost shrine of ugliness; narrow, treeless streets; dingy, flat houses; plain women smothered in finery; men in tweed caps bent double over the handle-bars of charging bicycles; ragamuffins screaming of murder and assault, committed within the last few minutes; omnibuses dressed from head to foot in advertisements; piano—

organs pelting the ear with tunes like stones; white waiters in greasy evening clothes staring out of the narrow doorways of cafés; a black funeral crowned with the ostentatious pyramids of plumes that had nodded already over the heads of a hundred corpses; a butcher's shop lined with red animals hanging upside down for the passing children to see; a row of patient waxen gentlemen in auburn wigs, clad in check suits at two pounds ten a-piece. All these idols of the great market-place Sir Reuben saw from his carriage. He had not seen them for years, but he had known them so well once that they were only familiar now. Even the motor cars had already greeted him in Paris. Nothing was quite new. And had there been anything new in the teeming thoroughfares those brilliant eyes would hardly have observed it. For, before them, shone the green light of an enormous emerald, and three faint engraved figures representing the soul being carried away by pleasures. They disfigured the liquid jewel with their rarity. To engrave a jewel is to make an insult preciously indelible. It is a work of decadence, of men who might wish to carve some legend on the sea, or to write a sonnet on the silver of the moon. But Sir Reuben loved this work of the engraver, not for its rarity, but for its subject. His rich and rank imagination was captivated by the faint suggestiveness, the ethereal cynicism, of those tiny figures floating on the shining and fixed water of the jewel; the legend of the soul borne away by pleasures stamped upon one of the most potent sirens that can lure it into dangerous paths. There was a sarcasm in the doing of it; there was a devil of mischief. And he saw the dead engraver at his artful work, as he had seen stern men at work in the shadowed bazaars of Cairo, Bagdad, and India. In his thin dark fingers—fingers alive with race—this dead artificer held the jewel, resting his long and lustrous eyes in the green light that Pliny loved, and that Theophrastus wrote of. And the jewel was clean and clear, unsmirched by allegory or by any human suggestion. It was a drop of shining beauty at which the sight, weary with desire, might slake its eager thirst. It was a shrine of perfection, beyond praise like all flawless things. But the dead artificer who held it saw in it but a fine material for his craft, a surface to support and reveal for ever his cunning. And he held it in lithe fingers that longed to change it, to compel it to show forth not only itself and its loveliness, but also him and his intellect. He had that strange desire, so common among men, to force a perfection that has no thought to seem to think, to induce a wonder that has no utterance to seem to speak. And of what should the jewel seem to speak, of what should it seem to think? And then surely the dead artificer smiled, with that dim and enigmatic smile of Eastern men, as the thought came to him: "Through me thou shalt give to men thy secret; thou shalt tell to women what thou art; a lure, a danger, a green light that beckons to darkness, a spark glittering upon the edge of the pit." It is a grim pleasure to force perpetual silence to perpetual revelation. And the artificer drew forth his tiny tools, and sat down in his corner, cross-legged, and alone with his untiring patience and with his secret irony. And the jewel yielded itself to him. And he stamped upon it, with infinite precaution, his faint legend of what he thought it was. Who were near him in the bazaar? A hundred buyers and sellers, a multitude of still and ardent workers like himself, and all the shadows that sit beneath the leaning pent-house roofs in those strange countries of the sun; dark men, veiled women, shadows, and this enormous jewel, on whose surface the tiny tools wrote slowly out their story. But the artificer must surely, in his toil, have sent out his imagination on the wing above the paths of the emerald's eventual pilgrimage, must have seen that light, which now he held in his long fingers, shining faintly in many places, beckoning to the eyes of many unveiled women. And perhaps, as he strove, he saw, too, the dim pilgrimage of those who would follow that light, and heard, as from afar, the softly beating footsteps of the crowding women who worship jewels and are borne away by them. He would never know them. He would sit in the bazaar, and grow old with the shadows, his nostrils full of the strange scents of the East, his ears full of those cries which are never heard in Western market-places. He would grow old and never know them, would die and rest in the Moslem paradise, attended by beauty and soothed by gratified desire among the roses of the other world. But they would know his handiwork, would read his legend, would smile, perhaps, at his graven irony, or would weep. And then, cross-legged in his corner, and leaning close above the jewel, surely the dead artificer fell into many dreams of smiling and of weeping women, soft dreams of triumph. For is it not the greatest triumph of a man when he can make a woman smile or weep at his will? And to be at rest among the roses of paradise, and still to have power over women in the world that is far from the roses, must not that be strangely sweet? And so in the shadowy bazaar the artificer dreamed, and turned the great jewel in his delicate fingers until his work was done.

. . . .

Sir Reuben's carriage stopped before the house in Park Lane; he got out slowly and entered his home. It was strange to him this summer, not because he had been absent from it for eight years—eight years are as the dropping of a handful of sand to an old man—but because his pretty Creole wife was no longer there.

Her absence made the house seem fantastically large to Sir Reuben; he shuddered at its immensity despite the warm, bright colours, the pictures, the dense carpets, the painted ceilings. His home was not only gorgeous in its wealth of strong and magnificent hues, its superb reds and blues, its subtle greens and rose colours; it was seductive also, for it suggested repose, enduring inertia, and contented rest. Many of the windows of the rooms were heavily latticed with carved wood. The air could enter, but it was difficult for the eyes to catch any disconcerting glimpses of the passing world of the town. Such glimpses disturb the mental peace and recall to the memory the convulsive energies of London. To a man of Sir Reuben's temperament there could be no beginning of comfort so long as one travelling cry could be heard, one flitting figure seen. But his precautions of past years had not been in vain; the men who had made his house what it was had set London very far away; its sounds were deadened, its sights were hidden. The tinkle of the fountain in the central hall was so ceaseless that it seemed at last to cease. There was a long perfume of flowers, instead of the short and violent rushes of scent that startle and confuse the senses in many English homes. Sir Reuben understood that the mission of perfume is to create atmosphere, not to tickle a curious nose or to enchant the inartistic lover of surprises. Draperies fell over the doors. There was no suggestion that because you had entered you must presently emerge. There was never heard a murmur of talking servants in the hall or a bang of a gate in the offices.

And in this house, too, there was a faint sense of mystery. It was so quiet, so coloured, so full of carefully subdued light, and so very large that it suggested to the curious mind infinite hidden possibilities. There might well be a harem here, concealed and guarded, as in the palaces of the East. There might well be pretty, chattering, empty-headed women living indolent and luxurious lives in unseen apartments concealed beyond the falling tapestries, the grotesquely carved wood of the tall lattices; but if there were, no one ever heard their laughter or the patter of their feet, no one ever saw the flash of their peeping eyes or the sparkle of the jewels that they wore. The great house seemed to be empty. If any houri dwelt there she made no sign; she sighed, smiled, wept, loved, slept, and played her little lute in some chamber that was utterly secret.

The intensity of the privacy in his house had pleased Sir Reuben in bygone years. After the passion of business that rages like a plague through the city, he had loved to pass abruptly into the stillness of his home, and to remain, sometimes for long hours, idle, sunk in a reverie through which no chink of money sang a grating tune. His power of work had had as companion a power of rest that belongs in the same degree to few Englishmen. But then Lady Allabruth had been alive; she had not been a clever woman, but Sir Reuben did not seek for cleverness in beauty. She had loved society. Often when her husband returned from the city she had been out, and he had sat alone; but such a loneliness did not weigh upon his senses, Oriental though he was, for he had trained himself in the codes of this society in which he lived, and this society gave unlimited freedom to its women—when they were married. And then Sir Reuben felt Lady Allabruth's presence in his house when she was absent. He felt the quiet contentment of possession and of power to give pleasure to the woman who pleased his senses. He heard continually the song of her beauty, continually renewed by her radiant re-entries from the outer world which she delighted by her gaiety and grace. If he sat alone he could indulge in the quiet luxury of recollection, presently to be corrected by actual vision of the beauty recalled. Now he could, it is true, remember; he could listen to the echoes, but vision and music were denied to him. And perhaps he did not care to remember; perhaps the echoes were hideous and harsh, like the reflected voices of ugly and wicked things—false witches of the Brocken.

When Lady Allabruth died suddenly, Sir Reuben sold all her jewels, all the trinkets she had loved and worn on her soft neck, arms, and bosom. He shut up his house and vanished. Perhaps he fled from the haunting memory of a tragedy, having given its souvenirs into strange hands that he had never clasped. Now his home seemed too large, and all its rooms were empty. To-night he had no engagement. He did not wish to have one. Yet the luxury of solitude weighed upon him, and he was unquiet with his mind, which could not cease from an intensity of thought that stirred and troubled him. The day drew on. He dined. After dinner he shut himself up in the smoking-room. He drank his coffee slowly. There was a reception at the house that adjoined his on the right. He went to the window for a moment, drew aside the curtains, and looked out through the lattice. In the distance, through the tall railings of his garden, he could see the lights of the carriages, a double chain of yellow eyes. He drew the curtains again, and sat down on a couch. He still saw the double chain of eyes, but now they were of a deep, translucent green. They looked like strings of enormous emeralds, and their light was soft and silken. As they moved on towards the house, they were continually replaced by others, by endless emeralds of immense size, and of an intense, soft lustre. The lamps in the smoking-room were carefully shaded, and were set high in the ceiling. Sir Reuben no longer noticed them. The room seemed lit by the fire emitted by jewels, and all these jewels were still emeralds. Even the iced-water that stood in a glass beside the porcelain coffee-cup had changed from phantom white to a wonderful green hue. And Sir Reuben remembered the saying of the old writer, that the emerald imparts its colour to water when dipped in it. Was it not, then, the most influential of all jewels. Had it not powers denied to other jewels. Possibly for this reason the dead artificer had chosen it as the imperturbable scroll on which to write his ironical allegory. For he had thought, perhaps, that it could bear away the soul more swiftly, more certainly, than the gems that gleamed beside it. And was that true? Sir Reuben meant to prove it presently. The green lights died out. They faded—as the pretty Creole wife had faded—and were gone. But, ere they faded, they seemed to crowd together, for one livid moment, all these great emeralds, and to rise in a wall of marvellous, implacable green, and to stand there before Sir Reuben, dividing his past with the pretty Creole from his future—with whom?

CHAPTER V

SIR REUBEN drove Aubrey down to Epsom on Sunday. The weather was fine and hot. There was a clear sky. It seemed certain that the musicians in the shubbery would not be rained upon, and that the torches borne by the bicyclists would burn bravely in a still evening. On the journey down Sir Reuben found his godson even more stiff and reticent than usual. He looked well in his light suit, with his fresh English complexion and thick, smooth hair, and Sir Reuben was rather proud of him, and of their curious connection. But decidedly the new Aubrey was difficult to get on with. His reserve of manner was singularly impenetrable. He was perfectly civil. Any desire to be unpleasant was certainly far from him. But he was rigid, and looked like an immaculate male puppet dressed for a highly conventional country life. As they drove along, he examined the passers-by calmly with his clear blue eyes, apparently taking no interest in them as human beings, but regarding them simply as the furniture of the streets stripped of the brown holland in honour of the Sabbath. He talked to Sir Reuben quietly, with a sort of gentle and sustained indifference. All subjects seemed alike to him, as they seem alike to those half-dead men whose minds slumber in bodies proud that they are flesh. Yet Aubrey did not convey any impression either of sensuality or of sleepiness. He was full, apparently, of a cold and attentive life, that could watch but could not respond, that chose neither to give nor to receive. There was no summer in him, one would have said, no sensation of youth, no desire of anything, good or evil. And to-day his invariable conventionality of manner was slightly accentuated. The stamp set upon him by society was more clearly marked even than usual. He resembled more closely than ever those many Englishmen, of whom one would never say they are intelligent, or bright, or amusing, or thoughtful; but of whom one would say, dismissing them in one fully descriptive word—they are thoroughbred.

Sir Reuben, when he was not attending to his spanking piebalds, thought over his conversation with Lady Rangecliffe. Was this young man really so unlike his usual companions? Was he, as his mother declared, imaginative, desirous of sympathy, even one of those strange and pathetic beings at whom the world smiles, calling them dreamers? It seemed unlikely, and yet reserve is curiously deceptive. It is like one of those maladies that manifest themselves in pain remote from the seat of the disease. You are aware of a result, but are often far from guessing its cause. Sir Reuben shot a glance at his companion out of the corner of his eye. Aubrey was settling the pin in his narrow tie, and gazing indifferently at a row of mean suburban villas along which they were passing. His face wore a weary expression. Sir Reuben began to rearrange his ideas, originally put in train by the incident in Bond Street, rejecting some despite the maternal evidence of Lady Rangecliffe. His first conception of the new Aubrey returned to him, the conception of a youth ground down in the ruthless mill of fashionable life, which finds the soul a jewel and leaves it a powder, a dust that disperses along the winds.

"Shall we have an amusing day, Aubrey, do you think?" he asked the young man.

"I don't know. I don't care particularly for opera-singers."

"I hope to advance in my acquaintance with Lady Caryll."

But this remark did not tend to any more vivid conversation. Aubrey merely replied—

"Lady Caryll is scarcely seen at her best on these occasions."

The garden of Lady St. Ormyn at Epsom was not very large, but it was very artfully laid out. The building which she called the summer-house stood in the middle of a good-sized lawn, and contained a music-room with a parquet floor, a dining-room, a billiard-room, three or four dressing-rooms, a kitchen and offices. Behind these were stables. On the lawn a tent was pitched; it was hung with Egyptian embroideries, and was decorated with palms and hot-house flowers. Beyond the lawn were large trees, copper beeches, monkey-trees, yews cut into conventional forms, and some fine walnuts; belts of rhododendron, shrubberies, a rose-walk, and a fish-pond, at the edge of which was a pretty tea-house hung with wisteria. Round the garden, on the outskirts, was a bicycling track. The garden was walled, and was entered through a very high iron gateway between brick buttresses covered thickly with ivy. A few village loafers hung about this gateway in the dust, watching the arrival of Lady St. Ormyn's guests. They stared with round eyes at Sir Reuben's piebalds, and one of them said in an audible voice—

"That's not a h'opera gent. Thems from the circus."

"Lady St. Ormyn's guests are very mixed, I suppose?" said Sir Reuben.

"Very mixed indeed," said Aubrey stiffly.

It was four o'clock as they drew up at the thatched porch of the summer-house, and the sound of many voices came from the lawn. English, French, German, and Italian mingled in the warm summer air, and two men servants were carrying out some tall music-stands and some portfolios. Lady St. Ormyn, in a pink silk gown and a large and shady pink hat, was standing on the verandah of the music-room engaged in violent conversation with three men. Her face was covered with paint, her white hair with powder, and she plied a huge fan of pink feathers as she talked in French. One of the men, very tall and broad, with a dyed beard and feverish eyes, was a famous operatic bass. Another, small and grizzled, and carrying in his hand a pair of blood-red kid gloves, was Barré, the fashionable composer. The third, a melancholy youngish man like a bird, with black hair and a deformed smile, was a well-known musical amateur, who was mystic, immoral, cultivated, and dyspeptic. He composed hymns and gave luncheon parties, doing both decidedly well. And he was always in Lady St. Ormyn's pocket. Beyond the verandah there was a vision of the lawn, spotted with conversing celebrities. Araki, the Syrian singer, was lighting a cigarette in a corner, and at the same time furtively examining his face in a mirror that was let into the wall.

"You are just in time, Sir Reuben. No, no, Barré, the one with the canon, about the monk and the nightingale! I love it! You are just in time. They're arranging Herr Kranz in the rhododendrons at this moment. Mr. Herrick, you must——Put the stand for Herr Kranz well behind the shrubs, James—well behind."

"Yes, my lady," said a man-servant.

"He's not to be seen on any account; it would spoil everything. Sir Reuben, you know Monsieur Anneau? The finest Mephisto since Faure."

The man with the dyed beard and the feverish eyes bowed very magnificently.

"Yes, Barré, after the quartet. And—no, not Araki's sobbing song—we'll have that after dinner. It sounds better in the dark, much better. Lady Mary, do come out, won't you? and you, Sir Reuben. Where's St. Ormyn, Mr. Fraser? He must be kept quiet during the music. I can't have him wandering about in the shrubbery trying to get up companies all through Barré's exquisite —where is he?"

The melancholy man with the face like a bird said he didn't know.

"Do find him. Yes, Barré, whenever you like now. Mind about Herr Kranz! Now, Mr. Herrick, come along. St. Ormyn! St. Ormyn!"

A very small man with a beard, who was skipping furtively across the verandah, stopped short.

"What is it, Fifi?"

"Where are you off to? Not into the shrubbery?"

"Well, but surely the quartet——"

"Nonsense, St. Ormyn, you don't understand anything of that kind. You are going to make a noise about money and disturb—Sir Henry, would you like to have a game of billiards? Yes! I thought so. St. Ormyn's longing for a——Now, Sir Reuben, will you come? It's quite safe now. My husband is so noisy when he's talking about investments that I have to—yes, it's a pretty little garden, quite small, of course. Mrs. Luffa Parkinson, will you come with us? You shall have a chair. Where's Caryll? Oh, there she is with Mr. Fane."

A light sprang up in Aubrey's eyes as he saw Lady Caryll, in white, standing by Mr. Fane on the lawn. He was pulling his beard slowly, and staring piteously at the guests who were gathering round an ambush of rhododendrons, in which Barré was now arranging four anæmic-looking men who carried stringed instruments. Lady Caryll was saying something with a smile. Aubrey could not hear what it was, but, as Lady St. Ormyn and her *entourage* came up, Mr. Fane's reply was audible.

"The prince don't like it," he said; "the prince don't like it."

"What doesn't he like?" cried Lady St. Ormyn. "Caryll, here's Sir Reu—Herr Kranz, you aren't comfortable. Put your chair a little more into the bushes."

Herr Kranz, an enormously stout German, with a yellow face and long mouse-coloured hair, secluded himself obediently, and began to tune his 'cello.

"Isn't his tone delicious, like a rich wine?" said Lady St. Ormyn. "He's quite hidden now. Barré! Barré!"

Meanwhile Lady Caryll had greeted Sir Reuben and Aubrey. Sir Reuben noticed as he took her ungloved hand that it was very cold. Aubrey brought her a chair, but she declined to take it.

"I can see Herr Kranz if I stand," she said. "Just his head surrounded by leaves. I must have something to interest me while they are playing."

"Don't you care for music, then?" asked Sir Reuben.

"Oh yes. But I have heard Monsieur Barré's so often."

"You are like Lady St. Ormyn—you worship Wagner?"

"Oh, Lady Caryll adores the Italian school," said a young Italian composer who was standing by an adjacent rosebush.

"Perhaps. But how did you divine it, Signor Rudini?"

"Because I heard you say that you would rather have a box for Madame Viva in 'Traviata' this week than for the 'Meistersinger.'"

"They say she's going to wear £80,000 worth of diamonds in the first act," murmured Mrs. Luffa Parkinson, the cinnamon-coloured lady, putting up a red parasol covered with poppies.

Sir Reuben looked across at Aubrey. But the boy was gazing at Lady Caryll with an expression that had become suddenly almost wistful.

"Oh, I like the tunes in 'Traviata,'" said the girl, in her calm voice.

"'Traviata' is a threadbare outrage. Hush! they're beginning!" said Lady St. Ormyn. "Mr. Harris," she added in a hot whisper to a dark young man who was moving away, "come and sit by me. I want you to write about this quartet in your paper. You'll love it."

The dark young man sat down in a resigned manner as the 'cello of Herr Kranz buzzed out from the bushes.

Sir Reuben and Aubrey stood with Lady Caryll while the music ran its course. Her grey eyes were fixed upon the flower-like face of Herr Kranz, grotesque amid the leaves, and transformed by various terrible expressions of hard labour as executive difficulties increased. A little smile of cool amusement hovered on her lips. She seemed unaware of the people round her. These whispered incessantly, unable to be quiet even for a moment. The air was full of faint ejaculations, half-smothered scraps of scandal, murmured bits of information that covered a wide range of topics, furtive utterances of praise and blame.

"Delicious in the open air? Yes. We go to Nauheim in July. My heart gives me so much trouble. My heart—only five balls this week—things are quieting down a little."

"This morning? Yes. He preached against Sunday-parties—it was very impressive—I never miss hearing him. I shall be glad when the bicycle races begin. A little heavy, yes, but still beautiful."

"Oh no, not at Ascot. I never bet in the ring. She lost three thousand last week. Will he back any bill for her? Really! Then there is something in it after all. Scherzos, yes, they're always delightful. I agree with you—I hate slow movements."

"No, I think he'll get fourteen years—he won't be hanged, oh no! He used to dine with us quite often, so we have been to the court twice. He cried when she was giving her evidence—most distressing. Yes, it's a killing piece. Algy roared. I thought he'd have to go out. Exquisite music—but Barré's always is—I could listen to it for ever."

"He's very strong in the leg—doosed strong in the leg, and don't know when he's beaten. Like a man like that, do you? Oh, as fast as they make 'em. Not a marryin' man; pity for her, yes. Gone on music? I should think so; dead gone! You're right there—too much butcher's meat about him for real stayin'. He's very ready with his fists, very ready, but he'll have to knock under to——"

"Three inches less than it was last season, and she's got three children. Wicked, yes, isn't it? so bad for her health. No, she's not naturally small; I'm much smaller by nature, but I don't choose to squeeze my——. I'm glad you prefer natural people; after all, sincerity is——"

"Yes, violins are perfect; nothing like them, no. Yes, the coach-horn is very gay. Well, perhaps it is for out of doors—perhaps it is; more fulness of tone, certainly. They're stopping; oh, what a pity! Three more movements! not really! But I thought —no, I'm not tired, only a little cramped from sitting so long. Shall we? An ice, well, perhaps. I love music, still I am a little cramped; let's go quietly."

Lady St. Ormyn listened violently, her ostentatious silence being illuminated by a great deal of very expressive pantomime, denoting passionate and almost wild admiration of Barré and all his works. Music, she said, was her religion; and, like many other people, she liked to have her religion brought comfortably to her door, planted among her own rhododendrons, and preached to her by famous male celebrities. Her soul, being diffused through the network of her nervous system, was only appealed to by the music of certain composers, of whom the chief was Wagner. She thought Mozart tiresome, just as many people who go to church think the Litany tiresome. Noise gave her an agreeable sensation in the small of the back. She always had an opera-box close to the stage, so that she could beck and nod to the singers, and ask them to lunch when they were kissing their hands before the curtain. And she valued her influence over a tenor or a baritone as earnest-minded maiden ladies value theirs over a vicar or an archdeacon. At present Barré was her idol, and his songs, which generally dealt with priests and birds, or nuns and Pierrots, or graves and ladies who were no better than they should be, moved her to tears as ostentatious as the popping of champagne corks. His quartets really bored her, but she said they were angelic. She had made Barré the vogue in England, and therefore loved him as we all love our own inventions. And Barré kissed her feet on every public occasion, and was at present composing a "Hymn to the Virgin" which was dedicated to her, and was peacefully scored for an organ and four trumpets.

A prolonged and sonorous rustling at length announced that the quartet was over. The four anæmic-looking men, bathed in perspiration like bicyclists, emerged from the concealment of the shrubbery, and Lady St. Ormyn began to exhibit Barré, as a conjurer exhibits the pigeon he has extracted from the bottle of wine.

"Isn't he extraordinary?" she cried to Mrs. Luffa Parkinson, a lady without the encumbrance of a mind, who was always "in the movement" of the moment, whether it made for immoral literature or for the extension of Roman Catholicism in England.

"Most extraordinary," said Mrs. Parkinson in a thin and fatigued soprano voice. "Most! How does he think of it? How do you think of it, Monsieur Barré?"

"It comes," said the little Frenchman, with all the modesty of a cock-sparrow. "I sit down at the piano and it comes to me."

"But where from?" said Mrs. Parkinson, with the peculiar earnestness of idiocy. "That is what I want to know. Where from?"

But Lady St. Ormyn had no idea of allowing her little god to be monopolised, so she broke in upon this searching cross-examination of genius.

"Barré, you want something to drink," she said firmly.

The composer smiled with greedy deprecation.

"Come with me to the tent. Caryll, bring Sir Reuben. And then Monsieur Anneau is going to sing 'Le Bon Dieu et les Oiseaux,' Barré's last song. Monsieur Anneau, you haven't forgotten!"

The famous bass, who was one of the wickedest-looking men in Europe, bowed and smiled.

"May I come with you also, Lady Caryll?" he said to her in excellent English.

"Please do," she answered. "And you, Sir Reuben."

She walked across the lawn between the two men, while Aubrey escorted Mrs. Parkinson.

"I love to sing about the little birds," said Monsieur Anneau. "They are innocent. They sing so exquisitely because they are so innocent."

He made his glorious voice intensely gentle as he spoke.

"Do you sing so exquisitely for the same reason, Monsieur Anneau?" said the girl.

He smiled pathetically.

"You should have asked me that question before I came to London," he answered.

"The little birds can be sarcastic," she said, smiling.

"Perhaps it is my lost innocence which gives me my passion when I sing," he murmured. "No one can be an artist who has not something to regret."

"Then you cannot regret your lost innocence."

"You are an artist in conversation; I am a blunderer. It is only when I sing that I have power."

He fixed his feverish eyes upon her with the expression that had turned America's head and put Russia into the hollow of his hand.

She laughed lightly at him and looked at Sir Reuben.

"Music is dangerous, isn't it, Sir Reuben?" she said, as they entered the tent. "I don't think I shall dare to listen to M. Barré's last song."

"I fancy you need have no fear," he said with intention.

She turned suddenly, and gazed at him for the first time with real interest.

"Am I not to be influenced like the rest of London, then?" she said.

"Yes—and no," he replied.

"Ah, you take refuge in enigmas. What a crowd!"

The marquee, large though it was, presented the spectacle of a polite battlefield. It was thronged with people, all anxious to be soothed with refreshments, and the heat, on which was borne the heavy scent of flowers, had become tremendous. Near the entrance a world-renowned prima donna, in a garden-hat and a white muslin dress spotted with mauve orchids, was eating pineapple and talking French with a vivid colonial accent. Her companion was a big boy who hated music. She loved big boys, and, as she hated music too, they naturally had a great deal in common. They were talking about the *Grand Prix*, and the boy was giving her a good tip for it. She cared more for a good tip than for all the operas ever composed. Yet she could sing with consummate art when she chose. She had been born with an iron will and with an inordinate ambition, and God had given her one of the loveliest voices in the world.

"I rather fancy the Comte de Gramont's 'Hirondelle,'" she said to the big boy.

"Not a chance. Take my tip and go for 'Sourisette,'" said the big boy. "Some more pine-apple?"

"My voice forbids. What a nuisance it is to have a voice!"

"Yes. Awfully hard lines for you."

"Well, it can't be helped. What stable is 'Sourisette' out of?"

Barré was drinking champagne and receiving the adulation of two elderly peeresses with auburn hair, sisters, who dyed their grey heads exactly the same hue in order to deceive society, at which innocent effort society was perennially amused. Lady St. Ormyn was standing in the centre of a circle of people connected with the opera, and was accepting from the hands of a great Italian conductor a plate of strawberries. A dull and impudent-looking man, with a turned-up nose and a curled moustache, was talking authoritatively to her, and to the group around her. He was a business man, totally unmusical, who had a great deal to do with the financing of operatic speculations, and who, in consequence, thought himself fully competent to teach mere artists their business.

"I heard her twice in Buda-Pesth," he was saying, in a slow and thick voice. "A perfect soprano. Not been spoilt by singing Wagner."

A very stout young woman in mustard-colour, who wore yellow thread gloves and a large red rose in the front of her gown, turned suddenly purple. She had been singing "Venus" the evening before.

"Really, Mr. Wilson!" she ejaculated.

"Spoilt! I repeat it," he continued calmly. "I shall bring her over next season, and then you will all see."

"But what's she to sing?" said Lady St. Ormyn. "Who cares for anything but Wagner? I'm sure I don't."

"Oh, this Wagner craze will blow over—it will blow over," said Mr. Wilson. "As long as it pays it's all very well; but it can't last. I know the signs of the times. It can't last for ever."

Three other stout people in the group turned pale and began to look unstrung. They were celebrated vocalists from the Fatherland, who knew quite well that nobody would tolerate their voices for a moment in any music but "the master's." Would they "blow over," too, when he did? Mr. Wilson wrinkled up his nose and continued—

"There will have to be great changes in the *personnel* of opera companies within the next few years. That's to say if money is to be made. And the whole question is really one of money, in this country at any rate."

"Well, I'm sure Wagner pays," cried Lady St. Ormyn triumphantly.

"For the moment," said Mr. Wilson, drinking some iced champagne. "But if I remain on the syndicate I shall take very good care he's not kept incessantly on the bills till the public gets sick of him."

"You're perfectly right, Mr. Wilson," said a light soprano in green, who couldn't be heard unless she were singing top notes or runs and shakes. "Heavy music can't last for ever. I always said so. The reaction must come."

"Ah, but we shan't go back to 'The Barber,' Signorina," said Mr. Wilson with a slow smile.

The lady in green hastily devoted herself to a strawberry ice.

"'The Barber!' I should hope not!" said Lady St. Ormyn.

"We shall advance, of course, though how any one can go farther than 'Tristan' I can't imagine."

"Nor I—farther in uproar," said an elderly judge, who had been educated on Bach, Mozart, and Haydn, and who thought the modern world was mad. "I wish Wagner had been brought up before me for sentence."

"I think salvation will come from the young French school," said one of the auburn-haired peeresses who had been petting Barré.

Barré, who was only just sixty-four, looked modest.

"Not if they go on giving us symphonic poems and rubbish of that kind," said Mr. Wilson. "The public doesn't want old beggars dying in attics on the flute and the kettledrum."

"Such a combination of instruments is practically unheard of!" cried Barré indignantly.

"The flute and the kettledrum!" repeated Mr. Wilson more loudly. "They want good, honest, sterling stuff, something they can take hold of and remember. That's what they want, and that's what they'll have in a very short time if I have my say."

The four Germans uttered a sniff that was like a blast. But Mr. Wilson was a power, and could prevent their re-engagement at the opera. They dared not offend him, so they waddled away in different directions, wondering what life would be like when they had "blown over" with Wagner.

"You're very hard on them, Mr. Wilson," said Lady St. Ormyn, while the light soprano in green bridled with satisfaction.

"These Wagner people want taking down," he replied. "And if nobody else will do it I will. I'm not afraid of them. They must learn to know that they're only so much material, and material that's very soon worn out into the bargain."

"What a way to speak of an artist!" cried Barré, who was not connected with the opera, and had nothing to hope for from Mr. Wilson.

"Yes, indeed," said Lady St. Ormyn. "The artistic temperament is a gift from the gods."

"And if the 'gods' get tired of it, it's not worth tuppence-ha'penny," said Mr. Wilson, strolling away to smoke a cigar on the lawn and talk about the rise in guano to another of the opera syndicate.

"I believe that 'Parsifal' is the beginning of the new musical era," said Mr. Fraser, the man like a bird, who wrote hymns and gave luncheon parties. "And that we shall have religious music dramas, full of passion, love, desire, but floating in a beautiful atmosphere of mysticism. Man must believe in something. He must aspire, even if the body holds him back."

If the world spoke truth about him, Mr. Fraser's body was very much given to holding him back.

"I should like to play St. Stephen, if an opera could be written round him, say by Bruneau," said Monsieur Anneau. "Think of the last scene. What a chance for a singer!"

"Oh, I fancy Herod, or some strong character of that kind, would suit you much better," cried Lady St. Ormyn. "But I hope we shall never have another oratorio era. I went once to stay with the Duchess of Grandon for a provincial musical festival. It was perfectly awful—hot weather, and one prolonged cry of 'Hallelujah, Amen!' from one end of the week to the other. We sat on cane chairs in a crypt for eight hours a day, and there was a collection going out. I was seriously ill afterwards, and had to go to Paris to recover. Now, Monsieur Anneau, don't you think we might have 'Le Bon Dieu'? In the music-room, of course. I know you don't like singing out of doors."

"I shall be delighted," said Monsieur Anneau, looking more like Herod than ever.

He turned to Lady Caryll, who, with Sir Reuben, Mrs. Luffa Parkinson, and Aubrey Herrick, was standing close by.

"You will come to hear me?" he asked her. "If you do not, I shall think——"

"What will you think?" the girl asked, calmly looking into his dissipated eyes.

"That you fear the power."

"I will come," she answered. "But I fear nothing."

"Not even the most dangerous of all the arts?"

"Not even that. Will you come, Sir Reuben? You must be justified of your faith in me."

As Sir Reuben left the tent with her, he saw Aubrey following Monsieur Anneau with his eyes. For a moment his calm face was transformed. A cold and yet fierce anger and disgust made it strangely vivid. Then the smooth and conventional expression returned.

"Would you like to hear 'Le Bon Dieu'?" he said to Mrs. Parkinson.

"Oh yes! It's sure to be delicious! Nobody can write about such a subject like Barré, or sing about it like dear Monsieur Anneau."

"Then let us go too. I agree with you. Monsieur Anneau is the very man to make the Deity popular in such a society."

"Yes, isn't he? I love his sacred manner."

They followed the crowd slowly towards the music-room.

CHAPTER VI

BARRÉ seated himself at the piano, ran his fat hands through his grey hair, and struck a chord high up in the treble. And Monsieur Anneau, leaning with his elbow on the piano lid, and fixing his eyes upon Lady Caryll, began to sing, or rather to recite on one note, in a beautiful, deep voice, a sentimental poem about dead flowers in the snow, starving birds, and the white terrors of the first frost of winter. Most of Barré's songs were on one, or at most two notes until quite close to the end, when there appeared a tiny tune of a very languid nature, to take you by surprise just as you had given up all hope. The singers of his masterpieces spoke till they reached the tiny tune, and then sang with all their might in order to show that they really did possess voices; and as Barré always took care to set very pretty words, everybody was invariably delighted, and said that the man who could interest you so much with a melody on one note must be a genius. On this occasion the dead flowers, the starving birds, and the frost were presented in recitative, and the little tune was reserved for the appearance of the Bon Dieu, with rain for the flowers, and crumbs —apparently of a supernatural description—for the attenuated sparrows and robin redbreasts.

Lady Caryll stood in the crowd, and met the fixed gaze of the fierce-looking singer with her calm and glittering grey eyes. Both Aubrey and Sir Reuben were watching her closely for different reasons. At the close of the song Monsieur Anneau's magnificent voice filled the whole room, and all the women present were thrilled with an emotion that was wholly sensuous. Their nerves danced, as the nerves of America had danced under the spell of this magician with the dyed beard and the feverish eyes. His shameful reputation, his evil appearance, and his gorgeous talent carried everything before them And then there was something strangely piquant in this immense, broad-shouldered man, with his great arms and mighty chest, warbling so tenderly about such tiny things. No more attractive could have been a magnificent blacksmith lamenting over the chagrin of a glow-worm, or Hercules shedding tears about the accident to a grasshopper. Mrs. Luffa Parkinson wept, and the paint on Lady St. Ormyn's cheeks glistened in the heat of her enthusiasm. Only Lady Caryll, to whom the whole song had been pointedly addressed, remained totally unmoved. When the last note died away she said to Sir Reuben—

"I think mother was right. Monsieur Anneau would make an admirable Herod. As the Bon Dieu he is hardly convincing."

"Have you a nervous system?" he said in reply, and there was an intonation of genuine wonder in his voice.

"What a strange question! Yes, I suppose so. Why do you ask me?"

"Look round. Look at the women in this room."

She glanced at the faces near her. They all looked the same as Barré struck the final chord of the symphony, for a peculiar staring excitement was in all the eyes, the undressed expression that displays the savage in civilisation. In many faces, too, the cheek-bones seemed unnaturally prominent, and the lips of the mouths were parted to allow the hurried breath to escape. The success of Monsieur Anneau was plainly written on these feminine faces. He had struck home, not to the heart, but to the senses. And that is the aim of singers like him when they sing in fashionable drawing-rooms. His voice had stirred the stagnant pools. There was a movement, the water eddied, the weeds below the surface, those tall, rank, secret things, swayed noiselessly. For the Bon Dieu had appeared to all these women in the guise of a man with feverish eyes and dyed hair, and they were enchanted. Aubrey had been right. Monsieur Anneau was the very person to make the Deity welcome in such a society.

Lady Caryll glanced round slowly. Then she said to Sir Reuben, "Well?"

"And now look at yourself in that mirror."

The mirror in which Araki had examined himself was close to them. She turned to it, and saw her white face.

"You mean that I look different. But I never feel the heat," she said quite simply.

"No, you never feel the heat," he said. "And you never will. No tropics could ever affect you."

"Sir Reuben, you speak about me with a great deal of assurance, as if you had known me very well for a long time."

"Do you know how I started in life?" he replied. "What my *métier* was at the beginning of my career?"

"No."

"I was a diamond merchant."

The girl suddenly fixed her eyes upon his worn and furrowed face with an expression of sparkling interest and animation. She opened her soft and narrow lips to speak.

"Did you feel the power, Lady Caryll?" said Monsieur Anneau's voice.

He had made his way to them from the piano, despite the noisy entreaties of Lady St. Ormyn and of all the other women in the room for one more song, the one about the nun who was unfaithful to her vows with pretty Pierrot, and who was eventually carried to Purgatory by laughing clowns, bound in a net of wild roses.

All the sparkle died away from the girl's face.

"Your voice is beautiful," she said.

"The voice! Ah! that is nothing. But my soul when I sing, my will, I myself—did you feel that?"

"In what way? In my heart, as a child might, or in my nerve-centres, like all these people?"

He bent over her, with his favourite movement suggestive of a stormy embrace barely checked by the foolish conventions of the world.

"In both."

"I don't think I have any nerve-centres," she said coolly, with just a glance at Sir Reuben.

"In your heart then?"

"I am too young to have one. This is my first season."

"The first season of a woman's heart is the most beautiful, is the only one worth having," he murmured gently.

"Shall I tell you really what I thought all the time you were singing, Monsieur Anneau?" she said, with a half smile that was full of mischief.

"Please do," he answered, folding his huge arms, and staring steadily into her eyes.

"That you and the Bon Dieu haven't even a bowing acquaintance, and that your voice is the finest in Europe."

At this point Mrs. Luffa Parkinson came up drying her eyes.

"We have all been in heaven," she said in her weary little voice. "Mr. Fraser is so upset by it that he has scratched for the bicycle handicap this evening. And all my money was on him. I ought to hate you, Monsieur Anneau."

"But you will not?" he said, transferring his passionate gaze to her.

She was immensely rich, and gave very smart little concerts at which royalties were often present.

"I am sorry Mr. Fraser is upset by being in heaven," said Lady Caryll. "Oh, good-bye, Lady Mary. Must you go?"

"I dare not trust myself to hear any more music, and I'm dining early at Claridge's to meet the new negro acrobat, Darkie Tom. He's going to be the rage this season, and I hear he's most good-natured about performing for charities. Your mother's very anxious to meet him. I'll try to arrange it."

An elderly American poetess who was standing near almost fainted, and afterwards published a terrible satire in verse upon the British aristocracy.

"You're not staying for the orgy?" said a captain in the Life Guards to a brother officer who had ordered round his cart.

"No. Wish I was. Goin' to be extra lively this evening, I'm told. They're goin' to have a skit on it in the *Pink Un.* Won't Lady St. Ormyn be jolly proud of herself?"

The big boy who hated music was staying on for the orgy. He was a noted cyclist, and the prima donna had plunged heavily on him.

"Thank heaven all the music's over," she said. "We shall have a little peace when these people are gone. D'you think I'm really not too heavy for the wheel-barrow race?"

"You're a feather-weight," he replied gallantly. "I wouldn't take the risk with one of those Germans."

"Fraulein Vogel, for instance! Did you see her Isolde?"

"Not I. But she don't come in my wheel-barrow, I'll swear."

He plucked at his tiny blond moustache with an air of martial determination, as became an arbiter of fates.

People were going fast, undeterred by the piercing shouts of the plump young woman in mustard-colour, who was singing, "Ocean, thou mighty monster!" in a voice that could be heard for miles around. Aubrey had at length shaken himself free from Mrs. Luffa Parkinson. He approached Lady Caryll, who was still with Sir Reuben.

"Can't you get away for a few minutes now?" he said to her in a low voice. "Come and have a cup of tea in the tea-house."

"Yes," she answered. "Sir Reuben, I want you to see it. You must tell me whether it is as pretty as the tea-houses of Japan."

Aubrey's face was like stone. She did not seem to notice it. Her manner had become more than usually animated.

"I feel quite domestic," she said, as they crossed the lawn, on which two young novelists were conversing about golf and American drinks in earnest undertones. "Walking between the godfather and the godson. Have you given Mr. Herrick a silver spoon, Sir Reuben?"

"Not yet," he said.

"But you are going to?"

"Perhaps—if you mean by a silver spoon a lucky chance."

His voice had become oddly significant. But Aubrey was not listening; he was feeling. Beneath the stone there was leaping fire. They passed through the shrubbery and the pond lay before them. In it red goldfish made everlasting tours, opening and shutting their bland mouths, and gazing at the water with strained eyes, in which seemed to flicker the hint of a faint and idiotic amusement. Aubrey looked at them. Their coloured bodies glowed like flames. And yet how cold they were. This thought came to his mind with intensity. He could not tell why. But in moments of emotion some insignificant object will often attract the attention with violence, acting as a magnet to the needle of the mind. And long afterwards such an object is inseparably bound up with our tragedy or with our rapture. It is the fly caged in the amber of our destiny. The largest of the flickering scarlet fish poised itself in the water with its blunt head turned towards Aubrey. It opened its vacuous mouth in a sort of smiling yawn. He remembered the exact expression for years.

"Those fish are like moving jewels," said Sir Reuben. "Their colour is alive like the colour of fire."

"Yes," said Lady Caryll. "I always feel they would be warm to the touch."

"And yet they are cold," said Sir Reuben, thinking of the moment when he had shaken hands with her for the first time.

Between them Lady Caryll and he had translated Aubrey's thought into words, and it dwindled at once, and seemed to become childishly obvious and insignificant.

The tea-house, a small and low building of wood with a pointed and thatched roof, was divided into four rooms, in all of which were little tables. The long locks of the wisteria flowed down its sides and rustled gently in the light summer wind. As they approached it seemed to be deserted, and Aubrey had a moment of cold hatred for his godfather. The young are lashed by agony when they see the flying chance as it escapes them. But often they do not see it. When they entered the tea-house it proved to be deceptive. They looked into the first room—a well-known tenor was playing Faust over the teacups to the Margaret of a pretty Russian princess, whose husband spent his life in taking baths for a complication of diseases; into the second—a little clergyman, who held that godliness is next to gaiety, was telling a funny story to a comic-opera divette; into the third—the elderly judge who hated Wagner was giving a little legal advice to a beauty whose husband troubled her by being faithful, and expecting in others the old-fashioned virtues he practised himself; into the fourth—a Jewess in rose-colour was looking through a lorgnon at a young artist who sat at one pace from her whispering that a portrait of her would make his fortune.

"How fond people are of tea," said Lady Caryll, recoiling

gracefully for the fourth time. "Shall we have ours out of doors?"

But at this moment the little clergyman and the comic-opera divette made a convulsive exit from their room, and disappeared in a peal of laughter that seemed to be the appropriate anthem of a consolidated Church and Stage brotherhood.

"How kind of Mr. Sebastian," said Lady Caryll, entering the room. "He has to get back to town for his eight-o'clock service. Miss Daisy Heriot is singing 'Blessed are the pure in heart' for him to-night."

She sat down at a round table by the window, and a servant brought them tea. They could hear the legal voice of the judge humming softly through the wall, and the final cries of the German prima donna made almost Italian by distance. The wisteria rustled gently. Aubrey listened to it, ignoring the other voices. There was a clink of china as the servant put down his silver tray.

"Do you like silence?" said Sir Reuben to Lady Caryll.

She gave him his teacup.

"I don't mind it," she said.—"Here, Mr. Herrick.—It is uncommon, and so it becomes distinguished. What do you say, Mr. Herrick?"

"I love it."

The words were on Aubrey's lips, but he checked them, and said—

"I hear it so seldom that I don't know much about it. I daresay it's all right."

"I have had years of it," said Sir Reuben. "Silence on the sea in my yacht; silence in the desert in my caravan; silence in my Moorish garden on the edge of the Bay of Tangier."

"Why were you away so long?" said the girl carelessly. "What did your diamonds do without you?"

Aubrey moved slightly and suddenly.

"I gave up my diamonds many years ago," said Sir Reuben, "for finance."

"That's what my father goes in for," she said.

The two men succeeded in not smiling.

"And I have been away in my own world," he continued. "You know I am not English. My blood is Oriental, and I am at home in places and with people who would frighten you."

"Oh no!"

Lady Caryll was stirring her tea gently.

"Well, then, with people whose habits, whose way of life, would at least disgust you."

"Do you think so? After the habits and customs of civilisation?"

"You forget that I have a husband, Mr. Hickson," said the voice of the Jewess in rose-colour to the artist as they passed into the garden.

"Won't you forget it too?" he replied. "Think what such a success would mean to me! Why, in ——"

Their conversation died away.

"You are very sarcastic, Lady Caryll," said Sir Reuben.

"I—sarcastic?" she said with calm surprise.

Aubrey longed to tell Sir Reuben that Lady Caryll spoke in simplicity and not in sarcasm, as when she had misunderstood an allusion to love in Hyde Park.

"How can he look into her face," the boy thought, "and think she understands the true meaning of this world in which she moves? She is a white flower with all the petals folded in a white sleep."

"Yes. Think of the position of women in the Western world," said Sir Reuben.

"What sort of women? Do you mean the typewriters? I know Lady Wickham said in her speech the other day that the true light has spread so far that now no less than—I forget how many hundreds of thousands of young women are 'typewriting happily in our midst.' Is that what you mean? I suppose women are not allowed to be typewriters in the East?"

"That is true; but that is not all I meant."

"Did you see many women from your garden in Morocco?"

"Yes, many—in the early morning, in the twilight, going to and coming from the Soko of Tangier. I used to watch them as I trimmed the roses that grew along my garden wall."

"Twilight!" she repeated. "Ah, listen!"

And she held up her small, cool hand, which he had touched for the first time that day. In the distance they heard the deep voice of Monsieur Anneau. He was singing "Crépuscule," Barré's last song but two. Evening was falling. They sat in silence. Aubrey's eyes were fastened on Lady Caryll, but his face preserved its conventional and rigid expression, the fixed expression of a mask.

"Let us come out on to the grass," Lady Caryll said, when the first verse faded away.

The voice of the singer sounded nearer to them now, and more beautiful. At their feet lay the water in which the glowing fish moved silently. Aubrey watched their bodies gleaming and growing dim as they vanished in the opaque shadows, and colour seemed to him then, as often before, to be music, as music often seems to be colour. The red gold of the fish was a song, and the clear pallor of Lady Caryll's face, the frosty yellow of her hair, the grey of her long eyes—these were a song too. And the evening light had a voice that blended with the voice that sang again and again "Crépuscule! Crépuscule!" His heart was stirred. Something within him seemed suddenly to live and to be restless in its life, as if all these voices called to it and cried, "Do you not hear us? We are calling to you." And he was filled with that strange and terrible sensation of a living thing that knows it has never really lived, and that scarcely knows what is the way to live, but that knows there is a marvel, a wonder called—living. But this new-born creature within him ached. It was in pain; yet its pain was beautiful, for he felt that he divined from its power to suffer its power to rejoice, and that, robbed of the one, he could never hope to possess the other.

The song was over. A gong sounded, and then the wild note of a coach-horn blown by the big boy who hated music. It was followed by a shrill peal of laughter and by loud voices raised in merry remonstrance. The *crépuscule* of society was falling!

"Dinner!" said Lady Caryll. "While we are at dinner they will light up the garden."

"I'm hungry," Aubrey said, merely because he felt that the blast on the horn, the dinner, the artificially lighted garden, were things hateful as the cries of hawkers would be along the ways of paradise.

"Are you going in for the bicycle races?" she asked him.

"No. Wish I was, but I drove down. Don't make me take in Mrs. Parkinson; she's the wrong colour for dinner."

They went towards the house.

The guests of Lady St. Ormyn who had waited for the orgy dined at little tables. There were eight people at each table. Aubrey took in the American poetess, and sat opposite to Lady Caryll, who was with Monsieur Anneau. Sir Reuben was at Lady Ormyn's table. The American poetess was a charming creature, with soft, snow-white hair and bright, observant brown eyes. She had travelled much and suffered much, and, like most sweet-natured women who have suffered, she had a very sensitive love for all young things. She looked forward for them, and hoped for them, and feared for them, and longed to preserve their purity, and the morning light in their eyes and in their hearts. She was of those who can shed tears in secret for strangers, who can have the heartache for vagrants seen only in passing by the roadside. Nevertheless she had many odd prejudices, and could write with a lively bitterness. Some of her readers thought her cruel, but all those who knew her knew her kind.

She and Aubrey had never met before, and Aubrey was not easy to talk to. In many ways he resembled his father, and his father was patrician and British to the core. Mrs. Reckitt—Adela Reckitt, as she was always called by the reading world—tried him on several subjects, and found him dull and abstracted. Yet she liked him. She liked what she would have called his atmosphere. She was quick to read character, quicker still to feel it. And very soon, looking round for the cause of this character's dissimulation, she found it in Monsieur Anneau.

Monsieur Annean was one of those many men who think ill of all women, who divine debauchery in every nature, and who believe that descending is the secret pleasure of every foot that treads upon the earth, whatever pretences to the contrary may be put forward to deceive a watching world. He loved to wallow, had loved to do so all his life. And he felt pleasantly certain that this affection was shared by everybody. Those who endeavoured to make him think otherwise he called hypocrites, and he considered himself better than they were because he was honest. Even talents he looked upon as aids towards the attainment of the slough. He was immensely gifted. He had a noble voice, would have had a noble appearance, had he not looked evil, was intensely musical, and had an emotional temperament. When he sang he could and did feel what he was singing, though he felt it often in a wrong way. But even in his art he was a libertine. When he sang of the Bon Dieu he thought of a woman, of some human being on whom he meant to cast his spell for one reason or another. And he had done more evil with his music than most men could accomplish with all the devilish weapons invented by the cruel artfulness of civilisation. Finding that he possessed something which could be made a great power, he perfected it. And ever since it had been perfected he had used it vigilantly in the service of ambition and in a lower service. And the use of it in this lower service especially had become an inordinate passion in him. If he was yielded to, he was agreeable at first and cruel at last. If he was resisted, he became dangerous. It was his continual desire to feel that his power was being effective on some individuality. Night and day some thought connected with this desire, some hope arising out of it, was with him. It filled him to-night as he sat by Lady Caryll.

Aubrey knew it, and Mrs. Reckitt grew to know it through Aubrey. Her companion, calm, self-possessed, and frigid though he appeared, was on the watch, was whipped by a keen emotion of manly anger. Mrs. Reckitt went back a great many years. She saw another man who had felt like that for her sake, and she knew Aubrey intimately, though he was totally unaware of it.

" Did you hear me summoning the twilight?" said Monsieur Anneau softly to Lady Caryll.

"Yes—even Nature obeys you. What's your Christian name?"

"Jules."

"Not Orpheus?"

"You are cruel. But I do not care for the twilight. It is an affair for Nature. I care only to have power over human beings."

"The people at the opera! Well, old Lady Groome never misses a night when you sing."

"But you miss many."

"It is so hot at Covent Garden."

"Ah, you love the coolness of night in open spaces. Come out with me after dinner. I want to——"

Mrs. Reckitt felt that a quiver ran through her companion. He lifted his glass to his lips, and she noticed that his hand trembled slightly. From Lady St. Ormyn's table came peals of laughter that were almost wild. They heard her saying at the top of her voice—

"No, no, I won't go in your barrow. Monsieur Anneau shall wheel me. His arms are as strong as his voice. Sir Reuben, you must—no, no, I won't—I won't. What, Sir Frederick? Margaret carried away by Mephisto! Absurd! But Barré's going to wheel Fraulein Vogel."

There was a scream of merriment.

"I'll make him. He'll do anything for me. What? Kill him! He's wonderfully wiry—quite a stayer! More likely to stay than go! Then he shall have a prize for——"

The conversation in the big room seemed to Aubrey to become a deafening roar, from which now and then voices detached themselves for an instant only to sink back eventually into the whirlpool. He heard Lord St. Ormyn's light and playful tones, suggesting to a rich Australian widow that there was any amount of money to be made in electric perambulators. Araki's mechanical and almost hyena-like laugh came to his ears, and then the guttural murmur of a German tenor talking about Bayreuth to one of the auburn-haired sisters. Some one near Aubrey said, "Yes, Lady St. Ormyn's parties are always so delightfully gay;" and he felt inclined to shudder. He tried not to look at Monsieur Anneau, but the feverish brilliancy of the singer's terribly expressive face tore at his attention. It was to him an utterly hateful face, but he realised its power, its magnetic influence. And it seemed to him that such eyes must stir a girl's heart to excitement, even if only to an excitement of repulsion. And then he remembered a song that he had heard, "If thou art sleeping, maiden, wake! wake and open thy door!" A sort of dull terror seized him. For he saw before him a sleeper, wrapped in the white dreams of early youth, of purity, of that perfect thing called ignorance. And he saw a brilliant, middle-aged *roué* giving way to his one inordinate passion—the passion for making an effect upon, for gaining control over, a new nature and a new heart. If it should fall to Monsieur Anneau to awaken that lovely sleeper! A sort of sickness of the soul fell upon Aubrey. The length of the dinner seemed endless, because he was resolved what to do when the end came.

"Night ought to be lovely in this garden," said the gentle voice of Mrs. Reckitt to him.

He turned to her mechanically.

"Yes, and there'll be a moon."

"Are you fond of country places?"

Aubrey thought of his annual tour of big houses, and answered, without enthusiasm—

"I don't know—sometimes. I'm fond of shooting and hunting." Then he added perfunctorily, "And you?"

"I love quiet, and I love animals, and thoughts—so I love the country. It is difficult to think in crowds."

"Do you find that?" Aubrey said, with a sudden quickening of the voice, aware of the ferment of thought in his own mind.

"To think rightly, that is," she said. "Of course the mind often works very rapidly in noise and a vision of multitudes. But we want quiet in order to find out the errors in our thoughts, just as we often need suffering in order to discover the errors in our conduct."

Aubrey looked into her face carefully, curiously, for the first time.

Rings of smoke rose softly over the little tables. People were sipping coffee.

"Is the garden lit?" said Lady St. Ormyn to a servant.

"Yes, my lady."

Aubrey glanced out across the verandah. He could see a small moon coming up above the chestnut trees, and a multitude of blood-red stars, like eyes, looking out among the leaves. Along the paths green glow-worms seemed crawling in multitudes, and the mauve spray of an illuminated fountain aspired between the earth and the dark evening sky.

"Don't forget the torches," said Lady St. Ormyn.

"No, my lady."

"Let me see," she cried. "How many do we want? You count, Johnnie!"

"All right, Fifi; don't you bother. I know all about it," said the big boy.

He was in roaring spirits, and was showing the prima donna a new game played with nuts and cherries. He threw her a cherry, and at the same time she threw him a nut. Opening his wide mouth, full of strong white teeth, he caught his nut and cracked it like a monkey. The prima donna made a wild effort, a terrible grimace, and missed the cherry, which fell with a splash into a silver bowl full of rose-water. They shrieked with laughter.

"Try again!" shouted the boy. "You nearly got it. Hold your head lower, and turn your face up towards the ceiling. No; that's not enough. Here — pardon — let me. Now open your mouth!"

"Make haste. It's worse than holding a high C."

Araki came up to Lady St. Ormyn, bringing his chair with him. He began to consult her about his songs, which always sounded best at night.

"Oh, give us your wickedest. Nobody here'll mind—besides, out in the garden it doesn't matter. What is it about?"

He murmured two verses of French with his sly and conscious smile.

"That's delicious—yes, very, very! But that's all the better. We must have it. Repeat the refrain once more, 'Ah, ma petite tu—' What comes next?"

He whispered. She smiled.

"It's like a song I heard in Vienna, only worse. Just the thing. Sing it and the sobbing song, and then we'll have the races, and a *punch* to finish up with. Now, good people!"

There was a general movement. The men began to light cigars. All the women had dined in their hats. A few of them began to put light wraps over their shoulders. The prima donna, assisted by the big boy, wound some lace round the throat that had made her fortune, and went off with him to see about the torches for the bicycles. Lord St. Ormyn patted Sir Reuben gently on the back preparatory to a conversation about a very promising new concern in the City. Araki surreptitiously arranged his hair before a mirror and looked at a new smile which he was going to try for the first time in the song he had recited to Lady St. Ormyn. It didn't quite do. He tried another, rather more obviously wicked, and contemplated it fixedly with anxious, inquiring eyes. Monsieur Anneau bent over Lady Caryll.

"The garden looks exquisite."

"Like Marguerite's garden. You ought to be dressed in red."

"Why? I am only a fiend when I'm paid to be one. To-night——"

"You are an angel—for nothing. What self-sacrifice!"

Mrs. Reckitt was trying to give Aubrey the chance of escaping from her without being impolite. He stayed beside her and spoke of Araki's singing, endeavouring to conceal the effort that it cost him. His eyes were fixed upon Monsieur Anneau, who was now moving towards the verandah with Lady Caryll.

"Yes, French songs are generally pretty enough," he said. "Absurd things sound pathetic in French—or gay. It's different in English."

Monsieur Anneau and Lady Caryll moved across the verandah and disappeared. Their figures threw a black cloud upon the mauve spray of the fountain for an instant, hiding it. Then Aubrey saw the coloured lacework of the water again.

"Would you care to go out into the garden?" he said to Mrs. Reckitt in a very calm and constrained voice. "Every one is——"

He looked round. People were flowing out. All of them were talking loudly and laughing. Even Mr. Fraser was in fits. His mysticism had disappeared for the moment under the humanising influence of champagne, and his melancholy was merged in a sort of hysterical and birdlike madness. He chirruped in a high soprano voice, and made extraordinary gestures with his thin hands as he accompanied a pretty Frenchwoman into the garden, which began to hum with the sound of voices.

"Yes, let us go," said Mrs. Reckitt, "and then I must find Lord St. Ormyn. I want to have a little business talk with him."

Lord St. Ormyn had been kind enough to lose a couple of hundred pounds for the poetess recently, "as a friend."

Aubrey thanked his kind companion in his heart, and they went out.

The garden wanted to be poetical, and the lovely night aimed at an atmosphere of tenderness and of reverent romance. The silver disc of the moon was almost cruelly bright against the black funeral of the chestnuts, and in the wind, delicate and vague, the scent of flowers hovered still, reluctant to depart. With it, ethereal, emotional, mysteriously pathetic, mingled the scent of Nature in night hours. Alone, the garden would have been a nocturne.

As Aubrey and Mrs. Reckitt stepped out, the big boy exploded a rocket without warning, and all the women screamed. The rocket went up above the trees and burst in the very face of the moon. A flood of golden sparks poured down upon the funeral of the trees. Every one acclaimed the big boy, who then prepared to entertain the poor, sad, old night with a few squibs of extraordinary detonating power. Meanwhile servants were getting ready the torches, and a piano had been carried out to the front of the verandah. The popping of soda-water corks gave a hint of what music ought to be to the untutored wind, and three-quarters of the men present began to think steadily of Scotch whisky.

As the rocket burst Aubrey found himself alone and free. His sweet companion had vanished under fire.

CHAPTER VII

ARAKI pulled his favourite lock of hair forward on his forehead, and whispered to his accompanist, a young man of talent who was doomed for the moment to play pigeon-music at the parties of fools. The accompanist nodded with a weary expression of reiterated assent. He was thinking all the time about the things he wanted to do in life. He began to play a tinkling prelude mechanically, and to improvise in order to attract the attention of the people who were shrieking and bounding round the squibs of the big boy.

"Johnnie, be quiet!" cried Lady St. Ormyn on the lawn. "Araki is going to——"

"Only one more, Fifi!"

Bang!

The prima donna clapped her hands. She was almost in love with the young roisterer, for he had just refused her offer of a box at the opera to hear her sing "Traviata."

"You're splendid at letting off fireworks!" he had said, "but singing symphonies—no thank you!"

And then he had trusted her with a "Pharaoh's Serpent." She began to appreciate his frank nature too warmly to explain that she had not yet begun to earn her living by singing symphonies. And she grew hot with triumph when she managed the "Pharaoh's Serpent" cleverly, although she was always cold before the fiery applause of an adoring public.

Araki began to fidget and to lose his conception of his new smile. The accompanist went on industriously improvising and kept his right foot firmly pressed upon the loud pedal of the piano.

"Johnnie, you naughty boy! you are only fit to be at Eton!" cried Lady St. Ormyn. "I insist upon——"

"Only one more, Fifi, 'pon honour!"

Bang!

"Play louder! Play louder!" said Araki to the accompanist. "They don't hear you."

"I can't," said the accompanist. "I shall break the piano."

"Break it, then! I must have it in the papers to-morrow that I sang my new song here with success."

"No, Johnnie, that must be the last. Mr. Fraser, stop him for me! Madame Viva, do try to."

Bang!

"Here, Madame Viva! You shall do the catherine wheel. Hang it on this rose-bush. Bravo! Look out for the sparks! You are a dodger and no mistake!"

Mr. Fraser fluttered away with the movements of a distressed canary-bird. He was afraid of everything, but especially of fireworks. And then big boys seemed to him like dangerous wild animals. He never asked them to his luncheon parties.

But now, acting under Lady St. Ormyn's shrill and laughing commands, two guardsmen made for the big boy amid peals of merriment. He took to his heels, his arms full of fireworks. They gave chase, leaping flower-beds, and deploying cleverly round rhododendrons and rose-bushes. Madame Viva, forgetting her voice imprudently, shrieked directions to the big boy. He doubled like a gigantic hare. But unfortunately he had no form at Epsom. So, after a prolonged chase, he was caught, seized, and robbed of his explosives, to the secret sorrow of all those who were laughing at his efforts to go on being naughty.

"Now, Araki!" said Lady St. Ormyn.

And the Syrian, quickly rehearsing the smile for the last time, touched an electric button which illuminated his expressive face, and signed to his accompanist to begin the new song which was worse than the song heard by Lady St. Ormyn at Vienna.

Meanwhile Aubrey was searching in the garden. He followed the winding paths, walking slowly and calmly between the green lines of the artificial glow-worms. And everywhere he found people talking violently and laughing as people only laugh at night after dinner. The elderly judge was being very funny to the Beauty. The Jewess in rose-colour was still arguing with the young artist about the possibility of his painting her picture. Barré, seated in a garden-chair, was receiving more exaggerated compliments from the auburn-haired sisters, and Fraulein Vogel was discussing Isolde with two compatriots in a voice that reached the stars. All the natures seemed stirred into a frothing turmoil, and on every side volubility was indulging in the luxury of a steady crescendo. Through the trees that concealed the stables moving lights flashed, and the voices of grooms and of footmen rose in a confused murmur. Then there was a shrill little shriek and a burst of soprano giggling. The maids were evidently following a long-recognised custom and were imitating the amusements of their mistresses.

Aubrey reached the shrubberies. Just then Araki began to sing. He had a thin and penetrating voice, very foreign in timbre, with a little break or catch in it, and he sang with a great deal of trickery, and uttered his words with almost hysterical precision and clearness. As Aubrey came into the black shadow of the trees he understood the meaning of the song, and a sense of disgust, often felt by him before, flooded his heart. This sense of disgust was quite distinct from prudery, but it was complicated by a feeling of wonder which seemed to set him very much apart from his kind. He wondered at his world. Yet, so far, it had never occurred to him that he might, if he chose, seek another world, make a trial of a different class of society from that which was his own. Day by day, night by night, he did a thousand things. Why? For no reason of affection or of desire. He was like a man in a climate that does not suit his health, who is vaguely aware that there are other climates, but who never dreams of going to them.

After the first verse of the song there was a confused murmur of approval. Many people who were pacing the paths of the garden stood still between the lights to listen. They whispered to each other, and smiled consciously while the accompanist played the interlude.

Aubrey passed into the shrubbery. He heard the birds shifting their places among the trees, and was sharply conscious of this other life, so strangely different from the human destiny, yet being lived so continuously and so ignorantly by its side and in its shadow. The instinct of these birds told them to sleep. Yet they remained in Lady St. Ormyn's woods while Araki was singing. He began his second verse. But here, among the trees, Aubrey could not hear the words. Only the nasal voice, with its shrill break, reached his ears. And from its inflections he gathered the progress of the historiette about the "*petite*." He followed a tiny path that curved among the chestnuts. It was deserted, and might have been a path in a forest. Only the red eyes watching from the branches of the trees created an artificial atmosphere. Aubrey turned a corner and saw two figures walking slowly in front of him. He recognised Lady Caryll and Monsieur Anneau. The girl's white robe was like the robe of a ghost that treads a sorrowful round on the dark nights of the year; and the huge form of the singer was almost blotted out against it. He was a towering vagueness in the night, and seemed to impend over his companion like the shadow of something tremendous and influential, that was too discreet to allow itself to be plainly seen. Aubrey hesitated to join Lady Caryll and Monsieur Anneau, although he had come to seek them. The reserve that was the guiding principle of his life took hold on him. He cursed it, but, for the moment, he could not fight it. He paused and watched the white robe of the girl grow faint among the trees. His exact knowledge of where she was seemed to arrest his power of action and to chill the impulses which had been leaping in his heart. To seek had been possible to him, and he had thought that he sought with intention. But he had not realised himself and his own sensitiveness. He stopped, stood still for a moment, then turned and retraversed the shrubbery, just as Araki began to sing his famous sobbing song.

This song had been the rage of London for an unusually long time. It was a tale of varying griefs, and once the Syrian had sung it well, with a real art, variety, and the touch of nature. Incessant repetition had, however, blunted his powers. He hated it now as a man hates an illness that is incessantly with him. The sound of his own voice in it filled him with a sickness of ennui that was almost insupportable. It was incredible to him that there should still be people who wished to hear him sob; and so his sobbing had become entirely mechanical, like the melancholy of a machine, and he cried in the refrain like a loud thing that is without life. Aubrey, who at this moment felt strangely sad, heard this lifeless noise of grief among the trees—the weeping of a young girl for her lost lover, of an old man for his lost youth, of a coquette pretending repentance, of a child who has broken a toy. And all these griefs sounded to him the same and sounded horrible. Laughter had oppressed him—the laughter of Lady St. Ormyn's guests, forgetful of the night and drowned in the influence of a good dinner. Now tears oppressed him, and, moved by Araki's poor and pitiful mechanics, he began to say to himself that both the gaiety and the grief of the world were equally horrible, that men and women wept without real sorrow, even as they laughed without real joy. All expression of emotion, even all emotion, became for the time ridiculous to him. He did not except his own. When you suffer physical pain, watch your pain, consider it, and often it will seem to cease to be yours, and become like an object outside of you observed by the eye. And so it is sometimes with the pain of the heart. Aubrey listened to Araki and watched his own grief until it became detached from him and he could dissect it coolly, as many a man dissects the grief of his acquaintance. He stood there in the shrubbery, and stared at and laughed at his heart—until the song ceased.

But then, in a moment, the atmosphere changed. The cessation of false expression caused also the cessation of that which was unreal in him. And he walked on, and mingled with the crowd, tormented, tingling with excitement, yet always pressed by the icy hands of reserve.

Araki, on whose forehead stood little beads of perspiration, was surrounded by people expressing their delight in the thing that he loathed. He smiled at them with his mouth, and could have struck them. The accompanist watched the scene with cold and lacklustre eyes. Two servants came out and carried the piano away.

"Thank goodness the music's all over!" said the big boy to the prima donna. "Now then for the larks!"

She looked at him with her unimaginative, greedy eyes, and almost loved him.

Lady St. Ormyn was now in a state of boisterous excitement. Talking always intoxicated her, and she had been talking ever since one o'clock in the afternoon. She began to give innumerable directions about the races.

"How many wheel-barrows are there?" she cried.

"One dozen, my lady," said a servant.

"Wheel them all to the top of the slope."

"Yes, my lady."

"Now, let's see! Who's entered? Sir Frederick, Barré, Monsieur Anneau, Johnnie." She counted on her fingers, which were covered with extraordinary rings, and rattled her bracelets, from which hung innumerable charms. For she was as superstitious as an Indian.

"Eleven!" she exclaimed arithmetically. "We want one more." She looked round. "Mr. Herrick, will——"

But Aubrey had disappeared. As he reached the outskirts of the little crowd he met Lady Caryll and Monsieur Anneau. The singer looked angry. His red-brown eyes were flashing. The girl was like a moonbeam, Aubrey thought. He stopped, and said to Monsieur Anneau—

"Lady St. Ormyn wants you for the wheel-barrow race."

The singer bowed, as he bowed on the stage when he took the part of a king or of a high priest. He was undeniably impressive. He stretched out his mighty arms with a smile.

"I shall win the race," he said, looking hard at Lady Caryll.

"With my mother," Lady Caryll said. "I will pray for your success."

He stared into her face with fiery impudence.

"In all things?"

"All things connected with wheel-barrows."

"Your prayers move only in a limited circle?"

"My prayers on your behalf."

"Monsieur Anneau! Where is Monsieur—Barré, you're to wheel Fraulein Vogel! Yes, you are. Now, Sir Frederick—No, no, you have the green barrow with the green lamp! The green barrow! Monsieur Anneau, where are you?"

The singer cast a last glance at Lady Caryll, and went towards his hostess with a slow and striding walk. Barré and Fraulein

Vogel were passionately discussing their chances amid peals of laughter. The big boy was giving the prima donna tips about sitting firmly, and helping him at the turn with her feet. Two of the men-servants were trying to conceal their convulsive merriment. They failed, but nobody noticed it. Lady St. Ormyn's voice grew continually louder. She shouted without being aware that she was not whispering, and made as many gestures as if she were arranging a pageant of elephants. She was quite happy because she was in the midst of noise and confusion, and confusion was her idea of gaiety. She liked to feel as if she were stirring people with a large spoon.

"Lady Caryll!"
"Yes."
"You have been in the wood with Monsieur Anneau?"
"Yes."
"Come into the wood with me."
"But the races?"
"We shall not see them there."
"Don't you want to see them?"
"Not to-night."
"But M. Barré and Fraulein Vogel?"
"Don't let us think about them," he said, trying to beat down his riotous and nervous impatience.
"Have you no sense of humour?" she answered.
"Perhaps not to-night. Will you come into the wood?"
"Do you know that there is quite a heavy dew on the grass?"
"A dew!" he said. "How strange!"
"Why?"

But he could not explain there those little sudden thoughts that glide into some minds, whimsically as it seems, or make her understand, in the midst of the laughing crowd, his sense of the strangeness of dew in that garden.

"Come into the wood," he repeated.
"Very well," she said, without either apparent eagerness or apparent reluctance.

They turned and went away from the people, who were now beginning to follow Lady St. Ormyn to the top of the slope where the wheel-barrows had been arranged in a gaily painted row. In the small wood there was loneliness for the moment. Aubrey bent down and put his hand to the grass. He withdrew it wet. He felt that he could have kissed his hand with the dew on it.

"Wasn't I right?" Lady Caryll said.
"Yes."
"Don't you pity the people who are spilt in turning the corner?"

"No. They deserve it."

"But why?"

"For romping on such a night as this," he answered slowly.

"Is it not like other summer nights?"

There was a little note of mischief in her voice.

"How can you say that?" he said.

And indeed he wondered. For to him now it was the first magical summer night of the world. He knew why; he wanted to tell her why. Yet to do so was difficult to him. His reserve made most things difficult to him; but he was almost feverishly resolved to cast it away, here and now under the moon. Yet he hesitated and was troubled. They heard a shriek of laughter in the distance. Fraulein Vogel was taking her place in the orange-coloured wheelbarrow, and Barré was seizing the handles with his trembling fat fingers. Aubrey said to himself that it was this noise of humanity that troubled him.

"How can they do that?" he said impatiently.

For he feared each little thing that fought against the holy influence of the night on his companion and on himself.

"Don't you like to hear people enjoying themselves?" said Lady Caryll.

"Not like that—not to-night."

"How peculiar you are, Mr. Herrick," she said.

They were in the darkness of the trees, but always the red eyes were watching them, and now Aubrey thought they looked like jewels.

"Don't you feel as I do?" he said.

"How can I tell what you feel?" she asked a little carelessly.

The remark seemed to explain Aubrey to himself, to set before him all the blunted and sick life of the reserved man who lives eternally alone, pacing uneasily the cage that his own nature has constructed for him to dwell in.

"Shall I tell you, then?" he said.

And his voice changed in uttering the words. It was no longer the voice of a special world, of a special society, but it was the voice of a man.

"Sit here," he said.

There were some chairs dotted about in the wood. She obeyed him.

"I brought you here to tell you what I feel," he said. And then again he hesitated. "It is difficult, but I know you will understand me. No one else could."

He had felt that about Lady Caryll ever since he had loved her, and he thought he loved her partly because he felt that. She was silent, looking at him with her long, clear eyes, that had so lately, and in the same shadow, met the angry glance of Monsieur Anneau.

"Do you care to understand me?" he added.

"Yes," she answered.

A faint sense of curiosity was really waking in her, and she wished him to gratify it.

"Caryll," he said in an uneven voice that sounded half ashamed, "it is awfully difficult to me to explain what I feel about anything to any one. I don't know why. Somehow I cannot ever do it without a sense that I am being ridiculous or violent If I seem so to you to-night, you must try to forgive me. But indeed I would rather seem absurd to you than continue to be silent. Monsieur Anneau has not been silent. Has he, Caryll?"

"No, not exactly."

"Then why should I be? Do you care to tell me what he said to you?"

"It isn't worth while. But he was very operatic."

There was ice in her voice when she said that—ice that made Aubrey grow hot all over.

"I can't be that. He's been practising an art of expression all his life nearly."

"And he insists on making every woman listen to his exercises."

"You don't like him?"

"Bravo! Anneau old boy! Well run!"

It was the stentorian voice of the big boy shouting on the slope.

"I like him when he sings. I don't care particularly for his speaking voice."

"And I can neither sing—nor speak."

"Try to."

Now she really wanted to know him. She looked up at the red eyes in the trees, and she thought how unlike jewels they were.

"I will try," he said. "Caryll, I daresay you think I am cold and selfish and idle. That fellow Anneau has worked. He's better than I. I've been a fool—dropping the Foreign Office, and all that. But I'm young and I can change. I—I love you—very much."

He grew scarlet in the darkness, and his reserve stung him like a flame. But he let it go on stinging him.

"I love you, and I don't even like many people. I say this only because I want you to understand how much I mean when I say I love you. Can you understand? You must feel it—for I can't really explain properly. I can't explain myself. I don't believe I ever shall be able to."

There was a tiny tinkling of bells in the garden. The bicycles were being brought out from the stables.

"Perhaps my hands can tell you," Aubrey said suddenly, after an instant of silence.

He bent down and took Lady Caryll's hands out of her lap and held them in his tightly.

"I never want to touch people," he said. "I always want to touch you. Do you understand what that means in a man?"

"Go on," she said.

And then, having her hands in his, he was able to. The flame of his reserve almost ceased from stinging him.

"Nearly all my life I have felt things more than people," he said. "Now I feel all those things in you; summer, and night, and the stars, Caryll, and silence, and flowers, and the sun, and everything that is beautiful. Whenever I feel anything that makes me happy, or that makes me think I could be worth something, it is in you too—and seems to reach me because I love you."

The sound of the little bells began to be drawn round the garden in a circle. Two or three of the bicyclists were exercising on the racing track. Aubrey thought of the rings of the fairies in woodland places, and the music seemed to make a home in which he sat with this young girl whom he loved.

"Music too," he said. "I feel that in you, but not in all these people who talk for ever about music. They don't seem to understand at all the thing they are discussing. I don't know anything about music, of course, but it helps me to feel. Isn't it meant only to do that? Like the sound of the sea and of wind in the night? Perhaps I'm talking nonsense. But I don't care, now I've got hold of your hands. I don't care for anything but to make you know how I love you."

The circle of bells became more complete as more bicyclists slipped round the track, and here and there, through distant trees, the torches flashed and faded.

"How can I make you? You are so young and so——" pure he was going to say. But he stopped. It seemed impure even to whisper such a word to her—"so good. I should like to take you away from everybody who is not as good as you are, so that you should never understand them. But I think you never will. You are so different. Perhaps you are too different to love me. I've often thought that too."

"I am different from you—yes," she said.

And she spoke with the voice of one in whom a slight surprise was waking.

"I know—I know. But I will try to be like you, or at least

not that, perhaps. But I'll try to be worthy in my way. That's all a man can do, for he can't ever be like a good woman." He thought of his mother just then, the mother to whom he never told his thoughts or his desires. "He can only follow her at a distance, but she can lead him into a life he would never know without her, a life different from this!"

He said the last words with a sudden impatience, for with the sound of the flying bells was now mingled another sound. The bicyclists were calling to one another; the torches they carried seemed to glare through the trees like spies. And the shrill voices of anxious partisans, yelling encouragement or condemnation to the racers, disturbed the beauty of the night, and stirred into angry ripples the still waters of its dream. Aubrey tried to be deaf to these riotous voices which strove to make everything vulgar and absurd. He endeavoured to forget these gay revellers, who were so near to him in body, so far away from him in mind, and with an effort he set them at a distance, until their cries became indifferent to him, as noises that come to one from a ship irrevocably sailing to some place that one will never see.

"Caryll," he said, "don't you hate this life too, with all its noise and its lack of real meaning? Don't you feel that though it never stops talking it has really very little to say to you?"

"Sometimes I do," she said.

Her voice was slightly less calm than usual. Perhaps his hands did begin to tell her something.

"I do always. And I have often felt that you do, for you seem outside of it all. These singers with their everlasting jealousies and intrigues, these actors who talk about the Church as if it were their profession, and clergymen who talk about the stage as if it were theirs, these beauties who can only see their own faces, and these City men who——" He suddenly stopped, remembering Lord St. Ormyn. "I don't know why I've any right to condemn, though," he said with sudden humbleness. "I'm no better than they are. Only, I do think life is nothing without some poetry, some romance, some one to understand and to love, some one to tell one's thoughts to, some one who will tell their thoughts in return."

He stopped, suddenly aware of her long silence.

"Have you nothing to tell me, Caryll?" he said.

She looked up at him in the shadow of the trees.

"Have you nothing to tell me?" he repeated.

"Of myself?"

"Yes. The things that you never tell to others—to most people."

A curious expression of reticence, almost of cunning, came

into her face. It was ugly and strange. A red spear of light from one of the lamps among the leaves lay across her face almost like a narrow bar of blood. Aubrey thought it was this red spear that tarnished her moonlight beauty. And he sprang up, detached the little lamp, came to her, and again took her hands in his.

"Why did you do that?" she said.

"That horrible light made you seem—seem——"

"What?"

"It gave you a false and dreadful expression, like a mask."

She was beautiful again now.

"Tell me!" he reiterated.

"The things I never tell to most people," she said, in a low voice. "You want to hear them?"

"Yes."

Now her face changed again and became mischievous, and the corners of her soft mouth turned upwards.

"Do you think a woman ever tells those things?" she said.

"Yes, to a man when—when she loves him."

He spoke with a quiver of proud shyness.

"Especially to him?" she said. "Aubrey, do you understand women? They love their secrets, but they seldom love to tell them to the man they love."

"Would you say that all women are so reserved, then?" he said.

He had been accustomed to think that no one suffered from that strange sickness of the soul as he did.

"I think all women are naturally secretive?" she said.

"You too?"

"I suppose I am like my sisters."

"How little you know yourself," he said. "You are strangely unlike them."

"Do you think so?"

"I know it. I feel it whenever I am with you. I never met any one like you. I never shall."

"Perhaps that is a happy fortune for you, then," she said.

"What do you mean?"

"You don't know at all?"

"No, Caryll."

"Perhaps some day you will know."

"Tell me now," he said.

A sudden sensation of mystery and of oppression had come to him, as if the night had grown more sultry, as if a storm were hidden in its breast. He looked up at the sky. The stars were clear and bright; then he looked down into her eyes, and the mystery and the storm seemed to be in them. But he saw them in shadow, and in a gloom that was flecked with dim light, both natural and artificial. He remembered that afterwards.

"No," she said, "I cannot. And it is only a fancy. Perhaps I am too young to know myself. Even if I do, I cannot tell you what I am."

"You do not know," he said.

And the sense of mystery and of oppression left him. She seemed only a child to him, a child whom he worshipped.

"Shall I tell you what you are?" he added.

"What you think I am!" she said with a smile.

"What I know. You are a dreamer, Caryll."

"A dreamer, you think?"

"A dreamer in the midst of the hot noise and bustle of the world you and I live in. You do not notice it; you do not understand it, and it cannot hurt you, because you are asleep—like a child asleep upon a battlefield or in a place of wickedness."

"How you weave your fancies round me!"

"You do not think them true?"

"And of what am I dreaming?"

"Of beautiful things."

"Things of the world?"

"Why not? There are beautiful things in the world everywhere—in this garden. You feel them as I do."

"Yes?"

"Don't you?"

"I want to hear you tell me what I feel," she said.

And that was true. Never before had she felt any real interest in that strange thing, the character of a human being.

"In your dream? But I want to wake you from it."

"Isn't that cruel?"

"I wonder!" he said.

It almost seemed to him that it was, that a man's love for a woman was, and must always be, in some degree cruel. But if so, that was ordained and could only be accepted. And, being a man, he was even conscious of a thrill of joy that came with the thought. There is always a violence in any love that seeks a reward. And Aubrey had his great purpose in view, though as yet he had not stated it. Two things made him go slowly—his reserve and his joy in this absolutely novel renunciation of it. Beyond the belt of trees the laughter and the cries of people grew louder and more incessant. The torches carried by the racers spun by like demon flames borne on a travelling wind. And the tinkle of the bells was ceaseless.

"Would you dream for ever?" Aubrey said. "But that too is

sad, because in a dream you never really feel. You only dream that you feel, that you act, that you are sad or joyous. You hear only echoes. You are not absolutely alive. Let me wake you, Caryll."

"To what?"

"To love."

There was a slight rustle among the nearest trees. They did not notice it.

"Others have tried, I know," he went on earnestly. "That man to-night—Anneau——"

"We need not speak of him," she said.

"And yet," Aubrey said, with an uncontrollable flash of jealousy, "he has great influence over women."

"None over me."

Again he looked at her with wonder, and thought that the difference between her and all other women was strangely acute.

"Could I have?" he said.

And he spoke doubtfully.

"Do you think so?"

And she looked up right into his eyes, as if she asked him for an answer that her own heart had not yet given her, almost, too, as if she asked herself the question, slowly, thoughtfully, with a vague activity of curiosity that was not merely idle. They were silent for a long moment under the trees, as people are when they sit close and alone and try to read each other's souls, to tempt the great enigma from its distant hiding-place. And through their silence came the ceaseless sound of the bells. Aubrey hated them then. They seemed to stand in his way and to obscure his power of clear vision. Their noise was like a mirage that rises and floats before the real scenery that lies along the way of life. And when he answered Lady Caryll his voice was still doubtful at first.

"Yes," he said, "Caryll, wake from your dream, wake to-night. Sleep to those people out there," he pointed towards the moving torches and the cries, "to their world. Wake to me and to the world we two will make for ourselves. It shall be a beautiful world; not cold like theirs, and full of noise and intrigue, but warm and calm, a real summer world for us. I will give up my contemptible, unmanly life. I will work for you. We shall be poor at first. But do we want what all these people want? Do we want to outshine our neighbours, to gamble and race, and cram our home with strangers, and go to every place that is the fashion, and entertain princes, and be in the front rank of this endless turmoil? Do we, Caryll?"

"No," she said, "not that. Not that. But——"

She paused and hesitated. An uneasy look had come into her eyes. He drew her towards him with an instinct that his moment, his great opportunity had come. He felt then, and all his life afterwards, that she could be susceptible to love alone, that she possessed that strange, divine something which is without self-interest, without greed or worldliness—that spark, red and glowing with pure and intense feeling, which can only be kindled into flame by another spark, red and glowing, pure and intense as itself. And he felt then that in his heart was that other spark, united with which the divinity within her would burn as God surely desired and decreed.

But, as she knew the pressure of his arms, the look of uneasiness, almost of fear in her eyes grew more definite. Never before had she known the greatest of all terrors. Never before had she thought it possible that she could fear herself. Was this hideous and slow stirring within her, this lethargic uncoiling, as of a serpent from its glazed and relentless reveries, a stirring of the flesh or of the spirit? She could not tell. She could only tell that a dreadful confusion began to fill her soul, like the confusion that beats in the ears of a drowning man who dies amid unutterable tumult in a silent and breathless sea.

"Caryll," she heard Aubrey's voice say, "you are waking at last. You are waking."

And that seemed to be true and terrible, as the waking of the drowning man from the life we call life to the life we call death. The tumult within her grew louder, as if she were sinking down in the last struggle of that sea-tragedy.

There was again a rustling among the nearest trees, then the sound of soft steps, and then a voice, elderly and grating, but clear and almost pitilessly distinct in the night.

"Yes," it said. "It is quite true. I did buy the great emerald yesterday. It really is a marvel, one of the most wonderful jewels in the world."

There was a silence. Lady Caryll drew herself away from Aubrey's arms. He felt, just before her movement, that her slim body grew stiff, as the body of one who is startled and who listens intently. Then the voice of Sir Reuben again spoke, apparently in reply to some question unheard by Lady Caryll and by Aubrey.

"It belonged to Catherine of Russia. I daresay she wore it often in that pavilion with the strange gardens that have become a legend. It is engraved"—the voice was more distant now, but still clear and clean cut on the surface of the night—"with three figures—the soul being borne away by pleasures."

Silence.

"Caryll," Aubrey whispered, "love me. I am so much alone in the world; you are so much alone. Let us——"

"Hush!" she whispered.

She held up one hand and seemed to strain her ears, as if she waited to hear again the voice speaking of the emerald. Her white brows were drawn down over her eyes. Aubrey felt his glowing impulse turn cold as if a heavy breath of winter mystery floated upon it and hung about it. Then she dropped her hand into her lap and turned to him.

"Leave me to my dream," she said. "Leave me—I do not wish to wake."

Her voice had become dull like the voice of a somnambulist.

The ice of Aubrey's reserve, broken through for a moment, began to close over him again. He struggled against it with a sense of despair.

"Caryll," he said. "Caryll!"

He caught at her hands. She avoided his touch, leaning away from him.

"Leave me," she repeated, and now her voice was intensely cold and repellent. "I will not love you. And if I ever did, it would lead to my hating you."

The wild blast of a coach-horn rang out, and the noise of many footsteps and of loud voices approached among the trees.

"You rode splendidly," cried the prima donna with unaffected enthusiasm.

"Oh, that's all right. The others were only duffers," said the big boy.

Aubrey stood up quickly.

* * *

The crowd in front of the summer-house was saying loud good-byes. The lights of the carriages gleamed.

"Monsieur Anneau—Monsieur Anneau," cried Lady St. Ormyn, "you're to come on the coach, and Caryll and Sir Frederick! Where's Barré? Still lying down in the billiard-room? Is he so bad as that? He must have some more punch to pick him up. Wait a moment—we'll all have some more, and—oh, an idea!—while we are doing it Mr. Whitney Brown shall sing 'Drinking, Drinking, Drinking!' Will you, Mr. Brown? Charming of you. Where's Caryll? Now——"

In the crowd Aubrey found himself beside Mrs. Reckitt. She looked at him with her kind and thoughtful smile.

"A characteristic close to a varied evening," she said.

"Yes," Aubrey replied, in his slightly mannered voice of society. "It's been great fun. Lady St. Ormyn knows how to do things."

He glanced round on all the faces that were flushed under the faint light of the moon, and he saw among them the grotesque brown features of Sir Reuben.

How ugly he seemed to the boy just then, hideous as a goblin perched upon a cathedral buttress to sneer at all the tenderness of religion.

"Now, Mr. Brown, please!" shrieked Lady St. Ormyn.

There was a clinking of glasses.

And then the moon heard " Drinking, Drinking, Drinking!"

CHAPTER VIII

ON the afternoon of the following day Sir Reuben had invited a few people to his house to see the famous emerald. Among them were Lady St. Ormyn and her daughter and Lady Rangecliffe. Lady Rangecliffe, having been asked to come at four o'clock, turned up at a quarter past three, on her way to Whitechapel, where she was going to assist at a bazaar in aid of some extraordinary charity connected with an obscure profession that most people have never heard of.

Fortunately Sir Reuben happened to be at home. He received her without surprise in a drawing-room full of beautiful things, whose effect was almost dimmed by the strong colours of the background against which they were set.

"I'm afraid I'm late," Lady Rangecliffe said, striding into the room with her curious gait of a middle-aged but still athletic boy.

"Not at all."

"I couldn't help it. Rangecliffe kept me. How odd it seems to be here again. It is so long since——" She stopped abruptly, fearful of rousing painful memories in her host's mind.

Sir Reuben led her to a huge red divan, and she sat down, a curious patch of black in the brilliant room.

"Aubrey isn't coming?" she asked.

"No. I asked him, but he is on the river to-day."

"On the river! Then last night he——You were at Lady St. Ormyn's?"

She stared into his face inquiringly.

"Till past midnight."

"And what do you think?"

"It was an amusing party."

"I'm sure it was. But Aubrey and Lady Caryll?"

Sir Reuben either was, or chose to seem, unable to grasp Lady Rangecliffe's meaning. Seated on the red divan he looked exactly like an old merchant in an Eastern bazaar, a seller of carpets from Bagdad or of perfumes from Mecca; and Lady Rangecliffe in her trailing and unfashionable black gown seemed an anxious tourist at the mercy of his Oriental cunning.

"They enjoyed themselves like the rest of the world, I suppose.

We had music, bicycle races, dinner, fireworks. It was a Crystal Palace fête in little."

"Aubrey hates Crystal Palace fêtes. You know what I mean, Sir Reuben. Did he ask her to marry him, poor dear old boy?"

At this question Sir Reuben looked up out of the corners of his bright eyes, which twinkled as if he were on the point of driving a hard bargain.

"It is difficult to say," he replied. "In such a turmoil——"

"Well, but you stayed till midnight," she interrupted.

"There were a great many fireworks."

"Still he must have had a chance. And rockets are nothing to a boy who's in love. He wouldn't notice them. Even a girl wouldn't, and girls notice almost everything."

"I think Lady Caryll noticed all the rockets," said Sir Reuben in a quiet and dry voice. "Do you wish to see the emerald?"

"What?" said Lady Rangecliffe, who happened to be sitting with her deaf ear turned towards her host.

"Do you wish to see the emerald?"

"What emerald?" said Lady Rangecliffe, entirely preoccupied and totally unaware that her visit was supposed to have any special object.

Sir Reuben shifted his position and came round to her other side. His brown face had become grave and wizened.

"In my note to you I told you I had just purchased the Catherine of Russia emerald at Murphy's jewel sale," he said.

"Oh yes, to be sure," said Lady Rangecliffe, recalling her wandering thoughts. "What made you want to have it?"

She spoke with her usual blunt directness, staring him full in the eyes.

For a moment Sir Reuben was glad that she was so short-sighted. Subtlety was apt to feel small and singularly mean in the presence of this plain and badly-dressed woman.

He hesitated obviously before replying to her question. To give a truthful answer was difficult to him. To give an untruthful one seemed impossible while her eyes were fixed on his. At last he said—

"You remember our conversation the other day?"

"Which one? About the old women and *Ally Sloper*?" said Lady Rangecliffe, going off at a tangent.

"No," said Sir Reuben, still hesitating, divided in mind between his natural love of working in the dark and the quick prompting to sincerity that Lady Rangecliffe was apt to rouse in the breasts of all those with whom she was brought into contact.

"About Persia, or Sunday and the poor servants getting a little air?"

"No; about Aubrey and this girl—this Lady Caryll."

He spoke more quickly now.

"I asked you if you thought I could have any influence upon her, any influence which might induce her denial of Aubrey's desire, her refusal to grant him the wraith of happiness which you said he was seeking, in the belief that it was a reality."

"Ah! now I remember. I said you couldn't have any influence. You see, Sir Reuben, you and I are elderly; and the elderly understand the merits of a sensible abdication. Don't they, if they've got any gumption?"

Her wide mouth smiled, showing two rows of large but perfect white teeth.

"You and I haven't waited to be given the 'chuck,' as the boys say," she added.

But his answer sent the smile from her kind and open face.

"Shall I show you my influence?" he said.

There was a note of bitterness in his voice. She heard it, deaf though she was.

"Your influence over Lady Caryll?"

"Exactly!"

"You mean that you really have any? Well, but she isn't here. How can you show it?" said Lady Rangecliffe, in perfectly frank bewilderment.

"Her absence doesn't matter. Wait one moment."

He got up and shuffled quickly out of the room, leaving Lady Rangecliffe alone on the red divan. She sat still, her long lean arms resting on the bright cushions, and glanced about this room, which appeared like a sort of excessively brilliant fog to her large dark eyes. She remembered having been in it eight years ago, when Sir Reuben talked to her of his dead wife, and she recalled a sentence he had spoken then: "This room will not easily forget her." He had said the words with a curious and hard emphasis which had graven them upon her rather fluid memory. In this brilliant fog the pretty Creole had passed many hours, chattering to her gay world of acquaintances, or alone with her strange and unattractive husband. To Lady Rangecliffe Sir Reuben was never unattractive. For he had once done her a kindness. She respected and was sincerely attached to him. But her respect and attachment could not blind her to the fact that his days of bodily vigour and of the prime of manhood were long over. He was but a shell, roughened by the action of time and beating waves of circumstance. Possibly, within the hollow of the shell the thin and murmuring voice of desire still sang with a faint and an unceasing ardour, still demanded many things of life. If so, that was melancholy. Those persistent voices, murmuring within the darkness of the strewn shells upon the storm-worn strands, are more pathetic than are the voices of ghosts. Lady Rangecliffe began to hear them, as she sat alone, till all the bright room, so dim to her, was full of murmurings.

The door opened again, and she perceived something dark like a man entering.

"Sir Reuben," she said, "do you know that this——"

Two more figures appeared. They rustled.

"I will tell Sir Reuben, my lady," said a cold servant's voice.

Lady St. Ormyn and Lady Caryll came up to the red divan and shook hands with Lady Rangecliffe.

Lady St. Ormyn, as usual, looked very hot and flushed, Lady Caryll very cool and clear. Lady Rangecliffe was struck afresh by the peculiarity of her beauty and by the delicacy of her colouring, which suggested transparence.

"What a house!" said Lady St. Ormyn. "I'm sure I'm in Bagdad—do I mean Bagdad? There is such a place, isn't there? It's more Eastern than anything I've ever seen before in the West End, or even at Earl's Court, or one of those other dreadful places where they have exhibitions, with Burmese natives learning English ways in public at so much an hour. And then it's got such an enchanting hermetically sealed look, that one feels it's a sort of extraordinary privilege to be in it. We're preposterously punctual, because we've got some musical parties to—— Ah, here's Sir Reuben! We are absurdly punctual, Sir Reuben, but we've so many things this afternoon. Monsieur Anneau is giving an opera tea at the Cecil, and Réné Mackintosh has one of her dancing Mondays, and—— I'm in love with your house. It's so very Bagdad! Did you bring it over bodily from Persia? Or who did it for you? This scarlet is extraordinary, and I adore scarlet. It reminds me of a superb military band on a hot afternoon, or the trumpets in the overture to 'Tannhauser.' Where is the emerald? All London is talking about it."

She fanned herself stormily.

Sir Reuben was holding something in his left hand. The expression on his face was difficult to read as he came in at the door and saw his visitors. For a moment he was secretly vexed not to find Lady Rangecliffe still alone. Then the dramatic possibilities of the new situation struck him, and he smiled like a man with many threads in his fingers, all attached to living things which he governs and restrains. He greeted Lady St. Ormyn and her daughter. Then he looked at Lady Rangecliffe.

"The emerald!" he said. "I have it here. I was just going to show it to Lady Rangecliffe."

As he spoke Lady Rangecliffe jerked abruptly on the divan

and made a quick movement sideways with her head. Sir Reuben sat down close to her, facing Lady Caryll and her mother. A strong, naked-looking gleam of sunshine stretched, like a sword slanting downward, from one of the tall windows to the place where he sat. In it a minute dust, like a powder of tiny living things, whirled and danced ceaselessly. The eyes of the three women were all fixed upon his thin and brown left hand. None of them spoke as he opened it, showing a white velvet case. Even Lady St. Ormyn was overtaken by a momentary silence of curiosity. Sir Reuben pressed a spring. The white velvet lid flew up, and the point of the sword of the sun touched the great jewel, and seemed to pierce without wounding it, and to fill it with fire, which it transformed from yellow into an exquisite clear dark green. It looked alive, and full of a sort of eager and yet calm animation.

Sir Reuben turned to Lady Rangecliffe.

"That is what I wanted to show you," he said, and he held the jewel up in the heart of the sunshine.

She jerked again, fixing her eyes on the emerald; but she said nothing.

"It's superb!" said Lady St. Ormyn. "It's finer than anything that racing woman Mrs. Turner's got. Do let me take it out of the case."

She stretched out her hand. As she did so, Lady Caryll repressed an almost ungovernable gesture of quick prohibition. Sir Reuben noticed it, and his eyes sparkled. The girl's eyes were fixed upon the emerald, like Lady Rangecliffe's, and they glowed as they had glowed in Bond Street when they looked into the diamond-shop. She leaned slightly forward, in a posture of one fascinated, still, passionately attentive.

Lady Rangecliffe watched her now as well as Sir Reuben. He gave the emerald into Lady St. Ormyn's sacrilegious hands. She snatched at it, as she snatched at marrons glacés, and celebrated baritones; took it out of the case and flashed it about in the sun, turning it this way and that with a rapidity that was irritating.

"What does the engraving mean?" she cried. "The soul going to heaven—is it?"

"The soul being borne away by pleasures," Sir Reuben said.

Lady Caryll seemed to hear again the hidden voice in the dark garden.

"Dear me! By pleasures? How very shocking! Isn't it shocking, Lady Rangecliffe? I know you'll think so, because you don't like parties."

But Lady Rangecliffe appeared to be absorbed in thought, or else her deafness prevented her from hearing the remark. In any case she made no answer.

"Caryll," continued Lady St. Ormyn, still fidgeting with the emerald violently, "take warning from this engraving. I'm sure it's meant especially for girls. One can't be too careful of one's soul. That's why I adore music, Sir Reuben. It does me so much good. A sermon makes me ill and cross, but music brings out all that is fine in one, doesn't it? Especially Wagner and Barré. What a funny little soul, and what funny little pleasures? Where are they bearing the soul to?"

"Where do souls go when they are borne away by pleasures?" he said, looking at Lady Caryll.

"That depends on whether they're male or female," said Lady St. Ormyn. "Men's souls go racing, or to Paris on business. Don't they?"

"And women's?"

"You mustn't ask me. It's just as well that men should remain in ignorance of some things. Isn't it, Lady Rangecliffe?"

"Yes," she said gravely.

Lady Caryll said nothing. The rapid movements of her mother's hands seemed to irritate her intensely. She looked at Lady St. Ormyn with unfavourable eyes, with a glance full of sombre jealousy.

"Well," said Lady St. Ormyn, "it's very wonderful, but we ought to be going. Here, Sir Reuben," she thrust the emerald into his hand. "Its marvellous, matchless. Mrs. Turner would sell her soul for it, and her horses, too, I'm certain. But what will you do with it? You can't wear it."

"No. What shall I do with it, Lady Rangecliffe?"

"Sell it again," she said.

Her voice sounded like the voice of one moved. She was looking at Lady Caryll, and the fierceness of the sun had filled her eyes with moisture.

"Oh, Lady Rangecliffe!" the girl said brusquely, and almost with excitement. "Would you sell one of your dogs?"

Then she burst into a laugh and sprang up.

"Mother, if we are really going to all these places we had better start," she said.

"Yes, we must be off. Well, good-bye, Lady Rangecliffe. I know it's no use asking you to Epsom on Sunday? Sir Reuben, this scarlet is the most marvellous thing in London. You are a magician with your wonderful house and your wonderful emerald. I'm half afraid of you. Aren't you, Caryll? Aren't you afraid of Sir Reuben?"

"Are you, Lady Caryll?" he asked her.

She met his twinkling old eyes gravely.

"No," she said. "I'm not afraid of anything."

"Not even of being borne away by pleasures?" he said.

When he said that there was a sound of mystery in his rather croaking voice.

"It's dangerous not to be afraid of anything, my dear child," Lady Rangecliffe interrupted suddenly.

She had stood up to say good-bye to Lady St. Ormyn, and now she laid her long hand on Lady Caryll's.

"It's awful dangerous," she said. "I've never forgotten what a boy once said to me—he had saved another boy's life in the sea and nearly lost his own in doing it—'I can't think what made me do it,' he said, 'for I was in an unholy funk all the time.' There's nothing cowardly in being able to feel afraid, and it's more human."

"Well, then, I'm very human now," cried Lady St. Ormyn; "for I'm afraid of this house. I'm sure there's a harem in it somewhere, and all sorts of mysteries. Don't blush, Sir Reuben; such a house ought to contain a harem as part of the furniture. I can imagine veiled women passing their lives in rooms like this, eating bonbons, and talking to parroquets, and playing on lutes and tom-toms, and wearing marvellous jewels and spangled trousers. After all, the moral sense is merely a question of surroundings. I always say that, especially to young clergymen. I think it braces them to hear common-sense once or twice a year. And we ought to speak the truth even to clergymen. They think me shocking, but I do them good. And we should try to do good to the 'cloth,' shouldn't we? Why are curates called the 'cloth'? Is it because they wear hats like puddings made by a chef who doesn't know his business? I always say——"

She talked herself into her victoria, followed by Lady Caryll, who had said good-bye to Lady Rangecliffe very coldly, and had looked at the room she was leaving as a child looks at a strangely painted butterfly, or at the shadow of a reality it cannot see.

Lady Rangecliffe had forgotten her bazaar. She was standing by the window when Sir Reuben returned, and looking almost stern and curiously angular in the summer light. He came up to her. The emerald was still in his hand. On his face there was an expression of rather uneasy watchfulness.

"I understand now," Lady Rangecliffe said. "I'm as stupid as an owl in these things, but I understand now. Why do you think so horribly of women?"

"Do I think worse of them than some of them deserve?"

He opened the case, and let the light flash once more upon the jewel, and as it gleamed he smiled.

"But why don't you try to help them, then?"

"As you would try to help Lady Caryll. It would be useless. Some of them are meant to be as some of them are."

THE SLAVE

"You're wrong."

"I like to know there's one woman who can honestly think so," he said almost tenderly.

"And you think so too?"

"No."

"You must. You helped me long ago when I was in trouble."

"What does that prove?"

"A great deal to me—a great deal more than you know, perhaps." She sat down again.

"Don't think I'm going yet," she said. "I'm not."

"I wish you to stay."

"Give me that jewel," Lady Rangecliffe said.

Sir Reuben handed it to her. She lifted it till it was close to her eyes, and looked at it for a long time in silence. At last she said, still looking at it—

"And this is the influence you spoke of."

"Yes."

"You believe in its power?"

"Do not you?"

"I don't know. I can't understand it a bit—this miserable, paltry little green thing, without a voice or a heart."

"Think of what some women are," he said. "You told me yourself that there was something inhuman in Lady Caryll."

"And I was ashamed of having said it afterwards," said Lady Rangecliffe vehemently. "I felt like a cad. And now I've been with her again, and she is so beautiful and young. I've been uncharitable and selfish, thinking of nobody but my own boy. Perhaps he's right. Since he loves her he sees what she is better than we can."

"Since he loves her he cannot see what she is. Lady Rangecliffe, you are trying to laugh at your own instinct."

"No. There is something fine in every nature, but it has to be found and awakened and developed. Perhaps Aubrey——"

"Has tried to awaken Lady Caryll and has failed."

Lady Rangecliffe moved her head quickly sideways.

"When?"

"Last night."

"And has failed?"

"I bought that emerald on Saturday. Lady Caryll knew it yesterday."

Lady Rangecliffe put the jewel down as if it burnt her hand.

"You think that if you hadn't she——"

"I am too old ever to trust to chance again."

He snapped the white lid of the jewel case, and the emerald was hidden from the sun.

"Sir Reuben," Lady Rangecliffe said, "a great many years ago you did something for me. Did you do this for me too, because I told you what I thought Aubrey's nature needed to be happy?"

He did not reply for a moment, but sat leaning his head on his hand.

"Perhaps I oughtn't to ask you," she said.

"No; I didn't do it entirely for you," he answered at last.

Lady Rangecliffe thought of Lady St. Ormyn's remark, that there must surely be a harem in this strange and Oriental-looking house. And then she thought of Lady Caryll—of this beautiful child, with all the possibilities of a free woman's life in England stretching out before her; love, satisfaction of love, motherhood, with its pain and its passion. She thought, too, of her boy and of what he needed. She looked at Sir Reuben, old, wrinkled, burned by hot suns, worn with travelling, with toil, with cynicism, perhaps with pleasure. As he remained motionless he was like an ugly idol in some heathen land, a deity carved from a block by superstitious, savage, and cunning fingers; a deity to whom the ruthless and the fearful bow down, creeping round the hewn feet in hideous attitudes of abnegation. And the little white velvet case which still lay in one of his dry and corrugated hands was like a gift offered up to him in condonation of some nameless crime.

She had spoken to this silent idol of age and of its sensible abdications. But does it ever really abdicate? Does it not cling frantically to power until it is rudely pushed from the throne, on which it has become, in the inexorable passage of time, a pitiful spectre, horrible beneath a tottering crown?

A chilly sense of sorrow, almost of hopelessness, ran over her, such as she had never felt before in quite the same degree. But Lady Rangecliffe was never hopeless for long. She was by nature too manly for that.

"Sell your emerald, Sir Reuben," she said abruptly. "You know what I mean."

"You think I am too old to possess a jewel?" he answered.

That was the truth, and she acknowledged it bluntly.

"Yes, I do," she said.

"Then you misunderstand men. No man is ever too old to possess that which he has the power to possess. Eight years ago I thought I had lost all power, and I sold all my jewels. I never told you why?"

"Never."

"Eight years ago," he said, speaking slowly and with a bitter distinctness, "I discovered that the jewel I loved most had not been really and entirely mine."

Lady Rangecliffe understood that he alluded to the beautiful Creole. She understood his Odyssey.

"Before I die," he continued, speaking more quietly and with a deliberate composure, "I wish to have a jewel that will be wholly mine. Is that wonderful? Is it wonderful that, having found a rare jewel that I could possess wholly, I should take the necessary measures to purchase it?"

"My friend," Lady Rangeclifffe said, "when you speak like that you make me feel as if I were stifling."

"You can only breathe in one atmosphere, in air that is perfectly pure. But many of us can breathe in dark places where you would die. Leave us to do so. You will always be seated by your open window."

"I want my friends to be there too with me," she said, "or I have no pleasure."

"Remember that I am of different blood, accustomed to hot climates, and to suns that never shine here in England. Remember that I have been deceived, that I have stood by the corpse of the thing I had loved and longed to strike it!"

For a moment his face was terrible and his eyes blazed with fury; then, with an abrupt change to inexorable softness, he added, "Lady Rangecliffe, I must—I must buy my jewel."

A man-servant showed in some more visitors.

Lady Rangecliffe remembered that she had to go to Whitechapel, to breathe the purest of all air—the air of charity.

CHAPTER IX

WHEN London heard, at the end of the month of June, that Lady Caryll Knox had accepted Sir Reuben Allabruth as her future husband, London was gratified. Its curiosity about the famous emerald was at length lulled to rest. Sir Reuben had bought it for no actress, for no mysterious slave of the harem, but as a gift for the young beauty who was to step into the place formerly occupied by the pretty Creole. Once again in the history of society youth was to mate with age, while all the world looked on. Once again the gifts of God had been bought with the gifts of man, and the shadows of night came forward to take possession of the twilight of dawn.

It was all very gratifying and customary, and Lady St. Ormyn was warmly and sincerely congratulated, while Lord St. Ormyn chirped about the City like a sparrow sunning itself upon a housetop after adverse storms and showers.

Aubrey happened to be in the company of his mother when she received Sir Reuben's note announcing the news, which she had long expected. He noticed her agitation, for Lady Rangecliffe was too natural to be able to conceal anything. She was expressive despite her wish, and, unfortunately, was always expressive of truth.

The note arrived just after lunch. Lady Rangecliffe read it about five-and-twenty times, endeavouring to do so with a happy air of carelessness that was not very convincing. Aubrey was smoking, for Lady Rangecliffe allowed all her boys to smoke in her boudoir, or in her bedroom, if they liked. The smoke of her children rose like incense to her nostrils. Aubrey observed that she was excited and distressed.

"Bad news, Mater?" he said.

"What, Aubrey?"

"Had bad news?"

Lady Rangecliffe grew very red, and looked and felt more guilty that most criminals. It seemed to her in that moment as if she had conceived a plot against her best beloved son on the day when she first told Sir Reuben of her fears that Aubrey was deceived. Yet she knew well that Sir Reuben had laid the snare for Lady Caryll to please his own decisive nature, that strange and relentless nature which desired as strongly in age as in youth.

"What is it, Mater?" Aubrey repeated, looking at his mother with calm astonishment. "One'd think you'd robbed a bank and just been found out."

"Nonsense, Aubrey," said Lady Rangecliffe desperately, and tingling all over like a young girl lashed by shyness. "It's only a note from Sir Reuben."

"Is that all?"

"Yes."

A silence followed, through which Aubrey smoked languidly.

"There's a piece of news in it," said Lady Rangecliffe nervously, and jerking her head sideways.

"Oh! What is it?"

"He's going to be married."

Aubrey was really surprised now. He had never supposed that his godfather would do anything so obviously absurd and in such bad taste as to link his battered and embrowned life with that of another.

"Well!" he said, letting his cigarette go out. "Who is the old lady?"

"Lady Caryll Knox. Now I must go and see about my Brompton Clothing Club."

She turned to hurry away, but before she could leave the room, Aubrey said—

"Mater, when I said 'old lady,' I was merely joking. You'll understand that."

"Yes, Aubrey, of course I understand that," she said.

And directly she was outside the door she burst into tears.

When Aubrey found himself alone, he put down the burnt-out cigarette in an ashtray, took another from his case very carefully, struck a match, lit the cigarette, and began to smoke again, looking straight before him. He had not changed his lounging attitude, but his body was stiff in the chair. He felt as if he were made of steel, and that within the steel was some little thing which was bleeding to death. He would have liked to see it, this little bleeding thing, hidden away in a seclusion that nothing could reach, dying there in its dark corner. It did not choose to be helped. It did not want any lint, or any bandages, or any hand to hold the lips of its tiny and deep wound together. It only wanted to be quite alone and utterly unsuspected. It required just that. Was it unsuspected?

Aubrey was afraid of his mother then. Was it possible that she knew of the little thing and of its hideous wound. He had heard no sound outside the door. But why had she hesitated and looked guilty? Perhaps it was merely for Sir Reuben's sake. Aubrey knew of her deep friendship for him. Perhaps she had been thinking only of him. Any other idea was insufferable to the boy. His uncertainty tortured him. But he was resolved to believe, to convince himself, that so it was; that Lady Rangecliffe, always very sensitive for those she esteemed or loved, was pained by fear that the world, and with the world her son, might be inclined to sneer at Sir Reuben's last effort to be happy.

People are so ready to laugh when they see the old and the weary trying to go on being happy.

And then, that matter forcibly settled, Aubrey sat there quite still and felt the awful pain of the little hidden thing.

How strange the pain of the heart is, the pain that is not physical, but that seems intensely physical as well as intensely mental. At first it is often humiliating. The creature crawls in the dust. It has heard that suffering is ennobling. It feels that it is degrading. It has read that the fire refines. It feels that the fire destroys. It has been taught that pain fits wings to the soul. It feels the soft powder of the dust. It breathes the breath of the dust. It smells the dry and acrid perfume of the dust. It is conscious of each separate, shifting, infinitesimal fragment of this shattered material in which it creeps, which floats about it in a mist of decay, blotting out all clear forms and transforming all things into a phantasmagoria of blurred and sickly activities.

The creature crawls in the dust, fit only—so it feels—to be trampled to death, that it too may form part of the dust and become for ever one with the uneasy powder of the destroyed.

Aubrey felt at this moment as many others have felt, that sorrow can be so keen as to be degrading. He could not have explained why, but that was his sensation. His heart, his soul, his whole nature grovelled.

Sorrow was not new to him. But this sorrow was wholly new. Since that evening in the garden at Epsom when Lady Caryll had refused him he had suffered, but not without hope. He had believed that he had spoken prematurely to a dreamer who must dream on a little longer, alone with the visions of maidenly ignorance and of youth. He had thought that he had perhaps been too impulsive, and had startled the heart he meant to win. Lady Caryll, for the moment, loved her dreams better than she loved any man. He had imagined that, and he had waited, allowing his reserve to close round him again. And indeed, in any case, it would have been impossible to him to speak to her once more as he had spoken in the garden until time had renewed the lapsed force of his unusual impulse. There was no failure of feeling, no cessation of internal vehemence of desire. But verbal expression of his true self was seldom possible to him with any one, even with this girl whom he loved. And his reserve had suffered acute pain from the check he had received. His passionate impulse, put aside, driven back upon itself, had become timid, self-conscious, and slow for the moment. It must pause to gather courage.

And through the pause came his mother's voice with this message.

This old man had put out his wrinkled hands to beauty, had touched the dreamer, and—she awoke.

Was that possible? Or had his voice, penetrating vaguely through her dreams, confused her, and had she answered idly, not knowing what she said?

In the degradation of his horror Aubrey began to think, or to try to think. But his imagination was at first stronger than his mind, and he could only see with mental eyes. He saw incessantly two dry brown hands, ugly with the peculiar rough transparency of age, grasping the soft young hands of his dreamer, stroking them with an abominable and greedy tenderness.

That was terrible. He felt sick; not romantically, but as a man may feel sick at the sight of blood flowing after some dreadful operation. His flesh shuddered when he saw the union of those hands. He underwent personally the evil and shrinking sensation that affects any sensitive person who is touched, felt, held by some live and ugly thing. That was an affection of the body calling on the sympathy of the mind.

But the eyes of the mind in such moments will not be content with but one watchfulness. They have seen one thing; they throw their piercing gaze farther; they seek to see more intimately. Aubrey began to lose sight of the hands. . . . With a sudden exclamation he sprang up, opened the door, and went out hurriedly. Gaining the square, he walked on heedlessly and fast. It was one of those curious, still, and almost black summer days that may be seen sometimes in London, a day on which everything looks sullen, and graceless, and unusually large. The sky was low, like a penthouse eyebrow lowering over a morose eye. The dingy pavement seemed another sky, dour and forbidding. Shut in between them was a sick and heavy world. Houses, churches, monuments in this atmosphere were all alike sulky and without apparent beauty of design. The trees in the square stood up like weary and discontented shadows enclosed within the sentinel railings on which the mournful dust lay thick. The leaves drowsed silently and did not rustle. Along the walks sad servant-girls and peevish children plodded, without activity and without perceptible aim. A little dog with fatigued eyes sat alone on a doorstep furtively regarding a stain of milk which was drying before the entrance of an area. Enormous policemen were rooted at the corners of the streets. They appeared to be vulgar effigies, ravaged out of some uncivilised ark, and set down to show how far absurdity in costume had advanced in prehistoric ages—an alphabet of dumb and staring puppets. Organ-grinders wandered here and there, and as their stretched arms mechanically revolved, a mechanical uproar made this world grow darker and more submarine in sentiment. A massive ocean surely weighed upon it and caused it to be heavy with this dulness, which was fearful, like a crime. In the streets there were many people, but in such an atmosphere faces do not seem to vary or to be expressive of changing or of quickly flowing thoughts. Eyes look stagnant and complexions faded and morose, and the movements of limbs seem slow, like those of an invalid who can never recover from the illness that oppresses him. The cabs went by, directed in their course by perched men, careless of gesture and of aspect. What could an accident matter in such a world? Although the atmosphere was so still, sound did not travel; the eternal noise of the metropolis seemed to be enclosed in a massive envelope of wool. Inside this envelope there might be a thousand different notes: of men, women, children, of beating hoofs of horses, of bands playing, of dogs barking, of birds twittering, and fountains falling, of the sirens of mighty ships calling in the black river between the wharves and warehouses, of trains roaring beneath the twisted iron bridges, of millions of doors shutting, of walls slipping under the blows of pickaxes, of steam-rollers grinding new roads together, of barrels rolling from vans into the dark embrace of hidden cellars, of girls singing love-songs over their sewing at open windows, of drunkards stumbling on the stairs of gin-palaces, of runaway ponies, of bicycle horns at dangerous corners, of hammers beating on square blocks of stone, of machinery whirring while a thousand wheels revolved, of motor-cars spitting, of furnaces hissing, of smartly dressed men shrieking like maniacs in the Stock Exchange, of bells tinkling on a child's rattle, of bottles and glasses jingling and clinking in restaurants, of an iron curtain falling in a theatre, of organs pealing in churches, of bells tolling for deaths, of cries of pain and of joy at births, of a crowd applauding some one who smiled, of many tears, of shrieks of fear and of anger, of costermongers snarling over their barrows, of anchors let down from steamers come from far, of the shattering crash of foundering houses—London's message written in music. But all these notes were ruthlessly blended together into one deep bourdon, which hummed with a blurred and an inexorable heaviness through the ebon summer day beneath the leaning sky.

People, things, the elements, distant and near views, all were hypnotised. The day was not a slumber, soft and refreshing, but a trance, artificial and forbidding.

So Aubrey felt, and, as he walked, he too was wrapped in this numb and dreary dream. He no longer experienced a keen sense of pain. No activities were alert within brain or heart. Only a continual oppression weighed upon him and swam around him. Everything was warm and black. That was his actual sensation. And the heat, in this silent and dull blackness was more sad and destructive of vigour than the fiercest cold could have been. Yet there was no feeling of storm in this atmosphere. That is exciting. It rouses anticipation, and sends the thoughts flying forward to meet the thunderclaps and to watch the hurried signature of the lightning dashed across the sky. This atmosphere seemed habitual, like the monotonous relation who sits for ever by the hearth, permanent as the hapless city over which it crouched. It was unnatural but enduring, and Aubrey could not imagine that there could ever be sunshine in this city, a smiling life, or the breath of a gay and fluttering wind.

All the world dreamed sullenly, and he, too, and Lady Caryll. And he had wondered at her dream. He had striven to wake her. How absurd that was. What is there to wake to in life? Only a black sky and a crowd of mournful shadows going heavily. Sir Reuben was but a grotesque among them, he, too, like some curious mandarin recumbent upon a woman's mantelpiece, nodding eternally a shaven head and curving his lips in a heathen smile. Aubrey saw him there. His legs were crossed like an Egyptian's, and his thin, old body was bent forward. His flexible lips were extended, and in one of his hands he held an emerald. And he bowed his head unceasingly as if towards some one who stood in front of him. And then Aubrey perceived that a girl was standing by the mantelpiece, and that to her the grotesque was eternally bowing. The girl was Lady Caryll. She stood motionless as if fascinated by this smiling mandarin, and by his obsequious and inviting genuflexions. But Aubrey noticed that she was not looking at him. Her eyes were fastened on the emerald that he held, and the expression in them was horrible and greedy. She was like a snake charmed by hideous music. And Sir Reuben smiled and bowed without ceasing, his hand inflexibly thrust forward towards the girl with the jewel in its palm.

"I am mad to-day," the boy said to himself suddenly.

Why do thoughts escape from our control and perform such insane gyrations? The world was still black, and warm, and sullen, but Aubrey's numbness was passing. He was no longer in a dream, though a universe dreamed around him. For a moment he was passionately angry with himself. Why had he seen Lady Caryll with her eyes fastened upon the emerald? Aubrey was one of those rare men who can seldom do a woman they love injustice even by a momentary and wandering thought. His sense of chivalry was not shifting, but permanent, although it did not concern itself with all women merely because of their sex. Many women seemed to him utterly unworthy of respect, and his chivalry died at sight of them. He would have given way to them or have defended them in any danger, but to be inspired to the mere beauty of chivalry by cold vanity, and boundless greed, and immorality was not possible to him. Nor did he wish it to be so. But Lady Caryll had been a goddess to him, and she was a goddess still. All the romance within him flowed instinctively to her— all his dreams clustered round her footstool. And now, waking to a sense of his own reality in this unreal world, he hated himself for his foolish vision of the nodding grotesque and of the watching girl.

He found himself near Kensington Gardens. The trees, with their black and motionless leaves, looked gigantic. The flowers were strangely colourless, as if they gained their hues from sky and sun, and, like the chameleon, were not sufficient for themselves. Aubrey entered the gardens, and began to retrace his steps between the lines of beds and the hedges of brooding foliage. Presently he saw a small white butterfly on the wing. It looked unnaturally white in this weather and his eyes could not leave it. Wayward, as butterflies always are, it flew for a while along the path, turning hither and thither, hesitating, resting, then fluttering on again. Its tiny wings trembled, as if it shivered at its own purity. It alighted on various flowers, but only stayed for an instant, as if dissatisfied or deceived. Aubrey began to feel that it had some definite end in view, and that its investigations were not pursued without a purpose. It desired, surely, some special flower or leaf on which its heart was set, and it would flutter on until it reached that flower. Presently Aubrey saw, growing among a tangle of shrubs, an ugly plant. He did not know its name, but it was squat, had flaccid, prickly leaves, and looked unhealthy and fatigued. The edges of its leaves were of a sickly yellowish-brown colour, and were ragged and thin, attacked apparently by a decay which, beginning at the limits of the plant, was eating its way stealthily towards the heart. Over this plant the white butterfly poised on flickering wings. Then it alighted, keeping its wings extended for a moment. Aubrey thought it was going to dart away as usual. He stopped in the path to see it fly forward again on its search. And while he stood there it folded its wings as if satisfied and submissive. He felt that its search was over. Yet he waited there for a long while. He knew that he was longing with intensity to see this tiny white thing fly away from its ugly home on the breast of the sickly plant. It was so near to the disease, to the yellow edges of the leaves. Even while he watched a film of the decayed matter detached itself from the rest and went to feed the rank black mould in the shadow. In time the disease, ever moving, must reach the butterfly. Yet it remained. It seemed at last contented. Aubrey stretched out his hand softly and touched it with the tip of his finger. It did not move. Perhaps it was asleep.

He walked on, and all the strength of his pain had come back to him.

It was terrible to leave the butterfly there with the ugly and the decaying plant. But if a thing wishes, what is the use of bodily force? One cannot lay hands on the mind and lift it into beauty and into safety. The free will of the weakest can laugh at the muscles of the strongest. Even a butterfly owns its awful gift, that gift which is the mystery at the heart of the mysterious world.

Lady Caryll and Sir Reuben! Always, when he reached that thought and tried to face it, Aubrey felt stunned and stupid, able to contemplate without being able to realise. This was because he could not alter his conception of what Lady Caryll was. She remained with her beauty unchanged, the temple of all things lovely to him. He could not allow her to descend. And it was this inability that afterwards led to his strange and—as many people thought—infatuated elevation of his godfather.

Why had she done this? What curious spring of human tenderness had gushed forth from her heart at the touch of Sir Reuben's wand? Even in his pain Aubrey could foreshadow the remarks of his world, could hear all the society voices saying the usual things with the usual little sneer tacked on at the end like the tail to a kite. When an ugly elderly man marries a beautiful young girl, the smallest child in a Mayfair drawing-room knows very well the proper thing to say and how to say it. But Aubrey brushed all the cackling voices aside and left all the time-worn remarks behind him. He knew Lady Caryll so much better than any one else could. He had always felt that. He felt it as strongly as ever even now.

And then he tried to think calmly of this old man, worn and travelled, who had done so much, whose eyes had watched so many activities in distant places, who had sprung from so strange a union, and in whose veins ran alien blood.

But his grief and surprise were too young. He recoiled before this effort, and the numb and stupid sensation returned upon him. He saw again the smiling mandarin holding a great emerald in its extended hand and bending obsequiously to a watching figure.

The heaviness of the black and sultry city, full of a multitude of hypnotised desires, dull in a weary trance of heat, rolled over his spirit once more, and he plodded on like those he saw vaguely around him. The pain within him had not gone. He felt it, but at a distance, as a man who has injected morphia feels the agony that is stunned within him for the moment struggling feebly after its former vivid life. He let it struggle. He knew well that the effect of morphia is but transient, and that his pain must be lasting. And the deadly day became like a hot and exceptional night to him; night without night's tenderness, romance, and starry charm, night only because the world was so black that it could surely not be day. The lamps were not lit, and the stupid, entranced world continued monotonously its occupations of the daylight. The children tried to play. Women drove to pay calls. Boys bicycled, and in the Park the nocturnal loafers had not begun to creep among the trees, like insects intent on mysterious and unholy errands.

But it was night.

The shops were open and the theatres were shut. No windows shone. Gardeners were watering their plants, and the omnibuses were full of women laden with packages. The early editions of the evening papers were coming out, and the City men still remained in their hot and hidden hive. In their dingy lodgings, behind the blinds tied with cheap lengths of gaudy ribbon, the birds who fly when the owls fly had not begun to assume their marvellous plumage, and all the bats hung still to the rafters, and the eaves sunk in a steady sleep.

But it was night.

And the great city could not understand that. For it was stagnant, emasculate, and overwhelmed in the hot and heavy gloom that increased upon it moment by moment. It moved, but like a sleepy cripple. It spoke, but like a man who is paralytic. It watched, but its eyes were surely glazing to blindness. It lived, but like a monster resting its head against the gate of death.

And in the centre of this tranced and sodden world the white butterfly with the folded wings dreamed on the haggard and sickly plant, and the pale and pertinacious decay crept softly along the edges of the drooping leaves.

CHAPTER X

Now it was actually night. The strange and unnatural darkness merged into the darkness the world knows and expects when day fails. The lamps were lit and society was dining. Lord and Lady Rangecliffe were at the house of a Minister, and poor Lady Rangecliffe, distraite, abrupt and—so her husband thought—even more angular than usual, was talking politics to an Under-Secretary of State, who wondered whether there had ever before been a woman so deaf to epigrams in the history of the world.

Lord and Lady St. Ormyn and Lady Caryll were dining with Sir Reuben Allabruth in Park Lane before going to the opera.

Aubrey was alone in his rooms in Jermyn Street. With the coming of the real night had come a deepening of his sense of loss. He began to know now that he had looked forward to a future with Lady Caryll as something that must come, as something beautiful and inevitable. Her refusal had delayed it. But he had not really believed that refusal was final. He had spoken too soon, too ruthlessly perhaps. It was true that he had thought little of himself, that he had felt himself unworthy of her. But this sense of unworthiness had not rendered him hopeless. For he was young; and when youth longs for one thing only, it cannot easily believe that life will never grant it that one thing. For life seldom seems utterly unkind in the morning.

Now it was really night. And Aubrey thought that he felt old. It seemed to him that he was looking back on his lost youth from a long distance, and that already it was something faint and pale and spectral. He was like some one who had missed the experiences that generally come with the years, and had gained only one, the true knowledge of what loss is. His days had fled while he slept, now he woke to age, and he had only a dream to comfort him.

The dull heat of the city had surely increased with the coming of night. In some vague way it entered into his grief, becoming one with it and deepening it. He found himself thinking—ridiculously—that on a winter evening his pain must have been less intolerable, and he longed to see white snow lying upon the ground. He thought of Sir Reuben. This new and brooding heat connected itself with him. Aubrey saw his burnt and lined face and his shrewd eyes in the blackness. He looked like some creature that had grown old in sunshine and fire. Now he sought the coolness of Lady Caryll's jewelled beauty. Aubrey saw him resting his wrinkled cheek against hers, and playing with the sparkling meshes of her hair.

Would he draw youth from her? Or would he give her age? One of those two chances was surely inevitable. For the link of marriage is so strong that often it induces an abominable imitation in bodies as well as in natures. Even features sometimes change insidiously, as under a spell, and the wife's face seeks to resemble the husband's, or *vice versa*.

Then Aubrey saw in the night Lady Caryll after—long after—this marriage with Sir Reuben. She was not old yet in years, but she looked old, horribly old. And she had the expression of one who has thrown youth away without using it. But that was not all. Her face had grown to resemble the face of her husband in some mysterious and hideous way. It seemed as if her features were becoming transparent and his showed vaguely behind them; his dark and twinkling eyes behind her clear and glittering grey eyes, his dry and parched mouth behind her fresh soft lips, his wrinkles behind her smooth cheeks.

All his age, his fatigue, his guile of an Eastern man, his sad cunning, were fastening upon her, and making her a dreadful and an unnatural travesty of him. And Aubrey saw in her, too, something of that fleeting and sensual curiosity that gleams in the eyes of veiled women who live in an eternal seclusion. They pass through the teeming streets of Constantinople and of Cairo, enclosed in smart European carriages, shrouded in their thin white veils. And the streets are full of men with whom they can never speak. But the expressive eyes speak sometimes eloquently above the veils. Aubrey looked at this new face of Lady Caryll, and he felt as if he were looking at a harem woman, at a slave covered with jewels.

Suddenly he knew that he could not remain alone any longer. The heat, the blackness, the hum of the city, and these visionary faces were becoming like the heat, the blackness, the noise and the visions of a nightmare. Aubrey felt that he was terribly unsafe with himself to night. A sensation of horror overcame him. He looked at his soul as a man looks at a stranger encountered in a lonely road by night. And he asked it silently, "What are you going to do to me?" He knew for the first time that there were within him abominable possibilities whose existence he had never suspected. They were stirring, they were rising up from their long inertia. He shuddered at the thought of their unknown activities.

He longed for some powerful distraction. He longed to hear music. He thought of going to the opera. Then he remembered that the visionary faces would perhaps be realised there. He dressed, and went out into the street. It seemed to him that Jermyn Street was the darkest and saddest street in London. He wondered how he had been able to live in it for so many months. An old beggar woman was singing in the gutter. She wore a black bonnet, pushed very far back on her head, which was nearly bald. Her face was red and wore a fixed expression of distress, and she was singing a coquettish song about a gipsy who was loved by a soldier. There were many high notes in the song; when the old voice reached them it cracked. The reiterated failures of this sad diva of the gutter were both pathetic and ridiculous; to Aubrey they were frightful. As he passed the old woman he felt terrified, as a child does when it passes the open door of an empty room at night.

His nerves were playing him stupid tricks. Why should he fear an old beggar woman? Yet he did fear her physically. He hurried on towards the glare of Piccadilly. He sought light, the noise of many people, the sight of a world of pleasure-seekers, the safety of crowds. He wanted to be jostled, touched. It seemed to him that human contact would break the spell that bound him, would force him to feel less painfully and dangerously unnatural.

He turned up a narrow street past a small and furtive-looking public-house which stood demurely at a corner. Three youths were lounging in front of it. As Aubrey went by he heard one of them say—

"Yes, I come 'ome Wednesday and we got called Sunday. I soon bustled 'er up. You take my tip, mates—allays drive the women, allays drive 'em!"

Aubrey longed to be a poor man leaning against a public-house. He had sometimes thought that the so-called lower classes are happier than is generally supposed, owing to a gift of devil-may-care insouciance which many of them undoubtedly possess. Now he felt sure of it.

In Piccadilly he found the usual crowd, and he walked through it very slowly. For he wanted to get help from it. He wanted it to touch him, speak to him, say to him, "Life is not altered. All is the same as ever. There is no dull trance over the city. There is no nightmare in the gloom. We are not shadows. We are human. We too suffer, like you, and are happy, as you will again be happy."

Above all, he wanted this crowd to say to him—

"We are natural. We are following all our little impulses

thoughtlessly, gaily, and you are like us. For a moment you have been apart; but the moment has passed. You are only a boy, and a boy cannot be broken on the wheel in an instant. Life is only beginning for you. It is not over. You will not walk in this black dream for ever."

He walked slowly, wading, as it were, through this mighty river of rushing life. But it meant no more to him than the painted stream that pauses, so hideously and artificially, upon the canvas of a scene at a playhouse.

His state was more unnatural than he had supposed. Even physical contact with those around him could not stir him to normality. A beggar laid a filthy hand upon his sleeve. He perceived the hand but did not feel its touch.

And again he felt afraid of himself.

When he gained Piccadilly Circus he saw one of those piteous and awful tragedies that are so common in London. A bright and rosy-cheeked young woman, whose sparkling eyes and dewy lips looked and breathed a fulness of life and of hopeful anticipation, was saying a gay good-bye to her sweetheart, a handsome young soldier. Aubrey heard them making arrangements to meet on the following Sunday. The soldier kissed the girl.

"Well," he said, in a hearty voice, "so long!"

"So long!" she answered.

She mounted into an omnibus and the soldier sauntered away down the street, whistling a lively tune. As he vanished, apparently the girl found that she was in the wrong omnibus. She jumped hastily out, stood on the kerb for a moment, glanced round her, then started to cross the Circus at a run. Suddenly in the distance there was a dull roar of men's voices. It seemed to startle the girl. She hesitated in the middle of the traffic. People began to shout to her. She got confused. The dull roar grew louder. A fire-engine came at a hand-gallop down Shaftesbury Avenue. Cabs, omnibuses drew aside, but the paralysed girl did not stir until the engine was close to her. Then, as if governed by some insane impulse, she uttered a cry and started forward in front of the stretching horses.

When they were pulled up, a crowd of women, cabbies, street boys, and policemen stood round something that had been a woman.

A little way off a young soldier was whistling gaily and thinking of Sunday as he strode to barracks.

Aubrey tried to realise him now—and later, when he knew.

But the soldier was a shadow, and the thing lying there on the pavement a shadow.

He walked on, and again he thought of music.

As he had once said to Lady Caryll, he was no musician. He

neither sang nor played. He could scarcely talk the usual jargon that the fool is at home with in the happy modern world in which every self-respecting person is a critic.

He only loved music, and felt it like a live thing in his veins.

It seemed to him now that music alone could break the heavy spell which lay, like a thing of iron, upon his numbed and inhuman spirit.

He turned into an immense playhouse which stood in a noisy square, bought a seat, and made his way into the stalls. They were nearly full, but the seat next to Aubrey on the left was at present vacant. He felt glad of this. He would have liked to be alone, to watch and to listen without being forced into a close and intimate contact with strangers. He carefully avoided glancing about him, for fear of seeing some one he knew. Almost immediately a stiff little grey-haired man stepped into the orchestra amid applause, and the musicians drew from their instruments a strong flood of sensuous melody.

Aubrey listened idly to this music, which sounded far away.

The curtain drew up, and strings of ballet-girls floated towards the footlights.

Aubrey watched them as a man watches little dolls manipulated by a showman in the street.

Some of them smiled at the audience. Some looked dull and waxen. Some giggled at each other, and whispered as they moved. A few wore a fixed expression of fatigued wickedness, which might have made even a young man up from the country understand the unrewarding lassitudes of sin.

Nearly all looked stereotyped and unoriginal, and as the ballet continued on its way, Aubrey's dream seemed to increase and to become denser. Even the music, expressive and beautiful though it was, made no impression upon him. It had no meaning. It was like a voice that did not come from a heart, but from a machine. He listened. He thought of the frightful accident he had seen in the street. He thought of Lady Caryll united with Sir Reuben. He thought of the emerald, and of its legend.

And all these thoughts were the same, and were nothing!

Music could not break the spell. Rows of glittering women could not break it. The death of a human being full of life and of love could not break it. Aubrey had become ruthless and heavy as an image. He sat there in his seat staring before him, and his face was so inexpressive as to be horrible.

The scene of the spectacle was now changed, and was laid in some island—probably mythical—of the East. The atmosphere and the colouring were exquisitely warm and sparkling. Huge red flowers drooped in the glory of a supreme sunshine, languorous and fatiguing, but thrilling in its completeness of golden heat and light. The sky was a hazy blue, clear, but clear behind an ethereal veil, that seemed born of waves and of clouds, melting together, and diffused along vast distances. In the vague background the sea lay, a blue mirror on which a jewelled dust had been scattered by the hands of the gods—mythical, too, and strange—of this fantastic region, in which life seemed at the same time intensely full and intensely dreamy, passionate and drowsy as a tropical flower that is heavy with the burthen of its colour beneath a piercing noon.

This island was deserted. Yet Aubrey looked at it with anticipation. For the first time he stirred in his dull dream. The fulness of this superbly imitated life of Nature in some distant region touched some spring within him that nothing else had been able to reach. This veiled sky, these mysterious flowers, this distant sea held in coral arms, this shimmering atmosphere moved him, almost excited him. There must surely be some spirit in this place, sleeping in the shadows of the mighty trees and listening to the voices of the eternal waters.

The music played by the orchestra now became very thin and plaintive and mocking. There was a little pipe that reiterated again and again a melody that was both droll and melancholy. This melody trickled like a thread of water, that winds and is lost in sand and reappears, imperturbable but never increasing, small and wayward and indiscreet. Then, from some hidden place in the empty island, there rose the mutinous beat of distant tom-toms, and from the sea came two huge black slaves, with mighty bodies and submissive velvet eyes. They stood in the background, like two statues of ebony, and between them, beneath the heavy foliage of the palm-trees, trickled a thin stream of girls, like the stream of the pipe's frail melody. They were clad in varying shades of yellow, the colour deepening down the stream from very pale primrose to very deep and lustrous orange. And their hair, which hung down in long, loose plaits, bound with jewels, was blond and red, curled at the temples, and crowned with small, coloured turbans. These girls came forward with sleepy footsteps, and as they drew nearer the music made a crescendo, becoming more full of colour, of intention, and of depth, but always remaining intensely languid, and full of a sort of exquisite fatigue. There was the beat of noon in it, the beat of marvellous life in the everlasting sunshine, where the flowers are sick with their own beauty, and the sea is tired in the glory of its depths; where the slaves are slaves in soul rather than in body, and the trees droop towards their faithful shadows; where existence is ever a kind of dream, women are a dream, and men a dream; where the wave is so quiet that it is like the sky, and the sky is so gentle that it is like the wave ; where decay is fruitful as birth, and all things are fused together without thought of moralities, obedient to one law only, the marvellous law of the sun ; where death itself is a sort of golden ecstasy, even as life is a golden trance. And in the sun these sunny girls, with their blond and red hair, their pale-yellow and orange robes— sunshine of spring and sunshine of summer—slipped forward as the stream slips down an enchanted garden. In their hands they carried long garlands of tropical flowers, and the jewels slept in the glory of their hair. They moved slowly, as if the heat oppressed them, and their faces were pale and dream-like, attentive to the dreamy music.

Aubrey watched them. And it seemed as if their dream awoke him. For he began to suffer once more. But now his pain was an intoxication. And the rocking music touched him. It gathered round his heart and puckered it together, as the fingers of a woman pucker silk into a rosette. When the two lines of girls approached the footlights they began to dance, or rather to posture rhythmically and drowsily, swinging their garlands of roses. Presently one of them detached herself from her companions. As she did so a new melody sounded in the orchestra. It was her theme Aubrey thought, and it was very sensuous and infinitely sad, sad with the rich sorrow of golden languors, and with the melancholy of desires satisfied. There was nothing classical about it, and there was nothing classical about this girl. But there seemed to be a sleepy depth of passion and of longing in both, a cry in her melody, and a cry in her. They came from far, and from mysterious places haunted by dreams and by strange experiences, and they affected Aubrey powerfully. The girl was tall and slim. She looked very young. Her face was oval and pale and full of tender fatigue, and the eyes beneath her red-brown hair were very large and dark. She fixed them on Aubrey as she danced. Perhaps she did not see him. But it seemed to the boy that she watched him, and that she too was sad. He fancied even that he saw tears welling up beneath her heavy white eyelids, and that the footlights glittered in them as fire glitters in water. While she danced some of the other girls smiled at the audience and whispered to each other; but she was engrossed by the dream of the melody and by the dream of her sorrow, which it related, and cradled, and concealed. She listened to the music, now as a girl listens to her lover when he speaks to her, now as a slave listens to the voice of the master in whose bosom she lies submissively whether she will or no. And she replied, catching its mood and reproducing it in her sinuous movements, and in her wide soft gestures, which were slow and exquisitely graceful. While she danced, her sorrow seemed to increase till the burden of it was heavy on those young shoulders. And the great eyes that looked at Aubrey spoke in the dumbness of an appeal that was like the appeal of distant things ; of an echo in the hills at the end of a valley, or a far-off wave of the sea. When her steps were finished, she floated softly away and merged herself in the yellow line of girls. But her great eyes still rested on Aubrey, and he felt as if he had been sitting with her in some hidden place hearing her sorrow and telling her of his. He glanced at his programme, and saw that the soloist of the island dance was called "Miss Di Manners."

"How are you?" said a voice which spoke with a foreign accent.

Aubrey turned and saw that the empty chair at his side was now filled by Monsieur Anneau.

He longed to get up and go out without a word. He hated the singer instinctively, and to-night he felt as if he could no longer control his feelings.

"You are not singing?" he said mechanically.

"No."

The scene on the stage was changed.

"That was a pretty girl," said Monsieur Anneau, looking at Aubrey with his fierce eyes, in which a red light seemed always flickering.

"There are always pretty girls here," Aubrey said coldly.

He felt as if a coarse hot hand was laid upon him. The singer smiled with the air of one who can divine at a glance all the secrets of the flesh. He lit a cigar.

"I am very sad to-night," he said. "I come here for distraction."

"Ah!"

"This news of Lady Caryll will make me hate emeralds for ever, and I have to wear them so often on the stage."

"I don't understand you," said Aubrey, putting his hand under the seat to find his hat.

"You have not heard that she has succumbed to Sir Reuben's jewel. It is all over London to-night."

And he smiled with intolerable satisfaction. Monsieur Anneau was always pleased when any fact seemed to prove to him anew that his low conception of all women was founded upon rock.

"And now," he added, still smiling and stroking his dyed beard, "now begins the drama."

Aubrey took his hat, nodded, and made his way out. In the portico, between the great china tubs of flowers, he stopped and stood still. He felt confused and almost stunned. The sudden meeting with Monsieur Anneau, just as the curious lethargy of his mind was giving way to a more natural condition of impulsive thought, had produced upon him a physical effect. He put his hand to his head, which ached as if he had just received a blow, and he had a strange sensation of having forgotten something, though what he could not imagine.

"Cab, sir?" said the gigantic attendant.

Aubrey shook his head. He still waited. He was trying to remember what he had thought of or desired just before Monsieur Anneau had spoken to him. Then before his hot eyes floated once more the girls of the island. He saw again the strange and sorrowful look of sympathy in the dark eyes of the unknown dancer. He glanced round. The attendant was still at his side.

"Which is the way to the stage-door?" Aubrey said.

The giant smiled, and his large hand instinctively curved itself into a suggestive cup.

"This way, sir," he said in a confidential murmur.

Aubrey followed him into the street. Some hideous boys were standing there staring in at the flowers and the thick carpets. They wore the sad and abominable look of those who have never had a chance. As Aubrey passed, following the giant, they eyed him with bitter scrutiny and made some coarse remarks which he did not hear. The attendant turned to the left up a side street, walked on for some distance, then stopped at the corner of another street which ran to the right.

"Straight up there, sir," he said. "But the ballet ladies won't be out for another half-hour."

And he smiled again. He thought he knew the aristocracy as an organ-grinder thinks he knows a monkey. Aubrey gave him a florin and he retired, wondering how any one can be so short-sighted as to wish to do away with the upper classes.

Aubrey stood at the street corner. London is full of worlds, all huddled close together, and different from one another. The few yards that he had traversed in the wake of the giant had taken Aubrey from a world he knew into one of which he was ignorant. He glanced at the street before him. It was narrow, dark, and at present quiet. The buildings on either side of it were immensely tall, and looked unkempt and blind, like the backs of warehouses. The one on the right of the street was the theatre. But no one would have supposed so, for it was blank and dreary, and though there were many windows, few of them were lit up. There were three or four loungers at some distance, and while Aubrey stood at the corner a little girl with a blond pigtail and meanly dressed ran by accompanied by a magnificent white poodle with which she was playing. This little girl earned twenty-five pounds a week for her father, and had travelled all over the globe as an acrobat. She tumbled down in the gutter and burst out crying. Aubrey picked her up. She thanked him in lisping German, ran on and disappeared into a doorway at some distance, wiping her blue eyes with her little knuckles. The poodle, a famous trick-dog, followed her barking.

Aubrey guessed that she had entered by the stage-door, and he walked slowly down the left pavement. He passed two or three men who were smoking and staring at nothing. They looked like his idea of stage-carpenters. He stopped near them and almost opposite to the stage-entrance of the theatre, which flamed with gas. As he waited he could hear music very faintly. It sounded ugly and sad, though it was obviously dance music. An omnibus loaded with baskets and drawn by a wretched horse drove up. It stopped, and five very strong and athletic-looking men sprang out. They all wore ulsters down to their heels. They were followed by a small boy with an abnormally large hooked nose and hair plastered down on his forehead. The boy squinted across at Aubrey, then abruptly stood on his head in the street, elevated himself on his hands, curved his body like a serpent and put his left foot in his mouth. One of the men gave him a cuff, picked him up by the waist with one hand and carried him in at the door like a parcel. The two or three loungers laughed, and one of them remarked—

"He's a devil that Alf!"

"He draws more than the bally," rejoined another. "All the nobs come for his turn. He and Vauxhall between 'em could run a show off of their own bat, could they!"

Aubrey wondered what was the connection between the boy with the hooked nose and the unfashionable locality alluded to. He waited. Two or three more badly dressed men slouched slowly up out of the darkness of the street and hovered upon the kerb, regarding their companions in expectancy sideways without turning their heads. One of them took out an enormous silver watch and muttered—

"'Tain't time yet. They're only in the wheel now."

He lit a penny-cigar. Owing to the direction of the breeze Aubrey received the smoke in his face. He moved a little nearer to the stage-door. Within he saw dimly a man with spectacles and a red nose arranging some letters in a rack, another man drinking slowly out of a bottle, and a boy in the livery of the theatre picking a walnut out of its shell. The distant music swelled into a soft uproar.

"That's curtain!" said one of the loungers.

Light sprang suddenly into the windows of the great build-

ing, which were modestly shrouded in thin white blinds. And, following the light as if in pursuit, came sound, the noise of dozens of feet running upstairs, of dozens of screaming girls' voices mounting from some hidden abyss. Peals of soprano laughter, cries of remonstrance, of gaiety, of anger, of fear, all swimming in the enveloping noise of feet on bare boards, poured out into the street. Aubrey could even distinguish words—
"Get away, Annie!" "Slow coach! let me get by then, can't yer?" "Yuss, I see 'im. Ain't he Slyboots!" "I won't be tickled, no I won't—Ugh, you 'orror!" "Madame'll give it 'er to-morrer—you see!" "Shan't, then, shan't I tell yer!" "I've got a thirst on me." "Thought I should a dropped in the wheel." "She's a nice 'un to carry a flag! 'Alf mast 'igh, that's what she is." "'Urry up, Susie, Lord sakes! 'urry up!" "Supper with a nob, well why not? What's supper?" "Lost 'er shoe in the wheel, and then says its cruel 'ard to mike a gurl go barefoot!" "Goin' on yer bike! My word, where's the broom?" "Did yer 'ear Madame shriek to 'er? She'll git the sack if she turns 'em in agine."

And then female shadows began to tower and diminish, waver, flicker, and gyrate upon the white blinds. In some of the windows, half-way up, the shadows were of feet and legs darting hastily about as if in some mad acrobatic performance, and in the lower halves of these windows were shadows of heads and raised arms and busts. For one long window often lit two dressing-rooms, and the dividing floor was midway up the panes. The voices continued to scream and to chatter, and there was something unholy and diabolic in this piercing uproar emanating from this crowd of shadows.

As Aubrey stood in the dark street watching the intense activity of the silhouettes upon the blinds, and listening to the screams, the loud laughter, and the broken ejaculations, he felt as if he were observing the progress of a nightmare. He saw arms thrust suddenly up as if in appeal to Heaven—really to get rapidly into sleeves; slabs of black, that were hair, rolling up and diminishing into roundnesses that resembled bullets but that were "buns"; draperies falling from shoulders, and vanishing like shapes dropping down into hell; shoes, kicked from eager feet, mounting into the air like birds; mouths opening wide as if demanding invisible morsels of food; waists enlarging as corsets fell, diminishing as other corsets were violently assumed; bent knees, like knees of statues carved to represent motion; backs dodging to and fro; sharp profiles; blots that were full faces; bending heads that suggested heads of mourners, heads thrown far back; a hand with thin fingers that held an immense pin; a hand grasping a brush that was like a weapon. Then, a little later, and when the knot of loungers in the street had increased into a tiny crowd, there were shadows of hats upon the blinds, ostrich feathers towering like feathers on a hearse; quaint shapes of fruit, of flowers, of knots of riband, butterflies of tulle, and straw brims curved like shells. And all the time the cries were unceasing, and seemed to grow louder perpetually, storming the heights of the silence of the night.

The man with the penny-cigar pulled down his shirt-cuffs and gave a sudden twist to his moustache. Two or three other loungers assumed alert attitudes that were almost military, and the boy in livery swallowed his fifth walnut with a gulp and emerged into the street conducting a bicycle, upon the handle of which he proceeded to tie a brown paper parcel. Far down the street appeared two huge yellow eyes, which slowly approached, and presently a horse became visible between them.

"Madame's carriage," said a lounger. "They'll be comin' now."

And then girls began to flow forth under the gas jet on to the pavement. At first they came in solitary units, then in twos and threes, then in a stream, hurrying downwards, stopping by the man with the red nose and the spectacles, then turning through the half glass door into the street. As they came they chattered and laughed, pulling on thread gloves, and arranging hair-pins and buttoning cloth jackets. Some of them were smart and majestic, and walked in a dignified solitude, though jostled by impertinent neighbours. Others—the majority—were poorly clad in dark dresses, and wore sailor hats of straw pinned carelessly on hair that was twisted loosely into inartistic knobs. They talked at the tops of their voices, screamed with laughter, and stood in knots on the pavement exchanging piercing good-byes, mingled with boisterous chaff, scraps of intimate conversation, or comments on the events of the evening.

"Well, so long, Alice. If he should, you give him the chuck. That's my advice. He ain't worth it. You take my tip. So long."

"So long."

And a great girl with red cheeks tramped off, moving instinctively like one who is born to carry banners.

The boy in livery appeared again, escorting a pretty girl with impudent eyes, and a large bunch of roses in the front of her drab jacket.

"You're a good boy, Jackie," she said. "I'll bring you some more nuts to-morrow."

"Thank you, Miss."

"Is the lamp right? What time's the call?"

"Half-past eleven."

"My word! they don't give us much rest."

She put her hand on the bicycle and arranged her skirt, keeping one foot on the kerb and one on the right pedal. Some loungers gathered round, staring at her with admiration.

"Give 'im 'is 'ead, Miss," said one.

"Jackie," continued the girl with calm indifference, "when you're a man I'll marry you. You understand bikes and you ain't shoddy."

She glanced contemptuously round her at the staring men.

"Here, Jackie," she said.

The little boy in livery put his head down to receive a whisper. The girl gave him a sounding kiss on his round face, rang her bell, and glided off in the direction of the Strand, while Jackie returned proudly to the stage-door amid the laughter and ejaculations of the bystanders.

Aubrey wondered what it felt like to be a child in livery, eating nuts and being petted by dancers. All that he saw going on before him still seemed dreamlike and unnatural. But behind the dreamlike sensation lurked an acute sense of disappointment. In this dark and flickering crowd of girls how could he find the pale face and the deep eyes that had looked at him with such thrilling sympathy. He felt that he was foolish to wait, that it was useless, and even humiliating. Yet he waited. For now he did not feel as if he could remain alone, as if he could go back to his rooms without having spoken to some one. And he wished to speak to some one who knew nothing about him, to a stranger, whom he need never see again. The idea had come to him. It was eccentric, perhaps, but it governed him. He was resolved to wait a little longer. More girls flowed out. Some of them were mere children, and began to play "touch" in the street, or to perform steps for the benefit of the diminishing throng of men. For many of the loungers had welcomed, and departed with, their womenkind. They were brothers, cousins, husbands, lovers of the dancers. A man in a top-hat appeared, ceremoniously escorting a middle-aged lady dressed in plain black silk and a bonnet, who walked very slowly with a queenly air. This was the ballet-mistress, famous all over Europe. A girl came behind them carrying some roses. An attendant darted forward to open the carriage-door. The lady in black stepped in majestically. She was followed by the girl. Several loungers raised their hats. As the carriage drove away Aubrey saw the lady smelling the roses. He noticed that she had reddish-brown hair arranged in bands, and that she looked clever and determined.

Most of the girls were gone now. The street was beginning

to look deserted again, and in the windows of the great building many of the lights were extinguished. The man with the penny-cigar had found his companion, and had walked off with her, arm in arm, in a contented silence. At last Aubrey turned to go. As he did so he heard a voice say—

"Well, Di, night, night! Try and cheer up, Di."

"Night, night!" replied a young voice with a weary note in it.

And then Aubrey heard light feet behind him.

He stopped. A tall, slim girl walked slowly past him. In her hand she held a letter. She had a white, oval face, and dark hair fluffed out over her ears beneath a sailor hat with a white riband. He did not recognise her. But she was called "Di."

He followed her.

CHAPTER XI

HE passed her. As he did so, the girl glanced at him with a sort of hesitating inquiry, and, seeing her eyes, he knew that she was the Island dancer, although her dark hair transformed her, and she now seemed a very ordinary young woman, by no means formed to attract attention in a crowd or in a dimly lit street. He slackened his pace till she was at his side. Then he took off his hat. The girl stopped on the pavement.

"Go away, please," she said, speaking in a pretty, soft voice with a London accent. "It's no use. You've made a mistake."

"Mayn't I speak to you for a moment?"

"No. What for?"

"I'm very unhappy to-night," Aubrey said.

Such a confession contradicted his character. Sometimes such moments of direct contradiction occur in a life. They puzzle our relatives and throw our friends into confusion. The girl looked startled.

"Are you?" she said; then, after a little pause, she added, "Why ever do you tell me?"

"I don't know," Aubrey said.

He wondered sometimes, afterwards, why he did not find himself and his words ridiculous at that moment. But, at that moment, he had no feeling of self-consciousness. The girl stared at him with her great eyes, which looked heavy and as if they had been weeping recently.

"If you're unhappy whatever are you here for?" she asked prosaically.

"Let me walk with you for a minute," Aubrey said.

"But I don't know you, and I don't walk with strangers. I don't care about that sort of thing."

"I've never spoken to any one in the street before like this,' said Aubrey.

"Then why d'you do it now?"

"Because—aren't you unhappy too?"

"What if I am?" she said. "It don't matter to anybody except me. Now please I'm goin'."

And she went on, but slowly, and almost reluctantly. At a

crossing she had to stop to let a cab go by, and she looked back. Aubrey joined her again.

"I'm going to walk with you," he said. "I saw you dancing to-night and you looked sad. I'm sad too. Let me talk to you just to-night. We shan't ever meet again, I daresay."

"Well, but," said the girl. "There isn't any harm, perhaps, but if Vauxhall was to see me, I don't know whatever he'd think. He'd tell Lill and——"

"Vauxhall!" repeated Aubrey, thinking of the boy with the hooked nose. "And Alf?"

"D'you know them?" cried the girl, brightening.

"I've seen Alf," said Aubrey.

They were walking on slowly now.

"Isn't he a demon?" she said. "You should see him do his tricks in our kitchen. The dad laughs fit to split his sides. Dad manages the lights at Covent Garden," she added. "He knows all the singers. They give him presents sometimes."

"But who's Vauxhall?" said Aubrey.

"He's married to Lill, my sister. He's Alf's brother. You know the 'Marvellous Flicks,' don't you? Well, he's the one that lies on his back and catches Alf on his feet, and does the corpse business and the bird act. He lives at our place with Lill and Alf when they ain't travellin'. If he was to see me——"

She looked apprehensively behind her. They were passing a restaurant. The light streamed out upon the girl's white London complexion.

"Come in here and have supper," Aubrey said.

"Oh no, I couldn't; I've never done such a thing—not with a stranger."

She spoke quite simply, without any of the coquettish affectation that touts for persuasion. But Aubrey was determined to have his way. To-night he was very selfish in his sorrow, and he would not part from this momentary distraction.

"It's quite early," he said. "After supper I'll get you a cab. You can go home and never see me again."

She looked at him with a sort of babyish inquiry in her pretty eyes.

"Well, but whatever's the good of that?" she said. "You are funny!"

For reply he took her by the arm and drew her gently into the café. They arrived at a little table covered with a white cloth. A waiter, with an ashen face and dark rings under his Italian eyes, hastened up to serve them.

"I don't think I can," the girl said. "And besides, I ain't hungry—really I ain't, only tired."

"Sit down then. I'll take your jacket."

He held out his hands. The girl looked at him again with inquiring eyes. Then she wriggled slowly out of her jacket, which was very tight, and appeared in a pretty white blouse with a frill down the front and little lilac flowers scattered over it.

"I made it myself," she remarked, seeing that Aubrey was observing it. "I always make my own blouses."

She laid the letter on the table and sat down on the red plush divan.

"It's a deal cheaper," she added. "And besides, I can make 'em more tasty."

Suddenly her eyes filled with tears.

"Oh dear! I am bad to-night," she almost whispered. "Cruel bad."

Aubrey gave the waiter an order. He skipped to execute it with a weary agility.

"You are tired with dancing."

"No, it ain't that. I love dancin'. Madame knows it. No, it ain't that."

"What is it, then?" Aubrey asked gently.

He was sitting opposite to her, facing the long mirror, in which he could see the back of the girl's head, the counter, at which sat a heavy-looking foreign woman with a black cat in her lap, two or three waiters staring at the street, and two elderly Jews who were eating kidneys and onions at a distant table.

"I've had bad news to-day, shockin' bad. I don't know how to bear it."

The tears in her eyes made them look larger and infinitely pathetic. For the first time that evening Aubrey almost forgot his own life and himself.

"What is it?" he asked.

The waiter planted a dish between them, and uncorked a bottle with mechanical violence. Aubrey helped his companion to a cutlet and poured some wine into her glass. Then, when the waiter had gone, he repeated—

"What is it?"

"I've been deceived," she said slowly, putting her fork into the cutlet. "I trusted somebody, that's all. No, I can't eat to-night, really I can't."

"You must try."

"Oh dear!" she said, and she leaned her face on her hand. "Why ever isn't a girl let be happy? And I don't ever do no harm to anybody. I never crab another girl, or curry to Madame, or try to make the orchestra gentlemen like me to get anything out of 'em. I don't, really I don't. I can't see why it is I've had this awful cruel letter. If I'd give him any cause. But I haven't. I don't never speak to the Acros."

"What?"

"Why any of the acrobats, or anything like that. I wouldn't do it. Except Vauxhall and them, and they're relations, aren't they?"

"Yes."

"We were engaged," she continued, speaking with the direct simplicity of a small child, "Bert and I, for over a year. I used to go to his place of an afternoon and make his tea, and look after his clothes and sew for him, and all. And now he writes that we can't be married, because I'm not educated, and because Dad's a common person! Why Dad's liked by all the singers, and Madame Patti's shook him by the hand. And Bert used to come and dine at our place and talk to Dad by the hour, and say afterwards how he was intelligent and all what a lot he knew. And now he turns round like this, and we aren't to meet any more. I don't know how to bear it."

She put up one hand to her eyes.

"Oh, I am silly," she said.

Then she began to try to eat in silence, cutting the meat into tiny lozenges in order to be able to swallow it easily.

"A thing like that hurts dreadfully," Aubrey said.

"Ah, you don't know! But it does. It come all over me when I was dancin'. It's like when snow comes, and makes you all shivery. And I did understand him so. He'll never find another to understand him like I did. And I've read a lot of books since I knew him. But it ain't easy, is it, readin' when there's calls every day, and dancin' at night and then tired afterwards. I'm not educated, p'raps. But then he can't dance, so in a way it's quits, ain't it?"

She gazed at Aubrey with pathetic inquiry.

"Yes, in a way it's quits," he echoed.

In all his life he had never before talked to a girl like this. He had never before been in contact with such childlike and unconscious frankness. He knew comparatively few theatrical people, and those whom he knew were fashionable actor-managers, and the opera-singers whom he met, and generally avoided, at Lady St. Ormyn's. Chorus-girls and ballet-dancers had never entered into his life. Until this evening he had never waited outside a stage-door. If he had ever thought of dancing-girls at all, he had thought of them as knowing minxes, sharp London children, with the allures of the stage grafted on to the fearful cleverness that has its birth in the gutter. The extraordinary and sentimental simplicity of this girl, the bourgeois respectability that floated round her like an atmosphere, and set her apart in a virginal region to which few society women could penetrate, her unconscious confidence in a total stranger and her curious unreserve —all these things touched and surprised Aubrey. His own sense of reserve dropped away from him as he looked into this girl's eyes, and in the sympathy that he felt for her frankly expressed sorrow there was a vague, if momentary, solace for his own.

"He writes for the papers, Bert does," she continued. "He is clever. He does police cases and weddins, and his father was a capting. That's why he's always held himself so high. He's had an education, but I never thought as——"

She paused, took out her handkerchief, which had scalloped edges and a purple letter D in one corner, and wiped her eyes.

"It's come so sudden," she added.

Aubrey thought of the abruptness of his sorrow.

"Bad things generally come like that," he said.

"Yes, don't they? Ma was never so well as just before she had that seizure."

"You live with your father and mother?"

"And Lill, and Vauxhall, and Alf, and Jenny, and Bob, and Susie, and Charley. I'm the eldest. I have a lot to do."

She sighed.

"However shall I be to-morrow?" she said. "I don't know what Dad'll say. He's so high-tempered is Dad, and as proud as Lucifer. And he thinks a lot of me. They all do at home. It's Di here and Di there from morning to night."

"Is your name Diana?" asked Aubrey.

"No, Diamond."

Aubrey was silent for a moment. He was thinking of jewels, and of Sir Reuben's remark about Lady Caryll, that she was a human diamond. And it seemed to Aubrey strange that to-night he should be talking to a girl with such a name, and that her name alone had had something to do with her entry into his life.

"Just before I was born, Ma was dancin' in the Jewel ballet at the 'Crown,'" said the girl. "She was one of the diamonds, so they christened me after her. Ma used to be first class on her feet. She's dresser now at the Opera, so her and Dad's together. Whatever time is it? I must be home before they are. Dad's that particular with us girls. He'd be for killin' you if he was to see us here."

Aubrey could not help smiling at the earnest tragedy of the last sentence.

"It's not late," he said.

"Let's see! It's 'Lohengrin' to-night, I know. But who's the Elsie?"

"Why d'you want to know?"

"Because it makes a lot of difference in the time. If it's Madame Sabini, they won't be out till after twelve. She goes so slow with all them high notes. Dad can't a-bear her because she keeps them all from supper. All the carpenters hate her."

"It is Madame Sabini," he said, wondering if that famous Diva knew of her reputation in the carpentering world.

"Oh, then we've got a little more time. I used to dance at the Opera, so I know 'em all there. I've held Madame Sabini's train many a time. She's that kind-hearted, and can't she sing? But she does go so mortal slow, don't she? D'you like singin'?"

"Yes."

"So he does, does Bert. Oh dear! everything brings him up, dancin' and singin', and books and supper, and everything. He loves cutlets like these with mushrooms. He always will have mushrooms. That's it. If you love any one, it's them with everything. Even if its eatin', you're put in mind of 'em. Ain't you?"

"Yes," Aubrey said.

Had he not tried, in different language, to express the same thought to Lady Caryll in the dark garden at Epsom? Had he not felt her in music, and in all beautiful things, like a presence sanctifying and being sanctified by them? It was strange to find this little dancing-girl touched by the same sensation in her so different love. And it seemed to close humanity round in a very small circle.

"When were you at the Opera?" he asked her.

"Oh, last season. Madame lent me."

"Did you ever see a Lady St. Ormyn there?"

"What! Her as thinks she bosses the show! You should hear Dad on her! Why, she come to him once at rehearsal with that there Mr. Wilson, tryin' to teach him his business. She says, 'At Bayroot—or some place or another—the lights is blue,' she says. Dad ups and says, 'If I make 'em blue, my lady,' he says, 'the singers'll look for all the world like a pack o' ghosts.' 'Nonsense,' she says—she's a high-tempered lady too. 'Nonsense,' says Mr. Wilson. 'Very well,' says Dad, and he turns on the blue. You should have heard Madame Sabini cry out. 'I shall not sing,' she says, 'if I'm to be made a corpse of at every moment,' she says. There was a rumpus. Oh, how Dad did laugh! When he come home that night he says to Ma, 'This ain't Bayroot, nor this ain't Madigascar,' he says. 'This is England, and it's no manner of use her ladyship trying to introduce them savage tricks.' Dad can be firm with 'em, I tell you. He does think nothin' at all of them amateurs."

"Have you ever seen Lady St. Ormyn's daughter?"

"Only once in a box. Oh, she is pretty. You seen her?"

"Yes," said Aubrey.

The waiter brought some grapes. The girl ate them slowly. Whatever she was saying, her eyes never lost their sad and clouded look, nor her manner its childlike and soft gravity, sometimes deepening into sentiment, or into simple and homely tragedy. She was utterly without self-consciousness. Her white face was roughened here and there by her undue violence in removing her false complexion at night, and in the corner of one of her eyes there was a black fragment of make-up. Her lips were very flexible and pale, and her slim body looked like the body of a child in the frilled and puffed white blouse with the lilac flowers. It was difficult to believe that she was the Island sorceress, for her red-gold wig completely transformed her. And it was difficult to believe that this simple little girl could command at will all the curious seductions of dancing. She ate her grapes mechanically while Aubrey watched her. He noticed that her hands were long and thin. A little artificial rose still tinted the nails here and there, and she wore two rings. She glanced up suddenly and met his gaze.

"He give me them," she said, alluding to the rings. "They were his mother's. I shall have to send 'em back to-morrow, I s'pose."

And she choked.

"I'm not fit to be out to-night," she murmured. "Whatever must you think of me?"

"I think you must try to be brave and bear it," Aubrey said.

And he felt, while he spoke to her, as if he were speaking to his own soul.

"Other people have sorrows like this," he continued.

"Do they?"

"Hundreds."

She shook her head slowly.

"Ah! but they don't love as I love Bert. There's Mr. King, though. It is odd."

"Mr. King?"

"Yes. Oh, he is good. He's wanted to marry me oh for ever so long, since I was sixteen. He's a ridin'-master in a very good way of business, and so quiet and respectable. I almost thought I could like him till I see Bert, and then I had to tell him 'no.' He did take it well, but he always looks at me so sad. Whatever will he say? D'you think he feels about me what I do about Bert?"

"I daresay."

"Oh dear! it is a world, ain't it? Why ever can't we be let happy?"

"I don't know," said Aubrey, wondering why.

"There's Mr. King," she continued, in sad and wide-eyed reflection; "he won't never like any one but me. He says so. He says he's tried, and it ain't no use, because he can't. I went with him once to Virginia Waters on my birthday, before I knew Bert. Oh, he was kind. There wasn't nothin' he didn't give me, first class in the train, and supper when we got back, and all. He is good. But it's no use. Oh dear!"

And again the tears welled up in her eyes.

"Dad always said that Mr. King was the one for a good husband," she added. "He taught a princess to ride once."

"Did he?"

"Yes, and he's always with high people, but not a bit uppish for all. He'll never love any one but me!"

"Some day, perhaps, you'll be able to care for him."

"No, not like that. You don't understand what it is to love."

"Perhaps not," Aubrey said. "What is it like?"

"Why," she said earnestly, "one ain't oneself, and one's in a rare takin' all the time. Now it's happiness and as bright as ninepence and up to anything, and now it's as black as ink, and feelin' ten times worse than when Madame's took you out of a step because you're awkward, or when you've lost your shoe in the wheel, or fell down—like Lizzie Gunnin' did to-night. You seen her?"

"No. Well?"

"She will get her feet too close together and goin' round like that sideways you must keep 'em more apart. See?"

"Yes."

"And you feel lonesome all the time if you're not with 'em, 'specially of an evenin' and when it's dark. Oh dear! All these evenin's coming! Whatever am I to do?"

She gazed at him, and her eyes were full of a terrible and childish questioning. They were afraid and wondering. And Aubrey looked at her, and silently asked himself her question, and tried to see his future in the darkness, as she was trying to see hers. But suddenly she said, in a dry little voice, that sounded almost like the voice of an invalid—

"Whatever time is it?"

"Half-past eleven."

"Oh, I must go. Vauxhall and Lill'll think that—I don't know what. And Ma and Dad'll be home soon. If you'll help me on with my jacket, please. It is tight."

She stood up, and, turning, stretched out her long arms behind her, seeking the sleeves which Aubrey brought. Her white face was towards the long mirror, and was puckered by the physical effort of getting into the jacket, and for a moment Aubrey thought it was like the face of a little child being tortured.

"Oh dear! I've left on some of my make-up," she said. "Whatever must you think?"

And then, with the tip of her little finger, she removed the tiny black fragment from the corner of her eye. She buttoned the jacket while Aubrey paid the bill. Then they went out. Diamond held her gloves, which were of white thread, in her hand. On the pavement Aubrey stopped.

"Shall I take you home in a cab?" he asked.

"No, let's walk. It ain't far, and I don't like you spendin' all this money for nothin'," she answered. "I was always careful of Bert's money. Oh dear! he will spend it without me. He'll run into debt, I know he will. He's no idea of money. It's this way. We live in Milk Court."

"Oh," said Aubrey, with an air of being informed. He had never heard of the quarter before.

As they started, Monsieur Anneau passed them. He wore a light overcoat down to his heels, in which he looked gigantic. He was smoking a huge cigar, and had white Suede gloves on his hands. He stared hard at Diamond, smiled, and took off his hat. She nodded.

"Why, there's Mr. Anno," she said.

"D'you know him?" said Aubrey, feeling secretly irritated.

"I've often spoke with him at the Opera. He's a gay gentleman, ain't he? He gave me some chocolates oncest. They come from Paris. He can sing, but I wouldn't walk with him like this."

"Why?"

"Because I wouldn't," she replied quietly.

Aubrey did not inquire further. He respected both her ignorance and her knowledge, which seemed, at that moment, equally complete. They walked on in silence, turning up side streets occasionally. Presently Diamond said—

"We're nearly there now."

And she began to walk more slowly.

"It'll be good-bye, I s'pose?" she said, with a note of inquiry in her soft voice.

"For to-night," Aubrey said.

In the distance he saw a court, surrounded with high new buildings of red and white brick. Diamond stopped under a gas-lamp.

"That's where we live," she said. "You mustn't come any farther."

"Well?" Aubrey said, and he held out his hand.

She looked up into his face. At this moment of farewell a certain self-consciousness seemed to dawn in her for the first time, and, looking into his face, a memory came back to her.

"But why?" she exclaimed. "You said as you was miserable to-night too! And I've never asked—oh, I am mean! Didn't you want to tell me?"

"No, no," Aubrey said. "Good-bye. Some day I'll come to the theatre again."

- "Will you?" she said. "Bert used to come every night, Oh dear! whatever will Dad say? He'll want to kill Bert. It'll be awful for me to-morrow morning. And there's a call too. Oh, it's all come back to me again now."

She stared at Aubrey for a moment with sorrowful eyes, like the helpless eyes of a very young animal in mortal pain. Then she nodded.

"Thank you," she said. "So long."

And she walked slowly away towards the high buildings. Aubrey stood watching her. Just before she went out of sight she turned to look back, saw him under the gas-lamp and made a gesture of farewell. It was a very pretty gesture, full of grace and meaning. For this little girl's body was as carefully and cleverly trained as her mind was untrained. She could say more in a pose or in a pirouette than in a sentence, or even in a speech. For she had studied since she was a baby the wonderful language of the limbs. And her movements were always grammatical, if her sentences were not.

Aubrey walked away down the grim and narrow streets, seeking an outlet into some great artery that he knew. He had gained a curious solace from hearing another's sorrow. It was momentary, he knew, but it was definite. When he had followed Diamond in the street, he had been driven by the desire of telling his own misery to a total stranger, to a girl of a different world from his, whom he would never see again. She had looked soft and sympathetic. And, in her dancing, she had seemed to reach out a hand to rescue him from the cold and implacable dream in which his agony had wrapped him. Then she was the blond sorceress of a sunlit isle, and she postured to the dull sound of tom-toms. In her red-gold hair were jewels and in her slim hands were roses. And her great eyes were surely heavy with the burden of noon, and her lips were pale with the kisses of a tyrant.

And then he heard the story of her sorrow instead of telling the story of his own. He heard how the blond sorceress was loved by a riding-master in a good way of business, and how she had given her heart to a newspaper man who had jilted her, because she broke the rules of grammar and had a father who was closely connected with lights. And now he found it strange, this knowledge that filled him as he walked alone along the gloomy byways of London—the knowledge that he had found more solace in the little girl who cried over her cutlet than in the houri who moved to music through the sunny languor of the enchanted hours. The one had summoned him like a siren. With her body she wove a dreamy spell among the huge red flowers of her Island of the East. And her sorrow was subtle and indefinite, as the tattered emotions that lie like shadows in the hollow bosoms of the waves of music. The other had summoned him as a woman who is budding out of a child. He had been roused from his cold reverie by a fay, and he had wished to tell the fay the tale of his misery. Instead he had heard an old street story from the pale lips of a street-bred girl.

And for the moment he was comforted. He had no longer any wish to tell the secret of his sorrow, having heard the secret of another's.

He wondered why that was.

As he walked, he thought of these old street stories which he had never realised before. Then he thought of the girl's name— Diamond.

And then he saw again the vision of the island, and a pale sorceress in yellow robes. But she had the white and glittering face of Lady Caryll, and in her hair was a great emerald.

The tom-toms muttered in the drowsy noontide. They sounded like the distant murmur of the tyrant's voice summoning his slave.

CHAPTER XII

AT the end of the season Lady Caryll was married to Sir Reuben Allabruth. Aubrey went to the wedding, which took place at St. Paul's, Knightsbridge. He escorted his mother, and people noticed that Lady Rangecliffe was very pale, and seemed deafer and more absent-minded than ever. Aubrey watched the ceremony with calm eyes, and listened to "The voice that breathed o'er Eden" with an air of cold attention. He had seen Lady Caryll pass up the aisle convoyed by her radiant father. On her breast burned the great emerald. As she went by there was a faint whispering and a rustling of women, and a murmuring voice behind Aubrey said softly—

"That was her price. Isn't it marvellous?"

He longed to strike the speaker, who was a woman. Yet, when he saw Sir Reuben at the altar, he could scarcely wonder at the judgment of the world. Some men always look their worst on the great occasions of their lives, as many women always look their best. On his wedding-day Sir Reuben appeared frightful. It was a bright afternoon, and the sun shone upon his face as if to show distinctly how old and how fatigued he was in his tightly buttoned frock-coat and his light and baggy trousers. As he stood looking at Lady Caryll, a strange and cruel expression hovered round his dry lips and flickered in his shining dark eyes. Some people thought it was like the expression of a slave-owner, rich enough to buy the most beautiful slave offered up in the market-place. But Aubrey only tried to read in this bending, elderly figure, this lined and foreign face, some fascination, some curious and Oriental attractiveness. He could not. He seemed to see a goblin. And then he gazed at Lady Caryll, and his heart seemed to shrivel within him. Yet he would not believe what the world believed. As she came down the aisle, now Lady Caryll Allabruth, she looked brilliantly happy and sparkling, and her eyes were bent down upon her breast, where the emerald and its story glowed on the ivory background of her wedding-gown. Sir Reuben shuffled along at her side. He turned his head slightly away when he was close to Lady Rangecliffe. But she was not looking at him or at his wife. Hot tears prevented her from seeing anything for a moment.

Aubrey's right hand was on the edge of the pew. The impulse to touch it with hers was irresistible. He turned and looked at her calmly.

"What's the matter, mother?" he said.

"Nothing, Aubrey, nothing," she answered hastily.

They mingled with the smart crowd. At Lady St. Ormyn's house they saw the wedding presents. Some of them were jewels. Aubrey had given an antique ring. It looked rather humble and mean among the diamonds and pearls, and some extraordinary rubies set in silver, which were Sir Reuben's gift to his bride.

In the autumn, towards the end of October, the Allabruths came back to town and settled in Park Lane. Aubrey was in London. He had found something to do in the City, and was now the secretary of a company. He worked every day from ten to four in the afternoon, trying to entangle his soul in the meshes of routine, and to still the voices of romance in the roar of the music of commerce. But he hated the City and men when they were there. The great matinal procession was like some mighty funeral to him. These thousands of men, with their high hats, their morning papers, their attentive eyes devouring the news of the day, moved him to a sort of pity for them, and for himself now that he was one of them. He saw life like a beautiful light which shines only for an hour. And he saw all these men and himself pulling down black blinds, and making all things about them gloomy and horrible during that hour. Was it only by doing such a deed as this that bread could be earned? That seemed an irony. Yet, for himself, it was different. He felt that life was indeed a beautiful shining light, or was meant to be so to human beings. But he knew also that circumstances had occurred which rendered it impossible for him personally to be gladdened and to be warmed by that light. For he had committed the fatal error of seeking joy in another who could not give it to him. And now he could not gain it from elsewhere, as other men. He was like some one who has a little fortune, and who places it for increase in hands that cast it into the sea, leaving him destitute. But these other men by whom he was surrounded were not in his case. Many of them had strong powers of enjoyment, yet they passed the greater part of their existence in this terrible and dreary court of intrigues and of lies, of bitter fluctuations and of evil triumphs. At this time Aubrey saw many things wrongly in consequence of the sorrow that lived within him. He perceived the horrible side of the City, with all its details of chicanery, stealthy cheating, covetousness of other men's goods, slanderings, grinding down of one's neighbours, plannings of ruin, cruel selfishness, and savage greediness. And he failed to see the other side, the sturdy honesty, brave perseverance, calm facing of misfortune, noble sense of duty, and fine effort that others—wife, children, relations—might see more of the beautiful shining light than the toilers in the grim and murmurous prison. We look at things generally through the windows of our own emotions, and if the windows are dusty and dim, the figures that pass are dreary or wicked to us, and they move in an atmosphere that is like the atmosphere of unholy places.

Aubrey sought peace in routine. He found not peace, but a sort of narcotic, which dulled his senses and taught his brain the lesson of lethargy. He sometimes forgot, not because memory had really fled from him, but because he sometimes ceased to think. He let the City dream float over him. He gave himself into the grasp of mechanism. At moments he thought that he was like some piece of machinery, a wheel ceaselessly turning with an eternal whirring music, or a steel rod rising and falling with the gloomy precision of inanimate things constructed for the uses of men. At moments he thought that he was like a mannikin, making gestures in obedience to a wire that was pulled far away by a ruthless hand. Sometimes he seemed to be nothing, not even a machine, or a doll imitating at the bidding of another the movements of that which is alive.

But then, again, there were periods in which sensation and thought came back upon him with the flowing of a tide like the resistless tides of the sea. These periods were brought to him by the hands of Nature. When he left the City, he often walked alone into the unfashionable quarters of the town, and saw the fading of the day among houses whose occupants had no part or lot in the life of his order. He saw the sunsets of the autumn skies wake over the long streets of Hammersmith cloudy and red, sometimes pathetic, sometimes mysterious and foreboding, glories on whose garments clung shadowy hands, in whose bosoms lay the winds, and the rain, and the bleak wild nights of winter. He saw the leaves fluttering down in parks where the people think of country places that they will never see, and wonder wistfully why any birds twitter in London trees, why any green things turn gold, and fall upon its sad and dusky earth. He stood by artificial lakes, and watched the dull stillness of their evening sleep while the mists ran along their trim shores and hid the aquatic birds that pursued endlessly their apparently aimless occupations, making little journeys for no obvious purpose, searching for things that were invisible, staring at the grey and sombre atmosphere with their round and unconscious eyes, or paddling upon the water like creatures on a treadmill. And sometimes, when he was thus alone, he probed to the very depth of his sorrow, and wondered why he had to bear it. At such times he saw it like a phantom rising out of the sunset above the tall houses where middle-class people lived, or moving restlessly across the sullen waters into the breathless mists, or pacing on the carpet of the faded leaves beneath trees that could no longer hide their nakedness. He saw it, and he spoke to it, and he went with it where it went, as we go with our sorrows drawn on despite ourselves. There were moments when it seemed to him that his sorrow wished to leave him, and that then he was compelled to pursue it, calling on it to stay, fearful of its departure, and obliged to be with it. He pursued it thus, and perceived that it was approaching a rim that seemed to him the rim of the world. And he imagined it falling over this rim out of his sight. Then he hastened and caught his sorrow, and they returned together through the night. For his sorrow was his fate, and we cannot let our fate go though we abhor it. When he was alone in these out-of-the-way places, he no longer schooled his face, and the people who met him and chanced to observe him could see that he was suffering, and could not doubt that he was sad. But, when he returned to his own quarter of the town, he resumed his calm and imperturbable mask, and he felt like a man stepping into prison.

When Sir Reuben and Lady Caryll were established in Park Lane, Sir Reuben wrote to Aubrey asking him to come and see them. At the end of the note were these words: "Caryll is your godmother now, she says, and you must pay your respects to her."

Aubrey tore this note up with violent hands. But afterwards he started for Park Lane.

He expected to find alteration in Lady Caryll. Marriage does alter very strangely the expression of women's faces. Often these faces blossom. There is a flowering of happiness distinct as the flowering of spring in an orchard, or there is a flowering of passion. Sometimes the face becomes almost insolent with triumph when the nature of the woman is evil or cruel. Sometimes it is wistful and supremely tender. Then the heart is pulsing for the days that are to come, and training itself to receive a great message of anguish and of joy. But always marriage writes some new meaning, however subtle, on the face of a woman. What had it written on the face of Lady Caryll? Aubrey wondered as he went.

It was five o'clock in the afternoon when he reached the house. The darkness was coming on. He entered the hall, and seemed to leave England on the doorstep behind him. It was warm here, and the warmth was faintly scented. The light was dim and evenly diffused; and Aubrey was aware of the sensation, once crudely expressed by Lady St. Ormyn, that in this great house there might be hidden places in which hidden and secluded lives were being lived. He heard the tinkle of a fountain falling somewhere at a distance. The footman drew aside a great curtain, embroidered with a huge design in red and gold, and showed him into a small and lofty chamber which was empty.

"I will tell her Ladyship you are here, sir," he said.

Aubrey looked round the room. He felt instinctively that it was Lady Caryll's boudoir. The walls were hung with green silk. Two or three pictures stood on easels. One represented a gaunt Arab shepherd playing on his pipe in a rocky nook of the rosy Libyan hills. It was the sunset hour, and the sky was radiant with the clear lemon colour so often seen in Egypt. The face of the shepherd was sad, and Aubrey thought there was even a sort of horror staring out of his wild and dark eyes, which were looking at Lady Caryll's boudoir. Another picture was of some veiled women at a well. Their faces were covered, but they too regarded this room with curiosity through the slits that served them as windows. Near the hearth, on which burned a wood fire, was a small ebony table. A number of watches lay upon it. They were set with various jewels. Diamonds sparkled upon the gold case of one. Another was enamelled and was spotted with turquoises. None of these watches were going. Green curtains were drawn before the tall windows. There was a grand piano, but it was shut, and Aubrey saw no music. The couches in this room were low and broad, with many cushions. There were no books lying about. In a large gilded cage two gigantic green parrots sat blinking their round and irritable eyes. They seemed to be dozing in the warmth and the silence. A beautifully shaped lute leaned against the green walls in an angle. On the mantelpiece there was a large photograph of Sir Reuben standing in the garden of his Moorish villa. He was in native costume, and was smiling as men smile in photographs without any appearance of being really amused. Aubrey approached the fire and looked closely at the photograph. Certainly Sir Reuben was much more natural and effective in a *djelebe* than in a frock-coat. In this costume one realised that in England and in English dress he was really masquerading as something that he was not and could never be. And this Oriental, with his sly eyes and his barbarous smile, was Lady Caryll's husband. She belonged to him, as possibly black slaves had belonged to him in those periods of his life which he had spent in distant countries. Had she changed already under his influence, in her intimacy with him? Whither would he lead her, through what mysterious and abnormal phases, to what unforeseen and perhaps undesired end? Aubrey was shaken with a wild passion of fear and of desire. He trembled and laid his hands on the mantelpiece on either side of the photograph. And it seemed to him just then that he had never before really understood that Lady Caryll was irrevocably gone from him, had never before understood the exact meaning of his loss.

He heard a door open softly behind him. Lady Caryll came into the room. Aubrey did not turn until she stood beside him. He could not. When she was on the hearth he moved with an effort, half held out his hand, then paused, arrested by the brilliant happiness that shone out of her face, and seemed even to emanate visibly from her whole person. She was dressed in white, and wore round her throat a tight collar of magnificent pearls, all of the same size but varying in colour. Some were milk-white, others were yellow, blue, green, and red. Her frosty yellow hair was dressed very simply but very perfectly, high on her small head. Her long grey eyes were sparkling with a radiance that was like the radiance of satisfied love. She held out her right hand. It was covered with magnificent rings. Aubrey drew in his breath. The glory of this almost insolent joy struck him. It was like a blow. He felt stunned by it and dazzled. There was violence and there was illumination in it, but no heat. It blinded. It did not warm. When he had recovered from the shock of her beauty and of her joy, he took her cold, white hand, and as he pressed it the rings upon her fingers came in contact with his. A shiver ran through him. The different shapes of those rings were strangely disagreeable to his sense of touch.

"Come and sit down," she said. " Your godfather is in the City, I believe, but he will be back almost directly."

She sat down on one of the low couches just under the high golden cage in which the parrots were dozing on their perch, and the wild, black eyes of the Egyptian shepherd in the picture seemed to stare upon her with horror, and the shrouded women at the well seemed to watch her, too, through the round eyeholes of their veils. So Aubrey thought as he sat beside her. He looked at the coloured pearls round her throat, and he remembered her pose before the diamond-shop in Bond Street, seeing her for a moment as a figure in a long dead dream. Then the necessity of speech came upon him.

"You are happy," he said bluntly, moved to express his sense of her almost terrible radiance.

She smiled, and the smile was her answer.

"And you have become a worker, Mr. Herrick," she said "Do you like it?"

"No," Aubrey answered. "I think the City is horrible. But I must do something."

As he spoke, he was wondering whether she remembered how he had talked of work in Lady St. Ormyn's garden. Then he meant to labour for her, and he felt that, under certain circumstances, even the City might be a joy.

"The City is a necessity of many men's existence, I believe," Lady Caryll said, "as the nursery is a necessity of many women's—women I don't understand."

She touched the pearls at her throat.

"I think Sir Reuben loves the City," she added.

"I suppose he must," Aubrey said, "or why should he go there now?"

"Oh, do you believe that any man ever feels that he has made enough money while he has the power of making more?" she asked him.

"You think our sex is born insatiable?"

"I believe most people of both sexes are. That's why life continues to be interesting."

"And continues to be sad."

He spoke the words instinctively, but almost as he spoke them the absurdity of addressing them to her struck him forcibly, and he resolved to make an effort to throw himself into the joy of this girl whom he loved. He would live in her, if only for a moment. He looked into her white and radiant face.

"But not sad to you," he said. "How happy Sir Reuben must be to be able to make you so happy."

And, in speaking the words, he saw Sir Reuben surrounded by a sort of supernatural glory, such as attends men gifted with supreme and beautiful powers.

"Sir Reuben!" she said. "Oh—yes."

She paused for a moment, and then she added—

"Sir Reuben understands me."

As she spoke she looked at Aubrey, and with the fingers of her left hand she softly touched the rings on the fingers of her right hand. Her brilliant eyes became more thoughtful than usual, and Aubrey found again in her something of the mystery that had oppressed him in Lady St. Ormyn's garden, some suggestion of strange and hidden depths that no man had fathomed. Far away down in these depths he felt that her soul, her real self, was still hidden, waiting—for what? For the voice that was appointed to call it upward to life, as the prince called the mermaid from the shadows of the sea.

"And you?" he said, gazing at her with a sort of awe in his young eyes. "Do you understand yourself."

"At least to the extent of knowing when I am understood," she answered. "I always thought Sir Reuben was clever, but it is only lately that I have realised how clever he is."

As she spoke her husband came slowly into the room. During

his journey to London he had caught cold, and his face had the blunted appearance that a cold imparts to many people. His usually keen black eyes were dulled and watery, and he looked less intelligent than usual, and consequently older. He greeted Aubrey affectionately and kissed his wife; she gave him her cheek to kiss. Then he sat down close to the fire and made a cruel remark upon the climate of London.

"It kills me after my long sojourn in the sun," he added.
"Well, Aubrey, so you have gone into the City?"
"Yes."
"Do you like it?"
"I can't say I do."
"It's an ugly mine, but one can dig up jewels in it."
And he looked at his wife's hands and at her throat.
"Hardly as secretary to a company," Aubrey said.
"You must get something better," Lady Caryll said.
"Yes, we must see what we can do," rejoined Sir Reuben. "My godson——"
"Oh, it's a good enough berth, thanks," Aubrey said quickly.

He felt himself stiffening with proud reserve as he looked at this beautiful girl and at the old, grave man with a cold who had been able, strangely, to make her so beautiful. For the change wrought by marriage in Lady Caryll was exquisite. It began to thrill through him with a strange power as he grew more intimate with it. And from this moment he sought, with the determination to find it, the hidden and remarkable quality in his godfather which alone could have had such a subtle influence, an influence akin to that of a soft rain upon a flower or of a gleam of sudden light upon a jewel.

"What company is it?" said Sir Reuben.

Aubrey told him with a reluctant voice. Sir Reuben pursed his lips and said nothing; then he took out his handkerchief and blew his nose sonorously. Tea was brought in by the Arab servant whom Aubrey had seen on his first visit to Park Lane, and almost immediately after it Lady St. Ormyn arrived. She was dressed in scarlet and furs, and carried a muff about two sizes larger than any muff ever seen in London before. As she entered rapidly she exclaimed—

"I feel just as if I were coming into a harem. Oh, you here, Mr. Herrick! And how is the sultan?"

She spoke to Sir Reuben, but did not wait for an answer.

"Caryll! Good heavens! are those pearls round your neck? Yes! How superb! Red pearls! How long have you had them?"

"Since yesterday."

"Do take them off and let me see them."

"They look better when they are being worn," her daughter answered. And there was a sound of inflexible obstinacy in her voice. She drew back from her mother, who was extending an eager hand towards her throat.

Sir Reuben coughed harshly. His cold was really very bad. Aubrey tried not to realise how extremely ugly the cough of an old man is.

"Well, Caryll, you are very selfish about your jewels, I'm sure," said Lady St. Ormyn pettishly. "Really one would think you were jealous of them, as other women are jealous of their lovers."

"Pearls look their best when they are being worn," her daughter repeated.

She began to pour out some tea. Lady St. Ormyn's round and staring eyes were now fixed upon her daughter's rings. Aubrey saw that she was on the point of speaking about them, and he was suddenly moved to interrupt her. He felt that her remark would be disagreeable to Lady Caryll.

"Did you go to Bayreuth this summer?" he asked.

For the next twenty minutes Lady St. Ormyn talked Wagner with all the volubility of a mill-stream. Some more people dropped in, and the eyes of the women present seemed totally unable to leave Lady Caryll's throat. They were hypnotised by the circle of perfectly matched coloured pearls. More than once Aubrey found himself absurdly thinking that the horror deepened in the watching eyes of the sad shepherd in the picture, who, from the loneliness of his rocky fastness, joined his gaze to that of these smart and chattering London women.

Presently Lady St. Ormyn mentioned Monsieur Anneau.

"I've just heard such an extraordinary thing," she said. "Monsieur Anneau has thrown up his American engagement and returned to Paris. The New York management is furious."

"What is his reason?" Sir Reuben asked.

"Nobody knows. I've wired to him five times without getting an answer. And this afternoon I've been with Ritz, the agent, trying to persuade him to engage Monsieur Anneau for some song recitals this winter here. Before Christmas, of course, because I shall go to the Riviera in January."

"And what does Ritz say?" said Sir Reuben.

"Oh, he'll do anything I want."

The other women present eagerly exclaimed that they would take seats, that they would go anywhere, do anything for Monsieur Anneau. Only Lady Caryll seemed totally indifferent about the matter. Yet she had received that morning a letter from Paris, in which the great singer explained very frankly the reason of his return to Europe.

"I find now that I can only sing well when I am near to you," he wrote. "Will you not let me come to England and give a concert in your beautiful house?"

When she had read this letter, Lady Caryll had touched the pearls at her throat and had given the letter to her husband. Sir Reuben read it slowly and smiled at his wife as King Shahrizar may have smiled on Shahrazad when her story pleased him.

"Let him give his concert here if you like, Caryll," he said.

"Very well," she replied, in her cool young voice that sounded so indifferent. "But I think there are too many draperies and hangings. They muffle the voice."

"I will have a music-room made if you wish it," he answered.

And in the afternoon, as he was returning from the City, he stopped at a famous shop in Bond Street and bought a marvellous amethyst comb.

Aubrey watched the eager light in the other women's faces as they talked of Monsieur Anneau, and remembered what Diamond, the humble little dancer, had said about him. She would shun him for the same reason that drew these society women to him. That was curious and traced a grim line between two worlds. Lady Caryll seemed to be in neither of them. In what world then was she? Still in the world of jewelled dreams in which Aubrey had set her before her marriage? He looked at the radiant happiness sparkling in her eyes. That surely was too definite to be a happiness of dreams. Sir Reuben coughed again, trying to stifle his complaint, and failing. He came over and sat down by Aubrey, and Aubrey noticed that there was an expression as of pity in his eyes heavy with the cold that oppressed him. Aubrey felt inclined to shrink away from this expression, but when his godfather spoke his sensitive reserve was reassured. For Sir Reuben said—

"My boy, this berth of yours in the City is fairly good, but it can never lead to anything."

Aubrey understood the compassion of a great business man for his very humble appointment, and did not much mind it.

"It is better than nothing, Sir Reuben," he said.

"You really mean to work now?"

"Yes, I cannot be idle any longer."

Sir Reuben was looking at him with a sort of watchful curiosity. He continued—

"I have got tired of the life of a lounger. It never really suited me."

"No! You are worth more than that,"

He was silent for a moment, still looking at Aubrey. At last he said—

"You are my godson. If you choose to work, I shall find you something to do that is worth doing."

Aubrey felt himself grow hot and red.

"Oh, I'm getting on all right," he said, almost with brutality. "Thank you, Sir Reuben, very much," he added uneasily.

"Why are you so proud, Aubrey? Why should you hate my helping you to a career?"

"Thank you, Sir Reuben," the boy said again. "But I like my present work. I've got accustomed to it."

Sir Reuben said no more. He deferred the expiation which he was, nevertheless, determined to offer as a solace to his busy conscience. He understood Aubrey's desire to avoid receiving a gift from the hand that had struck him a cruel blow. But generosity —which, oftener than most men think, springs from self-love— was determined eventually to have its way in Sir Reuben's nature. When he bade Aubrey good-bye that night he said to himself—

"I have hurt you in the soul. I will heal you in the body."

He had been brought up as a Christian. But whenever he thought of paradise, he thought of a paradise of the senses. Many very good Christians do the same secretly, dreaming of an ever-perfect cuisine, eternally fine weather, and natural surroundings as delicious as those in the Garden of Eden.

When all his visitors were gone, Sir Reuben told his wife that he had purchased for her a wonderful amethyst comb.

She gave him her lips to kiss.

Then he spoke of Aubrey and of his position in the City.

"I shall do something for him," he said. "He might be very useful to me in my affairs. One could trust Aubrey implicitly."

"Of course," she answered a little abstractedly.

She was standing by the fireside, and the light played on her beautiful hair. Her eyes were fixed eagerly on her husband.

"What is it, Caryll?" he said, with a sort of grotesque passion, coming towards her, drawn by the spell of her loveliness. "What is it?"

He put his arm round her waist.

"Will the amethysts be sent home to-night?" she said.

He laughed, and answered her. He was in England. He was surrounded by civilisation. But he had his slave. And that pleased him.

CHAPTER XIII

AUBREY had seen Diamond twice since their first meeting on the night of his tragedy. Once he had met her by accident in the street; once he had waited for her outside the stage-door and walked with her as far as Milk Court. He had found her unaltered, simple, sentimental, and childlike, despite her evidently full knowledge of certain sides of life, and her continued acquaintance with the rather unrefined existence of the "ballet ladies" of a great variety theatre. In those three meetings a strong feeling of friendship had sprung up between these two members of two far different societies. It was uncomplicated by any thought of evil. Diamond spoke to Aubrey, as at first, with the frankness of a child. He listened to her with a full and untainted sympathy rather rare in a young man. Her entire lack of reserve fell upon his reserved nature like a refreshing rain, and caused certain buds —folded hitherto—to expand their petals, and to blossom quietly and confidently. Already Aubrey had begun to think of Diamond as men think of the one woman to whom they could tell their troubles trustfully. Yet he had never confided in her. He had only received her full confidence. That was enough. As he listened to the details of her very real though very ordinary trouble, he had the sensation that he was telling his, and he seemed to escape from his prison when he saw the open door of hers. After he left Park Lane, stunned and confused by the happiness of Lady Caryll, companioned by the vision of the jewels round her throat and on her hands, drugged by the curious and brilliant atmosphere of the house that was now her home, he felt the need of the wide simplicity of an uncomplicated nature. He could not understand Lady Caryll. To-day he had felt absolutely that there was a mystery hidden in her nature, which formerly he had thought he understood. And his sense of this mystery drove his love on to a more remote turning of the maze in which he was caught. A profound curiosity was added to his passion, and seemed to become one with it, and to touch it with a fierceness foreign to it before. And this mystery, shrouded somewhere in Lady Caryll, was not the mystery which lurks in all women. It was peculiar, and even, perhaps, not natural to her sex. Aubrey was dimly aware of that. Had Sir Reuben divined it, and so gained his power to win her? But he had thought of her so cynically. Did he think of her cynically now. Aubrey's curiosity, his love that must be eternally repressed, fatigued him. He felt as if he walked in chains, and as if they were made of coloured pearls. But each pearl was heavy as a lump of iron. He wanted to rest, and he thought of Diamond, resolving to wait for her that night outside the theatre. When he reached his rooms, a note lay on his table. The envelope was light-mauve in colour, and looked very cheap. The address was written in a large, unformed hand. Aubrey wondered who his correspondent could be. He opened the note, and found that it was from Diamond:—

"DEAR MR. HERRICK,—It is my birthday to-day. I am going to keep it after the show, and Dad has let me invite Mr. King. Would you care to come? I have told Dad you are a friend, and that I've met you at the theatre. He's not angry. I did not tell him just how we met, and he says to me to ask you, too, if I like. But p'raps you will not want to come. I will look for you at the stage-door, but I daresay you will not be there.—Yours faithfully, DI MANNERS."

That night Aubrey was at the stage-door when the ballet-girls came out, chattering shrilly, and laughing as they buttoned their jackets and hastily pulled on their gloves. In his hand he held a small parcel wrapped in white paper and tied with pink twine. Diamond had dressed more quickly than usual, and he had not long to wait before he saw her crossing the road from the narrow doorway, beyond which the gas flared. She had on a white hat, with white poppies dancing on it, and white kid gloves, and she smiled with pleasure when she saw him.

"Oh, are you comin' to supper?" she said, "or have you only come to say as you can't? It's only us, and Mr. King, and Vauxhall, and Alf. Dad's not a bit angry, because I said how quiet and respectable you were. He won't have any one rowdy round at our house. He's that particular. Are you comin'?"

"Yes, and many happy returns of the day," Aubrey said.

As they turned to walk away, he put the white packet into Diamond's hand.

"Whatever's this?" she said. Then she looked at him reproachfully.

"Now I didn't mean you to do anything like that," she said. "You are naughty."

She stopped under a lamp, and untied the twine. Her face was eager, but not greedy. When she saw the little gold bangle curved in the velvet furrow of the red jewel box, she uttered a cry of surprise and pleasure.

"Oh, how pretty! But you oughtn't to."

Aubrey fastened it on her wrist over her white glove. Hanging from the bangle was the letter D in tiny pearls.

"There!" he said. "Now come along, or that policeman will move us on."

"It is lovely," Diamond reiterated. Her face had become quite red with delight. "It's ever so much prettier than the one Vauxhall gave Lill when they got married," she continued. "You are kind. But I never meant——"

"I know," Aubrey said quietly. "What did you say to your father about me?"

"Only that I'd met you at the theatre, and that you were so quiet, and that I should like you to be at my birthday. Dad says, 'Then ask him, child, if he ain't too much of a nob to come.' So I did. But I never thought you'd come."

"Why not?"

"Oh, I don't know. Gentlemen don't care for everything, do they? Why, lots of 'em don't so much as give us a hand when we go round in the wheel. And we do look nice then. The young gentlemen in especial don't seem to like anything much, not when they're together. When they're alone it's different. I believe they're afraid of one another—thinkin' they're enjoyin' themselves, I mean."

"That's it," Aubrey said, smiling at her shrewdness, which was as childish as everything else about her.

They reached Milk Court. Aubrey felt moved by a strange sense of expectation, which he had seldom known before a state ball or any great society function. Just as they got to the door of Diamond's abode she said—

"Oh, our name's Slagg, not Manners. I took Manners for dancin'. See?"

"Yes, thanks."

She opened the door with a latch-key, and, as she did so, Aubrey heard the sound of many voices, all talking very loud, and the running patter of wild feet.

"The children are awful excited to-night," Diamond said, as if in explanation. "Susie's half mad. Come in, will you?"

Aubrey followed her into a narrow passage.

"Put your hat here. I'll take your coat."

Just then a little girl, whose curly dark hair was tied up with a red riband, ran shrieking out of an adjoining room.

"Di! Di! it's all ready, and Vauxhall says——"

She caught sight of the stranger, and subsided with the

abruptness of one seized by paralysis, putting one finger in her mouth and drooping her head, while her face became a meeting-place of blushes.

"Here, Susie, speak to Mr. Herrick. Now, don't be silly. Say 'how dee do?'"

"How dee do?" whispered the child, drawing in her breath as she spoke, and drooping her head still lower.

"How are you?" responded Aubrey, taking her little flabby hand. "Now, you mustn't be afraid of me, will you?"

Susie stared with enormous round eyes.

"Say 'no,' Susie," said her sister.

"No," whispered the little thing, with the manner of one making a great concession from the motive of terror.

"She's shy with strangers," explained Diamond, "but she's awful noisy when once she knows you. Dad, here's Mr. Herrick."

They had entered a good-sized room, new, but furnished in a rather old-fashioned way. The floor was spread with oil-cloth. There was a table laid for supper. On it stood a large sugared cake with an immense "Di" in red sugar letters. The chairs were of solid wood with seats of black horsehair, and near the fire there was a broad settle with a high back covered with cherry coloured and white chintz. The only occupant of this settle was an exceedingly small china doll with a round head and coal-black eyes. It was dressed in yellow muslin. Its legs were extended. Its arms were stuck out in a gesture of surprise or alarm, and it appeared to be lost in the sad reverie of one abandoned by the world in desolate places. Upon the walls of the room hung two or three oleographs; one displayed several bright yellow chickens examining, with an air of meek astonishment, the broken shells from which they had recently emerged. Another was a Swiss valley, bounded by chalk-white mountains and intersected by a bright purple stream, beside which stood a lady tourist in a poke bonnet, a pelerine, and elastic-sided boots, with a small hairy dog, designed in a barking attitude. On the mantelpiece, painted the colour of the yoke of an egg, stood several photographs of a theatrical nature, and a red-glass vase containing a bouquet of chrysanthemums. On the hearth was a black cat. This room contained a number of people, from which, on Aubrey's entrance, a burly man of middle height, with a dark moustache and bright humorous eyes, detached himself. This was Mr. Slagg, who had "stood up" to Lady St. Ormyn. He was dressed in a black morning-coat with short tails, brown trousers, and a red tie.

"Your servant, sir," he said, in a strong bass voice to Aubrey as he came forward. "Proud to see you, sir. Any friend of Di's is welcome here."

And he held out his hand, with unembarrassed and straightforward cordiality. Then he turned and kissed his daughter.

"Mr. Herrick," she said, "this is my sister Lill."

A tall girl, very like Di but less simple in appearance, came forward and shook hands with a smile.

"And this," continued Diamond, "is Vauxhall and Alf, and Jenny and Bob."

All those presented came forward in turn to shake hands. Alf, in returning to his place, cut an attenuated caper, which was met by a cuff from his brother, and the remark, "It ain't your 'turn,' so leave it, Alf."

Alf left it with the grin of the incorrigible.

"Where's Ma?" continued Diamond.

"In the kitchen. So's Charley. And Mr. King hasn't yet arrived," replied Lill, who spoke with a certain slight air of superiority, having travelled on the Continent with the "Marvellous Flicks" since her marriage with Vauxhall.

"Won't you come to the fire, sir?" said Mr. Slagg to Aubrey. "Bob, make room for the gentleman."

Bob was the elder boy, a serious lad who was devoted to machinery and understood it. His family was proud of him, and he talked much of steel and electricity in the home circle, a fact which gave him a certain authority. He made room with quiet alacrity, while Susie, still in awe, proceeded to join the china doll on the settle. Aubrey, who felt slightly embarrassed, made two or three remarks about the weather, to which Mr. Slagg responded with great heartiness and an air of having considered the question from all imaginable points of view.

"It's a funny thing is the weather," was his eventual conclusion, "a very funny thing."

"That it is," said Vauxhall, a young man of about twenty-five, who held himself acrobatically, and looked daring but modest. "That it is. And it's just the same on the Continong. Ain't it, Lill?"

"So it is, Vaux," she replied. "Have you been in France, sir?" she added to Aubrey, while Mr. Slagg looked at her proudly, almost self-conscious at having a child so obviously cosmopolitan.

"Yes, often," said Aubrey. "Your sister tells me that you have travelled a great deal."

"Oh, we go everywhere pretty well, don't we, Vaux?"

"Yes, sir. Russia, Austria, Paris, Buda-Pesth, Berling. We haven't performed in Turkey, but them Turks is such a dirty lot."

> "Oh, them Turks, them naughty, bad Turks,
> Why don't they try to be good, be good?
> Why don't they——"

"Shut it, Alf! or I'll——"

The singing voice died abruptly away, while Mr. Slagg continued the discussion of the Turkish question with the remark—

"We English can't do with savage tricks, can we, sir?"

"No, indeed," said Aubrey, thinking of Mr. Slagg's episode with Lady St. Ormyn.

At this point in politics a stoutish lady dressed in black silk came into the room with a rather gliding gait, followed by a little boy attired in a sailor suit. Behind her through the open door followed a smell of roast beef accompanied by a scent of cabbages.

"Oh, Ma," cried Diamond, "this is Mr. Herrick, and just look what he's given me."

And she exhibited the bangle, around which all the company gathered, while Aubrey felt more shy than he had ever felt before. Mrs. Slagg shook hands with Aubrey and said—

"Oh, sir, you spoil Di, you do indeed. Glad to see you here, sir."

"Thank you very much. It's so good of you to ask me."

"It's only a little birthday spread, sir, in honour of the day. Where's Mr. King?"

"Not come yet," said Di, while Alf began to tickle Susie, who emitted a piercing cry of mingled joy and anguish.

"Susie, you naughty—there he is," said Mrs. Slagg, as a bell sounded. "Go to the door, Jenny."

Jenny, who was a pretty girl of sixteen, in training at "Madame's" school for dancers, complied, and speedily returned with a small, horsey-looking man, who walked with his legs very wide apart, and fixed his pleasant blue eyes on Diamond with an eager look as he came forward. He carried a toothpick in his mouth and a large bunch of hothouse flowers in his hand.

"For you, Miss Diamond," he said, presenting them to her, "and many happy returns."

While she was thanking him and introducing him to Aubrey, Jenny and Bob brought in the supper, a huge joint of roast-beef, with Yorkshire pudding, potatoes, and cabbages, beer in jugs and lemonade in bottles with green glass-stoppers. At this point Susie began to be painfully excited, and, seizing the china doll from its desolation on the settle, bounded several times into the air, uttering piercing cries expressive of wonder and delight.

"Now, Susie, Susie," said her mother. "Mr. Herrick, sir, will you sit here by me, and Mr. King on the left next to Di. Susie, put the doll down and go next your dad. You're not to eat too much. Charlie, don't you spill anything, now mind."

They all sat down with much rustling and movement of chairs, Alf vaulting over the back of his chair, and alighting in a sitting posture, with his knife and fork in each hand, and his mouth open as if to receive his food.

"Alf, you're a demon," said Diamond, while Vauxhall leaned over and smacked the offender's head. Susie giggled wildly, and Charlie looked at Alf with an expression of awful worship. To all children Alf was as a god. His complete aplomb and diabolic agility penetrated their souls like strange qualities of deity. After everybody had sat down there was a silence, in which Mr. Slagg took up his carving-knife and fork. All eyes were fixed upon him, and a certain embarrassment of expectation seemed to reign. Aubrey thought of the ordinary dinner-parties to which he went so often. He glanced at the lady tourist in the oleograph, and remembered the watching shepherd in Lady Caryll's boudoir. Then he looked at the faces round him; Mr. Slagg's rather grim with the effort of carving, Mr. King's red with adoration of Diamond, Diamond's a little sad, yet pleased with the festivity in her honour, Alf's solemnly mischievous, Lill's graciously cosmopolitan and educated. The faces of the children were excited and attentively greedy. Vauxhall observed Mr. Slagg's proceedings with the carving-knife and fork rather as he observed his brother's acrobatic feats in theatres and circuses, his lithe body braced and one hand on his hip. Mrs. Slagg smiled vaguely in the way of hostesses, and pursed her lips as she noticed some brown gravy splash over the edge of the dish on to the white tablecloth.

"Take care of the gravy, John," she said.

"All right, Harriet," responded her husband.

Susie burst out into a hysterical laugh, and somebody said "Hush." Mr. Slagg handed a plate to Bob, who, on account of his well-known sedateness of character, had been placed in charge of the Yorkshire pudding.

"Mr. Herrick, sir," said Mrs. Slagg.

And Aubrey found the plate in front of him. He began to protest but in vain. It was quite evident that he was to play the part of honoured guest. When all were helped, Mr. Slagg sighed heavily.

"Carving's no joke," he remarked; and he looked at Aubrey, on whom at once all eyes were turned with expectation.

"Not for such a party as we are, Mr. Slagg," Aubrey replied.

He wished to identify himself thoroughly with his very novel surroundings, but being very English, and so not very supple in nature, he found the task a difficult one. All the usual weapons of a young society man were blunted here. And he did not know how to be genially simple. When he was alone with Diamond he was quite at his ease. To-night, surrounded by her people, he felt intensely shy. He caught the solemnly observant eye of Alf, who was bolting his food as men bolt food in plays, for the benefit of Susie and Charlie. Alf winked, without moving any muscle of his countenance except the one necessary for the performance of this operation.

"Just look at Alf!" choked Susie, caught in a vice between sense of humour and love of food.

Her father patted her back and reproved her gently. Then he again addressed himself to Aubrey.

"London's a fine town, sir," he remarked.

"It is—a very fine town," said Aubrey.

"Not many like it; is there, Lill?" said Vauxhall.

"Indeed no, Vaux," she replied.

A silence again fell. Aubrey began to feel rather desperate.

"You've seen many cities?" he said to Lill.

"Yes; when we're not here we're always travelling. Alf, you bad boy, how dare you!"

Alf had poised a glass of beer upon two fingers, and was now engaged in drinking its contents after a novel fashion of his own invention, his lips being placed on its far instead of on its near rim, while the glass was gradually tilted forward towards the table until the last drop it contained disappeared down Alf's throat, which was turned sideways and looked like the wrung throat of a fowl.

"He practised for a year, sir, to get that perfect," said Vauxhall with brotherly pride to Aubrey.

"Did he indeed?" said Aubrey.

"Yes. It ain't so easy as it looks. That's often the way with our tricks; ain't it, Lill?"

"So it is, Vaux," she replied.

"It's the same dancin'," said Diamond.

"Verily," added Mrs. Slagg, who had grown somewhat Scriptural in her retirement from the stage.

"And in the light business," joined in her husband. "Susie, leave that fat; it'll upset you."

"Take it from her, John," said Mrs. Slagg.

Mr. Slagg complied, and then continued—

"The public, sir, don't understand what they're looking at half their time. They ain't sufficiently eddicated. That's what it is. Why, I ask you, how many gentlemen is there that can tell you how to bring on a twilight real natural like?"

"Or how to do a full wheel without catching your feet, verily?" said Mrs. Slagg.

"Aye, or how to lie still and do the corpse act?" said Vauxhall.

"Oh, they may talk," said Mr. Slagg, wiping his mouth preparatory to a draught of ale. "But I say as eddication ain't gone on as much as some think. Why, would you believe it, sir, I've had a ladyship, a real ladyship, at me in the Opera to turn blue lights on the singers! And when I says they'll look like a pack o' ghosts, she ups and says, 'It's done in Madigascar.' I tell you some of the ladyships are that ignorant you'd think they'd never been to Board School."

"That was Lady St. Ormyn," said Diamond to Aubrey.

"D'you know her, sir?" asked Mr. Slagg.

"Yes, I've met her," Aubrey answered.

"No offence meant, I'm sure, sir."

"And none taken," said Aubrey, making an inspired effort to play up to his environment.

"She's all for foreign ways, sir, that's how it is—foreign ways and foreign mounseers. She says one day at rehearsal, she says, 'Englishmen haven't no temperiment,' she says. 'P'raps not, my lady,' says Mr. Wilson, him as does the opera business, you know, sir, 'but they've got devils of tempers,' he says, 'and it's temper rules the world, not temperiment,' he says."

"A wise saying, be sure," remarked Mrs. Slagg, helping herself to cabbage, like an oracle. "There's a deal done through temper. My poor mother knew it well."

"And made others know it too, Harriet," said her husband with genuine feeling.

"She thought it her duty, John."

"And made it her pleasure, Harriet, as is the way o' thin women," said Mr. Slagg, without bitterness. "I often thank the day when you began to put on flesh."

Mrs. Slagg smiled good-humouredly. She turned in dignified fashion towards Aubrey.

"Fat and fun go together, they do say, sir, don't they? So, I daresay, my fat is all for the best."

"Certainly," said Aubrey, divided between the polite feeling that he ought to deprecate the idea of Mrs. Slagg's being fat, and the knowledge that, by doing so, he might seem to deny her possession of fun.

"Well, Ma, but Alf's awful thin," piped little Charlie at this juncture, "and lor', ain't he funny! Why, the boys in our court all——"

"Little boys should be seen and not heard."

His dad launched this quotation at Charlie, and the child lay low, devoting himself rosily to his gravy, and wondering when he would arrive at the majestic age at which it is permitted to humanity to address itself to the ear as well as to the eye.

The thinness of Alf was now the subject of discussion, and was thrashed out in all its bearings, while that self-possessed young acrobat continued to do what he named Food-tricks, without apparently being aware that a tempest of talk was raging around him. Mr. King, meanwhile, was speaking earnestly with Diamond. His sentiment for her was not concealed. But the Slagg family was evidently accustomed to it. Now and then Aubrey cast an eye upon his unreserve and marvelled at it. Mr. King leant his brick-red face towards Diamond, and fixed his small, honest blue eyes upon her with an intentness that did not confuse her the least. He was too deep in love to eat much, and only trifled with the beef and cabbage upon his plate.

"Why, Mr. King, you ain't eating anything," said Lill presently; "where ever's your appetite?"

Mr. King grew redder, and murmured something hastily, while Alf went through a pantomime of a man losing, searching for, and eventually finding an appetite, the final scene being almost glaringly pictorial and realistic, and causing Mrs. Slagg, as a thrifty housewife, a certain amount of scarcely concealed alarm. A rather peculiar atmosphere seemed to enfold Alf, emanating from the double fact of his sustained abnormal silence, and of his sustained abnormal activity. He appeared as one dumb, yet was so continually voluble with his body that he always seemed to be making a tremendous row. No speech could have been so deafening as his silence was, and his tricks constantly showed an inclination to perorate. At such divine moments Charlie and Susie were seized with a species of paralysis of adoration, and sat like heathen at an idol's feet, their supper in suspense and the vegetables falling from their motionless forks. Even the elders, who affected to ignore the proceedings of Alf as things beneath the notice of educated wisdom, constantly interrupted their intercourse to turn their eyes upon his juggling with knives and forks, his supreme manipulation of plates and tumblers, his exquisite interpretation of a napkin's true relation to its ring, and his intricate knowledge of the possibilities of toothpicks when brought into connection with the human mouth. Vauxhall, more especially, was intent upon this long and brilliant soliloquy of the body, which evidently rendered him imaginative. His daring eyes glowed when Alf became supreme, but he made no comment upon his brother, and, at this point of the meal, no further proceedings were taken to check the full expression of a nature which was evidently regarded by all with a scarcely concealed reverence and joy.

Apple-tart succeeded the beef, and, with the arrival of a second course, an added geniality prevailed about the long table. Mr. Slagg gave off—so he himself expressed it—a couple of anecdotes connected with lenses, and made a pun about the electric light, which was well received by every one. Mrs. Slagg, who was, it seemed, a lady of a romantic turn of mind, became more flowery in speech, and spoke aside to Aubrey of certain tender experiences that had waited upon her early dancing life, expressing the remarkable opinion that, " after all, there was nothing like love for making a young girl think of serious things, verily, dancing or no dancing ; " and Bob, the elder boy, described with grave minuteness and an almost alarming command of strictly technical language, the unseemly behaviour of a boiler which got out of order on board a ship named *The Happy Despatch* while cruising along the coasts of Java. Vauxhall, too, in the intervals of observing his brother's silent intercourse with spoons, forks, apple-pips, and squares of pastry, discoursed of back falls, double summersaults, the proper mode of standing on the head for lengthy periods, the art of flying leaps and of walking on the hands, the inward beauty of catherine wheels of a superior kind, and the best methods of balancing heavy men upon the stomach with the head thrown back and the arms extended. Mr. King, forcibly detached from his secret conversation with Diamond by the gay badinage of Mr. Slagg, described the efforts of a royal princess to ride barebacked under his supervision, and Diamond gave a gentle, and obviously unexaggerated, account of her first solo dance at the Grand Theatre of Varieties in Champion Square.

Aubrey was surprised to find how all this quite artless and sincere conversation interested him, although he was so often completely bored by the chatter of the set in which he generally moved. He found charm in the entire lack of all pretension, in the often complete and unaffected display of ignorance. When Bob spoke of machinery, all listened with a reverence which betokened frankly lack of knowledge of the subject; and when he ceased, the nods that ran round the circle, the expressive looks of pride in Bob, made clear a modesty and an anxiety to appreciate others that really warmed the heart of Aubrey; for he was accustomed to the far different demeanour of those who strive to hide their ignorance by volubility, and to conquer the admiration they have not earned by bluster.

He was surprised by the good manners of these people, and began to feel himself oddly at home in this long room with the oil-cloth floor and the cherry and white chintz-covered settle. Yet he felt that he had little to tell in return for the confidences of those around him, and, as he looked at Alf, now balancing a knife upright upon a spoon, and causing it, by almost imperceptible movements of his hand, to take a short walk without losing its equilibrium, he was conscious of an odd impotence that was almost crushing. For those around him were workers. Their spheres of work were perhaps peculiar, but the point was that they were really interested in their own labours and took a pride in them. Mr. Slagg, for instance, was a blazing enthusiast about everything connected, however remotely, with limelight and electricity. He grew hot with excitement when he discussed the manipulation of sunsets or the tutoring of a rising dawn. He would have laid down his life in defence of his theory that, to give a moonlight night its proper effect, radiance should be conveyed from directly overhead as well as from high up at the sides of the scene. His deep bass voice vibrated with quick feeling as he talked, and it was difficult at moments to bring him to a sense of the duties appertaining to his position as dispenser of the applepie. Vauxhall was equally passionate about all feats of the body and all questions connected with muscular development. When speaking learnedly about the beautiful mechanism of the human frame, he perpetually appealed to his adoring wife for confirmation, and Lill's equally perpetual "So it is, Vaux," was alive with a simple fervour of wifely admiration that delighted Aubrey. He had been for so long accustomed to wedded contempts, whether genuine or offensively affected, in adherence to a feeble and despicable fashion. The atmosphere that floated around this supper-table was warm with good-will and bright with loyalty even in the pudding stage. With the arrival of oranges and nuts, and the reverent uncorking of a dusty bottle of elderly—if not absolutely old—port, it became almost tempestuous with high geniality. Mr. Slagg called loudly for a song, and, after some pressing, Mrs. Slagg obliged with a high soprano rendering of " Gaily the Troubadour," which she gave seated and dexterously peeling an orange "all in one," so that the peel might afterwards be dropped on the floor, and consulted as the sign of a coming future. Then the little Charlie was set standing upon his chair to speak a piece. This was an elaborate business, not in respect of matter, for the piece was " Mary had a Little Lamb," but in respect of manner, since the little Charlie, overcome by a sudden and evidently very acute consciousness of the presence in the family bosom of an aristocratic stranger from the outer world, rose to tragic heights of emotion, which flushed his round face with purple, withdrew his habitually small voice to his boots, and obscured it there, and forced the tiny thumb of his right hand into the neighbourhood of his thorax. Nevertheless he won through somehow, supported by the inherent pluck of the Slaggs, and his final choke and infantine subsidence were welcomed with the applause due to heroism as remarkable as that commonly attributed to Casabianca and other youthful spectres of legend.

Mary and her lamb ushered in the era of tobacco, when chairs were pushed back and legs were frankly stretched to their fullest extent. Mr. Slagg and Vauxhall smoked pipes. Mr. King preferred a cigar, and Aubrey lit a cigarette. Bob did not smoke, but Alf now neared the summit of his glory. When smoking was mentioned, he was juggling with a knife and fork, a plate, and an orange. He made no remark, but his small eyes twinkled as he let his properties rest, and gave Susie a nudge which caused the child to swallow her thimbleful of port the wrong way and to tremble on the verge of suffocation.

"Alf," began Lill, "you'll choke the child. Upon my word, you——"

Her reproving voice died into silence, and an almost theatrical pause ensued, during which Alf proceeded to do a dozen amazing tricks connected with matches, cigarettes, and ash-trays. Throwing up a cigarette and catching it in his mouth, he spun a matchbox sky high, and made it fall upon an up-turned match in such a manner as to ignite it. The match then mounted like a firefly into space, and, in dropping earthwards, mysteriously communicated its glow to Alf's cigarette, the smoke of which, inhaled by the young miracle-worker, after a portentously long interval, wherein the expectation of Susie mounted like apoplexy to her head and flushed her face with lively scarlet, issued in an abrupt cloud from the porch of his left ear. This finale was also the finale of Susie, who was taken with something very like convulsions of surprise, and had to be removed by Mrs. Slagg and conveyed gurgling to another chamber, there to be put to bed. The little Charlie was bade by his father to follow her example, and a comparative calm ensued. Agility and surprise were followed by a gazing contemplation, during which the souls of men floated dreamlike in a haze of smoke.

Aubrey took this opportunity to have a little conversation with Diamond, who gently turned from the adoration of Mr. King.

"Let's come to the settle," she said, indicating the place of the doll, which had gone to bed with Susie.

Mr. King began to discuss equine problems with Mr. Slagg, who was "a bit of a sport," to use his own words. Lill, Bob, and Vauxhall, chattered seriously together of acrobatic and mechanical mysteries. Diamond and Aubrey were left to themselves.

"This isn't much of an evening for you, is it?" she said, and her big and pathetic eyes looked into his with inquiry.

"It's a very happy evening for me," he answered, "and for you, Miss Diamond?"

She nodded her head towards the talking group of relatives. "I want them to think so," she said. "But——"

The quick tears swam up in her eyes.

"He was here my last birthday," she continued. "And now—oh, it does make a difference, don't it?"

"It must. I understand that. But some day, don't you think, some day you'll be able to forget it?"

"Oh no. I ain't a girl like that."

She spoke with absolute certainty.

"There's some made so as they can't never forget," she added.

"That's very hard for them," Aubrey said.

"Not many of 'em are men," said Diamond.

"You think not?"

"I'm sure not."

"Why?"

"Because he's forgotten, I know," she answered simply, unable to get away from her own little personal experience.

"But men aren't all alike."

"No. There's Mr. King now," she whispered. "Do you like him?"

"Yes."

"He *is* kind. But it's no use. Oh, it is dreadful when I think of all the other birthdays I shall have—and never him."

She was silent for a minute, then she looked suddenly at Aubrey and said—

"You're happy, ain't you?"

"Not very."

"Oh, what a pity! But it—it isn't anything—it isn't like me over again?"

"Yes," he said, "it's something like that."

"You'll have to forget."

"But if I'm like you? If I can't?"

She shifted restlessly, as one under a burden.

"Perhaps we aren't meant to be happy, you and me," she said at length. "That's about it, I s'pose."

"I suppose that's about it," echoed Aubrey.

Suddenly he got up to go. A horrible sensation that he might lose his habitual self-control if he stayed had come upon him. Perhaps, in some dim way, Diamond realised this, for she did not try to keep him. But Mr. Slagg was loud in expressions of regret. Aubrey pleaded that he must be up early on the following morning, and, as he felt, with a certain shifty awkwardness, due to the uprising of fear within him, took his leave. He met Mrs. Slagg in the passage, and was cordially invited by her to call round again.

It was raining in the empty street. Nobody was about. Beneath his umbrella Aubrey tried to fight with his stupid, fierce, unreasonable demon of Sorrow. The London night seemed swollen with black despair, as eyes are swollen with tears. The rain grieved. It was the visible expression of some high, far-off and portentous tragedy that lay, perhaps, beyond the hidden stars.

A light run of feet behind him startled Aubrey. He glanced round quickly, and saw Alf in coat and cap. Alf joined him with a nod, and walked forward at his side with a springing step.

"Coming with me?" said Aubrey.

Alf nodded again. Apparently he did not want to talk. They went on in silence all the way to Jermyn Street. At his door Aubrey stopped.

"Will you come up?" he said to Alf.

"No, thank you, sir," said Alf.

"Look at the number, and come to see me another day, then," Aubrey said.

"Yes," said Alf.

He cast a piercing glance at the number on the door, cut a curious caper in token of farewell, and was off down the street in the twinkling of an eye.

Aubrey entered his rooms wondering why this little silent goblin of mysterious agilities had joined him. He found himself thinking that the boy was like some strange, scarcely tamed animal, full of odd impulses and droll whims. Diamond, and Alf, and himself— three lives pulsing on! Dark London enclosed them, as the tunnel encloses the life of a train. The train emerges presently into the light. Aubrey stood there on the wet doorstep when Alf was gone, and seemed to hear the roar of the train in the tunnel. But he could not think that it was rushing towards the light.

Good Christians thought so—his mother among them. But Aubrey was not a good Christian. He was one of the beings of to-day, who have to be restless in wondering, instead of being content, or at the least trustful, in believing.

As he put the latchkey into his door, Lady Rangecliffe was on her knees in the big, bare house in Eaton Square, praying for him with a strength as of one who wrestles with an angel. She told those secrets of her son that he had never told her—to God.

CHAPTER XIV.

Two or three days later Aubrey received a letter from Sir Reuben asking him to give up his poor little position in the City and to become his godfather's confidential secretary. Sir Reuben laid great stress upon the fact of his requiring such a person, and upon the extraordinary difficulty of finding any man who could be absolutely trusted, intimately confided in. He added that Lady Caryll begged Aubrey to accept the position, and concluded by a proposition that astonished Aubrey completely. This proposition was that, if he could see his way to accept the post, he should come to live with the Allabruths in Park Lane. In suggesting this change of life to his godson, Sir Reuben dwelt only upon the convenience such an arrangement would be to him.

"I am not so young as I was," he wrote. "There will often be days when I shall not care to go to my office, and important letters may arrive at any moment which will require to be dealt with. I must have my secretary upon the spot. The house is very large, as you know. You will have your own rooms, and will be as much your own master as you are in Jermyn Street. If you do not accept the position, I shall have to look out for somebody else, with whom I shall make this arrangement. I may add in conclusion, that Caryll is most anxious for you to accept this offer. She knows that my health is not always what it should be, and she wishes that my burthen should be lightened. You can lighten it more completely than any other man. I trust you will think it your duty to do so."

Sir Reuben then stated the salary attaching to the post. It was a very generous one. The busy conscience had been at work. The possessor of Lady Caryll was very determined to heal in the body him who had been so deeply wounded in the soul.

Aubrey's immediate and startled impulse was to refuse this offer, and the strength of this impulse was born of the strength of the desire within him to accept it. As he read the letter a hot passion of yearning flamed up in his heart, lit by the possibility of dwelling in that curious foreign London house with Caryll. What a transformation of life that would be, like a strange journey to some Eastern land, to some far-off home of rich colour, of rich silence. London, that great and ebony tide of life and crime and breathless activities, ceased upon the doorstep of her house, as the flowing sea-tide, spent in its journey onward, ceases when the hour of return, fixed, immutable, strikes for the ignorant wave. Aubrey longed so cruelly to accept that his longing told him to refuse. He sat down at his table and wrote a letter to decline Sir Reuben's offer. He put it into an envelope, and threw the envelope into the fire. Then he wrote another letter, asking for a week to consider the offer, for which he warmly thanked his godfather. He sent it to Park Lane by a boy messenger and received a reply—

"By all means. Take a week on one condition—at the end of it you must say 'Yes.'"

Aubrey went into the City, succeeded in obtaining a week's holiday, had his bag packed, and left London in the evening, alone. In the tremendous moments of our lives we often have an overmastering desire for complete solitude, perhaps because in the most tremendous moment of all we must be solitary. This invitation to a changed existence filled the heart and brain of Aubrey with feeling and thought that seemed to combine in flame. He felt that he must come to his decision alone and among silences. He went to the hills in Northern England, to a place that he knew as a child, that he had not seen for some years. This was a very narrow, very deserted valley, hidden at the feet of heights, barred in by obdurate grey and hoary crags. Midway in the valley stood a small inn, quite alone, by the side of a grey road set between grey walls of stone. A river crept behind it. Above, the sky was often cloudy. This valley was a place of clouds and of soft melancholies, where few passed by, where a man might flower and fade almost unnoticed. In the early morning Aubrey came to it through the cold air. The little inn was empty, its owner, once a shepherd, surprised, most cordially, to take the commands of a guest. Aubrey breakfasted in the coffee-room, listening to the trickling river's cry, looking at the clouds that leaned, grey it seemed with weariness, upon the shoulders of the hills.

Then he walked out, thinking that this place was an oasis of silence in the desert of the world's far-stretching uproar.

Strangely fast fled his days in the valley. He wandered very far among the hills, and looked at winter from the heights. Scarcely knowing it, he asked all the stealthy influences around him to help him in his decision. How did they answer? For surely they knew and listened. The indecision of Aubrey was not the ordinary indecision of the young man, in his case, desiring not to be wicked. He loved a woman, and she was wedded to an old man, but he did not fear the proximity to her now pressed upon him as would have feared it many a man touched by personal vanity and uncertain of his hold upon the moralities. He could not be so insolent in his thought of Caryll as to suppose her wrongly drifting to his arms from those of her husband, or impelled from purity by a wholly vulgar intrusion of immoral possibility. She stood upon the peaks, white as the morning when it faces aloft the longing sky.

What Aubrey feared was torture to himself in entering so intimately a life that he had longed to occupy completely. Yet she wished it. She was perfectly pure, he perfectly chivalrous. Youth in such hands is not a hammer plied for the breaking of commandments. Of the sordid danger feared ever by a world full to the throat of sordid imaginings, Aubrey had no thought. It was too far away, too impossible. But no man desires to suffer more keenly than is necessary. Aubrey in his long walks debated the amount of pain, to be avoided or endured, that hung in the balance of his decision against or for, and midway through the week he thought he had made up his mind to refuse Sir Reuben's offer.

Perhaps it was Nature herself who stepped in to twist his purpose. He never quite knew, though afterwards he asked himself the question. For one day he walked forth without purpose, moving in the open air that he might think the better, and it was at the beginning of this walk that he believed he had come to the final resolve. As he stepped out on the narrow grey road, hard in a frost, and glanced over the grey stone wall at the grey hills frigidly towering towards the sky in which lay snow as in a net, he realised strongly the iron-grey bitterness of pain, and he thought that he had settled to refuse the changed life offered to him. So fully did he think this that he dismissed the subject which had recently possessed him. He thought no longer of himself in connection with Caryll and her husband, but only of Caryll as he left the valley and mounted almost mechanically towards the heights. It was a mysterious afternoon, so deadly still that it produced upon Aubrey's imagination the effect of a great grey beast crouched to spring. The repose seemed to be that precedent to intense and cruel activity, immobility of a winter's day waiting its opportunity to wound or kill. He fancied that if he mounted out of the valley he would escape from this disagreeable impression which took fast hold upon him. But, strangely, it decidedly gained upon him as he proceeded. The beast now seemed crouched on the hill summits or in the lowering clouds. He stood and listened, as a man in a forest listens for the growl of the hidden creature whose near presence his instinct divines. But he heard nothing. Nature lay as one paralysed. He went on upward

When from time to time he turned to look back, he saw the valley, each time become more spectral than the last, as the faint mist shrouded yet one more detail from his eyes. Presently it was a grey blur. Then it was nothing. It ceased to exist for him. Only the heights had any meaning now, and they were full of mystery. He could not read them. Each hill was an enigma, intentionally, not unconsciously. Each grasped its secret with a portentous determination, a clear knowledge of all it meant or ever could mean. Aubrey felt that he trod in a cold world of secrets. The very stones, shifting like things alive beneath his feet, were stern with reticence. And the sky, leaking mist, was muffled in a bleak and almost perilous reserve. He was, indeed, quite alone, a wandering hermit in a world of secrets. The crescendo of an impression upon the mind is like the crescendo of a sound upon the ear. Each, to the mental vision, is a thing that climbs, as Fate climbs on its ladder. And since Aubrey was also actually climbing in the bodily sense, the crescendo was enormously accentuated for him. He felt as one who mounts to the top of things, and as if the noise of all the secrets of the world rose now to its highest and most piercing expression. Nature clamoured in his ears, " I am full of mystery."

Presently he came to the edge of the clouds, an edge so sharply defined upon the hill that he lifted his hand to feel it. His hand melted into the grey mantle, and he followed his hand into it. He was lost in the trackless waste of the sky, though his feet still trod the earth. Now he saw nothing except the wet grass, the wet stones immediately around and beneath him, and he breathed dampness and cold secrecy. He knew not why he still went onward. But he felt expectant, as if on some hidden summit he was going to meet a great personality. He lost the sense of time, the sense of fatigue. He walked eagerly, and the murmur of mystery rustled all about him, rousing a vital curiosity. Far off he heard the voice of a stream descending to the valley submerged in the clouds. It went in haste to tell the hollow its tale of the spirit of the summits. At last, looking upward, he saw the height curve and cease. He stood among rocks. He had gained the top of the hill. Resting against a boulder, he waited. He felt that he had something to wait for; and now that he had ceased from bodily activity he began to think, not vaguely of the vague mysteries of Nature, crowding here like shadowy figures in some gaunt circus lit by tragic fires, but clearly—of the mystery of Caryll. He saw her standing with the coloured pearls about her throat, her eyes glittering with a strange joy. He felt again, and more acutely than ever before, the profound curiosity which had seized him when first he saw her in her new home. This profound curiosity had indeed become one with his passion for her, and touched it with a new fierceness. And now he knew that all the time he had been mounting the hill so eagerly, he had been, almost unconsciously, dreaming of the activity of investigation which must lead him at last to understand the exact meaning of the soul of the woman he loved and had lost. Our thoughts often direct our limbs without our knowing it, drive them as a man drives horses. And when we cannot grasp the substance by doing that which we desire mentally, we often grasp the shadow by a grotesque bodily travesty of the soul-action we have to forego. So Aubrey's mind had led his body to the home of the mysteries of the hills.

He did not go wholly unrewarded. For while he stood on the summit the mist stirred under some prompting of Nature, crawled up and aside, broke, dispersed, was shattered into drifting fragments. Through many a rent Aubrey saw vague and far-off views, grey pictures of wild scenery. A jagged tooth of rock pierced through a cloud, a distant hill wandered into sight and stayed. And still the mist continued to disperse, shrugging itself together and shifting uneasily like an anxious creature stealthy in its departing. The country disclosed itself, cold and full of a wan and wintry pathos. Below lay a sheet of steel at the foot of an iron precipice. And then a curious and romantic greyness appeared, lying along the darker edge of the world. Aubrey knew this was the sea, and his pulses quickened, as they always did when he saw the sea far off. He could not discern its movement, but he divined the restlessness of its wave, the restlessness of its voice, the sway of its uncouth desire and half-strangled despair. And beyond and above it glowed a penetrating orange light — light of the sunset struggling in the hands of Winter, like a live thing being strangled by one who has caught it, and calling, in its dumb way, by a frantic and dumb manifestation, on notice and on help.

That light was like the cry of a voice, magnificent with apprehension and coming up out of the heart of things. Aubrey listened to it. And again he thought of Caryll. Was not her soul, perhaps, struggling like that sunset in the hands of Winter? Can any human being be happy with a secret that no one knows? The light faded and he turned to go. As he went down the hill he knew that he would accept his godfather's offer. The mysteries of the hills pushed him towards the mystery of a woman. He must learn the meaning of her joy ; he must go through the mist until, gaining the summit, he caught at last a glimpse of the light in the sky, and heard the cry of the inner voice that is the only voice worth hearing.

CHAPTER XV

When Lady Rangecliffe heard from Aubrey of his new decision and new plan of life, she was exceedingly upset, and, acting with her usual abruptness, she wired to Sir Reuben asking him to call upon her. He came promptly, and found her looking violently uncomfortable.

"Sir Reuben," she said quickly, "look here! Aubrey can't possibly go to live with you and Lady Caryll."

"Why not?" he asked, with a smiling serenity. "Do you think the world will talk?"

Lady Rangecliffe jerked her head upwards.

"I'm not thinking about the world, but about my boy. It's not right for him to do this. I know that."

"It is to his advantage."

"Oh, Sir Reuben," she said. "Aubrey loves your wife, we both know it. How can he live with you? How can he?"

Lady Rangecliffe did not understand what subtlety meant. Had she felt it to be her duty to commit a crime, she would probably have committed it in Piccadilly Circus at three o'clock in the afternoon. But her terribly true statement did not confuse her visitor.

"Aubrey is my godson and a gentleman," Sir Reuben said. "If he accepts my offer——"

"Why on earth did you make it?"

Lady Rangecliffe pushed forward her face till she almost touched Sir Reuben's, and stared at him with a directness well-nigh inhuman.

"Because I wished to have an assistant in my affairs whom——"

"No, Sir Reuben, no. I never thought you'd tell me a lie."

She looked much distressed, and walked about the room, which was littered with work for a bazaar, and had a confusingly calico appearance.

"Because I wished to make Aubrey happier than he is now."

Lady Rangecliffe turned, rather like a grenadier, and came up to him again. After a silent scrutiny of his lined face she said—

"Yes, that's your reason. But this can't make him happy, and it's wrong."

"Aubrey is to be trusted; he loves honour."

"Yes, but——"

"Caryll is to be trusted; she loves an emerald."

Lady Rangecliffe moved a step backward as if physically repelled.

"You can speak of her like that now?"

"Why not? Do you not love the truth? This is the truth then. My wife is not quite like other women of this London, of this epoch. She was born to live in a harem, petted as an animal is petted, adorned with jewels as a sultan's favourite is adorned. Such a life would have satisfied her nature. Her soul shines like a jewel and is as hard. Human sorrow will never touch her, for she cares for nobody. Ordinary pride will never uplift her, for I believe that social position, that great traditions, are as dust in her eyes. But she must have a life that glitters with jewels or she would die or become as nothing. There are certain foods, Lady Rangecliffe, that give certain powers to men. Well, my wife, to reach her highest and most complete development, must be fed upon a diet of precious stones,—not quite in Cleopatra's way, though. You realise, or perhaps, being so splendidly human as you are, you don't realise, that a certain class of women has breathed through so long a chain of years a foetid atmosphere of unintellectual selfishness, has sold itself, body, mind and soul, so repeatedly for hard things that glitter, for gold, for diamonds, for the petted slave-girl's joys, that humanity has absolutely dwindled in the race, just as size might dwindle in a race breeding in and in with dwarfs. In Caryll that dwindling light of humanity —though the light of a strange intellect burns—has gone out. My wife's not human."

"You can say that of the girl you've married?"

"I can do more. I can thank the Ruler of Paradise that she's not human. Lady Rangecliffe, I worshipped a woman once, and she was human. She married me, and loved me perhaps as only human women can love, for a little while. And that short time of passion put the steel ropes round me that held me to her. Then she deceived me, because she was so human, and because of this deadly truth that lots of you English won't realise, that there's such an enormous amount of the animal in humanity. And she went on deceiving me till her end. Why, her death—and she was atrociously afraid of death, too—her death was brought about by a lawless effort to deceive me. And when I saw this human woman I had loved in her coffin, I wanted to take her body out and trample on it."

Lady Rangecliffe was white with the horror of his words.

"My friend, you lie against yourself," she said.

"No. In that moment I vowed that I had done with humanity. I was away so long. You remember? I bought my slaves then. You can do that easily enough under the rose—the Eastern rose. I studied the slave-mind. Many slave-girls aren't human at all according to Western ideas of what humanity is. Then I came back, and I found a white fairy with a slave-girl's mind, for all her brilliance, standing before a jewel-shop in Bond Street. Your boy has dreamed lies about her, beautiful lies. In his mind, in his imagination, she has the magic that clothes the forms which flit through our happy dreams. He loves Caryll. He's unhappy because he loves her, because she is mysterious to him. Let him come to live with her. Let him get to know her really as she is, the white fairy with the slave-mind, or the white diamond with no more soul than has a diamond. He has a passion for the lie, thinking her human. I have a passion for the truth, knowing her inhuman. Let him come to learn the truth, and, in his horror of it, his love will die, as in my joy of it mine lives."

"But it cannot be the truth."

"It is. You yourself divined it. You yourself said to me in this room that there was something decidedly inhuman about Caryll."

"Something—yes, I didn't say she was a monster. Oh, Sir Reuben, you are horrible—you are horrible."

She was violently agitated. Her face twitched fantastically, almost as it had twitched when she was a child. She fidgeted with her long hands and tears stood in her short-sighted eyes.

"I can't let you speak like this of any woman," she said. "There is a chivalry of sex. No, I can't. I won't."

"Very well. But you can and will let Aubrey come to learn his lesson?"

The passion that had disfigured Sir Reuben's face while he had been speaking now died out of it. He spoke very quietly.

"I can't prevent him," said Lady Rangecliffe. "But I know Aubrey, although he's my son, and I know this, that were what you say true—and it isn't, it can't be—Aubrey has such a nature that he could never understand it, never believe it. He is too human to believe in inhumanity."

"Poor Aubrey!"

"Rich Aubrey! Oh, Sir Reuben, my friend, who once saved my brother from destruction, oh how poor, how bankrupt you are!"

For a moment he seemed touched by her vehemence and sincerity, then he said—

"Lady Rangecliffe, the poorest, the most bankrupt is he who turns away from the truth and makes a religion of sweet lies. Let

Aubrey look his world in the face and endure the cruelty of its expression. The happiness of dreams is after all only a mirage. He must know Caryll as she is—a soul, perhaps, but, like the soul engraved upon the emerald, made to be borne away by curious pleasures. When I desire to comprehend clearly the differences in the natures of human beings, I study their differing pleasures. Caryll would rather feel her soft hand resting upon a pearl than upon a heart that loved her. Let Aubrey once understand that, and he will escape out of the prison of his dream. Would you, who love him, desire that he should be a prisoner for ever?"

Lady Rangecliffe made no reply for a moment. Then suddenly she came to Sir Reuben and cried—

"But you—you!"

"I?"

"What are you, that, believing this of your wife, you can be happy with her?"

"I am an old man. I have seen hell through its open door. Henceforth if I can own a slave I shall be content."

She said nothing. Sir Reuben touched her hand and left her.

The return of Monsieur Anneau to London coincided almost exactly with the beginning of Aubrey's new life, and the two events gave to the modern wild beast some food to tear with its savage teeth. There are certain women who will never attract the close attention of the world, whatever may be their position. There are others who can never escape the staring eyes, the staring mind of Society. The question is one of personality rather than of acts. Lady Caryll was of the latter class of women. Had she sat doing worsted work through the circling years the progress of her worsted work would certainly have engrossed the attention of all who knew of her. Since she never did worsted work, her prominence was of a less matronly nature, and, at this time of her career, was connected with three men and her jewel-case. Why did she seem so happy with her goblin of the East? Why did the goblin attach to his household a man so young, so handsome, as Aubrey Herrick? Why did Monsieur Anneau throw up a magnificent American engagement in order to come to London and persuade the Eastern goblin to arrange a perfect music-room for a concert of French songs? These questions leaped on the lips of London as bubbles leap on the lips of a stream. And then there was the question of the jewels! For now at last the feet of Lady Caryll began to stray down the twinkling avenues of that cave of Aladdin to which the murmured words of a priest had been the open sesame. And what woman is not fixed in curiosity, if not drawn in passion, by the changeful light of gems? In the cold and black winter the romance of Caryll's life began to glow like the strange emerald she so often wore. And curious eyes observed the peculiar radiance.

The progress of this pilgrim of the world was now a fact. If her feet had rested hitherto, they rested no longer. She had begun to advance towards the fulfilment of her destiny, and the ear of the world heard the soft and secret sound of her first footstep.

The installation of Aubrey was quickly accomplished. Lady Rangecliffe did not try to interfere with it. She was in a strange confusion since her interview with Sir Reuben, and out of this confusion her inaction was born. Perhaps the old man had influenced her despite herself, and she began to believe that her boy might learn a lesson in the great and brilliant home of the being who had struck so stern a blow at his heart.

Aubrey was given a suite of rooms on the second floor of the house. It was called the red suite. Surroundings undoubtedly influence the mind. Living in these changed conditions, and amid these unusual surroundings, Aubrey felt as if he were another man. He never forgot his first evening as Sir Reuben's secretary. It was of course an understood thing that he should dine where he would, and, except during certain fixed hours of work, be absolutely his own master. But, on this first evening, he dined alone with the Allabruths. Sir Reuben called the meal the banquet of inauguration. Being a man of much ironic humour, and a born lover of the fantastic, his novel situation—a thorn, as it were, between two roses—delighted him mischievously.

"Wear the emerald to-night, Caryll," he said to his wife before dinner, "in honour of the new member of the family. And you are more truly yourself, more absolutely a human jewel, when you wear it."

She smiled at him, and the light of her smile was blinding. Presently he watched her fastening the emerald on the black dress she wore. She never allowed her maid to touch it. Sir Reuben always thought that her hands looked changed and far more lovely when they were touching precious stones, as the hands of a mother change and are more lovely when they clasp the round limbs of her little child.

"Don't wear any other jewel," he said. "For that emerald kills its rivals. Now let us go down. No, wait a moment."

He stood looking at her with his preternaturally bright eyes, and she remained quite still with the obedience of one who is perfectly happy. Her face was turned towards him. Its clear white tint gleamed under the electric lights. The frosty grey of her beautiful eyes looked almost magically Northern. Her neck and arms were snow. And as there can be a peculiar intensity

of life in a white landscape, so there was an intensity of life in
her. Her very soul seemed to emanate in radiance and to mingle
with the radiance of the emerald. Sir Reuben, gazing at her with
the deep attention of ownership, thought that to-night Aubrey
must understand ; and, going to his wife, he put his old arms around
her and said—

"How truly you are yourself to-night, Caryll!"

She only smiled in answer, and they went downstairs.

Aubrey thought that banquet of inauguration was like an
Arabian Night's dream. They ate strange dishes, and only Sir
Reuben's Arab servant waited upon them. The lights were low
and the table was covered with very strongly scented flowers.
And Sir Reuben talked. It was a monologue, and the most
uncommon monologue imaginable. For he talked of jewels, and
allowed his rank imagination to have full play, even sending it
on with a sort of deliberate violence, as if he desired to whirl his
two companions with him into another world. His knowledge of
gems was profound ; his exhibition of that knowledge was limitless. And it was impossible not to feel the strange fascination of
his peculiar mental powers. For he spoke of jewels as a man
might speak of those live things which, by their life, have influence
on the destinies of men. And he told tales of engraved gems
most curiously and imaginatively, and as if he fancied that they
might perhaps be changed, as the character of a living thing may
be changed, by the stamp put upon them. Thus he discoursed of
the little grove of seven trees seen by Camello Leonardo da Pesaro
upon a figured agate, and of the curious love of trees that probably
grew in the substance on which they grew. He described the
changelessness of this solitary grove, and pictured, fancifully, the
seasons passing in the heart of the agate, the sense of spring and
of young desires stirring within it, the rapture of summer and the
heavy golden noons, the whispering wistfulness of autumn full of
the premonitions of decay, the white calm of winter with its leaf-
less thoughts. He told them of Boece de Boot's agate, upon
which was the design of a mitred bishop, and wove curious and
sacerdotal fantasies about it, fantasies in which the bishop drew
inflexibility from the substance on which he rested, while the
substance became magically impregnated with the deep ideas, the
tragic doubts, the solemn purities and hopes that stir in the secret
homes of God. He described to them the fly agate, with its
wonderful insect patterns, and the amazzonite with its little straws
of green, like veins in which ran the blood of leaves. He painted
for them in words the silvery argirite, opaque and delicate, fairy-
like as a moonbeam on a midsummer night, and quoted the words
of Pliny about the asteria, which has enclosed in it a light, "like

that of the eyeball, which it sends out now from one place, now from another, as if moving about in the jewel.

" Ah !" he said, turning his intensely bright eyes from his wife, who listened absorbed, to Aubrey, who was listening too and watching her, "does it not seem as if jewels have in very truth life, not as we have it, but life of a different kind, still, intense, and reticent? Does not the asteria watch like a spy? Who knows? Can that mysterious light within it, directed now towards one object, now towards another, spring from no source of will and be motived by no keen mental desire to observe? I have seen a gigantic oriental ruby, which, when submitted to the influence of the sun, gave out a luminous star. The sun spoke to it, the star was its reply. So do the silent things have their intercourse, even as we have ours. And gems do not merely speak in their ordained way. They, like men and women, know the pride of possession. The green calcedonyx, Indian by origin, holds fast its drop of water. The chalcedony clutches its golden sand. The beryl is a revealer of mysteries, for men, looking through it, have beheld things otherwise invisible to the eye. The Brazilian carbon, when whispered to by heat, yields up its phosphorescent flame, yet never diminishes or dies. The obstinate cyanite declines to melt under the assaults of the blowpipe, and the clorophane, like a cat, pierces the darkness with its strange and terrible green stare. Can it not, like the cat, see those activities of the dark that escape the eyes of men? and cannot it, perhaps, consider mentally that which it sees? How men would laugh at the idea! But men, since the beginning of things, have spent their short time on earth in laughing in the very face of truth. Plants feel, flowers enjoy and sorrow. Who shall say that jewels, in their flaming inactivity, do not love and suffer, attach themselves to a passionate owner"—he glanced from the face of Lady Caryll to the great emerald shining on her breast—"feel terror and pain when the hands of the robber or of the thief who comes in the night tear them from the safety of their home?"

As he spoke, his wife, with a stealthy and instinctive gesture, lifted her hand and laid it upon the emerald. She kept it there while Sir Reuben continued—

" I have often thought of the possible sufferings of jewels in those long and fantastic journeyings which they have made from country to country, from hand to hand, and of the cruelties which they have endured for the pleasure of men and women. The biography of such a gem as the Kohinoor, written with power and sympathy, would surely make every one with an imagination tremble and weep. Think of the terror—to it—of its dreary reputation, haunting it for ever on its wanderings through the world, from the moment when the dark Hindoos whispered together of its malign influence, till that day in which the revolt of a great city and the death of a great prince were placed to the balance of its dread account. Think of its physical sufferings at the hands of its possessors, operated upon by brutal hands, forced to undergo the bitter deprivation of so much magical beauty, of so much legendary value, cut and hacked by the insolent tools of the ignorant, and of those whose only idea of improvement is massacre. What a life has it led in the past—at the court of the king of Anga and in the palace of Aurungzeb. It has seen the sacking of Delhi, the assassination of the greedy Persian into whose grasp it fell. It has dwelt with Ahmed Shah Doorannee in Afghanistan, and has watched his nameless crimes. It has been solemnly dedicated to the temple of Juggernaut, and ravished from its sacred home to see the Punjaub crawl beneath the British yoke. Exiled from the lovely lands of the East, it is forced now to dwell here in cold and sunless England, and to listen to the wild and hideous march of civilisation along the bleak and iron roads of vulgarity. Yet still it watches life with the same clear serenity of old, and still it stares upon the masquerade of men with the imperturbable lustre that long ago made it one of the celebrities of the universe. The Orloff diamond, too, has suffered dreary things. It was an eye in the head of Brama in the temple of Scheringham. Brama himself made it a vehicle by means of which he gazed out upon the kneeling crowds of them who worshipped him. Through it he perceived the French dastard stealing in with a hideous mockery of devotion to blaspheme among the pious at his sacred feet. He watched the fatuity of his chief priests, so ignorant despite their mysterious office. He saw them learning to love and trust the traitor. He saw the traitor placed to guard his very temple. He heard the rising of that terrific tempest which roared through the black night in which the diamond was torn from its socket and borne away to its fate; to those amazing vicissitudes which carried it from the English captain to the Whitechapel Jew, from the Greek merchant to the royal courtesan who sat upon her throne in the White North, and showed her silent victim to the lovers whom she snatched from the gutter, kissed for a while, and then sent forth to prison and to death. Can things so full of radiance and of colour, things so marvellously vivacious, so quick to grasp the sun, and to smile back to the smile of the moon—can they, who rest upon the throbbing breasts of the loveliest human beings, who assist at the fêtes of kings, and are borne tenderly in the processions of empresses,—can they who are made the heralds of love and the trusted messengers of passion, can they be insensitive? Can they be soulless, frigid, without life, or mystery, or wonder?"

He paused suddenly, looking sharply from his wife to Aubrey. Lady Caryll's steel-grey eyes were fixed upon him with an intensity that was piercing. Her lips were slightly parted, and, in the silence of this pause, he caught the sound of her breathing, which was strangely audible. One of her hands was still clasped about the emerald, on which her fingers closed tightly. The other lay clenched upon the tablecloth. She was leaning forward, and her white bosom rose and fell with a certain violence, as of one who secretly struggles for full breath in an airless room. Her whole attitude indicated an extreme fervour of attention, such as men give in great moments to a very great orator. And she did not stir during the silence. There was no relaxation of muscles, no sigh of the released, no throwing off of tension. The white lids did not droop over the gazing eyes. The parted lips did not softly join. Her whole body—absolutely, even wonderfully, expressive of the meaning of the spirit—demanded a continuance of that which had given to it so passionate a vitality.

Sir Reuben turned his bright eyes from her to Aubrey. He was as deeply absorbed in Caryll as she was in her husband. He too was leaning forward in his place, and the most profound attention was written in his attitude. He had taken some fruit from the Arab servant. It lay upon his plate untasted. His glass was full of wine. He did not touch it with his lips. He had forgotten where he was, despite the modern consciousness which so continually dwelt with him, making part of his nature at all ordinary times. The book that contained his lesson was open before him. At Sir Reuben's crafty touch it had opened wide. His eyes were fixed upon it with a gaze that was full of a sort of passion of inquiry. Could he read that lesson? Could he understand, learn it?

"I often think," Sir Reuben said, and his voice became low and more monotonous than before, "that everything on earth, whether it is dubbed animate or inanimate, that absolutely everything has some power, however stunted, of giving and of receiving. Jewels, we know, can give a thousand things—light, colour, brilliance, pleasure, torture, despair, envy, greed, jealousy. These things and others they give to the world, to the men and women who possess them. What do they receive, and how do they keep it? And, if they receive and retain gifts from men, and—Caryll—from women, how do they return them? Do you think that it is possible for anything, alive or dead, to receive a real ardour of love, keen passion, deep faithfulness, and to remain absolutely unaffected by it, absolutely unaltered? Suppose that a man worships a woman"—Aubrey stirred slightly in his chair—"She may not love him in return. She may not grant him any favour. She may even refuse his worship, turn away from his prayers, laugh at his tears. But do you think she is exactly the same woman as she would have been if the man had never looked at her? Is it in the power of anything to refuse to accept some kinds of gifts? If love, if passion, be given, it belongs to that to which it is given despite a thousand refusals. And suppose a woman loves a jewel"—Lady Caryll did not stir as Aubrey had stirred—" Can the jewel, in its hardness, in its glittering inflexibility, can it absolutely repel that love? Can it remain totally unchanged by that love? Does it not retain, amid its tinted fires, one spark from the fire of the woman's adoring eyes? Does it not seize a more mysterious glow from the glow of her soft hands when she caresses it? Does not the woman pour part of herself into the depths of the jewel, draw part of the jewel into her own depths? For the law of exchange governs the world and weaves the ropes that bind the universe together. And the secrecies of attachment, so often apparently inexplicable, are strung like beads upon these invisible ropes. There is always a road on which love sets his feet when he travels. But often we cannot see the road, or hear the sound of his delicate footsteps upon it."

Lady Caryll dropped her hand from the great emerald, which sent forth its mysterious green lustre into the dimly lighted room.

"Look at that jewel," said Sir Reuben. "Does it not seem to live, to live as strongly, as persistently, as you, Caryll, or you, Aubrey, or I myself? We watch it, think about it. Has it no thought, no gaze for us? And upon its bosom it bears its child—that faint engraving of three figures, the soul being borne away by pleasures. Good people are shocked by that engraving. To them there is something awful in that journey of the soul, and they dream of a far-off and hideous destination to which the soul must come."

"Yes," said Aubrey.

Lady Caryll started at the sound of his voice and lifted her hand as if to still an interruption. Aubrey noticed the gesture and his lips tightened.

"But who can tell if the destination of wrinkled duty, creeping about its unimpassioned task, may not be as hideous? If the cry that is born in a nature, when the nature is born, be eternally unheeded, will not the nature in eternity resemble that flower which is everlasting merely because it has none of the loveliness of the flower which fades and dies? Will it not be dry, frigid, without colour, without scent, dead in its eternal life because of the cry that has been starved to death within it? Some people cannot feel that they have power unless they are withholding something. I cannot feel that I have power unless I am giving something. And if I met with a strong nature, a nature fierce in its desire and crying for all the seas, I should like to pour all the seas into it."

THE SLAVE

His eyes were on Lady Caryll as he spoke, and in her eyes he surprised a look of almost terrible gratitude. Under that look he was silent, lest he should interrupt its speech. Then, at last, Aubrey took up the peach from his plate and began slowly to peel it. Once or twice his knife struck the plate, which emitted a tiny ringing sound. He divided the peach into two parts, keeping his gaze upon it all the time. And all the time Sir Reuben and Caryll looked at each other. At last Aubrey glanced up. He saw the expression in the eyes of Lady Caryll as she gazed into the eyes of Sir Reuben, and he mistook the passion of gratitude in them for the passion of love. And that evening, for the first time, he began, as he thought, to understand the attraction of the Goblin of the East. Within his small, withered, and sun-dried frame—his husk, old and ugly to the eye—there dwelt a cunning of magic that was peculiar among men. There was something of the fascination of a geni about him, a diabolic quickness and changefulness, an atmosphere of far-off lands and of secrets which are hidden from London eyes and are disbelieved by London sceptical hearts. His speech, like a thin dagger, pierced below the surface of ordinary life, and through the crevice the eye could dimly see deep down a multitude of passionate activities never before suspected, far less revealed.

"And would you ask for any reward, Reuben?" said Caryll.

Aubrey had never before heard her call her husband by his Christian name. Her doing of it seemed to establish a strange familiarity between husband and wife. Never had Aubrey felt so far away from Caryll as at this moment.

"Possibly I might," Sir Reuben said.

"And what would it be?"

"That the one who submitted to my power of giving should only receive from me."

"Ah!"

She smiled quietly.

"Is that too much to demand?" he asked. "What do you say, Aubrey?"

"Oh, I suppose that charity can be jealous like all the other virtues," he replied quickly.

He spoke a little bitterly, as a man whose hands are empty and whose heart is full. And he fixed his eyes upon the emerald on Lady Caryll's breast. Now he fancied that in the dim light it was cautiously regarding him with its green eye, as if it would penetrate his soul. Remembering Sir Reuben's strange monologue, he could for a moment almost believe that it was alive, and that by degrees it was establishing a curious sympathy with Caryll—

giving her part of its nature, taking to itself part of hers. Suddenly he leaned back in his chair and burst out laughing.

"Why are you laughing, Mr. Herrick?" said Caryll.

"At my own folly," he said. "As I looked at your emerald I found myself thinking of it as a mental fourth in our little party to-night. You see, Sir Reuben, that you tell fairy stories too well."

He went on laughing in a way that was not natural. In truth, this first evening of intimacy in this house tried his nerves terribly, although he scarcely knew it. A profound curiosity—the curiosity of love—had led him to this new life. But this new life wrapped him in a flame that burned, that seared his heart. He laughed now because a demon, with the face of death, seemed to sit on his knee and to whisper in his ear, "Look, look! you are nothing to her, scarcely even a shadow. Watch her when she smiles at him. There is love."

The Arab servant stole in with coffee and cigarettes. On the salver, beside the cigarettes, there lay a letter for Lady Caryll. She glanced at it and said—

"This is from Monsieur Anneau. He has arrived in London."

Sir Reuben turned to Aubrey and remarked—

"He is going to give a song recital here. We shall arrange a music-room for the occasion."

"Yes," said Aubrey.

He knew that he had nothing to say. He wondered whether the man who woke from the dreams induced by hachcesh in the Mediterranean isle felt as he did this evening. Afterwards, when he was in his rooms alone, he tried to understand from whence emanated the spell that had certainly enveloped him during his godfather's dissertation upon jewels. Why had he not more clearly felt the absurdity of such a theory as that jewels are perhaps alive although men know it not? A thing made of a mineral substance crystallised—alive! Why had not that commonplace common-sense, which so often mercifully assists men in their intercourse with dullards, shaken him to amusement at the notion of the sufferings of a Kohinoor or the tragedy of an Orloff diamond? A spell had been upon him certainly. For a moment he supposed that it had come solely from Sir Reuben. But, after silent consideration, he recognised that it had been laid upon him partly by Lady Caryll. Her attention had been so genuinely profound that his could not be insincere or half-hearted. Her peculiar nature had been so entirely absorbed by the imaginative possibilities with curious cunning presented by Sir Reuben, that Aubrey had been folded in the draperies of her thoughtfulness, had laid in the bosom of her fascination. He knew it now, and, more certainly than ever before, knew the existence within her of the strength of a peculiar force, unusual, almost unfeminine. Only strength can listen as she listened, only vigour can be absorbed as she was absorbed. Aubrey, sitting in this new room, which was a pageant of deep rich colour, and which seemed heavy with a perfume of peculiar personality, watched the dusky smoke of his cigar mount wearily towards the light that burned in an ancient Moorish lantern, and loved this being, who was a mystery to him, more deeply even than he had loved her in Lady St. Ormyn's garden.

Meanwhile she was alone with her husband, with her Goblin of the East, as society called him. A fire of wood burned brightly, and threw a dancing yellow light upon the walls and upon the bed, which was hung with thin Moorish draperies, full of faded colours, varied, yet so faint that they seemed slipping into one. Caryll, whose maid had taken off her gown and left the room, was putting the emerald into her jewel-case. She snapped the lid sharply, and then turned to give the case to Sir Reuben, who placed it in the heavy iron safe which was attached to the floor beneath the bed. To do this he knelt down. The attitude made him look so small, so shrunken, that he was almost nothing. Caryll, wrapped in a white dressing-gown, her sparkling yellow hair loosened, stood looking at this pinched and dry being on the carpet. She watched his brown hands as he placed the jewel-case in the safe and closed the heavy door. He turned, and made a queer movement to get up ; but suddenly she sat down on the bed, and put her two hands on his narrow shoulders.

" No," she said ; " I like to see you at my feet."

He remained kneeling, and looked up into her long and piercing eyes, that were full of a sort of cold, almost wintry excitement.

" How wonderful you were to-night," she said in a low, very clear voice. " You should always talk about jewels."

" To you, Caryll."

" Do you believe what you said ? Do you think it may be true ? "

" Do not you ? "

She was silent, and her white face became serious, almost grim.

" How can the opal be affected by the health of its wearer if it has not some secret life ? Change of atmosphere has almost as much effect upon it as upon a human being. It blossoms like a flower in the air and in the sun. It fades and faints in frost. Can a dead thing do this ? "

" And my emerald ? "

She pressed her hands more firmly upon his shoulders.

" The Peruvian priests in the time of Pizarro believed that the goddess Esmeralda lived in an emerald. Do you not live in an emerald, and if so, is it not full of your life? But be careful, my beautiful Esmeralda—think—if your home were to be lost, destroyed, stolen!"

A sudden horrible look, of terror and of resolution combined, flooded her face, and her hands gripped his shoulders till he felt pain. He loved to have the power to waken such violence in his slave.

"Hush! hush!" she whispered.

"Or think—if I became poor—if I took it from you!"

"You!" she cried.

And he felt that her whole body trembled. He put his thin arms round her and held her tightly.

"Do not fear, my Esmeralda," he whispered. "Do not fear. To you jewels give life, and I worship your life. Outside the cave of Aladdin you are nothing. You shiver in the emptiness of the world—your heart scarcely beats, and your soul lies still in a shroud of snow. Is it not so?"

She answered him with her eyes, from which the fire seemed to withdraw as he slowly spoke.

"But inside—inside the cave!"

"Yes!"

"You are a thing of magic. Your eyes flame. Your heart beats strongly. Your soul awakes, and all your powers expand. Inside the cave you are the most live thing that lives, and the farther your feet stray down its enchanted avenues, where all the jewels watch, where all the jewels are intent, the more brightly will burn the flame of your soul. Put your arms round me, my Esmeralda, and I will lead you for ever through the jewelled wonders of the cave."

Caryll put her soft arms round his almost fleshless and withered body, and rested her head upon his breast. The firelight shone over them, as the moonlight shone over Romeo and Juliet in the Italian garden long ago. Caryll half closed her eyes. And she seemed to see, in a dim and delicious gloom of hazy enchantment, the long procession of the lustrous children of the cave. She saw the emeralds, the jades, and jaspers, a troop of exquisite green beauty. She saw the pure rapture of the pearl. The diamonds sparkled at her from the shadows, and among the rocks the blood-red rubies lay asleep. Coloured lights shone, like fairy torches, from the opals, and the striped epidotes gave out their pearly radiance. The chrysolites, those golden stones, glittered, to tell their sweet romances, and the wavy spark of the cymophane twittered through the magic mist. Far off, the purple sapphire gleamed like a tropical sky at midnight, and the moonstone dreamed its pale dreams upon the breast of the silver clouds.

Caryll gazed into the lustrous eyes of the children of the cave, drinking their coloured beauty. She heard the murmur of their sparkling voices. And in her arms she seemed to hold, not a weary and wrinkled old man, fatigued with the years and with the burden of time, but a wondrous magician, a powerful geni, at whose touch the shell of the grey prosaic world opened, and disclosed the shining infinity that she had so long and so cruelly desired.

CHAPTER XVI

THE arrival in London of Monsieur Anneau created a sensation in that musical society which thinks and talks of performers, and practically ignores that which they perform. Large numbers of very worthy ladies became hectic when they read in the *Morning Post* that he was staying at Claridge's, and Mrs. Eldridge B. Mybrough, of New, York City, at once sent a boy messenger to the hotel, offering him his own terms if he would sing at an "afternoon" at her hired mansion in Belgrave Square. He declined. He could sing for no one. Mrs. Eldridge B. Mybrough informed all her acquaintance of this tragic fact, and three days later received a card from Lady Caryll to hear Monsieur Anneau in Park Lane.

Mrs. Mybrough was not a silent woman. She had a piercing soprano voice, on which scandal seemed to float like a touzled feather on a millrace. She spoke her mind, and London smiled quietly, thinking of how many French plays. It was all so right and improper. The foolish old Goblin of the East deserved his fate. Let him kneel at Lady Caryll's feet with his hands full of jewels. Those hands were ugly with age—the contrast between him and his gifts was hideous and absurd. And then his voice croaked when he made a remark. It did not boom like the deep and drowsy bell of the Cathedral of Granada. It was not at the same time manly as war and magical as peace. His figure had no authority, and though his eyes were piercing and full of lively cunning, they were never shadowy with melting sentiment, or feverish with an ardour that seemed like a song and a sword, the serenade of one who would slay by his sweet singing, and who was ruthless in his tenderness.

Many people had noticed Monsieur Anneau's observation of Lady Caryll's beauty before her marriage. They delightedly comprehended his sudden reappearance, and prepared themselves eagerly for the spectacle of his triumph. For the world has a curious love of seeing men live up to their reputations. To gratify it the Saint must press his hair-shirt ever closer to his tortured flesh, the Sinner must walk, without deviation, in the broad path, and never heed the destruction waiting at its end.

Very few of Caryll's invitation cards elicited refusals. Lady St. Ormyn was in violent commotion. She had quickly grown to believe that it was she who had drawn Monsieur Anneau from the eager claws of America, and she went about London demanding gratitude for this imaginary feat. Her victoria was incessantly before the great door of Claridge's, and the men on the box grew numb beneath their furs while she discussed the arrangement of the programme, and the respective merits of Barré and Bruneau, Chaminade and Massenet. Monsieur Anneau was magnificently tolerant of her. He murmured occasionally to a sympathetic friend, a mime from Montmartre, "Miladi—Mon Dieu! Quand elle parle elle se grise toujours!" And the mime went through a pantomime of an English aristocrat getting very drunk indeed on conversation, and passing through all the successive stages of uproarious intoxication to a finale of exhaustion and a frantic silence. But the singer never lost his superb self-possession, or his demeanour of a high priest who had ministered in all the known temples of darkness. He had much to sustain him beside the sympathetic mime. His large sense of drama, which made him so effective a figure on the stage, was stirred by his renunciation of a continent for one concert in a private house. His fighting spirit was in arms, remembering the shadows of Lady St. Ormyn's garden in the summer before Lady Caryll's marriage. His nature, made theatrical by Providence and operatic by Fate, was braced to a new and engrossing task, compared with which all previous tasks were as nothing. And the power of music itself was being weighed in his balance. This great art had been his weapon in life, and this weapon he had burnished, sharpened, tempered, tried. He had studied its uses, and learned all its most subtle possibilities, as the fencer learns all the possibilities of the foils, and though he might have been persuaded to acknowledge that there had been in the history of the world greater singers than himself, he felt unalterably convinced that there had never before been a man who had so ingeniously placed any art beneath the yoke of his own purpose. That yoke should not be lifted now.

In his pale-yellow sitting-room, crowded with flowers sent by his innumerable adorers, he lounged majestically, giving ear to Lady St. Ormyn's passionate chatter, and seeming to yield to her clamorous arrangements for his programme. In reality, his vivid mind was concentrated upon his idea of the nature of Lady Caryll, and upon the best programme for its subjugation. He had not renounced America to further the reputation of Barré, or to float into popularity any of Lady St. Ormyn's quite innumerable boyish protégés, who were all remarkable for their large eyes and their elaborate buttonholes, if not for their musical genius, and who were all far more devoted to her than to their art. He was at this period rather like an eagle at which a parroquet was pecking, while his tireless eyes stared at some far-off brilliant luminary aloft on the horizon. Lady St. Ormyn was enchanted by his shining imperturbability, which she mistook for a sublime deference.

"Monsieur Anneau's so delighful as a winter friend," she said to Mrs. Luffa Parkinson. "I had no idea—singers are generally so entirely suited to summer weather, aren't they? I mean the great ones. One never imagines—I always think of them as lizards on a south wall, because they make all their great efforts in the hot months, May and June, at least over here—of course in Paris it's different. Besides, the great stars aren't much in Paris—except to go to Paquin, the women. But Monsieur Anneau is so sympathetic—even in a frost, and quite as musical in December as in June."

"That shows great depth of character," said Mrs. Parkinson in her weary voice.

When she had stated this it suddenly dawned upon her that she had said something very profound, and she repeated the remark in connection with Monsieur Anneau's admirable winter qualities in half the drawing-rooms of London. His fame as a December friend spread rapidly, and his yellow sitting-room would have been thronged with callers had he not been almost always out. Just at present he did not wish to diffuse, but to concentrate, his intelligence and his will, and he had no intention of distributing his power in fragments to all the smart women of the town. On his arrival from Paris he had learnt of Aubrey's appointment as secretary to Sir Reuben and of his residence in the Park Lane house. And at first the news had thrown the singer into a silent paroxysm of secret anger. To such a mind as his there was only one inference to be drawn from this fact. He drew it, and for half-an-hour ground his teeth at the thought of his lost American dollars. But he was no bad judge of men despite his exaggerated conception of the wickedness of human nature. A couple of visits to Lady Caryll, during which he saw and conversed with Aubrey, convinced him that Aubrey was not playing the ordinary sordid game of the world. And his observation of Lady Caryll persuaded him that no man had yet entered into her heart. Her apparent satisfaction, if not joy, in the presence of her brown old husband only puzzled him for a moment. Then he decided that it was the brilliant deception of a very clever woman, and smiled at it with the gay eyes of the man who sees through the veil held up to blind him. The fact of Lady Caryll's growing celebrity, the crescendo of gossip about her jewels, whetted his insatiable appetite for dominion, and increased the ardour which had driven him across the Atlantic. When Lady St. Ormyn had mounted at last into the waiting victoria and told the numbed men on the box to drive home, he sat alone on a couch touching the grand piano with his large hand, so apt in ample gesture, and looked at his art as a man looks at his sword for the fight. He partially realised the strangeness of his adversary. He got up from the couch, struck the piano, sang—to test his sword. Improvising with his voice, he spread the passions out before him, in fancy seeing the panorama of the heart. He threw fear into his voice, exultation, pity, desire, content, and supremacy—all this with the quick ease that he had gained by the assiduous education of his natural genius. His sword seemed to him magnificently tempered and he could not doubt its efficacy. And then he meant to wield it with his soul. For he had the determination which is given only to the man of the fixed idea. Since he had known how to sing he had dominated women of the most diverse natures, the musically ignorant as well as the musically cultivated. Even the unmusical he had pierced, exercising his peculiar and illegitimate talent, almost surgical, upon the nervous system. But he felt that Lady Caryll was a perhaps unique subject for one of his experiments. She stood aloof from other women wrapped in a species of blinding white radiance which was very frigid and curiously repellent.

Aubrey, with the instinct of love, which sometimes can almost change the sex of a mind, giving to man the peculiar perception of woman, divined the purpose of Monsieur Anneau. He abhorred him for it, and the strength of his hatred for the singer was measured by the strength of his love for Caryll. Nor was it in any way lessened by his secret conviction that Monsieur Anneau's victorious weapon would quickly know defeat. Monsieur Anneau was perpetually in Park Lane, superintending the arrangement of the music-room or discussing the selection of the programme. It is true that Lady St. Ormyn was also perpetually dropping in. Nevertheless he had many moments alone with Lady Caryll. While he opened Sir Reuben's correspondence and wrote his letters, Aubrey's heart was hot with anger, almost as it had been hot with anger when, in the shrubbery at Epsom, he had seen the white robe of this white girl vanish into the darkness with the impending shadow, scarcely defined, at its side. Sir Reuben watched him, and understood much of what was passing in his mind, guessing from his scarcely concealed nervous irritability on certain days, judging by one or two mistakes that crept into the performance of his duties.

"That isn't quite what I dictated to you, Aubrey," he said one day, handing back a written letter to his godson. "Your memory is short this morning."

Aubrey reddened.

"I beg your pardon," he said. "I'm stupid. I'm not fit to be a secretary."

He held the letter crushed in his hand.

"Sir Reuben," he said suddenly, "you'd better let me go. You'd better get rid of me. I'm no real use to you."

Sir Reuben smiled. He was by the fire, smoking a long pipe. On his head he wore a skull-cap. The winter morning was cold.

"You're young to the work, my boy, that's all, and perhaps something has upset you this morning."

The twinkling eyes searched Aubrey's grave face, and a cloud of smoke rose suddenly from the bowl of the pipe.

"Would you like a day's holiday?"

"No, thanks. If I take a holiday from all this it had better be a permanent one. It's not fair on you this—this——"

"Don't talk nonsense, Aubrey. If you stay on here, you must soon learn all that it is necessary for you to know."

The croaky voice had become curiously significant. Aubrey looked up quickly from the writing-table.

"Is there much?" he said.

He hardly knew what he meant by the question. It sprang to his lips almost mechanically.

"There's a good deal," Sir Reuben said quietly. "Now write as follows to Burn and Woodcroft:—'Dear Sirs, Sir Reuben Allabruth requests me to say that——'"

He dictated a letter. Aubrey fixed his attention fiercely on the matter in hand. After that conversation he exerted all his will-power, and resolutely banished the thought of Caryll and Monsieur Anneau during working hours. Each day a sense of loyalty to his godfather deepened within him. Sir Reuben's kindness was great. Perhaps it may seem strange, but Aubrey never connected his passion for Caryll with disloyalty. His knowledge of its purity, his belief in her white stainlessness, were too complete. He could not doubt either. Sometimes he wondered, however, why Sir Reuben allowed, even encouraged, such a man as Monsieur Anneau to come perpetually to his house, and took so much trouble to oblige his musical ambition. But then Aubrey never succeeded in understanding Sir Reuben's curiously mischievous and complicated nature. And he would have considered incredible the fact, that Sir Reuben, knowing all the truth quite clearly, was daily delighting in the efforts of personality put forth by the singer, was daily anticipating, with a sort of goblin's glee, the finale that must certainly complete this very operatic crescendo of will-power manifesting itself through the greatest of the arts. It was like a Rossini crescendo, in which the music steadily quickens as it grows steadily louder.

There were rehearsals—to test the perfection of the music-room, which Lady St. Ormyn declared was inferior to the one at Epsom. At these rehearsals Monsieur Anneau, so he thought, proceeded cleverly with the education of Lady Caryll's heart. For he always insisted that she should be present as audience, and she happily consented. In the beautiful room, which had been lined with white wood, he gave his strong personality to music, and ordered the music to exercise it on this woman with the sparkling hair and the grey eyes. The art moved obediently under the yoke that he placed upon its neck, returning patient labour for patient labour undertaken in its service. For had not this man given to it the shining years of his youth? Sometimes he thought of it as of the sad-eyed ox, that one may see on an Italian highway, stirring the white dust between the cypress trees with uncomplaining feet. He seemed some swarthy vagrant driving it forward, and when he sang he could hear the crack of a whip.

Lady Caryll listened with the absolute repose that distinguished her among women, and that Sir Reuben loved. It was so Eastern. She sat in a white velvet chair. On her white hands, loosely clasped, as if the muscles were indifferent, jewels sparkled. Round her throat she wore her collar of coloured pearls. Her face was brilliant with a shining of content—brilliant through all the changing songs. Monsieur Anneau watched it as he sang, and, disappointed of the emotional panorama he desired, told himself that it was but a mask.

"She is the cleverest woman in London," he thought; "but she is a woman!"

And he sang again.

The winter twilight was falling. Sir Reuben shuffled in softly. He sat down on a chair close to the door at the end of the room. Lady Caryll moved her head and sent him a smile. He smiled, turning his eyes to Monsieur Anneau.

The singer's broad shoulders and mighty chest loomed up above the grand piano at which he was seated. He had not noticed Sir Reuben's entrance, for he was playing a prelude softly while he considered what song he should sing now while the dull darkness came into the white room. And the prelude seemed to cover and to assist his thought. He looked at the pallor of the sinking afternoon, and the existence of monotony in the world struck him. His fingers sought and found a monotonous music, and he began to sing a desert song. It was warm with sunshine, with the monotony of sunshine, with the long heat that will not leave its home, that stays out there alone in the land ocean, alone with solitary animals, and with solitary birds hideous in mind and ever on the watch. Only a few men live there, and they are fierce in heart. For the long heat is in their blood, and pulses in their veins like music. And the land lies under the sunshine like a slave. Day follows day, and still the sun goes not. And the desert nights hold fast its red fingers, when it seems to have wandered down some far mysterious hill, like a pilgrim going to the hidden shrine that has beckoned him over the seas. The few men there are fierce in heart in the night as in the day. This was their song and the song of the land that held them. Monsieur Anneau's eyes blazed as he sang it. He threw into his voice a fiery languor and the sound of a passion that has never feared a law. He sang this song seldom. But he knew that few civilised women could resist its desolate influence or listen to it untouched. For it gave to civilisation the violent shock of complete novelty, having nothing in it of convention. It had been composed by a young and half-insane Frenchman, who had wasted his life in wandering and had died young. All his life he had known that he would die young. That knowledge had set his feet in many places. For always he was haunted by the fear that if he remained long anywhere he would die there—and so indeed it chanced. Wherever he went he caught some vagrant inspiration, now from the ice of Norway, now from the fire of the Soudan, from the flowering orchards by the rivers of Touraine, from the white and scented showers of the thickets of the Morocco mountains. Everywhere he wrote verses, and to these verses he gave music. And his last song was this desert song, made in the desert that he loved too well. For there—out there in the long heat—he forgot his fear, and he stayed his feet, and he made this song, and gave it to a friend, and died. Arabs buried him in the sand, and bowed their shaven heads to the ground in their prayers to Allah where he lay. And his friend took the song and brought it back to his loved Paris, and gave it to Monsieur Anneau, who had known him. In the singer's armoury this song was the surest weapon. The wildness of it was the wildness of the desert and of its few men, mingled with the wildness of a young and haunted, alien yet sympathetic, heart. It stirred civilisation from its dreams of drawing-rooms and of restaurants, and fired the blood of women who got their gowns from Kate Reilly and from Paquin. Monsieur Anneau delivered it magnificently. He had known the madness of its creator, his fear of rest so strangely justified. And he sang it as a desert man might have sung it above the Parisian's sandy grave. He did not know that the East and Paris were listening to it, united in the old body of Sir Reuben, who sat by the door. It was growing dark when he finished and played the monotonous conclusion of the accompaniment, which suggested the endless flatness of the desert lying in the endless burning heat. He got up from the piano, walked towards Lady Caryll, bent over her, and said—

"Shall I sing that at my concert? Does it move you? Tell me—or let me see for myself."

And he bent lower to gaze close into her long eyes. They were shining calmly. Her white cheeks looked as if they would be cold to the touch, and her hands lay still. Monsieur Anneau stared at her with fierce astonishment.

"Do you not feel such music?" he said. "Ah! I sing badly. Mon Dieu! I cannot sing—if you can still look like that!"

His large and dark face was hot with the effort he had been making. Now tears rose in his great, staring eyes.

"You sang superbly," said Sir Reuben's voice near the door.

The creak of a chair was audible as he got up, and the shuffling tread of his feet on the parquet floor as he came forward. Monsieur Anneau was surprised, but he did not start. Sir Reuben's small figure stood by him in the twilight. The wrinkled face was contorted as if by emotion.

"You sang as if you had the soul of the East in you," he continued.

"I have it in me when I sing that song," replied Monsieur Anneau.

He had made so great, so exciting an effort, that even his body cried out for a little enthusiasm from some listener.

"It was very strange and beautiful," Lady Caryll said quietly in her clear voice.

As she spoke Sir Reuben stretched his hand to the wall and turned on the electric light. The two men with their emotional faces were standing on either side of the white velvet chair in which Lady Caryll sat so calmly. As the light shone they looked at each other and then at her. Sir Reuben smiled. Monsieur Anneau went back to the piano and shut its lid. Perhaps by accident he let it fall rather heavily, with a noise that suggested finality. Standing by the piano he said—

"The man who composed that song wrote it in the desert. He never heard it. He died where he wrote it, and was buried in the sand beside the tent door."

He came up to Lady Caryll again.

"Think of that when I sing you that song again at my concert," he said.

"Why?" she asked, touching the hand of Sir Reuben, which lay on the arm of her chair.

"It may make you feel its force more keenly."

"To think of the grave of a man I never knew, never even saw?" she answered.

Monsieur Anneau said good-bye.

As he went out Sir Reuben laughed softly to himself.

When Monsieur Anneau reached his hotel he shut himself up in his room alone, and denied himself to every one. He was in the strange and horrible condition of a powerful man who, for the first time, begins to lose faith in his power, begins to waver, and to feel weakness and irresolution. He flung himself down on a sofa and remained very still for a long while, looking older than he really was, despite his dyed hair and beard. After a time he began to hold a silent colloquy with his art, with this thing that he had for so long made the servant of his pleasures and of his vices. He seemed to look it in the face, and to question it, and to feel that it grew obstinate, or stupid, or elusive, that it held back something from him, and so was no longer completely his servant. Then he recalled, as if speaking to it, the memory of how, in the past, he had most diligently been its slave, toiling hereafter to have its services at his command. He felt like a man who has made a bargain—I will do all this for you if you will do all this for me—and who finds himself betrayed. He grew bitter, as men do grow bitter with their art, which can come to be like a living mistress, and to seem to have a person and a countenance even as it has a name. He reproached it, cursed it, most pitiful thing of all—furiously regretted the sacrifices he had made for it. He wished that it were china—to break, a dog—to kick, a woman—to stab. He was the more embittered because he was physically fatigued. Often had he sung through a whole opera to some great audience, and been at the end less tired than he was by his effort of the afternoon. Only his temper supported him against exhaustion. Lady Caryll drew his vitality from him and returned him nothing. His passion for influence over others, his music, his genius, his powerful appearance and impressive manner, his determination and energy, all these combined beat upon the senses of this girl. And she was like a rock, splitting a wave into a thousand white drops of spray.

As he had spoken his last words to her he had seen her touch the hand of Sir Reuben, and now he said to himself again, really with doubt—"Can she love that brown wreck—her husband?" He felt it to be impossible. But then how consummately she acted, with such quietude too, such absence of effort! And then suddenly he remembered that all the time he was singing his last song Sir

Reuben must have been sitting quietly at the end of the room. She must have been aware of it.

He sprang up from the sofa, and walked up and down the room, moving rather as if he were upon the stage and desired to fix the eyes of two or three thousand people upon his mere allure.

Of course she knew it, and disguised the impression that the song and its singing must have made upon her. Her glittering coldness was a marvellously clever trick. He felt comforted and forgave music, realising that he had done it an injustice. And he resolved next time he was alone with Lady Caryll to elicit from her some expression of the effect made upon her by the force of his genius. His opportunity soon came.

Three days before the concert he sat with her in the green chamber in which Aubrey had first seen her after her marriage. The weather had become excessively cold. There was skating on the artificial waters in the parks. Fog brooded over the snowy slopes that in summer were shady lawns, and wolves might well have felt at home in the thickets of Kensington Gardens. In such weather the whole atmosphere of London changes. It no longer seems an English city. Mystery deepens in its bleak thoroughfares where, by night, the demon linkmen flit, drawing wild patterns of colour upon the background of the fog with their flaming brands. The misery of the poor rushes to the surface of life, and the cry of the starving wails through the darkness like the cry of famished animals in a frost-bound forest.

But in Lady Caryll's green chamber the cry could not be heard. The fog could not enter there. The white eyes of the snow could not peer through the heavy curtains to watch her as she sat near the hearth, with the singer beside her. He had murmured a few commonplaces. She had carelessly replied. Now he said quietly—

"My friend was at peace in his desert grave when I sang his song to you the other day. For he knew what I did not know. You cannot deceive the dead, Lady Caryll!"

A faint expression of surprise came into her face. "I don't care even to deceive the living," she answered. "Nor do I try to."

"I can't believe that—forgive me."

"Men always think a woman is deceiving somebody. It is their favourite delusion."

"Do you say, then, that you are a frank woman, and do not care to be a mystery?"

"Certainly."

"Yet you are perhaps the greatest mystery in London."

She laughed softly, holding one of her white hands to the wood fire. The jewels in the rings on it flashed in the dancing light.

"To whom?" she asked.

He thought for a moment, keeping his eagle eyes on her face.

"To that boy who lives here," he said.

"Mr. Herrick?"

"Yes."

"To any one else?"

"Shall I say—to me also?"

She laughed again as if with a genuine amusement.

"You had better include the whole city. You had better include Sir Reuben," she said.

"I certainly should include him," Monsieur Anneau said.

"You would be wrong."

"I cannot think so."

"I assure you that no other husband ever understood his wife so perfectly and completely as Sir Reuben understands me. That is why we are so happy together."

"You are really happy?"

"Then you think I look sad?"

She shot him a glance that was radiant, that was luminous with a cold joy. He shivered, and drew nearer to the fire. He felt as if his force were turned to feebleness by this girl. She was like the snow that was falling outside, manifesting a soft and inflexible power upon the works of nature.

"If you were sad you might choose to look radiantly happy," he replied. "Many women do that."

"How foolish and absurd of them!"

"Perhaps it pays them to act. They receive their salary like the actresses upon the stage—like me."

"When you play high priests—people who would bore you to tears in real life."

"They are glorified by music."

"As those women you speak of are glorified by the paint on their cheeks, the belladonna in their eyes."

"Why do you speak like that of music and then claim that you are frank? Your husband is not here, as he was the other afternoon."

He spoke with a bold significance, drawing his chair quietly a little nearer to hers. She did not move, or appear to notice his movement. But, returning to his first remark, she said—

"What did your dead friend know in his desert grave? You haven't told me."

"'That you were acting indifference to his wonderful song, to his swan song."

"Why should I do that?"

"Because your husband was sitting in the corner of the dark room all the time that I was singing it."

"You give strange reasons for indifference."

"Not at all. But I am jealous for my dead friend's power."

Lady Caryll looked into the fire. Keeping her eyes there, and away from Monsieur Anneau's, she said, rather softly and carelessly—

"Ah! Not for your own?"

"Mine!" he exclaimed, and the almost childish pride of the worshipped singer peeped out in him. "Mine is in my own keeping. I can take care of it."

He paused—she said nothing.

"Well?" he exclaimed almost irritably.

"You wish me to say something. What? Tell me and I will say it."

He recovered himself. The trickle of sarcasm in her voice cooled the sudden heat of his mind.

"Tell me the truth," he said. "You were moved by that song the other day, but you would not show it."

"Why?"

"I have told you—because of your husband's presence."

"But he is fond of music, and was moved himself. You saw that?"

"I was not looking at his face, but at yours."

"And that——?"

"Expressed no feeling, no emotion. Yet, I had sung with my whole heart and spirit—never have I sung better."

"You think I did not choose to show how much you moved me because my husband was in the room?"

"I think so."

Lady Caryll laughed softly again, and just then Sir Reuben came in.

He had been in Hatton Garden, among the diamond merchants. His wife welcomed him with her happy eyes.

CHAPTER XVII

On the day of his concert Monsieur Anneau felt doubtful of himself, almost nervous. His operatic mind was generally fixed upon some "scene" in the future, and when he thought quite naturally, he was inclined to think in acts, and instinctively to lay out the episodes of his life as a stage manager lays out the business of a music drama or of a play. He had now arrived at the Lady Caryll episode of his life. It seemed to him a terribly important one. It had come to seem so from the cold and impenetrable opposition to his purpose that hung round her like a mist round a frosty day. And Monsieur Anneau, always on the alert for great finales, in which his mighty voice and loud, violent, and forcible nature stood him in good stead, had decided that the finale of this opera, in which Lady Caryll and he were heroine and hero, must be reached on the day of his concert in her house.

The day dawned in cold and fog. He was magnificently excited. He did not go out. He resolved not to receive any visitor during the day. He wished to test his force, to feel the muscles of his influence. So he tried his voice, singing some of the songs of the night. And he knew that as a vocalist he would be at his best, which meant that he would be at his best as a man. While he sang alone, he imagined Lady Caryll there, before him, fixing her grey eyes on his, listening to the superb warmth, the changing raptures of his voice. She would look cold as a diamond lit only by the moon. He knew that. He was prepared for it, and was determined that her aspect should not disconcert him. Yet he was doubtful of himself. Through a long career he had grown accustomed to judge of the effect he was creating with his eyes, to expect and to look for symptoms shown by the body; deepening or dying colour, the shadows that unshed tears paint in their home, the shifting of lips, the tension of hands that tell the tale of the heart.

Lady Caryll, he knew, would grant him none of these customary gifts. To be with her was to be with darkness, seeming to see it, because one sees nothing. He was prepared to sing to the changelessness of her serenity. He was determined to believe that this serenity told the tale only of her cleverness, and not the true tale of her exact emotion. Yet he was nervous, he was doubtful in this determination, haunted secretly by the wonder whether this glittering and joyous calm were her setting forth of a fact and not of a fiction. But it could not be, for she was a woman. He determined that he would not enfeeble himself by striving still, as he had striven, to obtain from this woman the visible tribute given him so often by so many others. Instead of doing that, he would believe in a secret performance behind the mask, in the wild and flickering action of flames under the snow, dancing in obedience to his will. He would divine what he could not see. It must exist. He would not doubt it. And, in some solitary moment, he would appeal to it. He would force the flames to pierce, like glowing spears, through the snow. He could not think that this action would be beyond his power for ever.

Yet he was strangely doubtful, and began to fear lest this timidity might cripple his effort.

Thinking of this, he got up from his piano, and strode to the window. The fog hung in Brook Street, yellow and lethargic. Beneath it lay the frost, wrapped in its icy dreams. London was strangely motionless, and was not singing, or, if it still sang, he could not hear the song. Had he not been himself a singer he would have opened the window, and leaned out into this spurious and dreary travesty of night. For he had the desire to stretch forward into something that comes to excited men. While he was standing by the window, he heard behind him the sound of the door of his room shutting. He turned round. By the door, close to the yellow wall, stood a pale man, atrociously dressed, with a terrified and yet determined expression upon his face, which was abominably thin. He held in his left hand a parcel wrapped in brown paper. Monsieur Anneau looked at him in silence, stiff with surprise. The man touched the parcel, and the singer noticed that he had the hand of a pianist.

"You are the great singer," the man said in English, but with a strong foreign accent. "To-night you give a concert. I am starving. I have written a song. It is here. I wish you to sing it to-night at your concert. I borrowed the money with which I bribed the servant to let me in. I gave it to him—all of it, and I say that I am starving."

The man was silent. He now began to tremble excessively, and Monsieur Anneau could hear the shuffle of the brown paper under his shaking hand. Then, with an effort that was hideous in its violence, he controlled himself.

"Sing my song to-night," he said. "Or I shall be dead to morrow."

And then he burst into a passion of tears, pressing his face against the wall.

Monsieur Anneau strode forward. He did not speak to or touch the man, but snatched from the trembling hand the song, and brusquely tore it out of its covering. Hearing him do this, the man wheeled round, a wild excitement dawning in his face, over which the shameful tears were running. Monsieur Anneau was reading the words of the song. They were French, and told of the last sea journey of a pearl-fisher through the still waters of the East. He went to seek the most beautiful pearl in all the world for the maiden he loved. It lay far down in the shadow of the sea. He stood upon the pearl bank, murmured his prayer and the name of the maiden, and cast himself into the deep, sinking down from the world where walked his dreams and his great desire. The water resisted him. He felt that its blue hands were striving to press him back, that its voices were telling him to begone. He heeded them not, but sank down with open eyes watching for the pearl. He saw it where it lay asleep in the purple shadows, and caught it softly in his hand. Then he turned to rise. But the depth to which he had come was very great, and he felt a terrible oppression stealing upon him. It seemed to him now that, while he had been sinking in the sea, the maiden had come to the pearl-bank where he had prayed—surely a thousand years ago—and was watching for his return, and was extending her little hands towards the wave, to clasp his gift and the gift of the sea. Her dark eyes were full of a passion of desire as she leaned down. And surely he could hear her voice faintly calling to him from above, as if from some heaven very far away. He strove to answer, to cry, "I have the pearl, my love, my love! It is here!" But the oppression deepened around him, and drew nearer. And the sound of her calling voice died away. Now he could no longer feel that the pearl was in his hand. Yet it was there. Mechanically he strove to rise. Then he strove no longer. Everything faded. He was a dead man drifting in the sea with its greatest treasure hidden in his lifeless hand. And always, far above upon the pearl-bank, the maiden leaned over the wave, crying, "Come to me, come! Bring me my pearl!" And her voice changed into a horrible wailing. And she held out her little hands for ever to the sea, growing ghostly with desire, and ivory wan as the days gave themselves to the years.

When he had read the verses Monsieur Anneau glanced at the music. His large eyes were blazing, and with one hand he pulled at his beard. The man stood by the wall gazing at him with an anxiety that was animal in its intensity.

"Go to the piano," said Monsieur Anneau.

He had not spoken to the intruder till he said this. And now he scarcely looked at the man. The song was everything to him. The composer was less than nothing. The man went to the piano, trembling. He stretched out his hands, which were horribly thin, and struck some notes.

"Wrong! wrong!" cried Monsieur Anneau, with harsh impatience.

The man started as if stung by the exclamation. There were still tears in his hungry eyes, and he was on the verge of complete physical prostration. But, with a pitiful effort, he controlled himself and played the opening symphony. Then Monsieur Anneau sang. He read music easily at first sight. But now he did more than this. He gave an interpretation of the meaning of the song that was superb. When he had finished, the composer's hands fell from the key-board before he could strike the last chord. He had fainted. He had not known that his song was so beautiful.

When he had revived, and had been given some food and wine, brought by the amazed servant whom he had bribed, Monsieur Anneau said to him—

"I will sing your song to-night at my concert. It will be the last thing in the programme."

The man said nothing. He felt as if he were the core of a world that spun like a zoetrope, and roared as it spun. Monsieur Anneau sat down at his writing-table, drew a cheque, and gave it to the man.

"I wish you to accompany your song to-night," he said. "Come to Number 100 Park Lane at eleven o'clock."

"I have no clothes," the man said. Monsieur Anneau wrote some words on a sheet of note-paper, and gave it to the man.

"Go to Winnington, New Bond Street, get some, and have them placed to my account. That will do!"

The man went out without another word, gazing at the cheque which he held in his shaking hand with eyes that were full of terror, the terror that seizes the imagination encompassed by the violence of change.

Monsieur Anneau, left alone, flung himself down on a couch and devoured the song with eyes that were full—not of terror but of triumph.

CHAPTER XVIII

THE fog that lay over London deepened as night came on. Lady St. Ormyn was in despair. She feared that people would be afraid to venture out, and that Monsieur Anneau's concert would be a fiasco. As her maid dressed her in scarlet silk, she said bitter things about the climate of her native land, and she almost burst into tears when she received a message from her coachman saying that nearly all traffic was stopped, and that he did not think it would be safe to attempt to get to Park Lane.

"Tell him to come round at once," she cried, smothering her flushed face with powder, and pushing up one of her thick and dark eyebrows which was drooping—perhaps from depression at the tragedy of the weather. "The horses are not his, but mine, and if I choose, I shall kill them."

Ten minutes later she hurried over the strip of carpet into the brougham. A thick, swimming blackness, like a gigantic witch's brew, stirred wearily in the cauldron of the town. Every landmark was submerged in it and utterly lost. There were no gas-lamps, no railings, no houses, no people. Even the ground, slippery with the frost, was scarcely visible under one's feet. Faint sounds, soft and spectral cries, ghostly footfalls, the thin grating of distant traffic in cautious and hesitating motion, shivered through the bitter atmosphere, suggesting some far away world full of timorous activities. Lady St. Ormyn's bosom quivered under the cold jewels that decorated it. She wrapped herself in her furs and lay back. The horses moved on slowly and stopped. She twisted the long gloves that she was beginning to draw on into a ball, and then frantically unwound them. The horses started. The left wheels of the carriage struck the kerb and grated against it. The horses stopped again, and she heard the gruff murmur of the coachman's voice speaking to the groom. She violently let down the window and put her head out into the darkness, exposing her astonished diamond stars to the terror of the night.

"Go on," she vociferated. "Chalmers, go on at once! Whip the horses, whip them!"

The coachman leaned sideways and backwards towards her. He was invisible, but she heard his thick voice.

"I daren't, my lady," he said. "It's a cruel night."

"I tell you to whip the horses."

"If I do, my lady, there'll be an accident."

"I order you to whip the horses. If you don't take my orders, you leave my service to-morrow."

The lash fell on the satin backs. There was a jerk, a moment of quick progress, then a crash and a battering of hoofs on pavement. Two flickering lights sprang up by the carriage window, and a voice that suggested innumerable casks of gin, cried—

"D'yer want to put 'em down the airey, stoopid? Where the blazes are yer a-drivin' to?"

The whip fell again. The coachman was losing his temper. Lady St. Ormyn, thrusting her head once more through the window, beheld two filthy and degraded-looking men holding torches.

"Give us a bob, lydy," said one, "and we'll tike yer anywheres."

"If you'll——" began Lady St. Ormyn.

There was another crash. The carriage lurched forward. One of the horses was down. Then there was a noise of smashing woodwork. He was expressing his surprise in the usual way of horses—with his hoofs. The tattered linkmen ran forward, swearing happily. They foresaw a fortune, and their oaths came in a most joyful profusion. A moment later a scarlet woman, whose hair bristled with diamonds, stood in the road joining a shrill voice to theirs.

That night was one of the tragedies of Lady St. Ormyn's existence When, half an hour later, she regained her house, escorted by an alarmed groom and the two roughs, who backed before her, as if before a royal personage, extending their grimy hands for lucre, anger and disappointment had almost filched the semblance of humanity from her disordered features.

The hysterics that preceded her retirement to bed were of so complicated a nature, and so many-sided, that her maid gave her warning on the following day, on the ground—as stated in the servants' hall—that she was "a Christian woman, and didn't want to know anything about the other place before her time came, if it was ever so."

Meanwhile Monsieur Anneau was very heroically bearing with the fog that had destroyed so many plans. His concert was fixed to begin at eleven o'clock. At that hour only sixteen or twenty intrepid people who lived close by had put in an appearance. The white chairs in the music-room stood ghostly and deserted among the azaleas and the roses. Lady Caryll expressed her regret. She wore a white gown, very plainly made. On her breast shone the uncut jewels of a marvellous Indian necklace that Sir Reuben had just given her—an emerald, a ruby, a blue sapphire, a turquoise, a diamond, a white sapphire, and a topaz in an old silver setting. In her hair was a silver ornament in which more jewels gleamed. As she stood in the almost empty drawing-room, she looked like a radiant spirit striving after a semblance of sorrow. Aubrey watched her while she spoke to the singer.

"It seems cruel to expect you to sing such a programme to such an audience," she said.

"I wish my audience were composed of only one lover—of music," he answered.

"Ah! you mean Sir Reuben!" she said, with an airy malice. "He admires your singing of that desert song. He can talk of nothing else."

"I have another song more beautiful for to-night," said Monsieur Anneau, glancing round as if looking for some one.

"What is it about?"

"It is about a woman and a pearl."

An intent expression floated up in her eyes.

Just then the drawing-room door was opened and a footman called unintelligibly a foreign name. A man, horribly thin, horribly pale, with painfully excited eyes and twitching lips, entered the room. He looked nervous and as if he were being hunted. He was well dressed, but wore his clothes so badly that they seemed ridiculous on him. Perhaps his age was thirty-five. His dark hair was carefully brushed, but his black tie was a flourishing mess, and his shirt-front was impossible. Lady Caryll murmured to Monsieur Anneau—

"I don't know this dreadful-looking man."

"I told him to come."

"Why?"

"He is the composer of the song about the pearl."

The man was standing with his terrible eyes fixed upon Monsieur Anneau, who now went up to him, asked his name, and formally presented him to Lady Caryll. The few guests examined him with scarcely concealed astonishment. Aubrey wondered who on earth he was, and how he had got in; wondered still more when Lady Caryll, with an eager smile, began to talk to him.

"You have composed a song?"

The man bowed awkwardly.

"About a pearl?"

"Yes, madame."

"The music only?"

"And the words, madame."

"When did you write it?"

"Yesterday, madame."

"Only then!" said Monsieur Anneau, in deep-voiced surprise. "What made you think of it so suddenly?"

The man hesitated, looking feverishly about the beautiful room, and at the few people gathered in it.

"I heard—I knew—I heard you were going to sing to-night, monsieur. It was in a paper," he stammered.

"Well?"

"And more. In the paper it spoke of jewels, of a lady who had wonderful jewels."

Lady Caryll was listening with deep attention.

"Go on," said Monsieur Anneau.

"I was—I was ill—starving—I thought if I could write a song about a jewel, perhaps you would sing it to the lady."

He was painfully embarrassed. Lady Caryll spoke to him in a soft voice.

"And so you wrote this song for me?"

The man bowed again.

"Is it pretty?"

A sudden fierce enthusiasm leapt up in the man's pinched face.

"When he sings it," he said, in a husky voice, "it is beautiful."

Suddenly he caught Monsieur Anneau's hand and kissed it adoringly. The singer looked delighted. Such a scene did not embarrass him in the least. Was he not a Parisian? He cast an impressive and powerful glance at Lady Caryll. But her eyes were fixed upon the pale and hungry man who was losing his head, overwhelmed by this great episode in his wretched life.

Mrs. Luffa Parkinson was announced. She entered in her usual rippling manner. She had come through the fog in a bath-chair attended by two footmen. It was past eleven. Lady St. Ormyn did not arrive. It seemed useless to wait, and Lady Caryll decided that the concert should begin. As her guests began to move towards the music-room she said to the starving composer—

"Come with me. I wish you to sit by me till you accompany your song."

Then, as she walked with him through the warm and scented corridors towards the music-room, she added—

"Tell me the story of your song. What happens to the pearl?"

He looked at her as if she were a goddess, he a poor beggar suddenly led into heaven. He stammered out the story, striving painfully to hide his emotion. She listened with intensity to his halting words. At the close her clear white face was like a tragic mask.

"Why did you not give the maiden her pearl?" she said; and her voice thrilled the man.

She had turned her head as she walked, and was glancing at him keenly. But now his fear seemed leaving him. He looked at her and replied, almost boldly—

"Ah, madame, when one is starving one cannot give, and then it seems to one too that death attends every effort, and that no one is really happy. Is there happiness on the earth, madame?"

"There is happiness in the sea," she said. "Your dead man is happy, for he has the pearl."

They were now in the softly illuminated music-room. Aubrey came into it last. He was greatly touched by Lady Caryll's treatment of the poor composer, and by her keeping him to sit near her at the concert.

"She is full of sympathy for the poor and friendless," he said to himself. His thought flew to Diamond and to her humble family; and for the first time he was able to imagine Lady Caryll in Milk Court, sharing in simple sorrows, partaking happily in simple joys.

The little audience began to settle itself in the room. Mrs. Luffa Parkinson was full of regret. As she sat down by Sir Reuben, she exclaimed—

"Why is it, Sir Reuben, that atmospheric conditions are allowed to destroy the calculations of genius? Who sends a fog like this to shatter the plans of the world's greatest singer? I shall ask my confessor, Father Grimble."

"Would it not be better to make inquiry of the clerk of the weather?" said Sir Reuben.

"Oh, I can't endure clerks, they are so uncultured. They read those dreadful farthing magazines that answer questions. Long ago, when I was an atheist——"

She chattered theologically. Sir Reuben listened with his eyes on Lady Caryll. The mental proceedings of cinnamon-coloured ladies when they were atheists had long ceased to interest him.

It seemed almost as if the snow that wrapped the outer world had entered into this room, had floated upon the white walls, the white chairs—so many of which were empty. Only the scented warmth, the sweet breath of flowers, destroyed the illusion. The grand piano that stood on the small platform was open. A mass of roses almost concealed it. The few guests rustled as they settled themselves down here and there in luxurious attitudes. Mrs. Luffa Parkinson began to look slightly abandoned in anticipation of the approaching orgy of the talent she loved. Sir Reuben, who sat very low, appeared strangely shrivelled at her side. Aubrey was with a typical London girl—all royal fringe, weary chatter and bare shoulders. She told him a story about a supper-party, and asked him a few dozen questions about racing. He spoke softly to her and looked at Lady Caryll as a man looks at magic, for he thought he saw the root-humanity, God in his creature, shining in her eyes as she gazed at the poor composer, who moved among the white chairs and the flowers as one who treads the mazes of a dream so beautiful that it is terrible. She sat down at the side of the room at some little distance from the platform. The composer sat timidly by her. Despite the good clothes he wore, it was evident that he feared to defile the whiteness of his chair. In his mind he still wore the rags of poverty. Monsieur Anneau, followed by his usual London accompanist, a thin gentleman with an English face and Polish hair, stepped upon the platform. There was a flutter of applause. Monsieur Anneau bowed as if to a continent. He glanced round for Lady Caryll, found her, and looked confident. Sir Reuben's flexible lips curved in a mischievous smile, and Aubrey involuntarily clenched his hands.

"I'm sure you're a dab at boxing," whispered his lively companion. "I like a man who can make good play with his tuppennies."

Aubrey wished her dead.

The accompanist ran airily about over the keyboard, making a light noise, as indefinite as the chirping of grasshoppers in the heart of a summer's day. Then he became definite. Conversation was hushed. Monsieur Anneau called on all his experience of music, on all his experience of women, and began his brilliantly arranged programme.

It was a procession of sentiment, a quick passing of the passions. Many composers had given their hearts to make this procession, and some their frivolities. For with the priests and the enthusiasts, mingling among the devotees, there must be dancers and those who posture and leap towards the fire of the torches. Monsieur Anneau soon felt that he had seized and held all the women in the white room except one. Mrs. Parkinson lay back as one who floats upon an ocean of soft, hysteric ecstasy. Even Aubrey's companion began to look grave, and to forget all about fists and horses. Her large eyes were dewy beneath her cloudy fringe. Her round cheeks shone with rosy heats. Monsieur Anneau felt an abrupt contempt for her easy emotion. Only Lady Caryll sat negligently in her chair, looking towards him with quiet and observant eyes. She seemed to watch the procession of the passions as a savant watches through a microscope the movements of insects, only she watched with less intensity. He sang of Margaret at the door, of the man who saw the Lorelei as he rode through the forest hunting, and who let his dogs leap on while he stood gazing through the leaves at the wicked and lovely angel singing above the rushing Rhine. He sang of Mimi, who died for her student lover; of Pierrette, who was lifted into the moon when she wept for the false Pierrot; of the little German peasant girl, whose life was ruined because she had once heard the jingle of spurs as a blond soldier rode by on the dusty highway; of Fatima, with the deep and long Eastern eyes, who crouched at evening in her coloured doorway of the mysterious Kasbah, and listened to the wailing of the pipes, and smelt the smoke of the incense and of the Indian perfumes, and thought of the Breton sailor, who had loved her for an hour in a black night, and who had sailed for France and his bright-eyed *fiancée* in the morning. He sang the desert song, watching for a shiver, or the parted lips through which escapes a sigh. He saw the poor composer, torn by his splendid singing, holding the arms of his chair with spectral hands, forgetting his fear, his poverty, his future as he gave himself to the influence of the music that was the air in which alone his soul could live. But the one woman escaped him still, even as a white ghost escapes the grasp of the man who adores and tries to seize an apparition.

Anger rose up in him again, and he forgot his resolution to expect no outward sign of feeling from Lady Caryll, and to divine the fire leaping beneath the snow. He forgot it because, with his quick intuition, he knew that this calm was not assumed, but was real and deeply rooted. Something like despair seized him as he stood there among the flowers. For a moment he slightly lost control of his great voice, and sang an ornament roughly. The slip recalled his artist's pride and gave him greater power, as one sin may increase the holiness of a deep hearted saint. All the white room swam before his eyes in a mist of shadowy faces and floating forms, as if the snow and the fog had entered. The flowers and the jewels worn by the women seemed to retreat. He saw their colours as from a long distance, and the sound of the piano was surely far away in the air. Then everything became painfully close and clear. Each note struck by the accompanist was unnaturally definite. Each form in the chamber was accentuated till it looked grotesque. His own voice hammered upon his brain murderously. When he finished the song he was singing, he retired for a moment from the platform. The feeble but continuous applause of the small excited audience recalled him. He bowed with shut eyes, and again retired. He sat for a little while alone in the room that served as the artists' room. The gentleman with the English face and the Polish hair approached him to adulate.

"Please leave me, Monsieur," he said, rather fiercely.

The gentleman contained his admiration with an uneasy smile, half deprecatory, half offended. Monsieur Anneau leaned his head on his hands; they were burning, and his temples throbbed. Was his fire to be overborne thus by ice? He felt on the edge of his faculties, strung up to something far beyond concert pitch, and as if he might either sing the last two songs on his programme better than he had ever sung in his life, or break down altogether. He was so uncertain of himself as he sat there that he absolutely debated for a moment whether to go again on to the platform, or to send a message that he was unwell and could not continue. He remembered all his triumphs over women and that his music had never failed him yet. Perhaps even now he was on the verge of his greatest success. Intense depression of soul often immediately precedes an exceptional triumph. What artist does not know that? He rang the bell, and asked the man who came to bring the composer of the pearl song to him. Almost immediately the composer entered; his thin face was alive with intense expression; he hurried forward and seemed about to fall at Monsieur Anneau's feet. The singer checked him. Looking into the man's eyes, in which an almost hideous fire of excitement was burning, he said slowly—

"I feel fatigued—ill."

The man's face turned grey as ashes.

"I am not sure whether I can go on again," Monsieur Anneau continued.

The man dropped at his feet, seized his burning hands, and cried out piteously—

"My pearl song, Monsieur—my song! You must sing it, you must—you must!"

"Why?" said Monsieur Anneau.

"The lady—the beautiful lady like a white dream; she is waiting for it. All the time—when you sing of Gretchen, of the Lorelei, of Fatima—all the time she is waiting for my song, for my pearl."

Monsieur Anneau hesitated. A sudden jealousy stirred in his heart. Then he looked at the man at his feet, mad with anxiety, feverish with fear and hope, haggard, thin, with the beast mark of poverty and of starvation on him. He burst into a laugh. How fantastic to be jealous of such a creature, ridiculous in his new, ready-made clothes.

"We must not keep the lady waiting," he said. "But I shall only sing your song; I shall omit the other. Come!"

The man bounded up and followed him trembling. Monsieur Anneau made no explanation to the audience of the change in the programme. He did not care whether people were disappointed or not. As he came forward he looked towards Lady Caryll. Her eyes were fixed on the composer; then she glanced at the programme, rose from her seat, and came close to the platform. She sat down softly near the piano. The composer turned his flaming eyes on her. An authority had suddenly come into his bearing and manner. He no longer seemed awkward, but powerful; not merely at home with his audience, but born to dominate them. His expression did not timidly ask, it demanded Lady Caryll's attention. He played a soft prelude that had much resemblance to certain Indian music. Lady Caryll leaned forward; her breast touched the red azaleas that made a bright cloud along the platform. Then Monsieur Anneau sang. He was fired by the sight of this creature who escaped him, close though she was, with her white breast against the red flowers. And, with the complete impudence that was one of his gifts, he sang to her, ignoring the rest of the audience. The composer played to her, but in a totally different spirit, with the delicate fervour of a young father showing to a friend his beautiful first child. Aubrey, watching, felt Monsieur Anneau's exclusion of the audience to be an insult, the composer's to be a compliment. Sir Reuben cared little for either. To him Lady Caryll was always in the harem, safe as a veiled woman of the East. As Monsieur Anneau sang the prayer of the pearl-fisher upon the bank above the sea, he saw that Lady Caryll stirred at last from her cold slumber of the soul, and he thought of her suddenly as the maiden for whom the fisher sought the pearl. He was the man looking down upon the shining water that hid the secret in its shadow. The song was a great drama of two passions. They acted it together. But it became real. He dived into the sea, the last cry of the prayer upon his lips. She knew, as he sank down out of reach of the sun and of her glittering eyes—she knew of his journey. The darkness of the deep sea came upon him, blue moving dimness, and all those murmuring voices that speak together in the bosom of the sea. And now he saw the pale gleam of the pearl, and he knew that Caryll stood upon the pearl bank far above him. The heavy waters prevented him from seeing her, but he knew that she was there watching for his return with passionate eyes. And he caught the great pearl in his hand. How smooth and wet it was. He held it with the tenderness of a woman and turned to rise. Then he felt the horror of the sea's resistance. It was pressing him down like one who presses violent hands upon the throat of a thief who seeks to rob him in the night. He fought against it. For Caryll was leaning down to the sea with outstretched hands. She was calling, and her faint voice mingled with all the angry whispering voices of the sea. He strove to answer her, to cry aloud that he had the pearl. But his voice was faint and frail, like the voice in a shell of the sea, and an immense weariness overtook him. Everything was dulled and all the world was full of heaviness. Still he strove to rise. Then he strove no longer. He died, holding the pearl fast in his hand. And it was after death that, as in a vision, he saw Caryll leaning ever over the wave with outstretched piteous hands, whiter, whiter, becoming spectral, thin, almost like a hag, but always with the flaming eyes of youth, the shining hair of youth. And, as after death, he heard her voice crying, "Give me my pearl!" At last it was hoarse and hideous. It might have been the faint howl of a wolf had there not been in it the thrilling note of a human soul.

"Hark, Monsieur! Oh, listen, listen," said the composer in the artists' room. "They are moved! You have touched their hearts! They cry 'Encore.' They cry it to my song."

"Those people would encore my death agony, if I showed them that I suffered the torments of purgatory," said Monsieur Anneau fiercely.

He flung himself into a chair and hid his face in his hands. The little, persistent noise continued, and increased in the hidden room.

"Go—go, bow to them, show yourself to them," he cried to the composer. "It is your song. Go, go!"

The composer went, shaking. He had composed much music, but never had he been applauded before, except by one or two friends, poor, wretched like himself. Monsieur Anneau sat waiting for him to return. He did not return. At length the noise of applause completely died away. Monsieur Anneau's attention was attracted by the silence. The intense excitement which had followed the superb effort he had made in singing faded within him. He felt seized by a reaction, cold and fatigued. Then he heard a shuffling tread, and he knew that it announced the approach of Sir Reuben. In fact, he entered smiling, held out his dry brown hand and clasped the hand of the singer.

"I have heard all the great vocalists of the world in many years," he said. "You surpassed them all to-night. And then, too, you are a discoverer of hidden genius."

"I! What genius?" said Monsieur Anneau.

"The composer of the last song. He is with my wife now. Will you not come to her? We shall go to supper in a moment."

He stood by the door, holding it with his hand and still smiling. Monsieur Anneau thought there was malice in the eyes that watched him. He got up and came forward, staring at Sir Reuben almost stupidly. He was wondering what could be the cause of the quick gleam of triumph in the face of his host.

They passed out into the music-room together. The few people were scattered about, talking eagerly after their enforced silence.

Mrs. Luffa Parkinson was ostentatiously giving way to the emotion wakened in her by the final song. Two young men ministered to her, while she lay back in a large, deep chair murmuring hysterically—

"Oh, poor thing! Poor dear thing! Oh, give her the pearl! Oh, give her the pearl!"

Observing the entrance of Monsieur Anneau, she had a relapse, and, grasping the sleeve of his coat as he passed her, she cried, in a piping soprano—

"Oh, Monsieur Anneau—cruel—cruel! Give the dear thing her pearl! Poor little me's so upset!"

He spoke suavely to her, but his eyes sought Lady Caryll. He saw her standing in deep conversation with the composer. And he was startled by the strangeness of her demeanour. She had unfurled a big white fan, which she moved mechanically to and fro. Her face was flushed. Her eyes were very bright and staring, and she was speaking with extraordinary animation, as if carrying on a violent argument or protesting vehemently against something. The hand that was not holding the fan grasped the folds of her dress tightly. The composer stood silently listening to her. His eyes were cast down, and his thin lips were pressed tightly together. There was a curiously obstinate expression about those lips.

"Go to Lady Caryll," Sir Reuben said to the singer. "She wants to thank you for your magnificent performance."

And he bent down to give some pity to poor Mrs. Parkinson, who absolutely declined to recover from the prostration caused by her too lively realisation of imaginary events.

Monsieur Anneau approached Lady Caryll. She was too much engrossed by the conversation she was carrying on with the composer to notice him.

"You must do it," he heard her say. "You must do it for me."

The composer looked down on the floor and made no answer.

"But why don't you answer me?" she exclaimed, almost angrily. "Ah, Monsieur Anneau!"

The singer was standing before her. She could no longer ignore him. Her hand fell from the folds of her gown, and the fire died out of her face as she thanked him for his singing.

"It was superb," she said. "You have no rival."

"You were moved?" he asked, looking at her with violent curiosity.

"Oh yes. Every one was moved."

"But you! For it is so difficult to touch your heart. It is so difficult even to stir—forgive me—your temper."

A very faint smile hovered about the composer's thin lips. Lady Caryll saw it.

"Those who can stir the dog that sleeps possess the opiate that can make it sleep again," she said, looking at the composer. "Just as the hands that can make a terrible crescendo upon the pianoforte can make an exquisite diminuendo."

Monsieur Anneau shot an angry glance at this man whom he had lifted out of the gutter, and who now seemed the hero of some curious and inexplicable intimacy with the woman who ignored the power that triumphed over others.

"Caryll," said Sir Reuben's voice, "shall we go in to supper? I will take in the Duchess, and you——"

Lady Caryll turned hastily.

"As we are so few," she said, "perhaps we had better be quite informal. Don't you think it will be pleasanter?" she added, speaking to one or two people near her.

They agreed. A heterogeneous move was made towards the supper-room, in which were several small oval tables. Lady Caryll had the inevitable big-wig at her right hand. She made the composer sit at her left. Monsieur Anneau's angry astonishment was so great that he stood looking actually confused and almost stupid.

Sir Reuben touched his arm.

"Will you sit with my party?" he said. "Here, on the other side of the Duchess."

Sir Reuben enjoyed that supper immensely. He forced Monsieur Anneau to talk. He discussed music. The singer, who hated his art at that moment more than he hated the thought of death or the approach of old age, could scarcely find conventional words in which to reply. His eyes, which looked as if they had been polished, were incessantly turned towards Lady Caryll's table. Aubrey, too, often looked towards her. He loved her that night as we love those who have been mysterious to us, and who suddenly seem to fulfil our half-timid ideal of them. Caryll's marked honour paid to the most obscure man present comforted Aubrey as a fire comforts a man who is cold. He felt like one who, reciting the Creed, suddenly beholds a vision of the Trinity whose existence his faith is affirming.

While Lady Caryll talked to the big-wig, the composer added one more excitement to the long list of his excitements of the day and night. Only when he was offered food did he know how near he had been to starvation. The first mouthful of soup sent a message to his poor body. It came like an animal to the cage bars. All the mental faculties were dumb, while the imperious body spoke. The servants glanced at the strange guest in cold astonishment. They were too well fed to be touched by pity for starvation. They simply thought that this extraordinary man was an unmannerly glutton. Lady Caryll knew better. She was not touched either. But she talked to the big-wig calmly, divining the new mental condition that would inevitably follow the bodily process going on in the composer. Towards the end of supper she turned and found, as she expected, a new man at her side. She spoke quietly to this new man on indifferent subjects, watching his oddly contented look, an expression so abrupt and novel in him that it rendered him almost self-satisfied in appearance. She was like a cat playing with a plump, sleepy, and ignorant mouse, that rolled beneath the velvet paw in voluptuous enjoyment. For a moment she felt the contempt for the physical side of men that almost every woman feels at some period of her life—generally at some period that immediately precedes a feminine triumph. The composer of the pearl song, in a condition of starvation, was obviously a man of genius. Well fed, he seemed a blinking, complacent bourgeois. She talked to him softly. He expanded, leaning back in his chair, sipping his champagne from time to time. She drew the conversation towards music. Easy tears shone in his eyes, from which the former fires had died away. He praised his goddess in flowing periods. Lady Caryll watched him impatiently. Then she spoke again of his song.

"You will change it?" she said.

A servant filled his glass.

"I will do anything for you, madame," he answered exuberantly.

He had a sensation that he was floating upwards on clouds, rather in the fashion of Margaret in Gounod's opera. Lady Caryll was the chief attendant houri. He blinked in the heavenly light.

"Anything," he repeated.

"Then let your diver rise from the sea and give the maiden her pearl. I hate these beautiful works of our day which end in unsatisfied desire. You must not be like all the others. You can venture to be original."

"I—I will be myself. Henceforward, madame, I will fear nothing."

He blinked again.

"Then change your song and bring it to me. It shall be sung everywhere. You shall be famous."

They rose from the supper-table. Around the composer the celestial æther swam and swirled.

Aubrey helped him to put on his tattered overcoat among the contemptuous footmen. Monsieur Anneau had only given him an order for a dress suit. He held Aubrey's hand and blessed him in French. Then he went into the fog sideways, singing—

"On a mis la graine en terre,
    Saute donc, la brune, au son du flûtieau !
En terre on a mis la graine,
    Saute donc, la brune, au son de la flûte !
En terre près du ruisseau,
    Au son de la flûte, au son du flûtieau !"

CHAPTER XIX

Lady Caryll's guests had melted away into the fog. Monsieur Anneau alone remained, and he lingered with the air of one about to depart and on the edge of his polite good-bye. Aubrey had disappeared to his rooms, and now Sir Reuben, with a hidden glee, said to the singer—

"I am going to have a cigar; will you join me? Ah! I daresay too much smoking is bad for the voice."

"And I must be going," Monsieur Anneau said.

He was standing up. Rather hastily Sir Reuben pressed his large hand and left the room before he could.

"I must be going," the singer repeated to Lady Caryll.

She extended her hand; as she did so the door closed behind Sir Reuben. Monsieur Anneau took her hand and held it.

"Good-night," she said. "A thousand thanks."

"Ah!" he exclaimed, "why are you so conventional with me, so unconventional with that wretched, hideous, absurd spectre who —who——"

He dropped her hand suddenly, flung himself down on a sofa, and leaned his face for a moment against his arm on the cushion.

"Why? why?" he repeated, looking at her with a violence he did not seek to conceal.

There was no surprise in her face. She sat down quietly.

"Who is the spectre?" she asked.

"The man I brought here, the composer of the song. I made his triumph; I gave him his success. He owes all to me, and then you ignore me, on such an evening. You devote yourself to him. Am I nothing?"

His jealous anger gathered while he was speaking. A sense of outrage overwhelmed him.

"Do you know what I have given up for you, Lady Caryll?" he continued, almost with bitterness. "Ah! you never read the American papers."

She smiled, rather as one smiles easily at a child when he shows his childishness.

"What did they say?"

"That I was mad to give up such an engagement—to lose so much money."

"Oh, money!" she said, with a note of profound indifference that stung him.

"You can say that?" he exclaimed. "You—but——"

He hesitated, looking at her. It was strange, but his habitual bold impudence with women began to waver before her bright and cold glance. Yet his excitement, engendered partly by the intense effort to conquer he had made in his singing, partly by the subsequent insult—so he considered it—that he had undergone at the hands of Lady Caryll, drove him on. He thought again of all he had lost in America and grew reckless.

"Do you wish to say that you are indifferent to money, then?" he asked, "that you think it is nothing to give up a fortune?"

The stress on the pronoun was bitter. She did not seem to notice it.

"I know that it is the accepted creed of men to-day that money is to be worshipped," she said.

"And of women? Mon Dieu! do you leave the women out?" he said. "Why, you—do you not love money?"

"I?" she said, and there was a note of genuine surprise in her voice. "Not at all."

"Yet you are here," he said.

The sneer was unmistakable and revealed his meaning completely.

"Monsieur Anneau," Lady Caryll said quietly, "do you know that though you are a genius you can be singularly stupid?"

In his excitement he had got up. Now he stood before her, and the dogged expression that came into his eyes made him look suddenly common, like a great dock labourer or a hulking navvy.

"You are here," he repeated almost threateningly. "You have given yourself, Miladi, for what you speak of so lightly in regard to others. I have yielded up a fortune to spend a few hours with you, to sing a few songs for you, to show you my heart and my desire in my music. Would you give up—ah! not even a fortune, I will not say that, but even one of your jewels——"

He stretched out his hand towards her throat while he spoke with the quick freedom of gesture that his nationality and his long training for the stage had made his second language. Lady Caryll's face changed. It looked peaked, pinched with a sort of shrivelled reserve and fear, as she leaned back farther in her chair. The transformation startled and arrested the singer. He was silent, dropping his hand; he had never supposed that Lady Caryll could look so ugly. The expression in her eyes reminded him of the expression in the eyes of a French maid-servant whom he had once discovered reading some of his private letters in Paris. And then he had thought of the half-recoiling, half-threatening aspect of a suddenly disturbed snake.

"Ah!" he exclaimed, after a moment's pause, "what I say is true—truer than I ever knew till now."

He felt like one who reads a page of some extraordinary book by the blinding light that comes from a great conflagration. The ugly reserve increased in Lady Caryll's face, but she said nothing.

"I say," repeated Monsieur Anneau, "that you would not give even one of your jewels to save the life of—shall I say of Sir Reuben?"

He sat down again. This new ugliness fascinated his eyes, and he wanted to probe the depth of its meaning. Lady Caryll laughed, he thought uneasily.

"Sir Reuben is in no danger of death," she said.

She laughed again, and the strange expression passed away from her face.

"If he were, you would not," repeated Monsieur Anneau obstinately.

He had a sudden sensation that she was slipping away from him like a snake in the grass. The light from the conflagration was dying, and the letters of the book were fading from his eyes.

"You need not answer me," he continued; "I know it."

He leaned towards her.

"But is this, then, your only passion?" he asked, in a lower voice. "And how deep is it?"

For he was conscious now of some mystery in her, and that there was darkness round about them both.

"How curious men always are," she said lightly. "More curious than children and vainer than women. I have no passions, and if I had, I should not discuss them with my acquaintances."

Monsieur Anneau was silent. The last few minutes had pushed him back from the angry declaration of what he called love, that he had been so near to. He scarcely knew how to return upon his steps. Yet he had decided that to-night was to find him triumphant. He would not go off the stage having missed his climax. He began to think, in his anger, that he had made a false move. Instead of attacking, he should have pleaded. Suddenly he assumed a softer manner, and said more quietly—

"You will not allow any man to read you. Yet I have given up everything."

"You can take back everything again."

"What do you mean?" he asked quickly.

"America has not been swallowed up by the sea."

As she spoke she got up and shot a deliberate glance at the clock that ticked softly upon the mantelpiece. Monsieur Anneau flushed scarlet.

"You tell me to go back to America? It is too late."

"It is late," Lady Caryll said.

Her grey eyes were still looking towards the clock. The singer felt as if all the frost of the cruel winter had entered into the room. He struggled against its influence upon him.

"I shall not return to America," he said.

"Paris, then?"

"Paris! I hate Paris!"

He spoke with intense bitterness.

"I never heard any Frenchman utter so crude a blasphemy before," Lady Caryll exclaimed.

She felt the gaiety that springs in the soul of one suddenly emerging from an undesired situation. Her face sparkled in a smile, and it seemed incredible that she was the woman who had looked so grim and starved with reticence a moment before.

"You will unsay that to-morrow," she added.

And she held out her hand.

"I will unsay nothing," he answered. "Nothing of what I am going to tell you now."

"You need not, for you are going to tell me nothing. I am not curious about you, Monsieur Anneau. Keep your secrets."

As she spoke she touched the bell. The singer felt like a withered leaf that is quietly shed in autumn by the tree that will soon face a new spring. For a moment he stood there. He opened his lips to speak. Then a footman appeared in the doorway, an enormous puppet with a powdered head, silently staring.

Monsieur Anneau strode slowly out. He felt as if, for the first time in his life, he had been hissed off the stage.

"Has he gone, Caryll?" asked the thin, rather drawling voice of Sir Reuben.

"Yes, Reuben."

She came up to him. He was curled up on a divan by a big fire, with his thin legs crossed and his feet tucked almost under him. A cloud of scented smoke hung round him, and his dry fingers grasped a pipe with a long wooden stem, on which was Arab lettering. On his head was a red skull-cap, whose brilliant colour accentuated the wrinkled age of his face.

"Ah! into the cold and the fog."

"We are safe from them."

She came up to the fire. He watched her slim figure lit by the fierce flames. And it struck him that he had never seen her in the light of the true sun, of the sun that gives to the desert its peculiar glory, of the sun that shines upon the land of the slave. Speaking from his thought, he said—

"And safe, too, from the sun."

"That! But there is none."

"Not here. But out there"—he waved his hand—"over the sea it shines. It shines on the barbaric jewels worn by Eastern women. Come here, Caryll."

She came and sat down on a stool by the divan. Sir Reuben put his hand on her bare shoulder. His touch was hot, as if the sun of which he spoke burned in his blood.

"Before I die I must see you stand in that sunshine," he said.

"Die! What are you saying?"

He felt her soft skin shift under his fingers.

"Did you shiver, Caryll?" he said, and he coughed after the words.

"The thought of death."

"The thought of my death!" he said, having heard her imperfectly owing to his complaint.

He closed his hot, thin hand more firmly on her white shoulder, leaned forward, bending over his crossed legs like a mandarin, and looked eagerly into her face, which was turned towards the fire.

"Would you miss me? Would you be sorry if I died?"

There was a wistful, almost shy, sound in his voice.

"Death is disagreeable to think of when one is full of life," she answered. "He spoke of it to-night, too."

"Who?"

"Monsieur Anneau."

"Ah! In connection with whom?"

"What, Reuben?" she asked, in the voice of one who is thinking deeply.

"Of whose death did he speak?"

She looked up at him, and answered quietly—

"Of yours."

Sir Reuben smiled with an air of disagreeable comprehension.

"He thinks that I am old; that I shall not live long, perhaps?"

"Oh no! He did not say that."

"What did he say?"

She pursed her lips together, considering.

"I scarcely remember. Oh, he was wondering what I would do to save your life, how much I would do."

"Well? What did you say?"

"Nothing."

"But to me you can say what you did not choose to say to him. Tell me, Caryll, how much you would give to save my life."

His hand was on her hair now, near the silver ornament in which the jewels shone.

"I don't know," she answered in an indifferent voice.

"Then, let us say, to save me from ruin."

"Ruin!"

Her voice changed. There was a sharp note of vitality in it, and she turned quickly, so that his hand dropped from her hair.

"Yes, ruin. You would give all, would you not—your dresses, your pictures, your horses, your jewels—to save me from ruin?"

She stared hard at him, all the muscles of her face set, her mouth and chin protruded, the whole woman at gaze. She was trying to read him. He knew it and enjoyed it, making his own face an enigma for answer to the question in hers.

"Are you——" she stopped.

He blew a cloud of smoke to shelter them in this odd colloquy. But she caught the mischievous flash of his eyes through the smoke, let her face go, and laughed gaily.

"When you are ruined, you will know, Reuben, what I would do to help you."

"And when I am dead—what shall I know then?"

"Nothing, I suppose. How late it is!"

She got up to go to bed. As Sir Reuben finished his pipe alone, he muttered to himself—

"Is one ever too old to be a fool? Can one ever know the world well enough not to hope for the impossible? That I—I should have looked into my jewel to-night to find a heart! Piff!"

He sat cross-legged in the scented cloud, sneering at himself.

Caryll was asleep when he came upstairs. She looked exquisite in her sleep, almost tender; diamond fading into pearl, he thought, and caught himself wondering what she would look like dead. He held a candle, and shaded it with one hand while he watched her. Just so he had watched his other wife years ago, in a night that stayed with him still like a hideous ghost, whispering rules of sad conduct to him, teaching him the behests of cynicism, murmuring to him the worthlessness of apparent virtue and the emptiness of noble dreams. He had gazed on her as now he gazed on her successor. But she had lain dead, her dark face on the white pillow, her dark hair—that looked so fearfully alive—flowing loosely over her icy shoulders. Flowers had been scattered upon the counterpane. He remembered brushing some of them away, and trampling them beneath his feet on the carpet. He remembered, too, bending down to strike the dead face, and then seizing the bed-curtains with his hands, and drawing back, and wondering if he were not mad to have had so filthy an impulse. Now, as he stood looking on this golden-haired girl, noting the regular movement of her body pushed by the breath of life, he found that his hand was tremulous. It shook so violently that the ray from the candle danced upon the white bed and across the face of the sleeper. She stirred and opened her eyes, stared for a moment, and said—

"Take away the light from me. I want to sleep."

He obeyed her with a sense of guilt, as if she could have read, in sleep, his memories while he stood there by the bed. Later, while he lay awake, he found himself incessantly repeating her words in his mind, and putting them into the mouth of a dying person.

It seemed as if Death must have paused on the snowy door-step of the house that night.

In the morning the fog had lifted, the frost was melting, and Lady St. Ormyn, glaring from her windows, gave vent to the bitter soprano invectives of an excitable woman to whom fine weather is sent ten hours too late.

Monsieur Anneau ceased to come to Park Lane from this time. He had returned suddenly to Paris. Lady St. Ormyn, who followed him there, and afterwards went on to the Riviera, wrote incoherent letters to her daughter declaring that he must be seriously ill. He went nowhere, declined to sing, and seemed to hate the very name of music. In one letter she declared—

"I asked him to-day if there was anything wrong with his throat. He said that his voice had been out of order ever since he sang at that dreadful concert of yours that was such a fiasco. I always said that it was madness for him to come to London in the winter."

Lady Caryll smiled over this, wondering a little at the straightforward ways of untruthfulness. She was still in London. She was so contented that she did not seem to wish to travel or to track the sun. Sir Reuben's cough was persistent, but he loved her content and did not seek to disturb it. "She is happy behind the bars," he said to himself, and thought of the blind windows of the harem. He fed her behind the bars with jewels, till all London rang with the fortunes he gave to the dealers in precious stones. Five thousand pounds went to an Indian for one pearl. It was this pearl that Lady Caryll showed to Paul Villet, the composer of the song sung by Monsieur Anneau.

"The maiden has her pearl," she said, smiling on him. "And you, too, have given it to her in your song."

The composer, well fed now, and quite commonplace in appearance, agreed almost unctuously. He had fallen under the spell of Lady Caryll, and had forgotten that once, when he was starving, he had been obstinate, inclined to put his artistic conviction of what was right on a throne above her. Impelled by food, by comfort, by a dulling sense of safety, he had given his song-maiden her pearl. Lady Caryll, pleased, had made him the fashion. He composed little songs—quite ordinary now—and smart women said they sprang from his heart. Really they rose wearily from a too satisfied appetite. Starving, people had thought him ridiculous, and he had been almost sublime, in the sincerity of his privation, in the honesty of his fiery talent. Satisfied, even satiated, he became contemptible, believed that he gained dignity by setting foot in certain famous houses, and that music adored by great ladies became, by that very adoration, great music. He had a lap-dog air and ogled when he played, like certain libertine musicians, who become the rage by their impudence of allure, and whose songs are veiled insults offered to delighted women.

Aubrey saw him spoilt and pitied his human nature, loving Lady Caryll's. She, in her charitable compassion, had picked this man up out of the dust that he might be free, that his genius might have nourishment and grow. It was not her fault if he, in return, sprawled in satiety and let his soul snore in the warm darkness of the black night that he found full of golden glory. Do we not often ruin the man to whom we give what is called his chance? One day Aubrey spoke of this to Lady Caryll.

"Isn't it strange," he said, "that by helping people we can do them irreparable harm?"

"How?" she asked.

He hesitated a moment, then he said—

"I was thinking of Villet."

Lady Caryll did not seem to understand. She answered—

"He told me to-day that he has taken rooms for the season in South Street, and that half the royal family are coming to his concert at Richborough House."

She smiled happily. Aubrey thought her too joyful in her charity to see the black side of its result.

And at this time she was too happy to see any black side to life. Her radiance grew as the radiance of jewels increased in the Park Lane house, till the sparkle of her and of them began to dazzle the eyes, and more, the mind of the world. The worship of the partially imaginative is roused by size or by quantity. An immense building kindles their fires, and bows them in adoration, or a fabulous number of banknotes, or of acres of land, or of palaces and castles possessed by anybody. The worship of the partially imaginative began to creep round the skirts of Lady Caryll at this time, fed by the vulgarity of the Press which wallows in narrations of what money can do. But the reputation which Lady Caryll began now to acquire, and which spread beyond her private circle, was never, even in its beginning, quite akin to the American millionaire's, or the South African Croesus'! From the first there was a touch of the magical in it, a suspicion of the fairy-like, as in the Peruvian priests' conception of the Goddess Esmeralda, who had her home in the great emerald. This arose, perhaps, from various causes, of which one or two may be suggested. Lady Caryll's beauty was peculiar, and had something of the cool glitter that many associate vaguely with fairy things and places. Then, too, the troop of her jewels was headed, as it were, by one which possessed a sort of definite personality. The knowledge of the great emerald and of its engraving was quickly spread abroad. The papers originally had recorded its sale to Sir Reuben, and the immense price paid for it, then the marriage of Lady Caryll, and her wearing it on her wedding day. Now, when they spoke of Sir Reuben's notorious buyings of famous gems, they seldom failed to allude again to the emerald and to its engraved soul being borne away by pleasures. And so its green light began, as it were, to pierce very far, and to men and women who had never seen, who would never see it. And in its green light generally danced a vision of Lady Caryll, till she became a sort of goddess of jewels to many who had never seen her. Thieves talked of the emerald in their ugly dwellings. Suburban people chattered of it about their decent tea-tables. Sometimes Wesleyan mothers, stern to improve an occasion, lectured and advised plain daughters—never likely to possess much more than a Cairngorm brooch on the danger of being led away by specious worldly things, or persuaded to sell themselves for gems even the most wonderful. And the daughters meekly acquiesced, aching dully with the desire for such leading away, for such persuasion, and seeing the probably very wicked Lady Caryll set in a terrible light of success on the edge of the flaming pit. In London itself the emerald and its legend appealed to the easy emotionalism of the many young, and so-called decadent, persons of both sexes who sigh vaguely after all that is strange, confusing that which is out-of-the-way with that which is desirable. Young versifiers, really not so far from being poets as some bulky men brought up on Byron thought, wrote rapid lines on the journey of such a soul as the emerald's, taking it each to his own delightful Vanity Fair, and setting it amid the most wonderful and vivid crowds of joys. And each, as he wrote, had under-thoughts of Lady Caryll, and was inclined to bear her away to these riotous places of the imagination. To others, more sombre in temperament, there was something dream-like and full of space in the notion of a thing borne away. They set the imagined Lady Caryll flitting through moonlit deserts on the way to some far horizon, beyond which lay unimagined things, such as many suppose to await them after death. Then there were the more sordid, who thought of her merely as a sort of Queen over the mob of rustling effigies of womanhood who trample and howl after money, and cling to the most loathsome man if he can but pay a dressmaker's bill. These despised her for her greed when they did not adore her for her triumph in its brilliant satisfaction, or envy her for being at the top of what they told themselves was a despicable world.

In any case, and to the eyes of all, a certain strange dazzle and sparkle of light began to concentrate itself about Lady Caryll. She moved in radiance, though there were some who chose to think the radiance vulgar, and to affect to pity the girl who walked in it with so imperturbable a contentment.

And thieves talked of her in their ugly dwellings, often and long.

Aubrey, settled in now to the routine of secretarial work, had not yet learnt the lesson Sir Reuben had spoken of to Lady Rangecliffe. The circumstance of the raising of that Lazarus, Paul Villet, from the tomb of his starvation and neglect to his present modishness, and the circumstance of Monsieur Anneau's sudden departure, had delayed the learning of the lesson. Sir Reuben, who had come to read his godson, understood this. The dismissal of Monsieur Anneau increased Aubrey's ideal of Caryll's purity, the raising of Paul Villet his ideal of her pity. And both these qualities endowed her in his mind with a fresh and beautiful humanity. She could resist what conquered her sister women, stoop to what they would have passed by on the other side.

Since he had lived in Park Lane, Aubrey had set Caryll higher. Sir Reuben knew it and wondered at the blindness of youth. But this blindness tended also oddly to his own satisfaction, for, since the evening when he had descanted on the virtues and the wonders of jewels, Aubrey had begun to look upon him differently, with a growing admiration and reticent regard that pleased Sir Reuben more than he had thought anything could please him. Aubrey no longer saw only, or chiefly, the ugly and withered body upon which Time and a past despair had set a dreary seal. He began to succeed in the effort to avoid the sight of the body by fixing his eyes upon the supposed nature it housed. Caryll had done this—must have done it—why should not he? He would look at his godfather more as she looked at her husband. It should be possible since they were one and the same man. Sir Reuben's great kindness to him was an assistance. He began to think that he too, like Caryll, was under the fascination of a peculiar and brilliant mind, where that which was ordinary scarcely found any lodgment for its heavy foot. He sought continually for reasons of admiration at least, if not of something more, in his godfather. Now and then Sir Reuben gave one, consciously or unconsciously.

One was connected with the little acrobat, Alf, to whom he showed kindness.

CHAPTER XX

AFTER Aubrey had given up his rooms in Jermyn Street, he received one day a card forwarded from them. On it was printed—

ALF FLICK.
"*The Marvellous Flicks.*"

In the corner was written, in pencil and a round, boyish hand, "Grand Theatre of Varieties, Champion Square." So it seemed that Alf had taken Aubrey at his word and come to see him. He wrote the boy a note asking him to call in Park Lane, but for several weeks received no reply. This did not surprise Aubrey, however, for he had seen Diamond one evening, and had learnt from her that the Flicks were fulfilling a special engagement at Marseilles, and would not be back in England till the spring. One day, in the spring, a rather astonished-looking footman showed Alf into Aubrey's sitting-room. He entered with his usual imperturbable assurance. Life had rendered him incapable of feeling abashed. His hair was carefully plastered over his forehead and drenched with cold water. He wore an enormous, loose bow-tie, bought in France, and carried in one hand a soft black hat. As the footman retired, Alf cut a caper at him, something between a Catherine wheel and a back somersault, with a touch of the comic Leotard on the imaginary horizontal bar thrown in, just to give the *au revoir* a delicate finish. The footman, who could not see well what was happening, depressed a fearful back, and, as he passed through the door, half turned and shot a pale glance of haughty inquiry mingled with terror at the extraordinary visitor.

Alf shook a leg at him with a violent suppleness that completed the man's discomfiture, and he closed the door, with an amount of noise that should have cost him his place, tremulous in the conviction that Mr. Herrick was closeted with one of the younger members of the lunatic tribe.

"That chap'd be hissed off the bar," remarked Alf significantly. "He's as soft as butter. Them calves ain't real. He couldn't stand on his head with all that powder on and grease on. Why, he'd slip! What's he for?"

"Show," said Aubrey, smiling.

"To look at?"

"Partly."

"He's like the fat chaps at our place what change the numbers."

He spun the soft hat high in whizzing circles, and let it fall on a peg in the shape of a big vase of oriental china. Then he winked solemnly at Aubrey, who invited him to sit down. Having accepted the invitation in a collapsible manner, he seemed to have no further mission, but sat regarding Aubrey with steadfastness and an unwinking stony gravity, yet with a hint of goblin humour that suggested the gargoyle. Aubrey, marvelling very much why he had come, started the conversation.

"Been at Marseilles, haven't you?" he asked.

"Yes, sir."

"Good audiences?"

"Thundering. Four calls every night after the corpse act. The Froggies ain't such fools as they sound when they're at their lingo."

He spoke some gibberish with a wonderful faithfulness to the singing sonorousness of certain French voices, and an accompaniment of exaggerated gesture that placed France accurately, if ridiculously, upon the carpet. Then he again relapsed into stony silence, steadily regarding Aubrey with his small grey eyes.

"They're glad to have you back in Milk Court, I'm sure," said Aubrey.

"Milk Court—ah!" responded Alf.

He nodded his head in a portentous manner.

"Milk Court," he repeated again in a voice surcharged with an intelligence that was mysterious. "That's it, ain't it?"

Aubrey was sincerely mystified. Alf's statement could not be controverted or his question greeted with a negative response, yet the evident sarcasm that lurked in his remark suggested his anticipation of strong refutals and denials. Aubrey waited for developments. He began dimly to appreciate the fact that the goblin of the halls sought his closer acquaintance with a definite object.

"That's it, ain't it?" repeated Alf with more stress, and a contortion of the face rather neuralgic in tendency. "Oh no, sir, not Milk Court! Rather not!"

This time his tongue went openly into his right cheek, and he regarded Aubrey with distinct suspicion. It was impossible to be offended with such an odd specimen of humanity. Nevertheless, Aubrey began to suppose that, for some secret reason, he was held in enmity, rather than in regard, by the hero of the corpse act.

"What is it? What's the row about Milk Court?"

"Don't Di live there?" responded little Alf.

"Miss Diamond! Why, of course she does."

"'Tain't your home, is it?" said Alf.

"My home?" said Aubrey, in complete bewilderment.

"Is it, then?"

"Of course not."

"You're a nob," continued Alf. "One of the lot that slopes in at nine o'clock, and couldn't be there at eight—oh no! not to see Queen Victoria do a tumble, or the Prince of Wales hisself go up the Juggins on his hands. Now, ain't you?"

"I didn't know it," said Aubrey, with difficulty repressing a tendency to laugh.

"Well, sir, I did d'rectly I see you helping yourself to cabbage on her birthday. The governor's no class for watching it. But them that's in the light biz never is. It's all them colours blinds 'em."

"What to? Watching what?" asked Aubrey, more and more bewildered.

"Oh, we can't guess! can we, sir?"

This time the neuralgic tendency of the face became even more definitely marked, and Aubrey was obliged to understand it.

"Apparently you think I'm trying to tell you a lie," he said, assuming offence.

"It won't be no good not if you do," the boy calmly rejoined. "I'm up to all the games, sir, ground and lofty, and all the rest of it. No offence. Remember the night I walked home with you?"

Aubrey nodded.

"See me watching of you? I was taking it all on."

"Taking what on?"

"Your game, sir."

"What game? What on earth d'you mean?"

"Well, sir, Di's dropped through the net once and very near broke her back. There ain't no reason why she's got to do it again, is there?"

Alf had begun to look quite old.

"Come now, sir, man to man without the gloves on, is there?"

Aubrey began at last to guess at his visitor's object in calling, and to like him for it, even though it might prove to be embarrassing.

"Dropping the nob, sir, now is there?" reiterated little Alf, a crescendo of old age and worldly wisdom being all the time apparent in his comical face, which was full of hints of the solitary chaperon.

"Miss Diamond isn't an acrobat, is she?" said Aubrey. "How should she drop through a net?"

"My way of putting it, sir. You twig? I'm the man at the rope what watches Di. See?"

His little grey eyes were very stern.

"You don't go to Milk Court to play ball with Susie, now does you?" he continued gravely. "Nor touch with Charlie, I'll lay."

"I went there because Miss Diamond invited me to her birthday party, and because I have a sincere regard for her," said Aubrey.

Alf contorted his face gymnastically.

"Sincere regard," he repeated. "So had the other chap, but she fell through the net all the same, and's never tumbled as well since. I ain't going to see her do it again, Mister. I tell you that straight. I'm the man at the rope what watches Di. So now!"

His face was rigidly obstinate. Aubrey thought he looked like a fierce little dog guarding the door of his mistress. The watered lock of hair on his forehead curled up slightly at its tip as if in defiance, and his hard, knuckly little hands grasped his knees as he sat staring fiercely at Aubrey.

"So now!" he repeated challengingly.

Aubrey looked at him with the half awkward admiration that the Englishman gives to grit in another when it is working steadily against himself.

"Alf, you don't understand," he said.

A low and piercing whistle greeted this observation—a whistle that rose high, ran down a scale with infinite incredulity, and died in a cooing jeer:

"No," Aubrey repeated, "you don't. Miss Diamond and I are friends, nothing more nor less. I have a sincere regard for her. That's all."

"Oh my! these nobs—these nobs!" was the boy's somewhat enigmatic rejoinder.

The exclamation made Aubrey feel slightly irritated for the first time.

"Go and talk to Miss Diamond, if you like," he exclaimed. "She'll soon tell you how foolish your idea is."

Alf smiled a terribly wise smile.

"The other chap said he had a 'sincere regard' for Di after he'd let her through the net," was his reply.

"He was a blackguard," said Aubrey with genuine feeling.

"Most of 'em are," said Alf. "There's more blackguards than one in the great theaytre, just as there's more fried fish than one in the Whitechapel Road of a Saturday night. That's how I look at it, that is."

And again he regarded Aubrey with convinced suspicion.

"Give it up, Mister, give it up," he continued, after a brief pause. "In the words of the song, 'Leave the pore young gal alone.'"

His manner was such a strange mixture of manly resolve and impish satire, his face, by turns, so keenly expressive of serious concern and bitter worldly wisdom, that Aubrey felt rather as if he were sitting with two or three persons of varying ages and mental qualities. He suddenly resolved to speak more frankly to Alf.

"I quite understand what you mean," he said.

"Really, Mister!" interposed Alf, with an inflection of studied surprise.

"And I daresay your idea is natural enough. But it's wrong all the same. Miss Diamond and I are good friends. I know that she—that she's—well—fallen through the net, if you like to call it so, and hurt herself. She'll never have such another accident through me."

"How are you to twig that, Mister?"

"How—because I tell you we are only friends."

"That's what you think, p'r'aps. But then you ain't a gal."

"What has that to do with it?"

"A lot. A man can hold up a heavy weight longer nor a gal, and so he can stay only friends, as you calls it, longer. While you think as Di's safe on the wire, she may be falling through the net like as she did before. Put your eye to it, Mister, if you're talking straight, and see what she's after. And anyhow, you take it from me that I'm the man at the rope what watches Di."

As he spoke he bounded up from his chair like one longing for active movement after a tension of enforced repose.

"I hate setting," he said, with an entire change of manner. "I'm off now."

He stood still for a second, and his demeanour, suddenly become boyish, suggested that he was impatient to pour forth his bottled-up vitality in some violent exhibition.

"Seen my new game?" he suddenly cried, and before Aubrey could make any reply he had seized a book from a table near him—it was Pater's "Marius"—gone down on the floor on his hands with his body rigidly extended upward, and his feet pointing to the ceiling, thrown up the book into mid air, caught it on his toe, and was tossing it from the sole of one foot to the other while he promenaded rapidly about wrong end up.

At this moment there was a tap at the door, and Sir Reuben entered to speak to Aubrey about some business. He met the feet of the little acrobat and the flying "Marius," and started in surprise. Alf curved his body slowly till it formed an arch, leaped backwards and forwards several times, alighting alternately on hands and feet, then came to a normal standing posture and faced Sir Reuben gravely.

"It should be a ball by rights," he remarked, calmly laying down Pater's masterpiece, "but most anything does."

"Ah!" said Sir Reuben, who was still in the doorway, glancing at the young performer with a smile, "you're studying gymnastics, Aubrey?"

Aubrey looked rather embarrassed.

"Mr. Alf Flick, a—a—"—he looked at Alf—"friend of a friend of mine," he concluded.

Alf nodded.

"The Marvellous Flicks, sir," he said to Sir Reuben in explanation. Then he caught up his hat, threw it to the ceiling, ducked his head to receive it, and prepared to go. But Sir Reuben stopped him.

"Are you in a hurry, my boy?" he asked.

"Not so very partic'lar," said Alf. "Want anything, sir?"

He shot a glance of cool inquiry at the little old man before him, observed Sir Reuben's red fez, and wondered if he were one of "them naughty, bad Turks."

"Like to see some tricks, Mister?" he added, apparently reading Sir Reuben's mind, and he was about to give a selection of somersaults when Sir Reuben stopped him.

"Not here," said Sir Reuben. "Will you perform before a lady?"

"Is it Her Most Gracious?" said Alf, assuming an air of dramatic excitement. "Her Most Gracious hasn't never seen the Flicks, and she must see 'em all together, she must see 'em in patterns. Ever seen the Marvellous Flicks in patterns, sir; the growing vine, the serpent before and arter he's eat the pore little rabbit, the engine what's going sixty miles an hour, and the bishop —that's father—falling out of the pulpit and pitching on his head, yet never hurt? Ever seen that, sir?"

"Never," said Sir Reuben. "It isn't her Majesty, so it doesn't matter about the patterns. To amuse Caryll," he added to Aubrey.

Aubrey nodded. It seemed to him as if Diamond were taking a step towards that other diamond, since the man at the rope was to be introduced into Lady Caryll's presence.

"Right you are," said little Alf, whose sincere pride in his profession rendered him easily amenable to such an offer, and whose existence might be called one prolonged trick performance. "If it ain't Her Most Gracious, it don't matter. But when she sees the Flicks, she's bound to see 'em in patterns."

He followed Sir Reuben out of the room with a jaunty step.

THE SLAVE

The last hint of the chaperon vanished from his lively aspect. Sir Reuben led the way to the music-room in which Monsieur Anneau had shot his useless shafts. The white chairs were ranged rigidly against the wall. A piano still stood upon the small platform.

"Wait here a moment," he said to Alf. "I'll fetch the lady." He shuffled off.

"A Turk, ain't he?" asked Alf of Aubrey.

Aubrey smiled and shook his head.

"Well," continued Alf, "he ain't far off it, I'll lay. Who's the lady? Them Turks is——"

His manner suggested that some scandalous allusion to the domestic habits of the average Oriental was about to flow from his lips. But at this moment Sir Reuben returned with Lady Caryll, who was dressed for going out. She wore black, which made her look even fairer and whiter than usual. Alf gazed at her with an obvious admiration that rendered his appearance almost sentimental.

"Well, I never, if it ain't Her Most Gracious, it's the Queen of Diamonds!" he whispered to Aubrey.

"A private performance, Caryll, such as the Sultan has in that theatre of his at the Yildiz," said Sir Reuben. "Master Flick, here's the lady. Will you show her your tricks?"

Alf ran sideways, as between footlights and a down-dropped curtain, smiling, ducking his head, and blowing breaths to his hand with pursed lips in the way of successful acrobats. In this fashion he gained the platform upon which he lightly sprang. He put his hands to his coat, then hesitated.

"May I off it, lady?" he asked, addressing Lady Caryll.

She nodded. This odd moment, breaking an ordinary morning, pleased her. Alf was out of his coat in an instant and spinning in the air like a ball. Lady Caryll sat close to the platform to watch him, as she had sat to hear the pearl song on the foggy night of Monsieur Anneau's concert. But now she looked gay, almost like a schoolgirl, Aubrey thought, as her sparkling eyes followed little Alf's amazing gyrations, all cleverly adapted to the small space. When he stopped to breathe she clapped her hands.

"Bravo!" she cried.

Alf sidled and ducked conventionally, again with his sliding air of aiming for invisible wings. Having reached the wall he stopped, fixed his eyes on Lady Caryll, to whom his performance and all his thoughts were evidently directed, and cried—

"Like to see me do a juggle, lady?"

"Yes," she answered.

Alf looked about him.

"I must have something to juggle, lady," he said.

He fixed his eyes on her again.

"You give me something, lady," he said, looking her over searchingly.

Lady Caryll wore, in the front of her gown, a long serpent of dull green enamel with eyes that were big yellow amethysts.

"The insect, lady," continued Alf, stretching out his hand to this. "I'll make it alive for you."

Lady Caryll had put her hand over it at his first words, and had shaken her head at his request. His last remark seemed to change her decision.

"Make it alive?" she repeated.

"Yuss," said Alf. "Crawl over me like as if it was real, and a pet."

Lady Caryll unfastened the serpent and handed it to him.

Sir Reuben, who had closely watched her hesitation, and its disappearance, shot a glance at Aubrey. Alf took the serpent very carefully, even delicately, into his hard and sinewy hands. He rolled up his shirt sleeves and bared his arms. Then he let the serpent run on them, slip through his divided fingers, creep into his curved palms. That was the effect of his performance. He allowed the green creature, with its prominent yellow eyes, to do what it chose, and it chose to run. The innumerable movements, graduated with infinite skill and deftness, by which the boy gave it the semblance of life, were so slight and so swift, that to the untrained eye they were almost invisible. Lady Caryll did not seek for them, or think of them. She was intent upon the little green creature that was hers, that had lain on her breast so still, and that now showed such curious and unexpected activities. At last Alf caused the snake to glide, with an appearance of infinite secrecy, into the pocket of his waistcoat.

"It's tired, lady," he remarked; "wants a by-bye."

And he turned down his sleeves, popped on his jacket, and jumped off the platform. Lady Caryll looked at him with more than admiration, with the peculiar and complete attention that a child gives to a magician. She said nothing, but presently she extended her hand towards Alf.

"Oh, lady, mustn't disturb him," said Alf, touching his pocket with a soft gesture. "What? He's awake again, is he?"

And with an extraordinary wriggle of his body he caused the serpent to emerge, shudder along his hand, and drop into Lady Caryll's lap. She picked it up and looked at it.

"I always felt as if it were alive," she said.

Then she fastened it into the breast of her gown again and thanked Alf for his performance. It was evident that Alf had completely lost his heart to her.

"I say," he murmured aside to Sir Reuben, as Lady Caryll got up to go; "I say, sir, I should like the lady to see us in patterns. I should like her to see the growing vine."

"She shall see it," said Sir Reuben, with a kindness that pleased Aubrey.

"When?" said little Alf anxiously.

For Lady Caryll had nodded to him kindly, had received his answering respectful bob, and was going.

"Caryll," Sir Reuben said, "Master Flick wishes you to see him in a pattern with his relations."

"With Vauxhall and the rest of 'em, lady," cried Alf with goblin earnestness. "The growing vine, the serpent—not yours, lady—before and arter he's eat the poor little rabbit, the engine what's going sixty miles an hour, and the bishop—that's father—falling out of the pulpit and pitching on his head, yet never hurt. There ain't nothing like it on the halls, lady, specially the growing vine. I'm the grape on the top spray."

Lady Caryll smiled at him, but now with a certain indifference. The idea of Alf in a pattern with his relations did not seem to excite her very much.

"I'd rather see you making my serpent show itself in its true colours," she said.

Alf's face fell.

"Then you ain't coming, lady?" he rejoined. "You'll die laughing to see father fall out of the pulpit, yet never hurt. Why, I've seen old ladies—regular churchers, too—split their sides at it, and they thinking all the time as it's wicked, because of him pretending to be the bishop. You haven't no idea."

"Perhaps I'll come some day," said Lady Caryll.

She went out, touching the serpent and looking down on it.

"Well, I'm——" began Alf. "Any one'd think she b'lieved it was alive."

Sir Reuben laughed.

"That's because you're so clever," he answered.

He took out two sovereigns and gave them to Alf, who spun them in the air and caught them as they fell in his two waistcoat pockets.

"I promise you I'll bring the lady to see you as the top grape of the vine," Sir Reuben said. "So don't make yourself uneasy."

Alf grinned with pleasure.

"I'd almost as soon do a turn for her as for Her Most Gracious," he said. "She's the Queen of Di'monds, she is, straight."

"Ah!" said Sir Reuben, "you've noticed that?"

He glanced at Aubrey and went out after Lady Caryll. Aubrey thought again of that morning in Bond Street.

"Is the Turk the lady's governor?" asked the voice of little Alf.

"That gentleman is the lady's husband," said Aubrey in a rather cold voice.

Alf renewed his peculiar whistle, prolonging it this time as one who must accompany the busy working of his mind with music.

"Well, I'm blowed!" he said, when at length he spoke.

He looked at Aubrey, pursing and protruding his lips.

"Ain't you?" he added.

"Am I not what?" asked Aubrey.

"Why—blowed!"

Aubrey made no reply, but led the way toward the hall.

"Right," said Alf behind him. "I'm off. Don't you worry."

Having arrived in the large space of the hall, instinctively he prepared for acrobatic exercises. But suddenly something seemed to intervene. He paused, pulled himself together, and marched solemnly onward till the hall door was reached. Aubrey opened it. Alf stood looking at him. It was a sunny day, and the light fell upon them both. Alf glanced back into the dim and richly coloured hall where the tiny fountain tinkled.

"So the Turk's her Jack—her husband—is he?" remarked Alf.

He glanced again at Aubrey.

"You her brother?" he said.

"No," said Aubrey.

"No relation?"

"None."

Alf threw up his hat and caught it on his head.

"Don't let him—the Turk—forget to bring the lady to see us in patterns," he said. "Morning, Mister."

He sprang down the steps. Just before he darted away a thought seemed to strike him. He turned.

"I'm the man at the rope!" he said. Then he spun round and was gone.

Aubrey stood for a moment in the sunshine. He scarcely knew whether he was angry or entertained. The little imp had intruded strangely into his privacy, digging a sharp, childishly quizzical glance, like a tiny knife, into his reserve. He liked him for his watch-dog defence of Diamond. But——

Aubrey shut the hall door suddenly and went back to his own rooms. When he reached them he sat down and thought of Diamond. He thought of little Alf's saying that she had fallen through the net once, and that he wasn't going to let her do it again. There could be no chance of that, surely. Aubrey wondered. He thought of his own fall through the net and again of Diamond. They were like two injured ones of different ranks, brought together in the ward of a great hospital, seeking to comfort each other in a community of suffering. To comfort each other! Yes, that was their mission. They must fulfil it. Neither must increase the suffering of the other. Not till that moment had Aubrey ever quite realised how much Diamond's sorrow, even though he grieved for her, had soothed the pain of his.

He was reluctant to forego this solace. Yet the small grey eyes of little Alf were keen. It was possible that they had seen farther than Aubrey's.

He cursed the imp, then saw him sitting with his hands on his knees, and almost loved him.

For, after all, was he not the man at the rope, watching in his odd way over the safety of more than a body?

CHAPTER XXI

SIR REUBEN was a man of his word. He did not forget his promise to Alf that Caryll should be brought to see that wonder, the growing vine. But London is very full of preventing circumstances. Two or three weeks passed before the promise could be fulfilled. During these weeks more jewels came to seek a home in the great safe in Caryll's bedchamber, and Aubrey found an opportunity of seeing Diamond. The visit of Alf had made an impression upon him and had awakened him to possibilities. As yet he declined to think of them as probabilities. But he wanted to see Diamond now that his eyes had caught something, perhaps, of the watchfulness of Alf's. And he resolved that his own desire for a continuance of companionship should not blind him to any danger signal.

He met Diamond after the theatre. It was a warm Spring night. The month was April. During the day there had been soft showers, those sweet attendants that lead forward the hesitating steps of the sometimes reluctant goddess. The breath of the night was exquisite even in the ugly streets, like the breath of violets in a cellar. As Aubrey waited on the pavement outside the stage door, the omnibus containing the Marvellous Flicks drove up heavily. Their "turn" succeeded the ballet. Aubrey drew a little further away. He did not want to meet Alf just then. From the distance he saw the lithe acrobats leap out and hasten off to their duty. Little Alf was last. He cut his usual caper for the benefit of the loungers. They laughed and clapped their hands as he vanished. Aubrey came nearer and waited. He was strongly conscious of the charm of the night, despite the hideous thoroughfare, dingy and narrow, in which he stood, and a longing came to him for country places. He thought of the pleasant street of a village, with its few cheerful lights, its cottage gardens, its atmosphere of peace and of safety. Scents would be rising from the baptized ground. Scents would be flying on the breeze, and all the black woods would be stirring in the happy uneasiness of their birth pangs. He saw, in fancy, the lights go out behind the window panes, and thought of all the villagers at rest; the rosy children breathing quietly and regularly, their apple cheeks pressed against the white pillows; their parents stirring, perhaps, in the anxious wakefulness that often comes with the coming of old age, when the soul, so near its flight, listens each night more keenly for the soft sound of the footsteps of the angel.

Aubrey thought of these footsteps. It seemed to him that he would like to hear them treading over the earth of spring, that he would wish to go away with the angel over fields that were expectant, not regretful.

Some one touched him gently. He started and saw Diamond at his side.

"Well, I never," she said, in her low voice. "Any one'd think you was asleep and dreamin'!"

"Dreaming, perhaps," said Aubrey.

"Whatever about?" she asked, as they walked on together.

"Something most people think very sad."

"Oh?"

"Death, Diamond," he said.

He saw a little flush come into her face, and wondered why it came. He did not remember that he had always called her Miss Diamond till this moment.

"I never see a dead person," she remarked.

"Nor I," said Aubrey. "Would you be afraid to?"

"No," she said simply. "Where are we goin'?"

Aubrey hesitated. It was not very late. The night was soft and warm; the longing for trees, grass, cessation of noise, came to him again and strongly. He looked under Diamond's sailor hat.

"Are you very tired to-night?" he said.

"Not a bit," she answered.

"Shall we go and sit in the Park? It's so warm, almost like summer, and we shall be away from the noise and the houses."

"All right!" said Diamond in a tone of perfect confidence. "But I've never been in the Park of a night before. What's it like?"

Aubrey scarcely knew. He had once or twice walked across it after dining in Great Cumberland Place or in Hyde Park Gardens. And then he had generally been with some friend and had talked London gossip.

"Like the country," he answered at a venture.

He hailed a cab and ordered the man to drive to Hyde Park Corner.

When they were there, Diamond sprang out lightly. She was quite gay, and amused by this little adventure. As they passed through the gateway a constable eyed them with a gaze that

P

seemed full of ugly humour. Aubrey noticed it, but the girl did not. They crossed the open space and reached the trees. There was a crescent moon in the sky, which was vaporous and full of mystery where the feeble moon rays touched the edges of the shallow clouds. Diamond looked around her cheerfully.

"It is nice," she said. "Where shall we go?"

Some boys in caps went by them, shooting impudent inquiry from their furtive eyes. Aubrey felt a sudden longing to attack them.

"Let's go under the trees and find two chairs," he said. "Are you afraid of the grass being damp?"

"Not I."

They found two chairs in a green silence, well away from the broad walk. It was rather dark here. The lamps shone far off. Far off the carriages rolled by. Diamond unfastened her straw hat to let the light wind play about her fluffy dark hair.

"This is lovely after the theatre," she said. "Quite a little holiday. Ah! you've never seen me on my holiday! I'm a different girl then."

"How long d'you have?" said Aubrey, watching the moon through the trees.

"A fortnight. I go to Minchester-on-Sea."

"Who with?"

"Susie. We go in lodgin's. Susie is mad. You should hear her scream at the window when we get in the station. Alf came down one year. And once *he* came."

She paused. Her eyes filled with ready tears. She took off her thread gloves and clasped her thin hands in her lap.

"Oh dear! we did have a time," she continued. "He took Susie shrimpin'. The child was half crazy when she got among the rocks and all them little pools. She fell in ever so many, but salt water don't hurt you—that's what he said. Oh!"

A dark figure had crept close in the gloom and stood before them.

"Tuppence, please," it murmured, turning its head aside and extending its hand.

Aubrey paid, received two tickets, and saw it creep away to search in the shadows for other couples.

"He did give me a turn," Diamond said, "comin' so sudden. I should be afraid here alone."

She had drawn nearer to Aubrey. He felt her slim body touch his arm.

"And Alf came that year too," she went on, "the year he was there. Alf got on rare with him then. They used to go swimmin' together. I was frightened to see 'em so far out in the water; like dolls' heads they looked, and the great waves rollin' up to 'em. Susie did howl, like she'd have a fit, and I thought——" She paused —" Well, I thought if he was to go under, how different it'd all be, them lodgin's, and tea of a night, and the walk afterwards, and all. We used to like to see the sun go."

She leaned a little sideways. It seemed to Aubrey that her attitude was full of recollection.

"Oh, Alf was funny," she went on. "Doin' all his tricks on the sand of a night when there was the moon, like a goblin he was. He frightened an old lady what was lookin' out of the window oncest. She screamed like mad—seein' him do his somersaults backwards, you know,—and she cries out, 'If there ain't the Devil hisself on the shore!' she cries. We died laughin'. I don't know whatever we should do without Alf."

"Are you very fond of him?" Aubrey asked.

"Yes. He's a good boy. He'd do anything for me, would Alf. Why, he wanted to——"

She hesitated.

"Yes?" said Aubrey.

"To go for him, when—you know. But for me, he would have, too. And he's no size at all. But he ain't afraid of anything. That's why they all say he can't never have an accident. Vauxhall'd give his life for Alf, he's that proud of him."

"Did he tell you about coming to see me?"

"Yes, and doin' his tricks to the lady. He's crazy to see her again."

"Is he?"

"Yes. Says she's the Queen of Diamonds, and ought to walk first in our march down. You know?"

"I know."

"The old feller—pardon, her husband——"

"Sir Reuben?"

"Yes. He's promised to bring her to see the growin' vine. Will she come?"

"Yes, I'm sure she will."

"You'll see how Alf'll perform that night. He's practisin' up some new tricks a-purpose, awful darin' ones. He says as the lady—Lady Caryll, isn't it?"

Aubrey nodded.

"As she's dead gone on him. Cheeky!"

Aubrey smiled. But Alf's adoration of Lady Caryll pleased him and made him almost love the imp. He was silent, thinking of her and of the fascination that had reached even the little acrobat. He thought of Alf busily practising his tricks in the hope of her coming to see them, and then of the beautiful legend of the poor and deformed tumbler, who was found on the fête day of the Virgin going through his performance before her shrine, since he had nothing else to offer to the Divine Mother of God. The wind sighed in the trees, and the flitting clouds created the illusion of a hastening, anxious moon abroad on some nocturnal quest. Aubrey still felt the touch of Diamond against his arm, and now he heard her say—

"Whatever are you thinkin' of?"

"I don't know. I feel as if I were thinking of nothing and of everything at the same time. That's the night and the moon."

"They make me think too."

"What of?"

"Why people should be so beastly to each other. Ain't it odd?"

As she spoke, Aubrey saw in the distance two dingy figures of a man and a woman. They were standing under a tree. The woman was making violent gestures to the man. The man shoved her away with his shoulder. The woman seized his arm. He broke from her and made off. The woman shrieked after him. Aubrey could just hear the hideous thin sound of her crying voice.

"It is odd," he said in answer to Diamond.

"We might have such a nice time of it," she continued, looking wistfully at him. "Mightn't we? And it ought to be easy, too."

"Perhaps some day it will be easy," he said.

"When?"

"I can't tell you. At any rate, we must never be beastly to anybody, either of us, Diamond."

"Oh, you wouldn't, never, I'm sure," she said.

And it seemed to Aubrey that again, and as if unconsciously, she drew a little closer to him.

"How can you be sure about anything a man might do?" he asked, "or not do?"

Her large, soft eyes were cloudy with a sort of childish wonder as he spoke.

"Eh?" she said.

"Men don't know themselves what they are capable of, one way or another. They have their kind moments and their cruel moments."

"D'you think they always know how cruel they're bein'?" she said. "D'you think *he* knew? I often wonder; and when it gets night, I wonder more," she added.

Aubrey felt that in her simple way she was imaginative. She was sensitive to the quickening influence of the dark and the silent hours, when the mind wanders as it never wanders by day, alone, like some fantastic figure on a mysterious heath, led by the winds and by the dim stars towards summits or abysses that are hidden in the light of noon.

"Ever so much more!" she continued. "Why ever is it? And sometimes I feel as if there was something inside of me beatin' round just like a bird. And I want to let it out and I can't. Isn't it funny? I told Mr. King that once, and he said——"

She paused.

"Well, what did he say?"

"Why, he says, 'That's only a form of indigestion, Miss Diamond,' he says. 'Don't let it go on,' he says, 'or it'll be difficult to cure,' he says. And after he sent me some pills. He is kind. I took 'em, but it didn't go. It's here to-night. I think it comes because of the moon."

"I think I've felt it," Aubrey said.

Already he had forgotten Alf's warning, and forgotten what he had meant to find out, carried away by the curious sympathy that emanated so ignorantly from Diamond. How much and how directly she felt! How little she knew!

"Whatever is it, then?"

"Not what Mr. King thinks, though lots of people would agree with him—that it was liver, or something of the sort."

"Ah! but you don't?"

"No, Diamond; don't ever try to stop your feelings. Don't ever try to have no feelings at all."

Without knowing it, he had spoken with sudden violence. She looked quite startled.

"Well, but we can't, however we get tryin'," she said.

"Yes, we can," he said, thinking of many people in his world, of many who were in Lady St. Ormyn's garden on the night of his failure and his loss. "We can laugh at all real feelings until we scarcely feel at all. Or we can be afraid to feel, and let our cowardice triumph till our nature changes and we grow hard and indifferent, until we can hardly even be sorry. Diamond, depend upon it, there's a great tragedy in that—in being unable to feel really sad."

He had turned sideways and was looking into her face. His arm was behind the tiny chair on which she sat. A cloud was travelling before the moon and the wind shook the branches of the tree above them. Two or three drops of moisture that had been clinging to the twigs fell. They were cold on Diamond's face, cold as tears. She put up her thin hand to them. Her face was looking puzzled, like a child's face when it listens to an elaborate story.

"I thought we was all able to feel bad—upset, I mean. We all can. Even Dad, if there's anything goes wrong with the lights."

She paused in thought. Then she said—

"I don't know about Alf, though. I never seen him down, as I can remember."

As usual, she went straight to her personal experience, and told the truth as she had found it.

"No, he ain't never down. Vauxhall says it's just the same when they're travellin'. He's laughin' and playin' his games all the time and don't seem never tired. They can't keep him still. Why, it wouldn't be Alf, quiet. I do like settin' here with you."

The words and the mention of Alf recalled Aubrey to duty, and to the remembrance of the intention that had led him to seek Diamond that night.

"Why?" he asked quickly.

"Oh, I can talk to you like I can't to the others, not even Lill. And then it is nice here, like the country."

She lifted up her pale oval face to the tree. The wind shook down two or three more drops on to her cheeks.

"It's jolly after the theatre and all them painted trees on our Island—palms, ain't they?"

"Yes. They grow in the East."

"Lill's seen 'em really growin' and lizards runnin' up 'em. Hark at them soldiers."

A long way off on the broad walk there was a gleam of wavering scarlet under a gas-lamp, and a subdued shouting of "Tommy Atkins" came to their ears.

"Whatever do they want to make a noise for here?" said Diamond, with a sort of soft pettishness. "You wouldn't?"

"No," said Aubrey, thinking of the uproar in Lady St. Ormyn's garden. "But lots of people would."

"Yes, because they think as nobody can't be feelin' happy if they ain't shoutin'. There's ever so many like that in our Court; and the girls at the theatre too. One of them says to me to-night in the dressin' room, 'Why, Di,' she says, 'you sit so quiet, any one'd think you was dead.' We can't be talkin' all the time, can we?"

"No," said Aubrey.

And then they sat in silence for a little while. He thought of Caryll's capacity for shining silences, when she sat looking brilliantly calm, and far away from the dense shadows of speechless stupidity. There was a link between her and this little girl, who, in her odd way, loved quiet too. Two or three couples glided among the trees, with arms entwined sentimentally or affectionately round each other's waists. They murmured foolish words or giggled among the dark trees. One girl, in a long black jacket and a hat brimming over with feathers and ribbons, broke away from her swain and ran off awkwardly, looking over her shoulder to see if he was following. He started in pursuit. She screamed in triumphant terror, tried feebly to escape him and tumbled against a trunk. He caught at her arm. She broke into a piercing music of mingled cries and laughter, jerked, fought, tumbled down and rolled on the grass. He picked her up, shoved her hat—which had come off—on to her disorderly head, put his arm round her and dragged her away cackling hysterically and pretending to resist. Diamond observed it all calmly but with no disgust such as Aubrey felt. She was perfectly accustomed to such vulgar doings.

"They will have their larks," she said, as the striving black figures tortuously disappeared. "I couldn't never care for anything like that now."

"I should think not," said Aubrey.

"And Dad wouldn't never allow us girls to make too free. Besides, he couldn't bear anything low. And I shall always be just as I should if—if it'd kep' all right."

"Do you care for him still, Diamond, as much as ever?"

"Oh yes."

"You are as unhappy as ever?"

He would prove Alf's suspicions to be unfounded. She opened her lips to reply, then she shut them and looked at Aubrey.

"Sometimes," she said at length.

"Not always?"

"Not now," she said. "Not when I'm talkin' with you."

She made the confession without the slightest hint of shyness or of confusion. Aubrey felt uncomfortable, beginning to recognise the prescience of Alf.

"Why's that?"

"I dunno. Because I like bein' with you, I s'pose."

"And if we didn't meet at all?"

"Eh?"

"Suppose we didn't ever meet at all?"

The pale moonlight filtered through the branches to a white face that had suddenly become anxious.

"Why shouldn't we? Ain't we goin' to? Now you know Dad, and Alf, and all of 'em, I thought——"

"Yes?"

"I thought you was real friends with us."

Aubrey let his hand fall on hers. Something in the nervous tone of her voice compelled him. He had felt, he always felt love —a love that was apart from all else in his life. But for no one living did he feel such warm and pure friendship as for Diamond. She had come, in a horrible moment, to stand, almost like a guardian angel, between him and the artificial monster that held and yet disgusted him. She had saved him, ignorantly, from the last hopeless depth of despair. He even loved her, as we love our truest friends, without obscuring passion, without defiant and persecuting lust. She curved her thin fingers up to hold his. Hers were cold and wet with the tears of the tree which she had wiped from her cheeks. Their damp and almost clinging touch struck a chill of apprehension through Aubrey. He thought of the man at the rope, and seemed to see the little grey eyes of Alf fiercely watching him from some dark nook of the Park.

"Why ever d'you do that?" asked the voice of Diamond.

"Do what?"

"Grit your teeth like that?"

"Did I?"

"Yes, just as if you was angry."

"Perhaps I was angry."

"With me? Whatever for?"

"Not with you, Diamond, never with you. With fate, with life, with the Power that has made us so strangely."

"What! our fathers and mothers marryin'?"

"No, the Power that has made all men and women."

"God, you mean. Naughty! You musn't be angry with God. That's awful, wrong."

She might have been rebuking little Susie.

"And it ain't a bit of good, either," she continued, still holding his hand within hers, that was growing warmer from the contact. "Any more than it's a bit of good me bein' angry with Madame when she don't give me a solo step. We have to put up with things."

"Of course. But—but—don't you give me anything to put up with."

He was bending over her.

"Me!" she said. "Whatever are you sayin'?"

"Yes, you, Diamond. Be my friend always."

"Why, of course. Whatever is it?"

"And—just my friend. Come along."

He got up. The growing warmth of her hand seemed to tell him that it would be dangerous to sit longer. Diamond obeyed him with obvious reluctance.

"Must we go already?" she said.

"It's damp under the trees."

"Then let's walk a little. I don't want to go yet."

Aubrey knew it would be better to go, but he could not refuse her pleading look of appeal. They strolled over the grass in silence and reached a broad path. Here several people were walking slowly, some together, some alone, furtively, like spies. These were badly dressed men with degraded faces.

"What are they after?" said Diamond.

"I wonder!" said Aubrey. "Perhaps they could scarcely tell themselves. Don't you know that London is full of people who come out day after day, night after night, with no real purpose, on the chance of finding something or somebody that will change their lives and lessen their miseries?"

"I seen 'em in the streets; but whatever can they find here?"

"I daresay they are wondering. Don't look at them."

She turned her eyes away obediently from the dark places and the prowling figures.

"I should like to walk like this with you every night," she said simply. "Can't we do a day in the country some time?"

"I'm very busy in the day," Aubrey said hastily, and almost brusquely.

She did not speak again for several minutes. They reached the Serpentine. Its brown waters were whipped by the wind into little hurrying waves. On the near waves there was a streak of moonlight, which emphasised the flowing darkness all around. The wind was rising, and there was a mysterious wet breath in it.

"It's going to rain soon," Aubrey said. "We must turn and go."

"Yes, let's go," Diamond assented.

Her voice sounded strained and less sweet than usual. Aubrey guessed why. He did not look at her. As they walked towards the gates he felt as if a gulf yawned between them. He knew she was sensitively suffering, like a plant that folds its leaves. When they reached the gates they found two women and a man having a violent quarrel. A small and laughing crowd surrounded them, and two soldiers were urging them on. One of the women was crying bitterly. The other cursed the man, who cursed her back in the loathsome language of the street.

"You did," shrieked the woman. "You devil, you did, you did! And now look at 'er! You 'ave got 'er money! I say you 'ave, and she starvin' and nowheres to go."

She flew at the man, knocked off his hat, and tore at his hair like a wild-cat, all the time screaming oaths and curses. The man got away. The woman attacked him again, and fastened her teeth in his hand. He yelled. A policeman came up, and took the woman into custody. She was marched off, shrieking and struggling.

"You'll get three months, you hell-cat!" said the man, following.

The other woman was left weeping. The crowd had forgotten her already, and melted away cheerfully, discussing the pleasant little excitement that had broken the dark monotony of the streets. Diamond, who had watched the affair, and heard all the blasphemies without the shadow of a blush, went up to the woman who was crying.

"Did he take your money?" she asked.

"Ye-ye-ye-es, the 'ound, the —— 'ound!" whimpered the woman.

Diamond put two or three pence into her hand and returned to Aubrey.

"Spoils all the niceness of the Park, don't it?" she remarked quietly. "I'll go on a 'bus, please. No, I won't have you come with me to-night, please. No."

There was decision in her voice. Aubrey helped her on to the step of the 'bus, and watched her climb the stair to the seats on the top. He had not seen Sir Reuben's brougham going by, taking him and Lady Caryll to a ball. But Sir Reuben saw him and Diamond distinctly, just as they were passing through the Park gates. He moved suddenly in the carriage and looked out of the window.

"What is it, Reuben?" asked Lady Caryll.

"A street row," said Sir Reuben.

He leaned back, and turned his eyes again to the jewels that gleamed in Lady Caryll's frosty yellow hair, and on her neck and bosom. When he felt very old and tired, as now he often did at night, it reposed him to glance at his radiant slave, in whom the very heart of youth was surely beating, in whom the most exquisitely perfumed blossoms of youth were surely flowering. He strove to drink in her vitality, to sun himself in her radiance, to live in her still and yet increasingly intense virility. And when the grey and aged feeling crept upon him he was angry. For the sensation was horrible. He felt like a man with some soft, but heavy and inexorable animal crouched upon his breast. He strove to shake it off, to crawl, to wriggle from under it. But it could not be stirred. Indeed, his violence of exertion seemed only to increase the burden of its dominion, which was always more noticeable to him at night.

A few days later he told Aubrey that he had got a box at the theatre in Champion Square for a certain night.

"Tell that little imp, your friend, if you like," he added. "He fell in love with Caryll, and may be glad to know she is to see him and his relations in patterns. By the way, I've asked your mother to come with us."

Lady Rangecliffe did not often come to the house in Park Lane. She was discomforted there. It pained her to see Aubrey in his new home. It hurt her to see Lady Caryll gleaming with jewels and watched by the dark eyes of her husband. Lady Rangecliffe's honesty seldom wore a veil. She refused several of the Allabruth's invitations for no very apparent reason.

"Your mother dislikes me," Caryll said to Aubrey.

"Oh no, indeed," he answered hastily. "But she's always so busy. You know she looks after poor people a great deal."

"Yes. But I know, too, that she dislikes me. If not, why should she not come here? Besides, I saw her eyes on my wedding-day. There were no congratulations in them. And yet she has been my husband's great friend. She ought to wish him to be happy. And I have made him as happy as—I have made him happy."

"Yes."

Aubrey found nothing more to say. He was glad when Lady Rangecliffe accepted Sir Reuben's invitation to the theatre. Aubrey wrote to tell Diamond—whom he had not seen since the walk in the Park—the date on which they were coming, and received her answer. She said—

"Alf is in a state. He's got the new tricks ready, and talks of nothing but the Queen of Diamonds—says as she'll be fair mad with surprise when she sees him do his dive. All the music's to stop when he does it exceptin' the drums, what's to roll. I says they only roll like that for funerals, when they bury soldiers. Susie and all of 'em are to be there to see him, because it's the first time he done it, and I shall get Madame to let me stand with Lill in the wings." The letter was signed, "Faithfully yours, Diamond Manners."

Aubrey told Lady Caryll of the excitement which her promised presence at the theatre was already causing, and of the special preparation that was being made in her honour. She smiled lightly.

"Your little friend is like a gnome," she said. "I believe he came out of a tree-trunk to perform his antics, and that some day he will disappear among the leaves of a forest and be seen no more."

"He quite worships you," said Aubrey.

"Oh, does he?" she answered.

Her voice sounded cold, and for a moment Aubrey felt chilled. But then he remembered that Lady Caryll had no acquaintance with Alf's family, knew nothing of the pedestal on which he was placed in his home circle, and could not be expected to realise that the night of her visit to the theatre would be a great night in the humble annals of Milk Court.

Lady Rangecliffe came to dine in Park Lane before the performance. After it Sir Reuben was taking Lady Caryll to a great ball in Portman Square, to which Aubrey was also invited. A Royalty was to be there. Lady Caryll was dressed in black, and wore the engraved emerald, and a quantity of emeralds mounted on a black ornament that stood up high in her yellow hair. She looked radiant, but Lady Rangecliffe noticed that Sir Reuben was again oppressed by a cold, and that his cough troubled him. He seemed very fatigued.

"I am sure you ought not to go out to-night," she said to him bluntly: "You're looking dreadful."

"I always go with Caryll," he answered.

Lady Rangecliffe heard the obstinate note in his voice, remembered the dead wife, and said no more. But once or twice, at dinner, when Sir Reuben coughed, she winced, and an anxious look came into her honest face. Lady Rangecliffe was always in a state of anxiety about other people, though she took her own buffets from life as a boy takes a kick in a football scrimmage. As she dined, she often glanced at the emerald on Lady Caryll's breast. Then she looked at the wearer, and she too was dazzled by the radiance that emanated from Lady Caryll. There was something fierce in the apparent completeness of her joy, and Lady Rangecliffe suddenly thought that joy can be very horrible. Then, mentally, she—as she would have termed it—caught herself up, rebuking herself for lack of charity, and tried to share in her boy's worship of the glory of this girl, who shone upon the ugly and withered old man opposite to her, so uncomfortable in his unromantic malady.

When the carriage was announced, Sir Reuben wrapped himself in an immense fur coat, in which he looked like some small and peculiar animal. He stepped wearily into the brougham after his wife. Aubrey went with his mother in her carriage. On the way they talked a little, but conversation seldom flowed easily between them. Lady Rangecliffe, with the marvellously quick delicacy of perception that often guides a mother in her dealings with her children, lost much of her bluntness when she was with Aubrey. She did not blunder with him as she blundered with others. All her senses were sharpened by his presence, because he was her son, and she became highly strung and perceptive as a clairvoyante. The second-sight of the mother is often more truly miraculous than are the so-called marvels of the occultists. But this second-sight, and a certain confused and dim knowledge of it by the child, scarcely tends towards talk. Lady Rangecliffe and Aubrey said little in the brougham. Once she remarked that Sir Reuben was looking very ill.

"I fancy it's only a cold," Aubrey said. "I expect England hardly suits him after those hot climates."

"Well, he ought to go back to them; but perhaps it wouldn't suit her."

"Lady Caryll? I don't know. She looks meant for the sun, I think."

The words would not have slipped out but for the darkness in which they sat and the street noises that roared round them, and Aubrey quickly changed the subject till they were silent again. Lady Rangecliffe wished she could talk long with her boy in the dark. His unreserve would have been a sort of foretaste of heaven to her, but instinct told her that she could never hope for it. She must be content with silence, and the secret knowledge that he loved her as a mother longs to be loved. The lights shone from the front of the playhouse. They were blown sideways by the wind. The party of four entered Sir Reuben's box in time to see the ballet. There was a full house. The Marvellous Flicks always attracted a multitude wherever they performed, and to-night a long and strange Frenchwoman was singing terrible little songs of the horrors of the Paris streets. Pale, simply dressed, and wearing mournful black gloves up to her shoulders, she chanted hoarsely, in a veiled voice, the tragedies of the poor and of the wicked. And the smart world hurried from its dinner to hear her, loving to learn from her almost white lips the downward progress of the morphia victim or the hideous dreams of the drunkard.

Aubrey sat between his mother and Lady Caryll, and watched the ballet. Diamond did not come on until the Island scene. As Aubrey anticipated it, he recalled his condition on the evening when he had first seen Diamond. Then he had sat benumbed, face to face with a tragedy; now he sat beside the tragedy. It was with him in this small room with the red walls and the open window, through which he saw the pleasure-seeking world, with its eyes often upturned to Lady Caryll. She leaned her arm rather idly on the ledge of the box, seeming unconscious that she caused any sensation.

When the Island was disclosed, Aubrey's pulses quickened. The tom-toms sounded, and the line of girls floated forward. Diamond was among them, transformed by her red-gold wig and by the lithe and weary grace of her dancing. She glanced up at Aubrey. Sir Reuben leaned forward and scanned her through his opera-glasses. He wondered if she were the girl whom he had seen with Aubrey at the gate of the Park. He could not help thinking of a vulgar intrigue, and the cold and tuneless voice of experience whispered within him that all men were alike. Then he looked at Aubrey and found that his eyes were fixed on Lady Caryll. Lady Rangecliffe, who very seldom went to the theatre, was entirely engrossed by the stage spectacle. She moved her head to the music, and had put up her eye-glasses to see better.

"That girl there dances well, Aubrey," said Sir Reuben.

"Yes, doesn't she?"

"I wonder what she's like off the stage," said Sir Reuben, watching his godson sharply.

Aubrey made no answer. He had looked away from Lady Caryll, and now seemed absorbed in the business of the stage.

"Very common and uninteresting, probably," continued Sir Reuben.

He noticed a spot of red flame in his godson's cheek, and said to himself, "Can he really be cured already?" and, in face of the possibility, he was conscious of a sudden contempt for Aubrey.

When the curtain fell on the ballet, Sir Reuben talked a little—between his coughing fits—with Lady Rangecliffe. Lady Caryll sat silent, looking about the house. Her content to-night seemed supreme. There was a quiet expression of complete happiness in her white face. Aubrey did not disturb her by any words. He thought of Alf's excitement and expectation behind the painted curtain, of the tenseness of that body preparing for new and terrific physical feats. Alf was going to do homage with the body to the happy girl to whom Aubrey's soul did homage. Like the poor tumbler before the Virgin's altar, Alf would offer his gift. And Aubrey had a moment of jealousy of the little acrobat, a flitting, ugly sensation of which he was ashamed. It passed, and he looked up towards the black human swarm crowded under the many-coloured roof in which the lights gleamed. Susie was probably there with little Charley. Aubrey could imagine their condition of childish excitement, and of exultant pride in. Alf and their relationship to him. Aubrey supposed them—as was, indeed, actually the case—busy in informing those around them of the great and almost awful fact that the celebrated Alf Flick lived under their roof and played his tricks in their parlour; that their own father's cutlery and glassware endured the fearful honour of miraculous tossing at his hands; that from their own small and fidgety persons he produced eggs and apples, knives and cheese-plates at will. In truth, the little creatures, carefully installed in the front row behind the rail, were indeed floating on clouds of glory, and all agleam with pride and triumph. Nor had they failed to inform their sympathetic neighbours of their identity. Quickly from mouth to mouth the wonder flew that the small and shiny children with the excited red faces in the front row were relations of the Marvellous Flicks, and on terms of the closest intimacy with the famous Alf, whose demon antics and most terrific feats had moved even those stony-hearted potentates, the kings and emperors of Europe, to applause and admiration. The serious-minded Bob had much ado to answer all the questions addressed to him by those around him; by gallery boys suddenly become most strangely respectful, by a couple of scarlet soldiers who had done their valiant part in the last military tournament, by several young women in elaborate hats, and by a stout lady in gold earrings and a silk pelisse who professed herself a whole-hearted admirer of "all brave fellers, she didn't care where they come from!" The little Charley, by no means disposed to hide his light under a bushel, lispingly spread on all sides the tremendous news that to-night Alf was to perform a novel and hitherto unknown miracle in a descent from the roof, complicated by a perfect whirl of somersaults, and accompanied by the portentous rolling of muffled drums.

"He's been at the somersets in our kitching," announced the child, swelling with innocent gratification in the circumstance of being able truly to make so magisterial a statement.

And he beat his little hands on the rail before him in a perfect agony of pleasure, self-importance, and excitement. Nor was Susie at all his inferior on the occasion. Indeed, by right of her sex, she claimed an even greater share of attention than the battering Charley. Once her rosy shyness was overcome, and with it the attacks of suffocation which impeded her power of speech, she began indeed to border on the garrulous, and babbled freely of Alf and of his doings to all in her immediate neighbourhood, addressing herself more especially to the two soldiers, who received her confidences with every show of sympathy, and returned them with a fine orange which Susie was nothing loth to suck. Bob played chaperon with his usual serious air, but inwardly he was scarcely less excited than his little brother and sister, for Alf had won the admiration of all the Slagg connection since first he entered Milk Court. Bob, however, thought it due to himself, and to the machinery with which he was so closely bound up, to maintain an air of slight detachment, and not to thrust his relationship to the hero of the evening too prominently into notice. It may be that he saw the putting forward of the fact might, with safety, be left to the initiative of Susie and Charley. As the ballet drew to an end, the excitement of the children increased. They thrust forward their small heads beneath the rail, and squeaked their comments on the crowded audience. Susie, with the sharp eyes of woman, spied Aubrey in the box next the stage.

"There's the gen'leman!" she piped. "The gen'leman as come to supper at our house!"

"And there's the pitty lady!" cried Charley, perceiving Lady Caryll's pale face and sparkling hair.

For Alf had made no secret of his adoration of Lady Caryll, and had transformed her into a sort of marvellous fairy queen for the benefit of the children. Bob leaned forward to gaze at her with unwinking solemnity, and the eyes of half the gallery were at once riveted on Sir Reuben's box.

"She's a rare one, and no mistake," said one of the soldiers.

"My, what stones!" cried the stout lady in the silk pelisse and the gold earrings. "A king's ransom wouldn't buy the like, I'll lay."

And she broke into an account of a certain cat's-eye brooch of great value which at one time had been in her possession, but of which she had been most basely robbed by an individual who, it seemed, had been a candlemaker, and with whom she had injudiciously walked out in the neighbourhood, by what one could gather, of Barnes Common, the result being a proposal of marriage— accepted—the loss of the cat's-eye brooch, and the mysterious disappearance of the candlemaker, whom the good lady more than suspected of having fled over the seas to America in order most profitably to dispose of the magnificent booty. The history of this priceless jewel, to which no one listened very particularly, lasted till a bewigged functionary thrust a gigantic number into a gold frame, and the orchestra struck up a lively measure that smacked of the circus.

"That's their toon! that's their toon!" screamed little Charley, and he turned and furiously thumped the nearest stranger with his doubled fists. Susie began to get up from her seat in order to crane her head farther forward, but Bob caught her skirts and held her fast.

A large net was stretched over the heads of the people in the stalls, and secured by some mysterious arrangement of ropes and pulleys. Above this net swung one small trapeze, from which a cord dropped.

"He's goin' on that!" cried Charley, beside himself with excitement. "He's goin' in the roof! Oh! oh!"

He shuffled his feet in a sort of frantic dance, while Susie, whose face, bright-red in hue, seemed suddenly to have swelled in an alarming manner, dropped her half-sucked orange to the floor and grasped the rail with diminutive hands, puffing like one attacked by a sudden asthma. The people around caught the infection of the children's excitement, at which they could not help laughing sympathetically, and the pelisse lady, blessing them for a pair of pretty ducks, dispersed her bonnet-strings abroad upon her ample shoulders, and declared she felt all of a tremble at the prospect of Alf's high doings. Then the curtain was drawn up and the Flick Family bounded forward, making elaborate gestures, and smiling in the most athletic and self-possessed manner possible.

"Where's the little 'un?" asked one of the soldiers.

"He ain't there yet," piped Charley. "He comes by hisself. That's Vauxhall, what married my sister."

And he glowed, like a hot coal, with vanity.

Vauxhall's magnificent figure looked very well in his tight black suit, which was decorated with silver embroidery in a "chaste design" invented by Lill, as Susie took care to inform the company in the gallery. He stood in an easy attitude at the end of the family line, and turned his face towards the wings. There was a moment's pause, and then, in obedience to a gesture from Vauxhall, Alf came running forward with his quick and sidling gait, ducking his head on which the watered hair was plastered, and blowing kisses with his hands.

"There he is! There's Alf! that's Alf!" shrieked Charley.

He turned sharply round to the pelisse lady, who sat immediately behind him, cried again, "That's Alf!" and gave her a punch in the ribs that made her catch her breath and ejaculate—

"Bless the child! if he ain't crazed with it all!"

Having made his habitual salute in the most solemn and mechanical manner, Alf cut an extraordinary caper which made the house rock with laughter, stood on his head waving one hand at the audience, regained his feet, and looked stonily round the house with his grim, yet twinkling eyes.

Aubrey could just see Diamond and Lill half hidden in the wings to watch their little relative's new triumph. And once he saw Diamond peep forth to stare at their box. Her big eyes rested on Lady Caryll and then on him. Aubrey wondered if, with those two swift glances, there was linked a quick woman's thought.

Lady Rangecliffe, who adored all feats of strength, all daring exercises, like a boy, sat forward in the box, jerking her head sideways.

"The little chap's well put together," she said. "Not an ounce of flesh. He'd have made a jockey. Wouldn't he, Aubrey?"

"Yes, mother," said Aubrey.

He turned to Lady Caryll.

"He'll do all his tricks to-night for you," he said to her.

She smiled a cool recognition at Alf. Alf saw the smile, and his small eyes gleamed in the glare of the footlights. At that moment he felt an intense pride in his physical abilities. It ran like fire through his veins. He knew that Charley, Susie, and Bob were watching him from the gallery. He could squint at Lill and

Diamond in the wings. And the Queen of Diamonds smiled at him from her box. It was quite the grandest day of his life, and he felt born within him an overpowering excitement, a devilry of daring. He felt inclined to attempt some feat that he had never practised, to trust utterly to the perfection of his trained and obedient muscles. His mind went to work busily while the music rang out. Mechanically he caught the tambourine that Vauxhall flung at him, shook its bells in the air, and beat it while his brothers and father performed their first evolution. And all the time he was thinking he gazed at Lady Caryll. She looked calm and gay. Her smooth cheeks were white, her yellow hair was frosty under the great emeralds that quivered in their black setting. Alf desired to bring the red to her cheeks and the fire to her eyes. The actor's longing to hold captive the least easily moved person in his audience came upon him. He could see with his trained eyes, which had watched so many watching multitudes, that the dark, blunt-faced—he called her ugly—woman beside Lady Caryll would swiftly be waked to enthusiasm by his daring, but he felt that he must do something almost miraculous to send a thrill through the heart of the Fairy Queen. All this shot through his brain in the twinkling of an eye, always accompanied by the glaring sound of the music. Then his bar came. He dropped his tambourine, stretched out his arms to attract attention, spun forward in catherine wheels, leaped into the air and alighted, rigid as a dead thing, on the upturned feet of his father, his arms pinned to his sides, his legs extended, his toes turned up towards the lights in the ceiling. This was the famous corpse act, during which Alf was kicked about from one relation to another, was spun high into the air, dropped nearly to the boards of the stage, saved just in time on a toe, set whirling like a top to the four points of the compass, jerked into a standing position on his head, all the time rigid, motionless as a bundle of dead limbs and a dead body sewn up in black and silver trappings for the grave. This act was always a success, and was sometimes repeated if the applause was very persistent. Alf prayed that it might be encored to-night, for while he was a corpse he could think out some daring deed, some exquisite and unrivalled feat of lofty tumbling, that must conquer that fairy woman on whose white breast the huge jewel shone. As the great audience gazed at his stiff horizontal body, while his father, propped on his back against a velvet stand, turned him with drumming feet as the Japanese turn their gigantic barrels, little Alf was thinking furiously. Mechanically he kept his body perfectly straight, perfectly motionless. His small, wide-open eyes were now staring at the stage, now at the ceiling and the blazing lights, now at the wings, now at the back-cloth, as his father's practised feet kicked him with apparent violence first in one direction then in another. Then Vauxhall took up a prostrate position at some distance, and Alf was tossed high in the air sideways towards his brother. While Alf went on thinking he made the necessary effort which turned him twice in mid-air. He alighted on the soles of Vauxhall's feet. Great applause burst out in the house. Alf scarcely heard it. What extraordinary thing could he do to startle into irresistible admiration the lovely lady? There was his great new dive, it was true. He had thought that would be a sensation. But now, in her cool presence, it hardly seemed enough. Vauxhall kicked him high, still cogitating, taking his thoughts with him far into the air. He spun like a ball.

"Any one'd swear he was dead," said the pelisse lady, the perspiration bursting out upon her large, motherly face. "Never did I see such doin's, never, no. Oh, law! I thought they'd dropped him that time!"

In her tremor of fright she had laid hold of those on each side of her. Charley and Susie had become perfectly silent. With round and staring eyes, as those that look on some sacred vision, they regarded the flights, the turns, the uprisings and the descents of their august relative.

"He do keep jolly still," said one of the soldiers.

"Like one dead and ready for the layin' out, I say again!" said the pelisse lady. "Oh! it's enough to send a body silly to look at him."

Her bonnet was cocked, and a button burst from her boot. She never heeded it. Now Alf spun with inconceivable rapidity above the tripping treadmill action of Vauxhall's feet. It was impossible to distinguish which side up he was. His face became a blur. The silver embroidery on his tights flashed in the light. Merely to watch his whirling body made people giddy. They would have been surprised could they have known the calm calculations, the daring projects that were seething in his mind. He scarcely felt the continuous soft drumming of his brother's feet against him. Yet, at each short cry of command, at each clapping of the hands that signalled some change in the nature of the feat performed, his alert spirit almost mechanically responded, giving the necessary message to the trained muscles that swiftly and surely carried out his will. And all the time the gay, familiar circus music rang in his ears which scarcely heard it. He could not see Lady Caryll. He wondered if she were watching him. She should watch him presently when he was drawn up to the roof. He flew high into the air, bent his body, turned twice with the speed of lightning, and stood on the stage calmly regarding the immense audience. His breath was not hastened. His cheeks were not flushed. He sidled to the fierce applause and glanced up at Sir Reuben's box. Lady Caryll was looking downward at the emerald on her bosom. Then the scarlet came into the boy's face, and he drew his breath hard as he retired to his corner. Nor did he come out of it in answer to the demand for an encore. His father glanced towards him, but Alf shook his head. The elder Flick did not insist. He knew that Alf did nothing in a public performance without good reason. Vauxhall took the field, and Charley and Susie were once again in glory, inspired by the ardent praises that came from those around them. Yet the affection of the gallery, even as the affection of Milk Court, flowed in greatest volume to Alf. The feats of Vauxhall, brilliant though they were, did not fire the blood as did the feats of Alf, whose minute size and impudent daring always caught the imagination of the public.

After Vauxhall's "turn," the Flick Family proceeded to go through what they called their "trick patterns." In this act they all six took part, the father and the five brothers. It was a kaleidoscope performance of the most brilliant kind. Nor was it devoid of a curious and swift grace. The Flick father, sturdy and stout as some rooted immemorial oak, was the magnificent foundation of each new combination. Planted firmly on his large feet, a gay and continuous smile upon his broad and masculine face, he served his sons as base, springboard, ladder, pivot. They leaped upon him like cats, planting their light feet on his broad hips, darting to his shoulders, ready, in their turn, to be a base for startling operations by their higher climbing brothers. Now they seemed a human tree with spreading branches, now a wheel, now a wavering plant blown aslant by a wind, now a fierce group of scowling gladiators, now a laughing ladder of gay souls ascending skyward, now a quivering fan with their black arms spread for sprouting feathers, now a trumpet broadening to give egress to some triumphant sound, now a comb with living teeth. The swiftness, the intense, almost angry vigour with which each new pattern was formed and broken, made the watching eyes blink as eyes blink at the monotonous raging of machinery, or at the goblin play of darting fires.

Lady Rangecliffe was completely absorbed by the performance. Her long, thin body twitched with a responsive energy to the acrobatic energy upon the stage. She jerked her head continually and blinked her short-sighted eyes. But Lady Caryll was in no way moved. Often her eyes were turned to the house or to the jewel on her breast. Sir Reuben watched her from the shadow of the box. Aubrey's attention, like his mother's, was fixed for the present upon the stage. He felt a strongly personal interest in the performance, much of Diamond's interest, some of the glowing enthusiasm of the little Charley and Susie, even a certain pride—that was very boyish—in the feats of this family, because he knew something of its inner history, and of the happy homeliness of its anxiety and sincerity.

Presently came the pattern of the growing vine. The Flicks arranged themselves against a back cloth which represented a great trellis against which they seemed to grow, while Alf stood quietly upon the stage apparently indifferent to their proceedings. Then the father clapped his hands. Alf turned sharply, came backwards to the footlights, took a quick tripping run, sprang at his father, darted up him, reached his shoulder, stood on his head, swarmed up Vauxhall, wriggled with amazing rapidity between the arms and legs of the various brothers, and finally came out at the top of the pattern on which he perched in the shape of a round ball, or grape, his head completely doubled under him. There was a moment's pause, during which all the Flicks remained motionless as black figures carved out of ebony, while the fiddles in the orchestra played a shrieking tremolo. Then there was a bang on the big drum. The black grape was shaken from its plant by the mighty sound. It rolled into mid-air. The pelisse lady in the gallery cried out in terror.

"My, he's done for!" she shrieked, covering her hot face with her fat hands.

She heard a burst of applause, looked up, and saw the Flicks in a row before the footlights, leaping and bowing, their faces gay with smiles. A bell sounded. The curtain slowly fell, concealing them from sight. The pelisse lady heaved a lengthy sigh.

"I thought he was killed," she murmured. "I thought he was in pieces, that I did."

The two soldiers and those around her laughed at her excitement, stamped their feet vigorously, gave forth piercing whistles, and clapped their hands. Susie and Charley banged the rail till their little fists were marked with weals of red. Up went the curtain again, and the Flicks were disclosed in surprised and half-deprecatory attitudes. They made a combined movement as if to retire, paused before the frantically renewed applause, hesitated, looked at each other, then simultaneously burst into a wild series of leaping somersaults, till some huge black and silver serpent seemed winding its way about the stage. Then, rising to their feet, they stood at attention. The moment of Alf had come. He stepped forward. Up in the far away gallery Bob, Susie, and Charley were quivering with expectation. Even the serious and reserved elder brother could no longer conceal his excitement. In the wings Lill and Diamond stood motionless, their eyes fixed on Alf. The band stopped playing, and, amid silence, Alf ran to the footlights, bounded into the net that roofed the stalls, and, leaping on the rising and falling floor with the prancing gait of an exceptionally agile dancing-master, gained the cord that hung from the trapeze. He grasped it, gave a signal, and was drawn up in mid-air, swaying this way and that, his body rigidly extended and his feet close together. And, while he mounted thus towards the trapeze that hung at present midway between the floor and the ceiling of the great theatre, he peered at Lady Caryll, whose attention was now at last fixed upon him. The cessation of the music had attracted her attention. Apparently she had forgotten the jewel on her breast. She had turned in the box to get a better view of Alf, and as she saw him looking at her she smiled slightly and said something to Aubrey, who was now standing up behind her.

A fierce boldness, that was like a storm, swept into the boy's heart. His muscles tightened. His small hard hands gripped the rope more fiercely, and his body seemed to become indomitable as iron. Lady Rangecliffe had put up her opera-glasses. Sir Reuben pushed his head forward to see better.

Alf gained the trapeze, caught it with one hand, let the rope go, swung in the air, threw his leg over the bar, and sat looking calmly round him. Vauxhall had stepped forward to the edge of the stage. He rested one hand on his hip and gazed up at his brother, with the fixed and impassive expression which hid so strong an excitement and admiration. Susie sat closer to Charley. She felt a little frightened, as children feel when it begins to grow dark and no lamp is lit in the room where they are playing. Charley wriggled, and stuck out an elbow to keep her off. He was absorbed in Alf and could brook no feminine distraction. Bob said "Hush!" to Susie, and the pelisse lady remarked "Law sakes!" twice, in a voice that was muffled and stertorous. The cessation of the music produced a rather uncanny effect upon the crowd. Only the little black and silver figure that dominated the multitude seemed totally unconcerned. But what a life was beating in it, what a hurry and turmoil of wild and happy youth and strength and power! Alf was like a blackbird looking down upon a city into whose heart he presently meant to take a daring flight. Like a bird, he whistled. The faint and clear sound made the pelisse lady jump. Her nervous system was more sensitive than could possibly have been supposed from her appearance. Vauxhall heard the whistle and replied to it. A cord was pulled from below, and the frail trapeze on which Alf was perched glided stealthily upward toward the lights that shone in the ceiling. All the people in the front stalls leaned their heads far back and turned up their faces, which looked peculiarly white in the cold illumination of the electric lamps.

And now Susie and Charley—Bob, too, in his more secret way—reached the apex of family emotion. For they saw their all-glorious relative, serenely ascending to their level, honour them with an almost fraternal wink—(which was observed with awe as testimony to their previous truth in narrative by those about them)—and pass on and up to the coloured ceiling, against which he seemed almost a tiny, summer fly.

Susie clutched Charley's damp little hand, and made an odd, childish noise, something between a gasp and a chuckle. The pelisse lady began to breathe hard.

"Whatever's the child goin' to do up there?" she said, rolling her pocket-handkerchief into a ball, and beginning to look almost sick with apprehension. "It turns a body giddy to see him. Whatever's he goin' to do?"

"Jump down into the net," said Bob, trying to keep his voice decently calm, as became a young man absorbed by day in complicated pursuits.

"Jump—what! He'll be killed. For certain sure he'll break his neck!" she cried, covering her eyes with one hand, and clapping the other over her ear.

Bob smiled.

"Oh, Alf'll never have an accident," he answered. "He ain't any more afraid of doing that than you might be of jumping off a chair, Ma'am."

"Alf won't never have no excident!" piped Charley. "Oh! oh!"

Below in the orchestra the silence was broken by a drum tap, sharp and short. Alf stood up on the trapeze. Vauxhall moved a step forward, staring steadily up at his small brother, who was to dive head foremost into the net, turning two somersaults sideways in the rapid flight. To accomplish this feat Alf ought to stand facing the stage, and at this moment he was so standing, with his eyes fixed upon Lady Caryll far down below him. Muffled drums began to growl, rising into a soft thunder, dying away into a cruel and suggestive murmur. Vauxhall clapped his hands as a signal. Suddenly Alf turned on the trapeze, and faced the other way. Vauxhall made a quick movement of surprise.

"What's he at?" murmured the Flick father, still preserving the stereotyped smile with which he always honoured his audiences. Vauxhall shook his head. The veiled roar of the drums rose louder. Alf took one hand from the red rope of the trapeze.

"By God!" murmured Vauxhall, "he's going to do it backwards! The little devil!"

And into his stony face there came a strong flush of scarlet.

The roar of the drums increased. Alf swayed, took his other hand from the rope, and dived backwards. There was a flash of silver in the light as he turned in the air, a thud as his body dropped into the net. The watching crowd broke into a tempest of applause. Vauxhall had advanced to the edge of the net to give his brother a hand as he leaped on to the stage. But Alf lay quite still in the net over the white, upturned faces in the stalls.

"Little devil! He's feigning, to frighten 'em!" whispered Vauxhall to the line of brothers behind him.

He knew the mischief that bubbled eternally in Alf.

The line of brothers smiled. The applause died suddenly away. Only the muffled drums roared on. The people in the gallery and in the boxes craned forward to look into the net, and the pelisse lady, taking her fat hand from her eyes, said—

"Law sakes! I'm glad it's over. I sy such things is wicked and oughtn't to be allowed, that I do."

The roar of the drums ceased. The drummers, as if paralysed by curiosity, dropped their sticks. All the red had died away from Vauxhall's face. In silence he sprang into the net and bent over Alf.

"Come out of it, Alf!" he muttered. "You're scaring 'em!"

"Carry me off!" whispered Alf.

His lips were white.

"God!" said Vauxhall.

He bent down and raised his brother in his arms. Then, walking with the frightful, tripping motion that the net forced on him, a sprightly dancing-master's gait above the staring faces in the stalls, he carried Alf to the stage.

"Put me on my feet," Alf whispered. "D'you hear, Vaux? I'll take the call."

Vauxhall held him up in a standing position. He smiled, lifted one hand, blew a kiss, tried to duck his head—and failed.

"Gawd! how it hurts!" he whispered.

The curtain fell. There was no applause. People were frightened. An intense silence reigned.

After a minute or two the curtain was slightly pulled back, and a large and glossy man in evening dress, and carrying a shining silk hat, stepped before the footlights. He lifted up his plump hand, on which gleamed an immense diamond ring.

"Is there any medical gentleman in the house?" he said in a loud voice. "If so, the management will be greatly obliged to him if he will come at once behind the stage."

Two or three men in the stalls rose and made their way out. The band struck up a march, and the curtain drew up and displayed a number of performing dogs barking round their trainer.

CHAPTER XXII

LADY CARYLL was talking to a royal personage about twelve o'clock that night. The royal personage paid her a number of rather heavy compliments. All the time he was speaking to her his eyes were fixed on the great emerald. He said afterwards to his hostess—

"The Princess has no jewel so magnificent as Lady Caryll's jewel. Sir Reuben must be another Count of Monte Cristo, or he must have discovered the philosopher's stone which can transmute every substance into gold."

His hostess smiled rather indiscreetly. Her face wore a demure expression of artfulness which excited the curiosity of the royal personage, who loved to know, in good time, all the scandals of London.

"What is it?" he asked in a low voice, leaning sideways from the hot quail that lay in his plate.

His hostess bent to him over the flowers.

"They say, sir," she whispered, "that Sir Reuben is not a Monte Cristo. The resources of Dumas' hero were limitless."

"Ah! And Sir Reuben's?"

"They say in the City that if he lives long enough he will be ruined."

The royal personage looked towards Sir Reuben, who was supping at a table near them.

"Sir Reuben! he does not look that sort of man."

"He is not that sort of man by nature, sir. But he is in the hands of a strange woman."

The royal personage smiled and resolved to see something more of Lady Caryll.

Aubrey was not at supper. He came into the ball-room about one o'clock, just as Lady Caryll and her husband were preparing to leave. His face was very white and there were red rims round his eyes. After shaking hands with his hostess he made his way at once to Lady Caryll.

"Please let me speak to you for a moment," he said. "Come and sit down."

He led her into an alcove. The orchestra played a valse.

"Caryll," Aubrey said, in a rather unsteady voice, "that poor little chap is dying."

"Horrible!" she said.

A quiet expression of pity had come into her face.

"I have been so wondering," she continued, "whether he was seriously injured. I feared he must be."

She glanced into the ball-room. A woman with wonderful diamonds in her hair passed before the entrance of the alcove, valsing. The light from the chandelier shone over the jewels. They gleamed. Lady Caryll leaned slightly forward to see the woman better.

"How terribly sad!" she added.

"Isn't it?" Aubrey said in an unsteady voice.

The sound of the valse gave him a dreadful feeling of nausea. The sensation was absolutely physical.

"Some frightful internal injury," he added, "which causes intense pain. They thought at first of operating. How abominably loud this band is playing."

"Yes. It is the fashion this season. Poor little boy!"

"But they have decided that it couldn't save him."

Aubrey cleared his throat as if he were suffering from a cold. There were beads of perspiration on his forehead.

"I don't believe any of the windows are open," he said impatiently. "The heat is insufferable."

"I don't feel it," Lady Caryll said. "We are just leaving."

"I'm glad of that, because—look here, he'll probably die som time in the early morning."

"This morning?"

"Yes."

"How shocking!"

"He wants—he'd like—you know people have strange fancies when they're dying."

"Do they? I don't like to think about death."

She spoke with a certain obstinacy. Aubrey did not notice it. He was painfully excited, though he appeared calm, and sat perfectly still by her side.

"They've carried him home to—to Milk Court. It's near the theatre rather—not so very far. Look here, Caryll, will you drive there now?"

She moved, and her gown rustled slightly.

"I!" she said quickly. "Why? What for? What could I do?"

"Nothing, of course, to save him, poor little chap."

"No—exactly. These things are horrible, but we cannot prevent them. The doctors are with him, no doubt."

The woman with the wonderful diamonds passed again before the alcove. Lady Caryll's eyes followed her eagerly.

"The doctors can do no good. Caryll, he wants to see you."

"Me?"

Aubrey cleared his throat again.

"My mother is there still. She knows a lot about nursing."

"But I know nothing."

"It isn't that. He wants just to see you."

"But—how extraordinary! Why?"

With each sentence the sound of her voice grew colder.

"Why? Because—well, Caryll, he did the trick that will kill him in a few hours—he—it was for you, poor little chap. He'd never tried it before. He thought—he wanted——"

Aubrey stopped, and pressed his lips tightly together. He was angry with himself. Speaking very quickly, he said at last—

"He wanted to do something extraordinary to please you."

"How very strange!"

"It was terribly foolish. But he was always the most—most daring little beast. Well, he's paid for it. But he wants to see you before he dies. Look here, Caryll, don't be afraid. There's nothing horrible to see. The injury—you understand, it's inside. He looks much as usual, really—only very white. He's quite——"

"I can't go," Lady Caryll said.

Her face was distorted by an expression almost of loathing.

"But, Caryll——"

"I can't—I can't!"

She spoke sharply.

"But, Caryll, why not? You needn't stay more than a moment. He wants to hear you say you—you—he—it is absurd, I know—he wishes to hear you say you enjoyed your evening—seeing him perform, you know. He'd like to know he gave you pleasure."

"Yes, yes. Tell him so. Go and tell him so, poor little fellow."

She tore some white lilies out of her gown.

"Take those with you—with my love. Say I've been wearing them to-night and sent them, and was grieved—shocked—that I loved his performance—thought it wonderful. Reuben—Reuben!"

She called to her husband.

"Take me down to the carriage now, please. Good night, Mr. Herrick."

"Why have you given those lilies to Aubrey?" said Sir Reuben, as they got into the carriage.

"To give to that poor little boy. He's badly hurt. I thought it might please him, comfort him, perhaps."

"Caryll!"

It was dark in the carriage. Sir Reuben's voice sounded moved in the darkness. He put his hand on his wife's.

"Why, how good you are!" he said.

And, when he said that, he seemed a little surprised, too.

"I hope it will turn out to be nothing very serious," he continued.

"Oh, I hope so. Acrobats often have these accidents, don't they—and recover?"

"I daresay. I trust it will prove so. I'm glad you sent those lilies."

He kissed her in the dark carriage. In doing so, he noticed that her cheek was unusually warm.

CHAPTER XXIII

AUBREY came out into Portman Square. His hands were full of Lady Caryll's white lilies. Their scent was hot and feverish, and seemed to him strangely artificial. He felt that he hated the flowers, but he held them carefully as he stood on the pavement before the rows of carriages, whose lamps glared in the night. A linkman ran to call him a hansom. While he waited for it he heard the band in the house behind him beginning to play a Lancers. A number of popular tunes tripped jerkily through the scheme of the music. Cruel and frivolous things they seemed to him just then. The crowd of footmen standing about the door stared at the flowers he carried, whispered to one another, and smiled. Aubrey was glad when the cab drove up. To-night he shrank from all watching eyes. The linkman shut the apron with a bang, touched his hat, and said, "Good luck to you, my lord! Good luck to you, Capting!" Aubrey gave him some money, and leaned back in the cab. He was startled when he heard the cabman's voice saying—

"Where to, sir?"

"Drive to Milk Court, Graham Street," he said.

"Where, sir?" said the cabman in an astonished voice.

"Milk Court—near Champion Square. Drive as fast as you can."

"Well, I'm blowed!" murmured the cabman, as he shut down the door of his peep-hole. "Milk Court!"

He whipped up his horse. The lines of waiting broughams vanished. Soon Aubrey was in Oxford Street. He saw people hurrying along, or standing at the street corners staring about them, as if vaguely expectant. A few belated bicyclists were darting homeward, bending forward over their lamps. The policemen marched heavily on their beats, turning their bull's-eye lanterns to the doors of houses, the windows of shops. Some lads slouched along, arm in arm, squalling a music-hall song. They had pale London faces, and wore caps stuck on the backs of their heads, and their hair brushed forward on their foreheads. One of them held a flower in his mouth, and jigged to the tune of his companions. Two women in shabby dresses and long black cloth jackets conferred mysteriously together at a crossing. While they murmured to each other they watched the street furtively. They parted suddenly as an oldish man went by slowly, smoking a cigar. One of them followed the man, the other stood where she was, staring after them. Aubrey noticed that she wore long gold earrings which trembled perpetually against her bloated cheeks. She moved wearily down a dark side street as a policeman lethargically approached her. Aubrey felt a deep pity for her, and for all poor women, and then a terrible sense of the hopelessness of great cities. He looked no more at the streets. The sickly smell of the lilies enervated him. He thought of the place where they would soon be lying, and an old wonder came back to him. Is there any sensation in a flower? If so, how helpless it must feel in the hands of men. These lilies were torn from a ballroom to lie, perhaps soon, on the breast of a corpse.

"This is Champion Square, sir," said the cabman's voice. "I don't exactly know where Graham——"

Aubrey directed him, and in a few minutes the high red and white buildings of Milk Court were in sight.

"Shall I stop for you, sir?" said the cabman, as Aubrey got out.

"No, thanks," Aubrey answered, paying him.

The cabman drove off, wondering how the deuce a young swell came to live in such a neighbourhood. Then the usual thought came to him, and he chuckled.

As Aubrey approached the big house in which the Slaggs lived, he was conscious of a sensation of cowardice, almost of terror. Sorrow is like an advancing and invincible enemy. He stood for some time on the pavement of the Court before he could summon courage to go and knock at the door which Diamond had opened with her key on the night of her birthday party. And he remembered that evening with amazing vividness; the rush of the excited Susie into the narrow passage, the china doll desolate upon the settle, the happy group of relations by the fire, the lady tourist in the pelerine upon the wall. He recalled the little remarks that were made, and saw Alf leaping over the back of his chair and alighting before the supper-table. It was vivid, yet it all seemed a long time ago. At last he knocked on the door. Immediately there was a noise of steps in the passage, and the door was softly opened by Bob.

"Hasn't she come, sir?" he asked, in a voice that was full of anxiety, as he saw Aubrey standing alone.

"No," Aubrey answered, stepping into the passage.

Bob looked at the lilies.

"When's she coming, sir?"

Aubrey shook his head.

"What!" said Bob. "Then he'll—I don't know——"

Aubrey walked towards the sitting-room, the door of which stood partially open. There was a whisper of voices within. As Aubrey entered he saw that the room was crowded with people, all of whom were standing up, as if in readiness for instant movement. All the Flicks were here, except Vauxhall. Mrs. Slagg and Lill were crying into pocket-handkerchiefs which they held up to their faces. Mr. Slagg, whose face was very white, and whose eyes were fixed and staring, had his lips pursed up as if he were going to whistle. When Aubrey came into the room the sound of whispering ceased instantly, and everybody gazed fixedly at him and at the lilies in his hands, with the exception of the two women, who, after a hasty glance, buried their faces again in their pocket-handkerchiefs, and turned towards the wall.

There was something peculiarly horrible in this crowd of silent people all standing up as if expectant.

Mr. Slagg was the first to break the silence. Speaking in a low and very unnatural voice—a voice as of one who talks in a church—he said—

"Mr. Herrick, sir, ain't the lady coming then?"

"She—she can't come," Aubrey said, trying in vain to appear unconstrained. "She sent these. She's deeply grieved and shocked."

How cold and bare his words sounded as he heard them.

"How is he?" he asked.

Mr. Slagg pursed his lips again.

"Cruel, cruel bad, sir. The doctor's just going, I believe. They can't do nothing for him."

The father of the Flick family suddenly sat down by the table and put his hand over his face. He was still dressed in tights, as were all his sons. Over their tights they wore the long ulsters in which they always went to the theatre. The pause that followed was broken by the entrance of the doctor. He came in softly, buttoning one of his gloves. He was an elderly, substantial looking man with a kind, though rather heavy face. Every one stared at him as he entered. Even the two women showed their tear-stained faces. He took Mr. Slagg by the arm and led him into the passage. There was a murmur of voices, the sound of retreating steps, of a door shutting softly. Then Mr. Slagg appeared again.

"John?" sobbed Mrs. Slagg. "John?"

Mr. Slagg looked round on those assembled and cleared his

voice like a man about to deliver a speech. Then he said, with great formality—

"Doctor says he can't do nothing more. He'll come back again in the morning—if necessary."

Mr. Flick suddenly looked up, and said, with a sort of dull anger—

"Necessary! What's he mean by that? Of course it's necessary."

"It all depends, Sam," said Mr. Slagg rather huskily.

"Depends—what on?"

"Why—on—why, whether he's—you know, Sam, as well as I do."

"I do not," said Mr. Flick quite fiercely, and pulling at the front of his long coat with a restless hand.

"Well, then"—Mr. Slagg appeared to gather himself together for some unusual effort—"Well, then," he repeated, "you'd better know, Sam. Them that's gone don't need no doctors."

Mr. Flick half rose from his seat. Aubrey thought he looked as if he were going to strike the speaker. Then he tumbled back in his chair, leaned his mighty arm along the table, and dropped his head on it. There was a slight rustling in the passage, and Lady Rangecliffe put her head in at the door.

"Please come here," she said, looking towards the women. "I want another poultice heated at once."

Lill got up trembling.

"Come, Ma," she said through her sobs.

She pulled her mother by the arm. Mrs. Slagg got up and followed her out to the kitchen. Lady Rangecliffe saw them go and then beckoned to Aubrey to come into the passage. Aubrey obeyed the sign and shut the door behind him. It was rather dark in the passage. Lady Rangecliffe stood close to her son and looked into his face with her short-sighted eyes.

"Where is she, Aubrey?" she said, jerking her head sideways. "He keeps on asking when she'll come."

A dull flush rose in Aubrey's face. He hesitated a moment. Then, for the first time in his life, he told his mother a deliberate lie.

"Mater, I didn't think it right to bring her here."

"What, Aubrey?" said Lady Rangecliffe, bending down her head to hear the better.

"I didn't think it right for her to come. She's too young. She's never—she's never seen"—(he whispered)—"death."

"Do you mean that you didn't ask her to come?" said Lady Rangecliffe, looking intently into her son's face.

Aubrey nodded. He held out his hands full of the lilies.

"She was terribly grieved. She sent these. She tore them out of her gown for him."

But Lady Rangecliffe did not take the lilies. She stood quite still, and her face looked strangely stern in the dim light. Then she pointed to a side passage.

"Aubrey, you can tell him your lie," she said. "Yes—let him—make him believe it. We mustn't hurt him any more."

She blinked her eyelids rapidly as she turned towards the kitchen.

Aubrey stood in the passage hesitating, considering what to do. He began to feel dazed and fatigued. After a moment he mechanically followed his mother, and looked through the doorway into the kitchen. A fire was burning there. The coals were red hot and cast a strong glow over the hearth. Lady Rangecliffe stood by a deal table waiting for the poultice. Some muslin was spread out before her. The light gleamed on some family jewels which she wore round her long, thin neck. As she waited she jerked her head, and the shadow of her head, thrown by the light upon the wall, jerked too. The shadow looked much more grotesque than the substance. Mrs. Slagg and Lill were busying themselves over the heating of the oatmeal, and sobbing bitterly at their work. The contrast between their practical labour and their deep distress struck Aubrey as singularly painful. There was a sort of comic element in it which was heartrending. Lill choked into her handkerchief and said—

"Give me the spoon, Ma, please."

And Mrs. Slagg, with trembling hands, pulled open the drawer of the dresser and fumbled among its contents like a blind woman.

"Which spoon, Lill?" she said almost inaudibly.

"The wooden one. Oh, Ma—this'll kill Vaux. Oh, it will!"

Mrs. Slagg sniffed. Her usually serene face was distorted by grief into a vehement mask of grief, undignified, almost absurd. There is often something painfully ludicrous in very sincere sorrow. The oatmeal began to steam. Aubrey could smell it from where he stood in the doorway.

"Is it quite hot?" asked Lady Rangecliffe.

She spoke in a practical voice.

"Yes, ma'am—my lady," sobbed Lill.

"That's right. Bring it here then and I'll put it in the muslin."

Lill took the wooden spoon, and with it put the hot oatmeal on to a plate. Taking the plate in her hands she came towards the table. But her hands trembled so much that she dropped the plate to the floor. It was broken. She fell into a chair and burst into hysterical weeping, repeating, "I can't—I can't. Oh, Alf! Alf!"

Lady Rangecliffe kneeled down on the kitchen floor, quickly gathered together the oatmeal and put it on to the muslin, which she folded twice over it. Then she got another plate, put the poultice on it, and turned to leave the room. Before going, however, she went over to Lill, bent down and kissed her, saying—

"Never mind, my dear. Try to be brave. Remember that we should do all we can to ease his sufferings."

"Yes, yes," sobbed Lill. "But oh! it is awful. I'm frightened." She rocked herself to and fro. Her face, down which the tears streamed, was red with the heat from the fire. Aubrey understood her fear. The dim passage in which he stood seemed to him to be alive with terror. Lady Rangecliffe paused for a moment when she reached him.

"When I've put this on him I expect you can come in, Aubrey," she said. "It will give him a few minutes' ease. Poor little chap! He's as brave as a lion—such pluck!"

She strode away, the steam from the poultice making a thin cloudy veil about her. Aubrey waited where he was. In about three or four minutes she returned.

"You can go in now," she whispered.

Aubrey felt horribly expectant as he walked down the passage. He saw some one peeping at him round the edge of the sitting-room door, which was slightly open, and realised the tall, strong brothers, in their tights and their long coats, waiting there, almost as they waited at the theatre for their summons to perform their feats. Then he turned down the passage and stood outside the door of the room where Alf was lying. He tapped. Diamond opened the door. Her face was always quite pale. Now she looked much as usual, except that her eyes seemed unusually large and strained in expression, as if, by a violent effort, she was opening them wider than was natural. When she saw Aubrey she nodded to him and looked at the lilies he carried.

"He's askin' for you," she whispered. "He knows she isn't comin'."

Aubrey felt again the sense of acute shame that had stung him when he lied to his mother.

"Vaux is in there," continued Diamond. "He won't go, not for a minute."

She opened the door wider, and Aubrey entered the room.

It was very small. The walls were covered with a cheap paper, grey, with red bunches of flowers sprinkled about on it. A washhandstand, holding an iron basin, stood close to the one narrow window, which looked on to the court. By this window, and leaning with his back against the wall, was Vauxhall. He had taken off his coat, and, in his black and silver costume, looked extraordinarily out of place and theatrical, like a man who has "dressed up" for a joke or to act in a charade. His strong, muscular arms were folded across his broad chest, and he remained absolutely motionless, fixing his eyes on the narrow iron bed where his brother lay. Aubrey looked with a sickening sensation of apprehension towards the bed. He expected vaguely to see something horrible. He scarcely knew what. But death was sitting by that bed-head, and death is fearful to the young. So Aubrey looked with fear.

He saw Alf lying flat on his back, his head on a pillow which, being soft, stuck up on either side of his face, partially concealing his ears. His hair was still plastered forward over his forehead, which was covered with perspiration. His face was white. In order to ease his frightful pain, he had drawn up his legs under the patchwork coverlet, and the soles of his feet rested flat upon the sheet. His arms lay outside the coverlet, straight against his sides. His hands were clenched. His mouth was partially open. Now and then he panted, almost as a dog pants in hot weather when it has been running with a carriage. When Aubrey looked at him he turned his head slightly to one side and tried to nod. His attempt made the pillow give forth a scratching sound. There was a cane chair by the bed.

"Sit down, sir, won't you?" Alf said.

His voice sounded much as usual, only drier.

Aubrey sat down. Alf looked at the lilies inquiringly. Aubrey laid them gently on the bed.

"What's them for?" said Alf, staring at the flowers, which he did not attempt to handle.

Aubrey felt as if he could not control his voice sufficiently to speak for a moment. So he made no answer.

"Eh, sir?" said Alf.

"She sent them to you with her love."

"She—what, the lady?"

"Yes. She was wearing them. She took them out of her dress and gave them to me to bring to you."

"Ah!" said Alf.

He drew up one hand, put it inside the clothes and shifted the poultice, shrivelling up his face as he did so till there were masses of wrinkles round his small eyes.

Vauxhall watched him with a stern, staring gaze, frowning when he moved.

"Lay still, Alf," he muttered. "Lay still!"

Alf looked at his brother sideways, with difficulty.

"Get out for a minute, Vaux," he said. "Will you?"

Vauxhall shook his head.

"Yes, Vaux, you must," said Alf almost peevishly, and moving his feet to and fro in the bed. "Do get, I tell you."

"What for?" said Vauxhall, never moving.

"I'm going to talk to the—Cr'rr!"

He stopped speaking, and ground his teeth together. His face was contorted. Aubrey shivered as he sat in the chair.

"For God's sake lay still, Alf, and don't talk," said Vauxhall.

He, too, began to tremble where he stood against the wall, and he passed his tongue across his lips.

There was a silence in the room. Beads of perspiration ran from Alf's forehead down his cheeks. He had caught the counterpane in his hands. His eyes stared up at the ceiling fiercely. The expression upon his face seemed one of anger. At last he spoke again.

"Get, Vaux—get!" he said.

There was something in his voice this time that constrained his brother. Vauxhall moved slowly to the door. Aubrey remembered afterwards the strangeness of seeing him walking heavily, almost slouchingly, like a man whose body is flaccid, untrained, enervated. He did not look at his brother again, but opened the door and went out. Then Alf glanced at Aubrey and at the lilies.

"She ain't coming, I s'pose?" he said.

Aubrey shook his head. He did not feel as if he could put Lady Caryll's refusal into words.

"Why wouldn't she come?" asked Alf. "Eh?"

He seemed for the moment easier, and unclenched his hands.

"It was very late," Aubrey stammered.

Somehow he could not obey his mother. He could not tell a lie to this little being who was hastening towards the Great Truth.

"She didn't want to come?" said Alf.

He paused. Then he added—

"Well, it don't much matter, I s'pose."

As he said this, whether by design or accident he moved, and Lady Caryll's lilies fell from the bed to the floor. He did not seem to notice it. Aubrey bowed to a storm of pity.

"She might come to-morrow," he said.

"What's the good of that?" said Alf.

Aubrey could not answer him.

"It don't matter," he repeated, as if speaking to himself, and for the benefit of his own mind.

Then he looked at Aubrey.

"Did she enjoy it?" he said. "The Show? Eh?"

"Yes."

"Sure?"

"She did. I know she did. She thought it—she thought it wonderful."

"Right."

He lay quiet for two or three minutes, always with his knees hunched up. He appeared to be thinking hard. Presently he said—

"You know King?"

"King?" said Aubrey.

"The riding chap that's after Di."

"Oh yes, of course!"

"He's the right sort, is King. Think so?"

"Yes," said Aubrey, wondering.

"Means biz," continued Alf, clenching his hands tightly.

Aubrey saw that he was suffering a paroxysm of pain. He bent over the bed.

"Can't I do anything to ease you?" he asked, tortured by the sensation of awful helplessness that comes so often to those who are forced to watch human agony.

"Shut up, sir—please," Alf said. "It—it ain't no good to—worry."

He jerked in the bed, and his face twitched. His teeth were fixed on his under lip and his eyes were nearly shut. After two or three minutes the paroxysm passed and he spoke again, but in a lower voice, as if weakened.

"King means biz," he said. "You know that—eh, sir?"

"Perhaps he does," Aubrey replied. "But——"

"Well, sir!"

"But does Miss Diamond care for him?"

Alf turned on the pillow and stared at him fiercely.

"But for you she would, sir."

"Me! I only want her life to be happy."

"Ah! That's what you say."

"Alf," Aubrey said, "that's the truth. You ought to believe me."

Alf looked him full in the eyes.

"Look here, sir," he said. "We'd better fix it. I've got to give up watching Di. That back fall's done me."

"But you may get——"

"It's done me," he repeated. "I ain't heard what the doctors say, nor don't want to. I knew when Vaux took me out of the net—so that's all right enough. Give me a drop of the jug, will you?"

Aubrey went to the washhandstand, poured out some water, and brought it to the bedside. Alf drank eagerly.

"It's all hot—it's reg'lar Hell inside me now," he said, giving Aubrey the glass.

Aubrey felt a sickness of pity, but he said nothing. He was cruelly preoccupied by the sense of his own utter uselessness. Any expression of sorrow, of sympathy, would, he thought, seem conventional and heartless. He put the glass back in its place and came again to the bed. Then he laid his hand on Alf's, which was burning hot.

"You want something of me," he said. "Just tell me what it is."

"You leave Di alone, sir. Leave her alone. Give over seeing her. She likes you, does Di."

"We are friends."

"You're a nob and she ain't. Give over seeing her and she'll get spliced to King. She would now if 'twasn't for you."

"But——"

"Oh, she don't know it. Gals never do."

He spoke with a sort of old man's contempt and worldly knowledge.

"King ain't much to look at, but he's the man for Di, and you ain't. You know that well enough."

"What d'you want me to do?"

"Don't have Di for a friend. Don't pal up to her any more. It ain't no good. Let her cry and think you're like the rest of 'em—like that cad what wrote for papers."

"That's rather hard," said Aubrey.

"Ah! And it's a bit hard on me leaving the rope."

For the first time he seemed to think of himself with pity, and two tears glistened in his small eyes.

"But I've got to put up with it, and so must you with the other, if you don't want to start in as a beast."

He shifted the poultice again. Aubrey looked away. The vain effort after relief was terrible to witness. He heard the movement beneath the bed-clothes and then a long and bitter sigh.

"I'll leave Diamond alone," he said. "Perhaps you are right. But I never meant her any harm."

"I know as you didn't,—poor old Di!"

There was silence in the room. A faint light glimmered at the window, which was only partially covered by a thin white blind. It was the light of the moon, which would soon die in the dawn. Alf sighed heavily again. Aubrey turned suddenly to him.

"Alf," he said almost passionately, "I wish to God I could do something for you."

"You have, sir. I feel easier, that I do. Vaux can come

in again now; and you might ask the—you might ask the tall lady to give me that stuff the doctor left for when it come on mortal bad."

He hurried the last words and ended in a sort of stifled cry. Aubrey got up and hastened to the door. He opened it on Vauxhall, who was just outside in the passage. Vauxhall looked at him and sprang into the bedroom.

"Mater! Mater!" Aubrey called, "where are you?"

Lady Rangecliffe came hurrying from the kitchen, and at the same time the sitting-room door was flung wide open and Mr. Flick strode out. He stood in the light that streamed after him and stared at Lady Rangecliffe and at Aubrey.

"Mater," said Aubrey hurriedly, "go in and help him. You've got something from the doctor—he wants it—horribly."

"What are you doing to my boy?" said Mr. Flick, with the harsh incivility of dread and love. "I won't have him done anything to. What's the doctor mean by leaving him?"

And he stood right across the passage, barring the way to Alf's room with his great bulky form, while Alf's tall brothers crowded in the doorway. Lady Rangecliffe showed him a cardboard box.

"This is morphia," she said. "It will ease his pain. Please let me go in and give it to him."

"Will it hurt the little 'un—the taking it?"

"No. It is to save him from cruel suffering."

Alf cried out from the bedroom.

"Lady! Lady!" he called.

His voice was terrible.

Mr. Flick shuddered and stood aside. Lady Rangecliffe passed into the bedroom. Then the Flick brothers came out into the passage. Their strong and manly faces were grey with fear. The whole company stood listening in a breathless silence. They heard Alf gasping, and the rustle of Lady Rangecliffe's gown as she moved about, and then a low, uncanny sound.

It was Vauxhall sobbing as he leaned out of the window into the Court, holding his hands over his ears.

"What's it?" said Mr. Flick.

Diamond pushed her way into the passage and took him by the arm.

"Come back in," she whispered. "Come!"

She led him into the sitting-room again.

"Now, you all keep quiet," she said gently; "the lady's makin' him better."

She forced him to sit down, and stole out again. Lady Rangecliffe met her in the passage.

"The morphia will do him good in a few minutes," Lady Rangecliffe said. "He's asking for you now."

Diamond went into Alf's room. He was still in great agony and had his eyes turned towards the door. Vauxhall was leaning on the window-sill with his head in his hands. He made no sound now, but his shoulders were shaking. Alf beckoned to Diamond to sit by the bed. She took his hand and held it in hers till presently the morphia began to take effect. He stretched out his legs in the bed, and sighed once or twice.

"Better now?" asked Diamond.

He nodded.

"I want to see Susie," he said, "and Charley."

"They've gone to bed. Jenny's with 'em."

"They ain't asleep, are they?" said Alf.

It was evidently incredible to him that anybody should be asleep in that house.

"Why d'you want to see 'em, Alf?" said Diamond.

"Because I should like to. Can't I?"

Diamond got up and went to the children's room

"Jenny," she said, gently opening the door. "Jenny!"

Jenny came and showed a white, tear-stained face, full of terror.

"What is it?"

"Are the children asleep?"

"Yes. They've been cryin' fearful, but they've dropped off at last. Whatever is it?"

"Alf wants to see 'em."

"What for? Oh, Di, is he gettin' better?"

Diamond shook her head.

"I don't think it's that."

The tears began to roll again over Jenny's cheeks.

"Shall I wake 'em?" she said between her sobs.

"I dunno," said Di, hesitating.

She stepped into the room and contemplated Susie and Charley. They were fast asleep in their little beds. Susie's rosy fists were doubled on the white sheet. Charley had one finger in his half-opened mouth. Their breathing was soft and regular.

"It seems a pity," Diamond said. "But then—Oh, Jenny! if we don't wake 'em now, in the mornin' it'll be too late, p'raps."

"Too late! What for, Di?" Jenny asked in a nervous voice.

"For Alf," said Diamond.

Jenny said nothing. She had sat down on the edge of the big bed, in which Mr. and Mrs. Slagg slept each night between their little ones. Diamond was considering deeply.

"Jenny," she said, at length, "we'll lift 'em up and carry 'em in to Alf. Try not to wake 'em. Then he can do what he likes. You take Susie."

And she leant down and, with infinite precaution, lifted her small brother in her arms. He murmured and moved his hands, but did not wake. Nor did Susie. The children were utterly exhausted after the unusual excitement of their evening at the theatre. The two sisters then went out softly along the passage to Alf's room. He moved a little as they came in and towards the bed.

"Was they asleep?" he whispered.

Then he saw their closed eyes.

"Shall I wake 'em?" asked Diamond.

"No, I wouldn't. Bring 'em down to me."

Diamond bent down with Charley in her arms. Alf looked hard at the little fellow, touched his flabby hand, and said—

"Now Susie!"

Jenny followed Di's example, bent, then knelt at the bedside. But suddenly she began to cry. Alf said "Hush!" Jenny strove to check her grief, but Susie had opened her eyes. She stared hazily at Alf and pouted her rosy lips. With great difficulty Alf raised himself up enough to kiss her.

"Bye, bye, Susie," he whispered.

"Bye, bye," responded Susie in a muffled, tiny voice.

Alf lay back. The children were carried off to their beds. When they woke late in the morning Alf could no longer kiss them.

The morphia fulfilled its blessed task. For a time he felt but little pain. When the sun began to rise, however, his agony recommenced, and he was obviously much feebler. Again he drew up his legs in the bed, and his features were contorted. His face had become almost slate-coloured. Lady Rangecliffe whispered to Diamond to summon his father and brothers. Vauxhall had never left the room. He stood quite motionless, and looked half stunned. There was little expression in his eyes. The Flicks stole in, trying to walk softly. They stood round the bed, looking down on the boy who had been the pride of them all. Only Vauxhall never left his post by the partially open window. Mr. Flick, whose face still wore its former expression of dull anger, leaned over Alf and looked hard at him without saying a word.

"Well, Guv," Alf whispered. "It's a go, ain't it?"

Then the father spoke.

"Why did you try it, Alf?" he said, in a tone that was full of chiding. "Whatever was you after?"

Alf made no reply. The father saw Lady Caryll's lilies lying faded on the floor. He bent and picked them up, and put them rather awkwardly upon the outside of the bed.

"See what it's brought you, boy," he continued.

"Ah!" said Alf, touching the lilies.

He did not speak again for a long time. Diamond was the last to kiss him. She tried to draw Vauxhall to the bed, but he refused to come. He seemed now to be under the spell of an ungovernable horror.

"Come, dear Vaux," she whispered, pulling at his arm.

"Vaux," said Lill, trying in her turn to persuade him. "Vaux!"

But he still resisted, holding fast to the window-sill with one hand, and keeping the other on his hip, as he did when he watched Alf performing. At length Alf whispered his name. Then he came slowly, and stood by his brother's bed. Alf made a feeble motion with his hand.

Vauxhall took his brother's hand and shook it hard, almost brutally.

"With a day's practice you'd have done it, Alf," he said in a loud voice, bending over the bed.

Alf moved slightly, and lay still.

Then Vauxhall raised himself up and turned to those in the room.

"He would, I tell you," he said proudly, and as if daring any one to contradict him. "Just a day at it and he'd have brought it off. There never was one to come near Alf!"

So the epitaph of the little acrobat was spoken.

CHAPTER XXIV

COVENT GARDEN is strange in the dawn, strange in its activities of men, in its mingling of the sordid and the sweet, in its suggestion of the darkest slums and of the most perfumed country places. It is a maze of vans, wagons, roses, swearing half-dressed men, running boys, palms, orchids, violets, police. Bow Street and the tropics meet under the slowly brightening sky, and the people who live in glass houses are ruthlessly dragooned by those at whom they would probably like to throw stones. Aubrey walked through Covent Garden in the dawn, after the death of Alf. And the shouting of the market porters, the heavy rolling of the vans on the paving-stones, the cackling of the loungers round the coffee-stalls, the hoarse laughter of the men perched high in little eyries above the mighty, labouring horses, mingled in a dreary confusion that stunned his ears. The sky was grey and cold, and a wind blew up the dirty rubbish that had accumulated among the greasy cobble stones. Filthy bits of paper whirled by, straws floated aimlessly up and settled again in crevices. Lady Rangecliffe strode along muffled in her cloak, with a black lace shawl tied over her head. She held her gown high, and the men in the market stared ruthlessly at her ankles, and made crude remarks to each other in obscure, though strident, voices. Presently Lady Rangecliffe stopped before an open van, in whose dark shadow were ensconced hundreds of red roses. A small, pale man, crouched in the van, was handing them with mechanical rapidity to a mate who stood outside. He glowered at Lady Rangecliffe from his rose-bower.

"I want some of your flowers," she said abruptly. "Give me a handful, please."

The man gave her a red crowd of his wares, naming their price.

"Have you got enough money, Aubrey? I haven't," said his mother.

Aubrey, whose hand trembled, fished out a sovereign with difficulty.

"That cove's been out on the spree," thought the wise little man in the rose-bower.

He chuckled to himself, looked again at Lady Rangecliffe,

and thought she was a curious companion to choose for a spree.

"I want these flowers taken at once over the way," said Lady Rangecliffe.

"Where to, ma'am?" said the little man, with growing surprise.

Lady Rangecliffe mentioned the number in Milk Court, waited till a dirty messenger had departed with the flowers, and then walked on with her son. Presently they met a four-wheeler, on whose box a purple-faced old man, in a patched cloak, drowsed under a shining round black hat. Lady Rangecliffe woke him up and got in. Aubrey shut the door on her.

"You won't come, Aubrey?" she asked.

He shook his head. His face looked grey in the growing light. He leaned his arms on the top of the door for a moment.

"Why did you send those flowers, Mater?" he asked.

Lady Rangecliffe made no reply.

"I know," Aubrey said. "You wanted to—to cover up her lilies."

"The little chap deserves fresh flowers," she said.

Aubrey took his arms from the ledge, and the purple-faced man whipped up his degraded-looking horse.

In that moment Aubrey realised what his mother thought of Lady Caryll. He was too confused, too benumbed by the quickness and horror of recent incidents, to know what were his thoughts of her. Yet he was aware of one fact—that he felt an intense disinclination to return to Park Lane just then.

Presently he was standing on the wide step of the house in Eaton Square. Lady Rangecliffe let him in before he had time to ring.

"I thought perhaps you'd come, Aubrey," she said quietly. "Go to your father's room. He's away."

She made no further remark, but turned and went quickly upstairs. Aubrey loved her for her silence and her abrupt departure.

When the world was awake it was necessary for him to go to Park Lane. He recognised sternly his duty as his godfather's hired servant and did not mean to shirk it. A footman brought him some of the clothes he kept at his father's house. He dressed, had some tea in his room, and took up his hat and gloves. It was eleven o'clock. He waited for a moment, considering whether he should go to see his mother before he went out. Then he opened the bedroom door, descended a flight of stairs, and stood outside Lady Rangecliffe's boudoir. He heard her rustling about, and the bang of a lid as she shut something; then he went in. Lady

Rangecliffe turned round and stared to see who it was. Aubrey went up to her and kissed her rather roughly.

"Thank you for last night, Mater," he said, and bolted out of the room again, leaving his mother standing all red with emotion like a girl.

Near Hyde Park Corner Aubrey met two or three men he knew strolling towards the Row. He nodded to them, but did not stop to speak. They observed his tired eyes and abrupt avoidance of them.

"Herrick's been on the spree," they said. "Looks deuced cheap this mornin'."

And they smiled, having echoed in words the thought of the little man in the Covent Garden rose-bower. The "classes" are very like the "masses," and misjudge with much the same gay certainty.

Aubrey let himself in to Sir Reuben's house with his latchkey and made his way to his rooms. On the writing-table lay a quantity of letters for him to answer. He sat down and set to work.

After about half-an-hour Sir Reuben entered. He noticed at once the expression of fatigue and almost of horror in his godson's face. His first remark referred to the incidents of the night.

"How is that poor boy?" he said, sitting down by the table, and drawing his fez a little forward over his scanty hair.

"He died early this morning," Aubrey replied, tearing open a letter, and glancing over its pages.

Sir Reuben looked genuinely shocked.

"Dead—how dreadful!" he said. "Did he suffer much?"

"Very much," said Aubrey. "Here's a letter from Perkins about that mortgage."

He read it aloud. Sir Reuben looked at him in astonishment, then in pity, recognising from what cause his strangeness sprang. After the nature of the reply to the letter had been settled, Sir Reuben stopped work authoritatively.

"I wish to speak about that boy," he said.

He saw that Aubrey winced, but he went on.

"Caryll has been so anxious about him. She will be fearfully shocked."

Aubrey said nothing.

"Was he sensible to the last?" said Sir Reuben.

"Yes," Aubrey said.

"Did he have the lilies?"

"Yes."

Aubrey's voice was chilly and constrained. Sir Reuben felt surprised at its tone.

"It was a kind thought of hers to send them," he said, almost as if asking a question. "Did they please the poor little chap at all?"

Then Aubrey looked up at his godfather suddenly.

"I don't know," he said. "I don't see how they could."

"Why? I don't understand you."

"Well, you see they were instead of something he wanted."

"What was that?"

"Lady Caryll herself."

There was a moment's silence. Then Sir Reuben said—

"What d'you mean? Had he wanted—had he asked——"

"To see her before he died? Yes. I came to the ball-room with his message—and she gave me the lilies."

Sir Reuben pulled again at his fez. There was an odd expression in his eyes, half tragic, half bitterly humorous. He was thinking of the kiss he had given his wife in the carriage as they drove home from the ball. Just then there was a knock at the door and Lady Caryll came in. Aubrey stood up to receive her.

"How is he?" she said. "How is the poor little boy? Did you give him my flowers?"

"Yes," Aubrey said.

"Was he pleased? What did he say?"

"I don't remember."

Sir Reuben was struck by the resemblance between Aubrey's voice and his mother's when he spoke that blunt sentence.

"How is he now?" continued Lady Caryll.

She had come up to the writing-table and was resting her hand on it.

"He is dead," said Aubrey, speaking without emotion.

Lady Caryll moved backwards.

"Dead!" she exclaimed incredulously. "Dead—already!"

"He died hours ago," Aubrey said.

"How horrible!" she said.

"It was much more horrible before he died," Aubrey said.

"Don't," she said, holding out her hand as if to stop him. "Don't!"

"He had your gift of flowers, Caryll," Sir Reuben said. "They were not too late."

"I am glad—I am glad."

She spoke hurriedly, and moved towards her husband.

"I will send more. Poor boy!"

"You need not trouble about flowers," Aubrey said. "My mother has sent a quantity. She was with him till the end."

"Your mother!" said Sir Reuben. "Till the end!"

He looked across at his wife. In reply to his look Lady Caryll said—

"Lady Rangecliffe has studied nursing."

"Ah!" said Sir Reuben. "I see."

He could almost have laughed, when he thought again of his kiss in the carriage. Lady Caryll stood there. She did not seem as if she could decide what to do.

"Poor—poor little boy!" she said again.

Aubrey took no notice of her. He was looking at the letters on the writing-table as if he wanted to go on with his work. Lady Caryll took advantage of his glance.

"I must not interrupt you," she said, turning to go. "I've no business here in the morning. But I could not resist coming to learn the truth. I have been so anxious. And now—how horrible —horrible!"

She left the room. Aubrey sat down to resume work, and Sir Reuben sat on the opposite side of the table. He lit his pipe. He did not refer again to the tragedy of the previous night. Now and then he stole a glance at Aubrey. His face was white and grim. And Sir Reuben thought, "He has learnt the lesson at last. He knows her now." But then again Sir Reuben wondered, remembering his own facility for being deceived—that eternal facility of man which woman adores in him. Even he had looked into his jewel for a heart—he, with all his worldly wisdom, with all his bitter experience, with all his corroding unbelief. He had caressed Caryll after Monsieur Anneau's concert, thinking for a moment that she would miss his ugly presence if he died. And he had kissed her in the darkness of the carriage after the ball, loving her for her gift of lilies to the dying acrobat. Yes, even he had been deceived. And this youth—would he ever learn a lesson that must be strangely difficult, since an old man, who thought he had learnt it long ago, forgot it so easily?

"Sir Reuben," Aubrey said, when the morning's work was over, "I want—I wish to say something to you."

"What is it, my boy?"

Aubrey looked down.

"I want to give up my position here."

"Ah!" said Sir Reuben.

"You have been too good to me. But I must resign it."

"Without giving me any reason?"

Aubrey still looked down, almost like a man terribly ashamed of something, and trying to conceal his shame.

"I don't know that I've got any reason to give," he answered in a low voice. "But I wish to go. I'm very sorry."

Sir Reuben understood the flood of bitterness by which Aubrey's youth was overwhelmed just then.

"I will not try to keep you," he said quietly. "But I shall miss your assistance very much."

"I'm very sorry," Aubrey reiterated.

Nothing else was said. It was not a time for talking. That afternoon Lady Rangecliffe received a telegram :—

"The lesson I wished to teach is learnt, I think.—REUBEN ALLABRUTH."

Later, Aubrey arrived with luggage.

"I should like to stay a few days, Mater, if I can," he said. "I've thrown up that berth at Sir Reuben's. He only made it for me, you know. He doesn't really need anybody in the house."

Lady Rangecliffe did not discuss the matter. But she was, unostentatiously, very tender to her son that night.

When little Alf was buried Aubrey went to the funeral. It was a strange ceremony to him. He had never been to a funeral before. He stood at Brompton Cemetery in the midst of a heterogeneous crowd of people whose like he had scarcely even imagined. Among them were many performers connected with "the Halls." These had come to pay a last tribute of respect to one who had been at the head of his profession, child though he was. There were ladies of the ballet carrying flowers, which they were going presently to strew into the grave. Tears streamed down their cheeks. They were of the class in which emotion is a matter of habit, and by no means a thing to be ashamed of or to conceal. No doubt many of them were genuinely moved. But some would have wept as copiously had the coffin been occupied by a wax doll that had been famous. A huge girl, who carried banners in the ballet, sobbed mechanically at regular intervals, and pressed a pocket-handkerchief bordered with black first to one cheek-bone and then to the other. Her grief was as ostentatious as would have been a singing of the Marseillaise. Never before had Aubrey seen so strange a collection of men. There were low comedians with broad faces that looked almost as if they were made of india-rubber; lion comiques in elaborate costumes, and strange shaped hats with curly brims, and gigantic mourning ties suggesting bogs in which one might almost have floundered; clever deformed people, whose desperate exploiting of unsightly defects had rendered them dear to the great, unhealthy minded public; strong men who lived by breaking chains; pantomime gentry with red noses, who struck strange attitudes as if they had just been shot up out of the bowels of the earth through traps; boxers, bull-necked pugilists, "Sports," and patrons of the "Ring," who had loved Alf for his mischievous daring and contempt of danger. There was a melancholy serpent man who performed in striped tights and an artificial viper's head. There were several "knock-about artistes" in their Sunday clothes, and one or two ventriloquists with pursed lips and high Jewish noses. Few of these people were accustomed to hear solemn words or sacred sentences, or to think seriously of any life unconnected with their own professions. And this lack of custom made them shy and uncomfortable, as well as unhappy over the loss of a "good little pal." They shifted uneasily about as they stood near the grave, darting furtive glances at the coffin, and shooting their voluminous cuffs as if in an effort after severe respectability. Some of them squinted at the ballet-girls, began to smile, then, recollecting themselves, violently composed their countenances into what they hoped was an expression of resignation to the will of the Almighty. The professional humourists looked especially tragic, and were most ostentatious in their mourning. It was, perhaps, a genuine relief from their public labours.

All the Marvellous Flicks were there in the forefront of the throng. They were deeply disguised in their suits of decent black and their high silk hats with broad mourning bands. But these were doffed now, and they stood bareheaded. Their clothes made them appear much more common than usual. Their magnificent figures, their superb muscles, were concealed from view, and they stood awkwardly in their shiny leather boots. Their painful grief bowed them down, and had drawn all their normal elasticity from them. By way of hiding it they endeavoured to assume a sternly cold and manly demeanour, which, in the case of the father, became defiance. Mr. Flick stared hard at those near him, with bloodshot eyes whose rims were red and puffy. His thick moustache was carefully arranged, waxed, and curled upward at the tips in a martial manner. He carried his hat in one hand, a pair of black kid gloves, an umbrella, and a prayer-book bound in black in the other. At the grave side he assumed an indifferent, almost an irreverent posture, looking away from the clergyman with a pretence of easy carelessness, and glancing casually about from time to time like one who examines some country scene that happens to be novel to him. His tall sons stood with him—the troupe without the "star."

Perhaps instinctively, from their many performances, they had formed up in line as they did on the stage before they leapt into patterns, or sprang to airy feats. Vauxhall stood at the end of the line, and Aubrey thought that once he shot a hasty glance sideways, as if to summon his little brother to run in from the wings, ducking his head to an applauding audience. Vauxhall was the youngest now. He stared down at the hole in the ground, and then at the coffin, in which lay the boy of whom he had been so generously proud. A dazed expression came into his face, his shoulders rounded themselves, and his head drooped forward. It is always terrible to stand before the stillness of a being we have been accustomed to see in perpetual activity. In this case the change was peculiarly startling and fearful to Vauxhall. He had been constantly with Alf, and Alf had been constantly in quick, most often in violent, movement. To watch his bodily feats, to observe his infinite powers of juggling, of sleight of hand, to assist at the growth of his extraordinary and vehemently complicated tricks, had been Vauxhall's daily occupation and engrossing pleasure. Alf had been not only alive himself. By his goblin ingenuity he had made all the inanimate things within his reach seem alive also. Therefore his present stillness was the more unnatural and appalling. The sensation that gripped Vauxhall was one of absolute horror. He stood with his brothers and gazed at Alf's coffin, and his legs trembled. He did not know whether he was sad. No tears rose in his eyes. He thrust forward his head, looking at the coffin, and trying to realise that Alf was inside it, lying perfectly still with his eyes shut.

All the Slaggs were present, with the exception of Mrs. Slagg, who was too much overcome to leave Milk Court. Lill stood near her entranced husband, looking at him with frightened eyes. Diamond had little Susie and Charlie on either side of her, holding fast to her hands. Susie was crying. But Charlie was too much excited by the novelty of his situation to give way to grief. His eyes were round and protuberant as they looked first in one direction, then in another, trying to take in the whole tremendous scene. Sometimes he was hypnotised for a minute or two by his new black suit, and by the short black stockings which made his small legs look so white where they were uncovered. Then the box in the centre of the throng occupied him. He pointed to it with his thumb, tugged at Diamond's merino dress, and whispered, "What's in there?"

Diamond looked down at him, shook her head, and sobbed. That frightened Charlie, and, seeing all of a sudden that Susie was crying, he began to cry too, and to hide his face in Diamond's skirt. Mr. Slagg picked him up, and muttered incoherent words of comfort to him. Then, being in a coign of vantage, he recovered a little and stared at the clergyman, who had black whiskers of a surprising size.

Aubrey's attention was now mainly preoccupied by the little circle of which Alf had been the centre, the pride and joy. He looked at the pale and tear-stained face of Diamond, and remembered her saying—" It wouldn't be Alf—quiet." Then what was in that coffin, and what was going to be lowered into that grave? He felt as if it could not possibly be Alf, or anything to do with him. A few drops of rain fell. The ladies of the ballet began hastily to put up umbrellas and to pat in their skirts with their hands. The serpent man took the huge girl who carried banners under his protection. She went on whimpering heavily, and looked as if she wanted to lay her large, round face on his thin shoulder.

When the last moment came, when the coffin slowly disappeared from sight, Aubrey thought of Caryll. Her beauty and cold charm had given birth to the tragedy of Alf, and so had, directly, brought about this ceremony. She had in fact dug this grave and provided it with an occupant. He looked once more at all the faces opposite to him. Susie and Charlie were terrified by the lowering of the coffin, and were crying loudly, as children cry when fear wakes in them something of protest that is akin to anger. Alf's father still preserved his desperate travesty of unconcern. But the effort, the fierce determination not to show any natural emotion, now caused him to look actually sinister, almost malignant. One might have supposed that he was about to strike the clergyman. Vauxhall followed the slowly descending coffin with strained eyes, leaning forward as if he were attracted magnetically to fall into the grave after it. Now some of the ballet ladies moved forward under their umbrellas, on which the rain pattered, to throw their flowers into the grave. One of them, an affected-looking, thin girl, with a cloud of fuzzy hair snakily curled upon her narrow forehead, performed the action dramatically, then suddenly threw up her arms, screamed, and seemed to faint. Her friends assisted her, and there was some confusion, in the midst of which Aubrey noticed Vauxhall still staring fixedly down at the coffin with dull, yet horrified eyes. He looked almost like a man who had drunk too much, and who was at the same time stupid, and alarmed by something he could not understand. The last thing Aubrey noticed before the crowd separated was a well-known droll, familiar to the world as "Little Gee," and to all children as a source of perpetual laughter, putting up the collar of his coat hurriedly to protect his black satin cravat from the rain. He performed the action with a quick anxiety that was intensely ludicrous, and turned to leave the cemetery with the comic briskness of movement that had roused uproarious mirth in thousands of people both in England and in America. Yet there were tears streaming down his pasty and closely shaven cheeks. The rain beat on the umbrellas, and the ladies of the ballet hastened away, trying to make themselves small, and drawing their skirts forward into bunches, which they grasped with solicitous hands. The serpent man and the big girl who carried banners murmured to each other as they departed under one umbrella. Already they had become dear friends.

. . . .

Aubrey kept his promise to the dead boy with the unnecessary sternness of youth. When the young make up their minds to perform a distasteful duty they often perform it deliberately in the way that will hurt them most. Aubrey did not go to see Diamond after the funeral. He wrote a letter of sympathy, to which she replied rather formally. Then he let the acquaintance drop. Alf had asked him to be cruel. He was cruel, perhaps most cruel of all to himself. The man at the net was gone. But now Aubrey told himself Diamond should need no one to watch her. His own loneliness did not matter.

Lady Rangecliffe wondered why he never alluded to the family in whose tragedy he had been mingled. She sometimes paid a visit to Milk Court, and she noticed that Diamond did not speak of Aubrey.

The double silence perplexed her. Aubrey had never told her how he had come to know Diamond. She wondered how. But she thought no evil either of this simple, and now very sad, girl or of her son.

Sometimes she drove to Brompton Cemetery and put some flowers on "the little chap's" grave.

CHAPTER XXV

THE true history of but one gay pilgrim through a London season would be strangely interesting, could it be related exhaustively and with absolute accuracy. Lady Caryll was a fascinating pilgrim through the three brilliant months that immediately succeeded the tragedy in Milk Court. Afterwards, when her life was changed, and she struck society a stinging blow in the face that set its eyes watering, its tongue stammering blasphemies, many people looked back to this season and acknowledged, with reluctant truth, that it had been hers, in a manner had belonged to her. For she performed the rare feat of rising up definitely from the whirlpool like some goddess rising from the sea. And all the flotsam and jetsam spinning on the surface of the whirlpool, and all the engulfed, saw her predominant, and felt as if they could only perceive her clearly at all just then by looking above them. Few lives flash, few careers sparkle and shine, few existences blaze bringing memories of fire, unless the imp of recklessness is near them with his torch. Caryll had her own young recklessness to do her service. But she had more—she had the old recklessness of her husband. That was a strange spectacle, a fury of the Orient. Caryll's youth waking in her, Sir Reuben's age waking in him, these two opposites, coming together like two chemicals, gave birth to flame which illuminated society. Youth held out its hands in a passion of acceptance, age held out its hands in a passion of prodigality. The two recklessnesses fed each the desire of the other. That was an orgy of giving and of receiving.

The publicity of a London season is almost like the publicity of a ship, in which all the berths are taken and whose course is set towards the tropics. A madness of proximity in warmth comes upon the voyagers, the bias towards the frantic which swims up in heated crowds. Watching becomes a disease, talking a vice, laughter a jackal's necessity, exertion an intemperate monotony. Thought is trampled under boots with high heels. Reserve is driven away with whips of tulle. And as, on the before-mentioned ship, when the first white flying-fish are seen, human nature breaks loose from its irons, and all the secrets are told, while the quartermasters gaily listen, and the very Lascars fall to sarcastic grimacing behind their dusky hands, so, when June is hot in Hyde Park, and Mayfair is red with roses, does the book of revelation open, does the staring world bend over the pages to read.

Amid the recklessness of this season Lady Caryll and Sir Reuben stood out like forms seen in a firework. The great audience stared at the woman with her white hands held out to take at the man with his brown hands held out to give. And be sure that the quartermasters and the Lascars, ignored by the passengers, did not forget to play their time-honoured rôle. Those who swab the decks of London have sharp eyes and sharper tongues. But what do the occupants of the state-rooms care for that?

Once Sir Reuben had said, at the banquet of inauguration, "If I met a strong nature, a nature fierce in its desire and crying for all the seas, I should like to pour all the seas into it." Now, at last, he yielded himself entirely with a sort of old fury to this satisfaction. And he had no desire to yield in secret. He wished the world to be on the watch. That watchfulness made part of his joy. When he first married Lady Caryll he enjoyed giving her peeps into Aladdin's cave. Now he took from her the jewels that had been given to her by others as wedding presents, saying, "The one who submits to my power of giving must only receive from me." Then he flung the doors of the cave wide open and led her in to be wrapt in the enchantment of its jewelled wonder. And often he looked back to enjoy the spectacle of the world trampling about the entrance. Aubrey stood there with the rest.

Lady Caryll's jewels were the wonder of that season, the constant subject of discussion among women in boudoirs, among men in clubs and on racecourses, among both sexes in general society.

"Allabruth treats his wife as if she were a courtesan," said a married man, who admired King Solomon.

"He puts very rotten ideas into the heads of respectable women," said his companion. "Their expectations will become absurd. If virtue is to be rewarded by such a cataract of precious stones what encouragement will be left for vice? I think some one should speak seriously to Allabruth."

Lady Caryll's virtue was acknowledged even by the cynical. A famous Spanish dancer, who usually dressed in diamonds and very little else, said of her that she was the cleverest of all Englishwomen, because she was the mistress of her own husband. The jewellers thanked God for the madness of Sir Reuben, and longed to infuse a little Eastern blood into the veins of all millionaires. They recognised in his proceedings the gorgeous fantasy of an Oriental. He grew almost barbarous in the violence of his generosity. There was something fearful in it, as there is in unbridled avarice, the hint of wickedness that exists in all uncontrolled passions. He was like some monstrous figure of a dangerous legend scattering unceasing largesse on the woman whom he had chosen to be the recipient of his desperate bounty. Some people began to think of her as strangely fearless, facing this storm of jewels that fell about her almost like hail. Her serenity astonished them. Sir Reuben was not serene. The recklessness of his generosity sprang up, like some quick, licentious tropical plant, growing out of the peculiar rank richness of decay. For still the grey and the aged feeling crept upon him. The heavy and inexorable animal lay crouched upon his breast and could not be stirred. The permanence of its repose sometimes appalled him, and he underwent that most intense agony—the supporting of that which man tells himself is insupportable. In the paroxysms of his prodigality he found a sharp solace. Some felt that there was terror in his giving because he sometimes gave in an effort to escape from terror. Caryll was not one of these, and he knew well that she never could be. The woman who had stood before the diamond shop to gaze into the hearts of jewels, never stood before that larger house, the worldly house of many mansions, to gaze into the hearts of men. She knew very little about Sir Reuben, but he knew a great deal about her. At this time she looked upon him as she would have looked upon the Geni who led her through the cave. The magic of the jewels that came from his hands lingered about him. She always connected him with jewels. Some people thought that she was unnatural and loved him, others that she was politic, and pretended to love him. She neither loved, nor did she pretend to love him. He completely contented her by his actions. She lived happily with his passionate generosity. She had no wish to understand his complicated nature. It was enough for her that she was understood. The under-currents of his life were nothing to her. The ghost of the dead Creole never haunted her. Nor did she notice the unnatural vehemence of his desire to satisfy her, the fury of his kindness. The abandonment which began to amaze the world simply did not strike her. That was all. But then she did not hear the voices in the city, the mutter of the hard-headed men who trod the devious ways of finance. Nor did she hear the mutter of the thieves in their quarters, or understand the depth of the attention that was slowly concentrating upon her. She met the staring eyes of society easily enough. Staring is a sort of profession among well-bred people. They look at each other as a savage would look at the moon if you gave it into his hand. Caryll was accustomed to create a sensation and to meet unflinching eyes. She probably never thought that she was an object of intense interest to people, often the strangest, who had never seen her.

Yet so it was. In very humble, in very sinister quarters she was ardently discussed, as a woman of great possessions, as a woman who had infatuated a man to the point of mania, as a woman who was utterly careless of many things that meant much to her sister women, yet who was intensely solicitous about the shining things she loved. Certain tragedies were attributed to her. Truths float up on the surface of London sometimes almost as strangely as lies. Thus the truth of Alf's death became generally known. He had performed the feat he had never practised, the feat that killed him, to please Lady Caryll, and she had refused to stand for a moment by his deathbed, and to tell him that his performance pleased her. In some subtle fashion, from the bosom of a broken-hearted family, this fact penetrated into the world and was discussed there. The scent of those dead lilies went abroad upon the air.

Another and far more piquant fact also became known during this season. It caused great tumult in the feminine world. The death of an acrobat was of very little consequence. Alf had been a god in Milk Court, and ladies of the ballet had wept over his grave. Monsieur Anneau was a god in a larger sphere, and ladies, not of the ballet, were disposed to weep when he was attacked, or was rudely shaken upon his throne.

Monsieur Anneau had accepted an engagement at the Opera for the summer. He had not sung anywhere since his concert in Park Lane, nor had he been seen in Parisian society. Newspaper gossip had been busy with his name. Rumours had gone about that he had lost his voice, that he had been ill, that he was going to retire from the stage and take up farming. These rumours died comfortably when it was announced that he had arrived in London, and would sing for the Syndicate through the whole season. Lady St. Ormyn was in raptures. She had returned from abroad with several new protégés, and a conductor whom she had "discovered" at Monte Carlo, and intended to force upon London. The summer-house at Epsom was prepared for her famous "Sundays." She had brought a quantity of marvellous gowns from Paris, and was now to be seen everywhere perpetually talking opera, and getting her newest geniuses known. Her face was redder, her hair was whiter than ever. A pair of new eyebrows of a most startling blackness put a brilliant finishing touch to her always striking appearance, and, since she was already bacchanalian in May, her tribes of friends were busy in anticipating a more than usually remarkable July, and a series of Epsom Sabbaths rivalling the witch's sabbaths of legend.

Monsieur Anneau made his first appearance at the Opera during the third week in May. As usual he took the part of a high priest, and his admirers assembled in force to acclaim him. Lady St. Ormyn was in her box next the stage on the grand tier. The Allabruths were not far off. Mrs. Luffa Parkinson, in cinnamon-coloured velvet and yellow jewels, was in the stalls. All the critics were buzzing about, or scratching their comments in surreptitious note-books. At the end of the third act one of them said to another—

"What on earth's the matter with Anneau?"

"Temper, I should think," said his confrère. "The most sulky singing I ever heard."

"And all the sweetness, the luscious quality, seems gone from his voice."

"He sings like a man who hates music, I think," said the second critic, who was not without acute instincts.

"I'm afraid he must have caught cold in crossing the Channel," Lady St. Ormyn was saying to a young composer, whose eyes were like saucers, and whose compositions were as sweet as chocolates.

Sir Reuben leaned towards Caryll, whose blazing diamonds distracted even the honest music lovers who thronged the gallery.

"Caryll," he said, "can you hear what you have done?"

The curtain had gone up again. Monsieur Anneau, attired in flowing robes heavy with embroidery, stood upon some uneasy operatic temple steps. His mighty arms were raised towards heaven, and he began to declaim a solemn chaunt, which was taken up by a crowd of unwashed Italian gentlemen below. Caryll listened. The voice of Monsieur Anneau sounded harsh and dry, like the voice of an angry priest.

"Listen—listen!" said Sir Reuben, and he touched his wife's arm. "Do you hear? That note—and that!"

He smiled at her, twisting his brown face which seemed to have shrunk, as a sheet of paper shrinks and is brown after a flame has run over it and died away from it.

"You mean that he is out of voice, Reuben?"

She glanced about the house, then lifted her opera-glasses to look at some sapphires that shot purple fire from an opposite box.

"Shocking, shocking!" said Paul Villet, the composer of the Pearl Song.

He sat in a box on the ground floor, with a heavy Dowager Countess, a black-haired ex-actress whom he had lately married, and a sleek and rosy young man, with manicured hands and an ostentatious manner, who sang in drawing-rooms under an assumed name, and cut every one who knew that his father was an upholsterer at Greenwich, and that he had been known as Albert Sprigg before he went to Paris to become Sebastian de Rameau.

"Really disgraceful," continued Villet, who had grown very fat and authoritative; and who now earned eight guineas an hour by giving singing lessons, and "producing" voices by a new and acrobatic method, which, he said, had been revealed to him in a dream.

The Dowager Countess agreed that the chorus sang atrociously.

"No, no—Anneau!" cried Villet. "His voice is in an awful condition. He ought to come to me. Mon Dieu! Hark at that F."

He turned to Albert Sprigg, who was talking to Madame Villet about a well-known princess whom he called "Poor little Toto."

Mr. Sprigg waved his manicured hands in a French gesture of sarcastic disgust.

"Anneau is finished," he cried, "quite finished. We won't look at him in Paris. We won't hear his name. But here in London you will stand anything."

And he resumed his conversation about poor little Toto, who, he let it be understood, was dying for love of his fat, rosy face.

Madame Villet, who had forgotten that she had been an unsuccessful actress a year ago, and who now posed as a wit and an eccentric genius, was very sarcastic about the princess.

"She's asked herself to lunch with us on Thursday," she said, "to meet some of the singers—Jacques, you know, and Henri. Such a bore! princesses are like Scotch Sundays, always so wearisome. D'you admire my hair to-night? I want to look like a grouse."

"You look delicious," said Albert Sprigg, staring at her with the pig's expression that was so fascinating. "A gem in the midst of these heavy English women, with their everlasting royal fringes. Why is it that one can't see a forehead in England? Do the English consider foreheads indecent?"

He always spoke as if he were French, and many people thought that his parents were Parisian.

"Monsieur Anneau ought to be brayed in a mortar," said a clever girl in the stalls to a large hunting man who was half asleep at her side.

"The mortar'd have to be a bit large," said the hunting man, with a yawn.

"Yes," said the girl; "and the fragments would fill more baskets than contained the remains of the loaves and fishes. His voice sounds like an asphalte pavement to-night."

Up in the gallery, where a good deal of real intelligence and true sensitiveness to music was sitting on wooden benches, there were more murmurs and sincere regrets. A man with broad shoulders and a flowing beard, who carried a score, and wore a loose mustard-coloured suit, said that Monsieur Anneau was singing without sincerity.

"The voice is out of order," he said. "But there's something worse than that. The nature of the man's out of order. And he used to be so great in this part."

He shook his large leonine head, while a little woman in green linen by his side murmured, "Yes, William, I've noticed it too."

Bedford Park had divined something of the truth; but Bedford Park never knew the whole truth, nor even so much of it as eventually went, distorted, through Mayfair and Belgravia.

Monsieur Anneau's nature was forcible and violent. He had a fierce mind, and he had been accustomed for many years to triumph in all his undertakings. Whenever he had set out to do evil, that evil had been eventually wrought. Whenever he had sung, he had been travelling along some road towards a goal. And so he had had the sensation of jocund triumph from which, along how many roads, springs the carolling voice of man, the voice of the gay traveller, of the human bird in sunshine. Always with him had been his obsequious and efficient servant—his art. Now all was changed. His art had revolted. He had called upon it to perform an act. It had failed him. It had left him in the lurch. Lady Caryll had remained unmoved by his musical powers. He hated music. He held it in contempt. He cursed the long and patient service he had given to it. The memory of his years of pupilage—years which the locusts had eaten—was intolerably bitter to him. Now, when he sang, he felt as if he were giving his life to an enemy, or were performing menial offices for a loathsome master. All the sacrifices he had made for music came round about him like a troop of phantoms, like creatures pale and sneering, tragic and forlorn. They had the awful aspect of utterly useless things. He lived in the midst of them. He counted incessantly their numbers, and passed them in eternal review, and grew sick because he had been their creator. How drearily they tripped about him. Here was a pale year of his life, a full flower of time, laid, with its every petal, at the feet of music; and here a night of pain that might have been a night of pleasure; and here a cold day of aching self-denial; and here a black hour of passionate despair, that, but for music, might have been a golden hour. In youth, when life had called him to the open door, he had shut the door, had thrust away pleasure, had given himself to hard and unremitting toil. And this was his reward. He forgot all that he had gained in remembering the one thing he had lost. And whenever he sang he saw his enemy, music, the thing he longed to strike.

The alteration in his art became a thing of note, a tragedy in the London of Lady Caryll's year, one of the hoarse and sinister voices of the whirlpool above which she radiantly rose.

There were many voices in that whirlpool, and some of them were sad. Was there not the whispering voice of a little acrobat calling her to see him die? Were there not the voices of those whom he had left, the voices of Diamond and of Vauxhall? The voices of thieves muttered in the whirlpool, and of the city murmuring its chorus to the wild solo of Sir Reuben. Sometimes there was the growl, far, far down it seemed, of the creature that lay ever on his breast, and strove to gain the attention that he would not give to it. And Aubrey's voice, a little strange, a little doubtful, was there, and his mother's voice, as it sounded when she said "the little chap deserves fresh flowers."

Lady Caryll heard none of these voices. Women with their feet on the world are the deafest of all the creatures of God. And her feet were on the world now. She and her great emerald stood there together. For of all her jewels she still loved it the best, even as Eve probably loved in secret best of all fruits the apple which she gave unto the man. Had the Peruvian priests of the time of Pizarro been yet alive they would surely have acclaimed Caryll as the goddess Esmeralda. For she lived in her emerald on whose surface was graven the story of her fate. Sir Reuben, throwing jewels instead of dust in the eyes of the world, at length saw the scales fall from those eyes. Voices called from the whirlpool. They clamoured of the love of Lady Caryll and where alone her heart was given. She was elevated into a shining mystery. The strangeness of her attachment to jewels struck the imaginative, and came to the knowledge of those curious beings, the occultists, the mystery-mongers, the star-gazers, the card-dealers, the clairvoyants of London. Fringed men in Bond Street sought to read the lines of her hand. Suburban hermits, closeted in Clapham villas, or secluded in semi-detached residences near Barnes and Broadesbury, were fain to cast her horoscope. Wisps of women, dwelling above grocer's shops in Hornsey, or lurking in Whitechapel lairs, laid out the dingy cards for her, and wrote illiterate letters to Park Lane, describing the wonders they had discovered and asking for small sums of money. Thin females, of Mexican appearance and Jewish temperament, fell into trances on her behalf, and, on recovering, noted down the circumstances of their dreams, and the pale future that had shaken far off, like a mirage, before their sleeping eyes. One of these called on Lady Caryll, was admitted, and spoke this prophecy :—

"I see you happy in a dark place where none of your friends will ever come, with a man whom none of your friends will know. In this dark place you wear a great jewel, you have much money, and you are deserted by those who are about you in your present existence."

Lady Caryll smiled, gave the prophetess tea and a sovereign and told Sir Reuben the tale that evening after dinner. He frowned, looking at her strangely.

"Do you believe in prophecies, Reuben?" she said.

"I have known them to come true," he replied. "There are magicians in the East."

"This woman said she was a Mexican. Do Mexicans speak with a Cockney accent?"

"In a dark place," he said musingly. "In a dark place."

That night, when they had returned from a party, he referred again to his desire to see Caryll in the sunshine of the Eastern world.

"Next winter we will travel," he said. "I will take you over the sea."

"To the villa on the bay of Tangier?" she asked him.

"To a place where I have lived with slaves," he answered.

Suddenly he caught her by the arms and looked into her fair face, while all the jewels she wore flashed in his eyes.

"Happy," he said, repeating the prophecy, "in a dark place . . . with a man whom none of your friends will know. Caryll, where shall I be then?"

His face became disfigured with passion as his eyes broodingly watched hers.

"The great jewel will be your emerald," he continued, like a man talking to himself. "Yes—the emerald. You will be happy with it. I understand—I understand. But I gave it to you. I should be there. I should be that man."

He let her go, and sank down on the divan, still staring at her, with eyes in which suspicion flickered like a spitting flame.

"Where I go," he continued, "I should be able to take you with me. That is only just. You ought always to travel with me—always, whenever I journey. For I have made you happy— I have made you happy."

"Yes, Reuben," she said. "And I will travel with you."

She came to the divan.

"What is the matter?" she asked. "Why do you look like that? I will go with you."

"But suppose it is impossible," he said, in an under-voice.

"How could it be? You are strange to-night."

Now his eyes were fixed on her jewels and on the great emerald which she was wearing. An expression of intense hatred came into his eyes. He pointed at the emerald with his brown finger.

"That will last," he said hoarsely. " My gift will last. And I—go to bed, Caryll—go to bed!"

He turned his back on her suddenly. She obeyed him, and left the room. Some instinct told her not to wear the emerald for many nights after that interview with her husband. She looked at it in secret and wished him to forget it.

Through all that season Sir Reuben accompanied her everywhere. People grew accustomed to see the small and shrivelled figure shuffling into crowded reception rooms, leaning wearily back in his chair at the Opera, driving in the Park almost hidden at her side, even waiting patiently about ball-room doors till the dawn came up in the sky over faded London. For Lady Caryll was gay, and he chose that she should be seen everywhere. In the publicity of her life he found pleasure. He had learned to pity those Easterns who seclude their treasures. Civilisation was gloriously blatant. He rejoiced in that, the more keenly because he was never really civilised. He rejoiced, too, in the misfortune which lay about Caryll's feet. When people spoke of Monsieur Anneau's downfall, he thought of the dead Creole and was glad. It is good to triumph, to be secure in old age, when one has been tortured and deceived in younger days. And the greatness of the compensation lies partly in the added burthen of the years.

All the world talked of Monsieur Anneau's misfortunes. Some women were in despair, and showed him solicitous pity, driving daggers into his soul. The Opera directorate began to treat him cavalierly as a waning star. Other singers, over whom he had formerly exulted, were very anxious on his behalf. They spoke to him, quite casually, of certain throat doctors in whom they had every confidence, and of the undoubted advantages of prolonged rest when the voice became fatigued; never hinting that he was in question, but on the contrary alluding to his giant strength and immunity from such troubles as came to others. The papers struck hard, and, when he sang,·Monsieur Anneau faced a row of busy gentlemen, in whose note-books was being nightly recorded the serial story of his downward progress. His private engagements as a concert singer were far less numerous than in former years. But—Sir Reuben wrote to invite him to sing in Park Lane. And Paul Villet came to suggest that he should undergo the new method of training the voice. Sir Reuben offered him a large cheque, Paul Villet a series of lessons for nothing. Monsieur Anneau cursed Villet, rang for a servant, and ordered him to show Villet out and never to admit him again. Sir Reuben's cheque he refused, declining to sing at Lady Caryll's concert. Sir Reuben smiled over the letter. Villet went about everywhere abusing Anneau and speaking of his ingratitude. "For did not I," he cried, "give him his greatest success when I let him·be the first to sing my Pearl Song?" And all the people who had once admired Barré, and who now adored Villet, sympathised with their fat and authoritative pet. And Albert Sprigg, waving the manicured hands, and talking English with the slippery and gliding French accent of Paris, inveighed against those who are ungracious to the men who have helped them up the ladder. He forgot, no doubt, that he never went near the Greenwich upholsterer, whose savings had sent him to France, and who had certainly—at one time—been his father.

Who was it set afloat the sly and whispered story connecting the great singer's ruin—already people called it ruin—with Lady Caryll's virtue? London, at least, never knew. But the story certainly did float forth, a cockle-shell on the whirlpool, floated forth and lived in such an angry sea. Monsieur Anneau's innumerable successes with women had extended to a failure. People whispered that he was broken-hearted. Villet babbled memories of that foggy winter night when there had been a concert in a white room, when he had triumphed, and the singer had—what? That concert soon marked a turning-point in Monsieur Anneau's life in the minds of men, and especially in the minds of women. Lady St. Ormyn now spoke of it as if she had been there, and declared that she remembered acutely how hoarse Monsieur Anneau had become towards the end of the performance.

"It's his nature that's hoarse," said that critic who had spoken of his sulky singing.

And the critic, who was young and old, conceived the idea of writing a book about the influence of the passions upon the singing voice.

Mr. Wilson, the snub-nosed man, to whom music was merely a thing out of which money could be made, declared that Monsieur Anneau should never again be engaged to sing for the Syndicate.

"The public don't want high priests who bawl like a navvy in a passion," he said delicately in the hearing of the stage hands.

They sniggered, to please him, and Mr. Slagg, somewhere up in the flies busy with his lights, thanked heaven that he was not "one of them opera gents."

Monsieur Anneau, the vainest of men, lived in a veritable Inferno, and, as the season grew, felt that he was passing on and on from one circle to another. The disorder of his mind became as the disorder of some hideous lumber-room, in which the Furies rummage at their will. When he entered the stage door of the

Opera House when he appeared at rehearsal, his eyes were wild and suspicious. He looked about him when he sang as if expectant of some outrage. His gaze searched the crowding chorus, and if two women whispered together, or a man smiled at his neighbour, Monsieur Anneau stopped the whispers, cut through the smile with a glance that was like an attack. When he appeared in society he was defiant and incessantly on the watch, angrily fearful of neglect, of any sign that his empire was passing away. London is very active in contempt of a waning celebrity, very callous of personal sensitiveness. Monsieur Anneau now had the joy of seeing Paul Villet surrounded by adorers while he was scarcely noticed. One night he was engaged to sing at a concert given by Mrs. Luffa Parkinson. The Allabruths were there, Monsieur and Madame Villet, Lady St. Ormyn, and all the smart musical world. Monsieur Anneau sang harshly and unsteadily, without real finish or any subtlety of expression. He saw Villet shrugging his shoulders, and whispering to Albert Sprigg, whose sleek face was screwed into an answering grimace of contempt. Towards the end of the concert a new baritone from Paris sang the altered Pearl Song. Villet accompanied. Everybody was in ecstasies. Monsieur Anneau left early. Two or three days later he called on Lady Caryll and found her at home and alone. She held out her hand to him. He bowed without taking it. When the servant had left the room he said—

"Are you satisfied, Miladi? Are you pleased? Tell me."

His voice was rough and uncontrolled. His expression was disordered. He stood there looking down on Lady Caryll, who glanced at him with a quiet surprise.

"What do you mean, Monsieur?" she asked.

"Are you not laughing at my ruin? Are you not laughing with Villet, with all London?"

His chest heaved with excitement. He clenched his hands together, dropping the gloves they had held upon the carpet.

"Your ruin! You are not ruined. What are you saying?"

"What every one is saying. My singing power is gone. It is gone. They say my talent is broken. You—you have broken it. They say I can no longer govern my music. Was not music my servant till I met you? I say it was, Miladi. I commanded it to do what I would. It obeyed me. It made the world—the world that laughs, Mon Dieu! obey me too. I conquered whom I would—till I met you. Do you know what you have done? You have made my art revolt against me. I gave all to my art—my youth, my brain, my strength, my soul's strength, and my body's. I made sacrifices—ah! the sacrifices I have made! You cannot understand. You have never made sacrifices. You are content

to exact them from others. But I—I was music's slave—
I tell you so, to make music my slave—do you hear—mine?
All I chose to have I got through music, all—all, till I met you."

"Monsieur Anneau——"

"I loved music—I say to you I loved it for what it did and
had done for me. Now I hate it for what it will not do, and
because I hate it, I fail—I fail always. My voice is here."—With
a wild gesture he raised his hand and laid it on his throat.—
"People, fools say it is gone. I say it is not gone. But how can
I govern the thing I could tear out? How can I use the thing I
am cursing? How can I—how can I? Tell me—you! They
laugh at me—Villet, too, the man I saved from starving! They
will not listen any more. And it is because you—you have laughed,
you have not listened, you have resisted, you have had contempt
only for my music, as you have contempt for everything, everybody,
that boy who is gone from here, your husband, every—everything
except your jewels, except your great emerald."

He had become passionately excited. His eyes were almost
like the eyes of a crazy man. Lady Caryll, who at first had tried
to interrupt his torrent of words, now sat silent. Her face had
become very cold and hard, but her eyes were fixed on his face
with an expression of uncontrollable interest.

"Your emerald," he repeated. "People say that is the only
thing you love, the only thing that moves you. Ah! now you
listen! Now you hear! It is so! It is as they say!"

Suddenly he lost all control over himself. He leaned down,
and with an oath, he exclaimed—

"Ah! Ah! if I could tear it—if I could tear it from you, as
you have torn all from me! If I—if I——"

He stretched out his hands as if furiously to seize something,
stretched them out to Lady Caryll's breast.

Suddenly she sprang up. All her calm deserted her. She
looked horribly excited, too, horribly afraid. She clasped her
hands over her breast and rushed towards the door. As she
reached it Sir Reuben opened it from the hall and came in. She
caught him by the arm with one hand, keeping the other still
upon her breast.

"Reuben! Reuben!" she cried, in a stifled voice that was
thick and veiled with terror.

She turned, and looked at Monsieur Anneau.

"Thief!" she whispered at him.

She looked down at her breast. No jewel gleamed there. Sir
Reuben supported her feebly, glancing at the singer for an explanation. Monsieur Anneau strode up to them. A sort of ferocious
curiosity had come into his face. He stopped close to them.

"She has it there," he said. "She has it there—hidden—the only thing she loves! Search and see!"

He put his hand on the door.

"Are you not afraid?" he said to Sir Reuben. "Afraid to let her touch you? What is she? What is she?"

He did not utter another word. He seemed seized with fear of Lady Caryll. He hurried out of the house.

Sir Reuben touched his wife's breast under her hand. He felt something hard, hidden beneath her dress.

She cried out and thrust away his hand.

"Ah! Caryll," he said, "keep your treasure. But do not quite forget I gave it to you—and do not fear me."

Then she threw her arms about his neck and hid her face against his shoulder.

CHAPTER XXVI

Monsieur Anneau did not sing again at the Opera that season. He asked the Syndicate to release him from his engagement, pleading ill health. Mr. Wilson patronisingly announced to him that he might go when he would without let or hindrance.

"Take my advice, Anneau, old chap," he said; "give the voice a rest. Grow roses, farm, try a country life, potter about your garden. Good luck to you. Bernardine will take your parts."

Bernardine was a new man discovered by Mr. Wilson in Lapland, or some remote place. He was burning to step into Monsieur Anneau's shoes.

"He's been training with Villet," added Mr. Wilson, curling his moustaches.

Monsieur Anneau bowed. As he turned to go he was seized by an intense longing to perform some act of violence, to commit some crime for the perpetration of which great physical force would be necessary. Of course he controlled this desire. Next day he was in Paris. He had many strange acquaintances in Paris, and, as has been said, when he was resisted he became dangerous. Mr. Wilson had genially advised him to potter about a garden.

Instead he lived, for a while, a rather hidden life in the Gay City. Each week there was forwarded to him from London a certain paper which gave him a bird's-eye-view of the smart world. From Paris, then, he followed the career of Lady Caryll. He read of the entertainments she gave, of those given by others at which she appeared. He read glowing accounts of her dresses and of her jewels. One day he read a paragraph about the great emerald. At a party a modern magician had touched it and had told Lady Caryll something of its past, something, too, of its future.

Monsieur Anneau showed this paragraph to a man with whom he was sitting in a café.

Aubrey's intercourse with the Allabruths at this time was not very intimate. He often met them in society. He often talked with them. But, since the episode of Alf's death, he had come to feel a certain uneasiness when he was with Caryll. He believed,

as he always had believed, that she was misunderstood by others,
by the world. He thought he knew that she was not the cold
and glittering creature—strangely far from humanity—that she
was supposed to be. Yet he could not find the humanity in her.
He had sought it at the ball, when Alf lay dying. He had not
found it and, at the time, he had been repelled. Later, he had
argued with himself. He had told himself that Caryll was only
a girl still, and that she had feared the horror of a thing she
had never seen, of death! Was not that natural? He knew
that, silently, his mother condemned Caryll's refusal to comply
with Alf's request. But then his mother had a sort of manly
strength in her character. She would never "shirk" an unpleasant duty. Caryll had been afraid, and probably she had not
at all realised the effect her peculiar beauty, her peculiar personality, had had on the little acrobat. Aubrey found in her a fine
lack of personal vanity. She never seemed to think much about
her influence over others. Nor did she appear to realise, as a
beautiful woman, her power over men. She was utterly careless
of the sensation she created. That made the sensation greater,
and made Aubrey place her high. The episode of Alf had caused
him to shrink from Caryll for the moment. Even now he seemed
set far from her. But his allegiance was not broken. He stood
with the crowd, and gazed into the cave, through whose jewelled
mysteries Caryll wandered on with her attendant Geni, going—
so Aubrey felt—farther and farther away. Would she fade down
the twinkling avenues? Would she disappear in a mist of gold?
There was a remoteness in the magic of her content. The crowd
hummed about her, yet she was distant, lonely with her Geni who
was her husband. She loved him. Aubrey did not doubt it. And,
this season, he placed Sir Reuben on a throne. His power over
Caryll gave to Aubrey dreams of him, imaginations of a hidden
splendour that must be like some hidden splendour of the East.
Then Aubrey discarded the shell of the soul on which all men
fix their eyes, and many women their hearts. The ugliness of
Sir Reuben, his creeping, his shuddering old age, these became
but as the ragged trappings of a king, who wears them for
a freak, or from a superb indifference, for a while, or for a little
moment. Aubrey felt that Caryll's eyes could see the truth of
the soul through the riddle of the body. What she doubtless saw
he tried to divine. He thought of his godfather as a being remote
from others. And many wondered at his reverence for the little
shuffling old man, and some supposed that he was acting a part.

And so, through all that season, Caryll wandered farther and
farther among the jewels of the Cave. Her hands were filled with
the jewels. They shone in her hair. They glittered on her neck

and arms and bosom. And still Sir Reuben sought for more wonderful gems. And the jewel merchants were ever in Park Lane. The strangest people came to the door; foreigners, Easterns from over the seas, Swedes bringing pearls, Indian dealers, and Jews seeking custom for their masters in Paris, in Vienna, in Tunis, or in Persia; Siberians and Caucasians, men from the steppes of Asia, from Gogaz, from Cubaja and from Brazil. For reputations, like migratory birds, travel far, and the name of Sir Reuben, his supposed gigantic wealth, and his undoubted mania, had become known through the world to the men who traffic with jewels. And whenever a man brought to Park Lane a strange gem, a precious stone with a history, a jewel that was very beautiful, or that was very curious, in colour, in shape, in gleam of light or depth of mystery, Sir Reuben bought it and it passed into the soft and eager hands of Lady Caryll. She never heeded the prices that were given for the things she loved. Sir Reuben never spoke to her of money. But on the Stock Exchange men talked of the magnitude of his speculations, and of the wildness of his financial dealings, of his buyings and sellings, of the almost frantic greediness he showed for investments bringing in dangerously high interest, and of his continual gambling with stocks and shares.

"Allabruth wants money," they said. "And he doesn't care how he makes it."

The risks he ran appalled the prudent and woke admiration in the breasts of the younger men who knew of them. These younger men laughed about Lady Caryll, and applied to Sir Reuben the proverb of the old fool. Yet they were captured by the magnitude of his mania. There was something almost great in the force of his concentration on one object—the filling up of the measure of one human being's joy. There was something almost great too, in, that human being's apparently measureless depth of desire, in the calmness of her unending readiness to receive. She was like a deity whom no sacrifice could ever persuade to cease from waiting expectantly for further propitiation. She was like a deity and she was like a slave. But the world forgot the slavery, for the world is ever inclined to see discontent in a slave. Yet the happiness of many slaves has been, and still is, one of the most astounding of facts.

Could any one have seen quite clearly into the heart and mind of Sir Reuben, the view must have startled him, had he been cynic, philosopher, or—most cruel thing of all—mere determined watcher of his brother man. For the man who rages near his end, and in his grey old days, is fearful as one struggling to escape from the bosom of Abraham into the last abode of Dives. Old age, we think, must be calm or weak, querulous or holy. We dwell on the supposed merciful dispensation by which men's earthly desires drop—again in our supposition—from them by degrees as they approach the tomb. Door after door is shut between them and the things of this life, the things of the great street. The door of deafness shuts out the voices, the sound of the beating footsteps that go for ever by. The door of blindness closes, and the people in the great street are seen no more. The door of forgetfulness bars from the old man even the recollection of the actions without, the accidents, the bloodshed, the assignations and the joys. And then, too, do we not suppose, comfortably, that the memory of the flesh grows beautifully blunt in these, the grey old days, and that the withered creature of the Lord, wrinkled, bent, bony, and fatigued, is become but a material for the divine preparation, which will make of it presently a mere film of matter fit for its kneading by the fingers of Eternity.

Sir Reuben was neither calm nor weak, querulous nor holy. Nor was his fleshly memory blunted or dimmed. He was living now as he had never lived before. He was living desperately, recklessly, as a man lives in a fever, or when delirium catches him by the hand and bids him come away into the regions of the wildest dreams. All that there had ever been in him seemed to have started up, to be fermenting. All his qualities had become exaggerated, all his desires excited, all his mental faculties alert. He was the man having his last fling in the great street, not the man dozing behind the shut door, dozing away into the darkness. Something had enabled him to stir beneath the imposition of the heavy, crouching creature that had been lying on his breast, to struggle, to fight, to escape from it with a cry. He rushed out like one emancipated.

He rushed out to buy jewels for his slave.

Daily his fury of unnatural vitality seemed to increase. Nightly the vehement memory of younger days burned brighter.

Caryll as she yielded to his fantastic generosity yielded also to his other desires.

The Geni who led her ever through the wonders of the Cave was, indeed, her husband.

He thought of the dead Creole and, when Caryll lay in his arms, he flung defiance at the watching shade.

And when he came to Caryll softly, with new and curious gems in his brown hands, he looked back over his shoulder to see if the shade came enviously behind him.

And when Caryll kissed him, he thought of the singer's downfall. And when she spoke sweetly to him he heard the singer's voice, harsh and tremulous and full of fury. Then he shook with joy in the faithfulness of his slave, and he thought that here, in Park Lane, with the English popinjays all round about him, he was a veritable Sultan. Savagery bubbled up in him and a contempt of these cold, pale people who knew him not, who had never understood him. He had come among them. He had bought their friendship and had twined them into the meshes of his golden nets. But they were not his people and they could never know his glory.

Caryll was one of them. He knew that. But she was a being apart, like none other, one of those abnormal beings who rise up occasionally, who sometimes pass to the grave unnoticed, and sometimes pass through lines of staring eyes and muttering lips. He thought of her as belonging to no nation and having no ancestry. What had Lady St. Ormyn to do with her, or what the little man who chirped about the city, and fluttered gaily above the ruin he had caused? The geni longed to take her away. She was a slave. She ought to see a slave's land.

At the end of the season he spoke of his desire, which grew ever upon him, his desire to see her among women of a different race and of far different traditions. She listened to his passionate description of the lands in which he had travelled, of the strange surroundings among which he had lived. But no fervour of interest flashed in her long eyes. Thoughts of wild scenery and of wilder people, of untamed, cruel men, and of submissive, burdened women, or of harem women, hidden, and lives of golden ease—such thoughts did not stir her, or flush the whiteness of her face.

"You do not care, Caryll," said Sir Reuben. "You do not care to go."

"Oh yes, Reuben," she said, smiling at him. "I should like to see such places, such people."

But he saw that it was not so. He had contented her so much that no new, changed prospect moved her. For a moment he sat silent, feeling chilled and almost repelled. Then a light of mischief, of cunning, blazed up in his eyes. He leaned forward to her, as he had leaned at that dinner when he had told to her and to Aubrey his thoughts and his wandering fancies about jewels.

"Would you not, Caryll," he said softly, "would you not like to see the lands where jewels come from? Tavernier and Jaubert visited the home of the diamond. Why not you? Do you care less for the children of India than did they?"

Her face changed. Instantly a look of eager interest stole into it.

"Do you know," he continued, "that one of the most famous of the world's sapphires was found in Bengal by a poor woodcutter. He did not love jewels as you do. Yet you are ever here in this cold England, where the jewels come, it is true, but where all the jewels are in exile. Did not he know something of jewels that you do not know? Was he not nearer to them even than you—that poor wood-cutter who found a gem that has been one of the glories of Europe? And think of your emerald, your second self. Cailloud visited long ago the mountains of the emerald, near the Egyptian city of Asna. Will you not see Egypt? Will you not see Peru, where once dwelt those priests who spoke to the people of the Goddess Esmeralda—of you, Caryll, of you. For who can say if you are not, indeed, the Goddess Esmeralda come again strangely, mysteriously upon the earth? Perhaps you have been reincarnated to be one with your great emerald, here, in my house with me."

A strong excitement was awake in him. She had caught it now. This little man could fascinate her in moments like these. Her eyes shone as she thought of the far-off homes of jewels. He saw that he had lit the torch, and, holding her soft hands in his, he made her travel, travel with him on the wings of a storm of words. They went together far away that sultry summer night, while London revelled and slept, while the women slipped along the streets, gazing into the shadows with their hollow, hungry eyes, and the beggars crouched on the Embankment, and in the Parks the weary children—having hidden among the trees as midnight passed—lay upon the grass by the water and dreamed. They travelled and saw strange things. They stood with the old negress at Bogagem, in Brazil, and saw the round amazement in her bulging, velvet eyes as she found the great diamond that Paris called, long after, "the Star of the South." They stood by the Afghan chief, and watched him give into the hands of Schafrass, the Armenian merchant, the marvellous jewel called "the Moon of the Mountains." And, in the market-place of Bassora, they looked upon the merchant returning with his trophy to his home in the night. In Upper Hungary, and in Arabia, they lingered to gaze upon the triangular reflections of the harlequin opal, and at Limapan they rejoiced, with Humboldt, in the discovery of the fire-red Mexican opal that glows with such a vehement and almost murderous glory. They heard the crying prayer of pearl fishers by Indian waters, and in Siberian solitudes the topaz smiled at them, as smiles the yellow jonquil in an English happy valley. In the Islands of Mount Caucasus they perceived the turquoise eyes protruding from the "inaccessible and cold banks," to stare upon a frigid world. And in Ortosia they wandered through the red crowds of the rubies.

And that night Caryll said to her husband ere she fell asleep—
"Take me with you, Reuben. Take me over the world."

And he laughed, and held her fast in his small, withered arms, and answered—

"I will take you first to the land of the sunshine where once I lived with slaves. For are not you a slave, my Esmeralda?"

"How?" she asked.

"Slave to your jewels, if not to me?"

She felt his dry lips on hers as she fell asleep, and the last thing she heard was her husband laughing softly beside her in the dark.

CHAPTER XXVII

When the world fled from London in July, the Allabruths stayed on in Park Lane. Since the night of Sir Reuben's outburst, Caryll's perfect content had left her. She had become restless, desirous of a wider horizon. The heavy lattices that bounded her view when she was within doors now gave to her mind unquiet thoughts of prison. Sometimes Sir Reuben, coming in upon her unexpectedly, found her pacing softly to and fro. He smiled, and thought of a beautiful animal in its cage. She stopped when she saw him.

"Why do you smile like that, Reuben?" she asked.

He did not tell her that he was thinking how cleverly his words had caused her uneasiness.

"The desire to wander has come to you at last," he said.

"Yes, it has. When shall we go?"

"Where do you want to go?"

"You know, Reuben."

She did not try to tell him. She trusted completely to his comprehension of her.

"Yes," he answered, "I think I know. Caryll, we will stay on quietly here in the dead months of London. We will rest as people rest in the long heats of the East. We will rest, you and I, with our companions."

She smiled now.

"And," he continued, "I have affairs to arrange, things to wind up, people to see. In these dead months all can be set in order. Then, in the autumn, we will start for our tour to the homes of the jewels. It will be a strange pilgrimage, will it not? London will not know why we go, where we are going, what is our aim in setting forth. We will cherish our mystery."

"Yes, yes."

She was quiet now. She had sat down and was smiling almost dreamily. Her grey eyes, turned towards the latticed window, seemed to gaze on far-off things.

"Rest, Caryll, rest a little while," he said. "For our pilgrimage will be long, and we shall visit many lands."

As he spoke the last words some bitter thought seemed to

THE SLAVE

strike him. A shade came over his face. He paused. Then he repeated defiantly—

"Yes—many, many lands."

One of the last things people heard, as they bade good-bye to the season, was that the Allabruths were going to make a tour of the world. They refused all country house invitations; they would not even go to Lady St. Ormyn in Hampshire. She had taken a Grange, and was about to fill it with French composers, Italian singers, Russian authors, and English people who knew how to remain in an attitude of extravagant worship. She was horribly shocked to think of her daughter in London during the month of August.

"You'll be obliged to dine with caretakers," she cried, "and spend your afternoons at the Cattle Show. I always say that—— What, Mr. Fraser? The promenade concerts! Oh, but it's wicked to walk about and drink—what do the lower classes drink? Bottled something, isn't it?—while Wagner is being played. Besides, everything is in brown holland in August, and brown holland has such an awful effect on the mind. People who live much with brown holland always turn out badly. My great aunt, Lady Rimmington——"

She described various ancestral tragedies directly springing from the influence upon weak natures of that material which drapes dead seasons, and leads autumn into the echoing reception rooms of great cities. But she could not shake the decision of her daughter and her son-in-law.

Lady Rangecliffe, and the three men in the hall, departed to Beechin Castle in Shropshire, Lord Rangecliffe's country place. Aubrey went up to Scotland to stay with friends. Monsieur and Madame Villet and Albert Sprigg hurried to Homburg in the wake of royal dukes. The deliberate heat of an exceptional summer crawled upon London, sank down heavily upon the empty streets, leaned against the blind houses, brooded wearily over the great river, breathed, like a panting dragon, through the narrow alleys of the poor, filled each yellow day with a slumberous discontent, and each black night with a wakeful dreariness.

Through the town men went with tired feet. Women sat by open windows watching the white children quarrel in their play, and thinking of sea-places, where the winds were salt and vivid, and the waves were whispering blue. Government nodded, like an old man in the twilight. Commerce dozed with its chin upon its breast. The flies buzzed against the hot and shining windowpanes, where usury looked out with heavy-lidded eyes. And religion, from the pulpit, yawned to its yawning devotees. And the silence of Park Lane was almost as the silence of those ruined highways that the lion and leopard keep.

The long line of empty houses stared gloomily on the almost empty Park, where a few carriages, filled with stiff, conversing servants, passed self-consciously in circular promenades.

In the newspaper offices perspiring men in shirt sleeves wrote the columns on the "Annual Exodus," and waded through the ungrammatical letters that the silly season brings.

And behind the carved lattices of Allabruth House Sir Reuben and Lady Caryll enjoyed their long siesta before their flitting to the countries of her dream.

For now she had lost the restlessness, and spent many hours alone, wrapped in reveries or reading diligently in books. These books were given to her by Sir Reuben. They were histories of jewels, accounts of those countries in which jewels are found, imaginative tales of the supposed virtues, vices, influences and constitutions of gems. One of these books was very old. Its dingy brown cover and tattered label at first repelled her hands; but when she read it she was fascinated, and mused of a new science of healing. For it gave many instances of the curative properties of precious stones.

One evening she talked much to her husband of this book and of the beliefs that had come to her from reading it.

"If I were to choose a profession, Reuben," she said, "do you know what I would be?"

"What, Caryll?" he asked.

"I would be a jewel-doctor. I would heal my patients with my jewels. My medicines should be gems."

And then she related to him many curious instances of people cured of horrible complaints by precious stones. She told him of the scholar who was brought to the door of death by loss of blood, and who was saved by the gift of a blood-stone the size of a pigeon's egg, which was brought to him by a woman who loved him, and which he wore about his neck. She described minutely the pitiful condition of a young girl who was fading in a fever, and must have died had not an old sage who lived in a tower placed some oriental rubies upon her burning breast, whereupon the fever left her and she arose and went about her occupations. She grew eloquent as she enlarged on the appalling dreams which haunted the sleep of a certain Persian prince rendering his existence terrible to him, till he grew fearful and tremulous and nervous as a female child, and wept when the dark night fell upon his palace, and called to his musicians to play, to his slaves to sing eternally to him, that he might not sleep and enter into torture. One day an old crone, begging for alms at the portal of the palace, heard of the desperate condition of the prince. "Let him wear on his breast a spinel ruby," she croaked. And she turned and went upon her way. The prince obeyed her injunction, and henceforth the dream-goblins departed from him and he suffered no more.

Sir Reuben listened to such tales. They seemed to him as the tales of the thousand and one nights. He thought that their narration made Caryll seem still more like a lovely slave. And he leaned upon a divan, smoking his long pipe, sipping his Turkish coffee, and listening to the soft and eager voice that sang the long praises of all the precious stones.

The nights were hot and still. A great August moon looked down on the city. Sir Reuben ordered the Arab servant to draw back the curtain from the door of the room in which they sat, in order that he might be able to hear the tinkle of the fountain in the hall ripple on with the voice of Caryll as she talked. One night, recurring again to the subject of the medicinal virtues of gems, she said to him—

"Reuben, I shall study this subject, and then if you are ever ill I will heal you with one of your own gifts to me."

He lay on the cushions of the divan and said nothing. She looked closely, curiously at him. For the first time, and because of this pre-occupation of hers, she noticed that he had the peculiarly alive expression of a man in an unnatural condition of health.

"Are you quite well, Reuben?" she said.

"Why do you ask me?" he answered from a cloud of smoke.

She drew a little nearer to him, put out her hand and touched his.

He trembled, and sat up on the divan.

"Do you wish to find me ill, Caryll?" he asked slowly.

"No, no, Reuben."

She talked of other things. But after that night he noticed that she began to observe him with new and attentive eyes, and that she read more deeply in her books than ever.

The sultry days went by. Sir Reuben received a good many visitors. He was often closeted with city men. The news of his approaching departure on such long journeying had become generally known. It seemed that a vast number of persons wished to see him before he went. He never spoke of their visits to Caryll, and she had no sort of curiosity about them. Only those who brought with them jewels woke any attention in her.

Sir Reuben's yacht, the *Emerald*, was fitting out at Southampton. They were to start in the last week of September.

As the days went by Caryll noticed, with those new doctor's eyes of hers, that the peculiar expression of unnatural life increased in her husband's face. When he lay quite still in the evening after dinner, he appeared to be in movement. When he was silent it seemed as if he spoke. Although at this time he was generally one of the most motionless of men, Caryll found herself thinking of him steadily as one of the most restless. She came to believe that this strange vivid effect of movement where there was no, or so little, movement, must be produced by some very unusual condition of health. In former days she would not certainly have noticed the matter at all. She noticed it now because it connected itself with the fancies created in her by her reading in jewel-books. Her mind went busily to work. But she said nothing to her husband of the subject that now began to engross her.

She watched him, and he knew it, as he knew everything she did, everything almost that she thought. And this new personal watchfulness in her was disagreeable to him. It altered her, and he had no desire to find her altered.

"Never change," he said to her one day.

And he resolved to shut his eyes to change in her if there were any. He told himself that he was becoming fanciful, that certain affairs of his, of which Caryll knew nothing, were producing deceptive impressions upon his mind.

Then he fell again into the fury of living that sometimes attacks the old. He pretended that this seclusion in the great, silent, brilliant house, and in the dead season of the great town, was the seclusion of a honeymoon. Caryll was young, as a bride should be. He recalled the saying that no man need ever be old if he does not choose to be so. And he sought to play the youth. Caryll observed that, from this date, the peculiarity of aspect, noticed by her, markedly increased on him.

She thought of herself in a new relation with jewels. Mentally she began to regard herself in a novel light. When she was sitting alone her mind was filled with thoughts of the way of a jewel-doctor's life.

So the August days all slipped away, and went with the August moon.

September came, bringing the altering hints of autumn that always seem to come with it into the London ways.

Sir Reuben talked more and more of their travels as the time of departure drew near. He spoke with the eagerness of a man longing for emancipation. Already the sound of the sea was in his ears, the flash of the tropical sun was in his eyes.

"I hate London," he said one day.

As he said the words a look almost of horror came into his face. Caryll was sitting in an arm-chair, reading a jewel-book, a treatise on the supposed virtues of the emerald and the beliefs cherished by the ancients about this stone. She looked up. They were in the green boudoir, where Aubrey had first seen her after her marriage.

"Why?" she asked.

Her husband opened his lips as if to speak, but he said nothing. It was quite evident that he had checked himself abruptly on the edge of some quick remark. Seeing Caryll's eyes fixed upon him, he considered for a moment, and then said—

"I am tired of it. That is all. My temperament inclines me to wandering."

"Are you always restless?" she asked rather quickly.

"Why? Have you thought me so?"

"Sometimes—lately," she answered.

"It is the knowledge that we are going to start on a journey so soon," he said.

Caryll returned to her reading. After she had read a page or two, she heard her husband say—

"Do you fancy that I am in any way abnormal, Caryll?"

His voice sounded suspicious. She put down her book.

"Abnormal?" she said. "How?"

"That is for you to say."

"I don't think you so," she answered, wishing to please him.

"You are certain the thought has never come to you lately?"

She shook her head smiling. But now she felt that he, too, had secretly recognised that some curious process was going on within him. Was it physical, or mental, or both?

"I think you have seemed—well——" she paused to consider. What did she think exactly?—" Unusually young lately," she concluded.

He looked pleased.

"Is that all? Yes, I feel young. You keep me young. Since I have married you I have dropped a weight of years."

All that evening he was gay. He talked much, mischievously and imaginatively by turns. But when Caryll was next alone she sought among her books until she found one which dealt with "The strangeness of that which is familiar." This was a curious and rather wandering work, written by the editor of a certain paper much read by occultists. It dealt with the mysterious qualities possessed by many things with which mankind is well acquainted. One of the chapters was devoted to a discussion of the strangeness of jewels, and to their power, fantastically affirmed by the author, of giving information to those who understand them. Certain persons—he stated that he was among their number—can, by merely holding a jewel in their hands, receive mysteriously from it the knowledge of whence it came, of the people to whom it belonged in the past, of the circumstances and surroundings among which it had been preserved. And, he went on to say, this communication is a deliberate act on the part of the jewel, which can at will either impart or withhold such information. A jewel then possesses life? The author declared his absolute conviction that life exists far more generally than most men suppose, and that a certain amount of life—different from our own, and misunderstood by us—is present in things generally pronounced lifeless.

He brought forth a number of facts to support his contention, but acknowledged that this unemphatic, and intensely reserved or modest life is so mysterious, and often so faint, that it seems impossible at present to discover clearly much about it. He concluded his chapter by a reference to the life in a human being which, so unreserved and so blatant in comparison with the life in a jewel, or in the materials of a house (in this connection he had dealt already with so-called haunted houses), is nevertheless so misunderstood, so often unheeded when it is trying to tell the most important truths.

The following-paragraph struck Caryll very forcibly. Indeed, her vague memory of it had prompted her to get down the book from its shelf and to search again through its pages.

"The Spirit of Life is continually speaking to us, and we decline to hear it. In jewels it exists and speaks; in trees, in flowers, and in plants. Sometimes our indifference to its voice angers or distresses it. This is often the case when it speaks in a human body. Never more anxious is the Spirit of Life to convey to us a message than during the period which immediately precedes that moment in which it is obliged to go elsewhere. It rises up then like a departing visitor, holds out its hand to us, and says 'Farewell!' How often do we decline the hand and fail to hear the adieu! How often afterwards do we complain that the abrupt departure of the Spirit of Life has taken us by surprise or has stricken us to the earth with grief and terror! So-called sudden deaths generally startle and amaze us. They do so because most of us have never learnt to be truly observant. I am convinced that the Spirit of Life seldom or never departs from a body without previously giving definite signs of its intention to do so. One of the most common of these signs is any very unusual or seemingly unnatural symptom of brightness, fierceness, flaming vigour, or intense restlessness manifested by man or woman."

The author then proceeded to give instances of persons who had displayed such unnatural vigour and restlessness immediately before their so-called deaths, and when they were apparently in perfect health. Afterwards he sought to show that certain jewels sometimes foretell the death of their wearers. He claimed this quality more especially for the sapphire, which, since it can protect against death—as the ancients believed—can also indicate when its power of protection is being drawn from it. Then, he said, it becomes dull in appearance, clouded and almost black, as if perturbed by its own uselessness and weakness.

When she had reached this passage Caryll laid down the book and sat absorbed in thought.

That evening, at dinner with her husband, she wore a wonderful sapphire ring which he had given to her in the early days of their married life.

Sir Reuben did not talk very much during dinner. But it seemed to Caryll that the silent vivacity of his appearance, the extraordinary atmosphere of energy that seemed to emanate mysteriously from his inactive body, had decidedly increased. She thought of the book she had been reading and looked at the sapphire, turning it gently round on her finger. She wanted her husband to wear it. She wanted to watch it while he wore it.

A profound curiosity was awake in her. It was not touched by or mingled with fear. It stood quite alone in its intensity.

She wanted to prove to herself—what? That there exists in certain jewels the curious life, even the knowledge of coming events, affirmed by the author of the book she had been reading?

Perhaps she scarcely told herself at first what she desired. She looked at the great sapphire—jewel of Roman cardinals in modern days, jewel sacred to Apollo in days of old, jewel that had murdered asps and pacified enemies, that had given liberty to slaves, and delivered the sad victims of enchantments. The gem was marvellously clear and flawless, neither absolutely blue nor absolutely purple, but full of a mingled beauty of two wedded colours. Translucent and serene it looked as if it would be soft to the touch like velvet. Caryll gazed at it with a passionate interest. Then she glanced up at her husband.

He was leaning back in his chair, in which he sat very low. In one hand he held a glass of wine, which he was in the act of raising to his lips. Often his hand trembled slightly when it held anything. To-night it was steady as a rock. He sipped the wine slowly. Then he put down the glass and said—

"I bought you a present to-day, Caryll."

"What? A jewel?" she asked quickly.

"No, a travelling-case to hold your jewels. I knew you would want to take them, or many of them, on the yacht."

She thanked him.

"I will show it to you after dinner," he said. "It is marvellously arranged, and full of ingenuities."

When he had smoked a cigarette and drunk his coffee, he told the Arab servant to bring down the case into the smoking-room where he and Caryll were sitting. He unlocked it, and showed her all its multitudinous drawers and recesses, its little doors, its nests for necklaces, and tiny wells for rings. She examined it with some eagerness, but with less than he had anticipated. The case was so contrived as to hold an enormous quantity of jewels and yet to be comparatively small. Some conversation took place between Caryll and Sir Reuben as to the amount it would contain when it was full. Suddenly an idea struck Sir Reuben.

"Let us pack the case with jewels," he said, "and then it will be ready for our journey."

"For our journey," she answered. "Yes."

Her manner was certainly preoccupied to-night. He wondered why, and the desire came to him to stir her to a shining excitement. He therefore determined to proceed at once to the jewel packing. For he felt certain that the sight, the touch of her gems would wake Caryll from the cloudy dreams that seemed so strangely to beset her. He went upstairs himself to bring down her jewels. All the time he was out of the room she sat looking at the sapphire on her finger, drinking, with her eyes, its exquisite clear purplish blue. Could so radiant a jewel ever look misty black? That seemed impossible. Sir Reuben returned. The Arab servant took away the coffee.

The travelling-case stood open on a divan.

"Now, Caryll, come and help me to take your jewels out of their cases," Sir Reuben said.

He had put them down all about the room, upon the long divans. Now he went to the wall near the door and turned on all the electric light. Caryll got up. She opened two or three of the cases. The jewels they contained flashed in the light, flashed red, white, pink, yellow, green, purple fire. Sir Reuben opened the other cases. The huge engraved emerald shone from its snowy velvet bed. The big, smooth, milky-white pearl that Sir Reuben had bought from the Indian for five thousand pounds gleamed gently in the midst of the fiery or more showy jewels that surrounded it, the strings of rubies, the diamond chains, the quivering sprays of sapphires and amethysts, the ornaments thickly set with turquoises, with emeralds, with harlequin opals, with beryls, and with vivid blood-red garnets. The chamber shone with varied and distinct brightnesses, with silky brightness, with pearly brightness, with brightness adamantine, resinous or vitreous.

Caryll stood looking at the coloured sparks that flashed at her from all sides.

"I love to see you standing in the midst of your jewels, Caryll," her husband said. "Now we are together in the Cave of Aladdin."

To-night he was full of changes. He became quite gay, almost childish now, and took her hand.

"Yes," he said, "this is indeed the Cave. No one can come into it but we two, but you and your Geni, who obeys all your behests."

"If you are the Geni of the Cave, Reuben," she cried, apparently falling into his mood, "if you are the geni of the jewels, you should be covered with jewels. They should cling about you as if they loved you."

She burst into soft laughter.

"Let me make you like a geni," she exclaimed.

She seemed to be full of a gay excitement. Sir Reuben was not loth to submit to her pretty desire. All this was like a game in a harem—and London lay around, hot and black, and wearily drowsing.

"Do you want to dress me in jewels?" he said. "Would you make me like an Eastern potentate?"

"Yes, yes. Are you not Eastern?"

"I feel so to-night. And you—you are surely a beautiful Circassian, with your gleaming skin and your bright eyes."

He wanted to kiss her. She drew back hastily, and a momentary expression of dread, or of disgust, flitted across her face.

"No, no," she cried, "not till you are really my geni."

She looked at the sapphire on her finger and at her husband's hands. Then she went swiftly to the divan and began to lift the jewels from their cases. He watched her eagerly, thinking, almost like a boy, of the kiss which she had refused but which he would give her presently. She turned and came towards him. Her hands were full of jewels.

"There is a diamond chain for the geni," she said, hanging one round his neck; "emeralds for his fez"—she fastened an emerald ornament into the front of the fez that he was wearing—"rubies for his robe."

Slowly, with a deliberation that was almost sensual, she covered all the front of his silk smoking coat with gems. She put no sapphires among them. But each jewel fastened upon him was a step on the road to her purpose. She journeyed quietly, with a deep joy in her anticipation of arrival, with a passion of interest such as she had never felt before. Presently she turned him about under the lights. His brown face was smiling in the midst of the jewels. His brown hands touched, with an Oriental delicacy and gentleness, the precious stones that gleamed on his narrow chest.

Caryll noticed that their vivid fire, instead of dulling the effect of his appearance, seemed, on the contrary, to increase the violence of the life in his face, the quickness of vitality that seemed to emanate from his whole person. She watched him furtively with wary eyes.

"Now I am a Rajah," he said. "Do I wear my jewels well? Tell me, Esmeralda."

Again he sought to touch her lips with his. She avoided him, with an agile indifference that sprang from her secret intention, unknown by him.

"Wait, Reuben, wait!" she exclaimed. "You have no jewels on your hands."

As she spoke, she slipped the sapphire ring from her third finger.

"You must wear this," she said.

"It will be too small," he replied. "I could not get it on."

"Try—try your little finger."

He made a grimace at her, as, almost with roughness, she pressed the ring upon the little finger of his right hand.

"How strong and determined you are, Caryll," he said. "Yes, it is on. But it is very tight. Now am I quite a geni? Caryll, do you hear? Am I quite a geni, I said?"

For she had not answered him or seemed to hear him. She had been looking intently at the sapphire on his hand. She glanced up hastily, impatiently.

"Yes, Reuben. Now you are a geni. Let us sit down on the divan."

She led him to it. He sat cross-legged, with a deliberate assumption of an Oriental attitude. He was still smiling. To-night all this folly amused him, because it was connected with her, and with the price he had paid for her. It had delighted him to be dressed in jewels by her soft hands. It delighted him now to squat, like some old Moor or Egyptian, upon the big cushions of the divan with all the jewels sparkling about him, while she sank down at his side. It chanced that the hand on which he wore the sapphire was hidden beneath one of the cushions. Caryll sought gently to remove this cushion.

"Why do you do that?" he asked.

"Are you comfortable?"

"Quite. I could sit like this for hours."

His hand was still hidden. Caryll frowned. It was evident

that something displeased her. She moved uneasily on the divan. Sir Reuben began to talk about their approaching journey with the extravagance, the half fantastic, half serious eloquence that was natural to him. He poured forth a flood of words about the foreign lands they would visit, about the many aspects of the seas, the variations of weather they would encounter, about the differing races of men among which they would sojourn for a while. As he talked the vivacity of his appearance increased. Caryll noticed that. Never had he seemed so curiously, so almost unnaturally young and vigorous. Could it be the brilliant effect of the jewels that made him look so brilliant? Again and again, while he talked, she asked herself that question. His hand was still concealed beneath the silken cushion.

She could not see the sapphire.

This circumstance irritated her intensely, and preoccupied her so much that she scarcely knew what he was saying. When she did know, when she heard him elaborately describing the possibilities—he faced them as certainties—of their future, a curious sensation of pitiful doubt overwhelmed her. But her mind was really given not at all to him but to the hidden sapphire. Curiosity as to its condition crept upon her till the fact that it was invisible caused her physical pain, and she could have struck her husband for remaining always in one position while he talked. She interrupted him brusquely at last.

"Reuben," she said. "How can you sit hunched up like that? You ought to rest after dinner. Do lie down, and I will pile up the cushions behind you."

He shook his head.

"Why should I rest? I am a geni; I am no ordinary mortal. You are not romantic, Caryll. Your conception of a geni who has to lie down and repose after dinner does you no credit."

And he went on talking about their travels. He was in Ceylon now. She set her teeth. It was only with great difficulty that she could refrain from tearing the cushion away from the hand it concealed. The marvellous colours of Ceylon all rushed together in a flash of glaring yellow before her eyes. For a moment she shut them. She lifted her hands to her ears, then hastily controlled herself and sat listening with apparent attention. From Ceylon Sir Reuben passed to India. His dissertation seemed as if it would be endless, and he was evidently under the impression that Caryll was enthralled by the prospect before her. Both his imagination and his memory were now fully awake. There was a glow in his words. There was an onward movement in his sentences. And Caryll, noting it, compared it with the repose of his body, and found the contrast intolerable. Suddenly an idea came to her,

"Reuben, you aren't smoking," she said. "I will get you a cigarette."

"Thank you, Caryll," he answered.

She got up from the divan. He sat watching her as she moved across the floor to a table on which lay a box of cigarettes. He let the lids droop over his eyes till she was misty, and looked like a vision in the distance of the big room. And, with half-shut eyes, he continued to regard her sensually, while she lifted the silver lid of the box, took out a cigarette and began to return, holding it lightly in her soft hand. She approached him.

"Here it is, Reuben."

For a moment he did not move, but sat gazing at her. He was enjoying his possession of her more keenly, more fiercely tonight than ever before.

"Reuben!" she said.

And now her voice sounded irritable. He took his hand from under the cushion and held it out for the cigarette. She gave it to him, and was bending to gaze at the sapphire when he said, drawling the words with a kind of lazy passion—

"A light, my Esmeralda."

Caryll started. She turned sharply, went again to the table and fetched the little silver cup in which, red hot, the fire glowed against the metal. Sir Reuben bowed himself forward like a Mandarin. He had put the cigarette between his lips and had once more hidden his hand against the cushion. The cigarette touched the cup and gleamed. Caryll could scarcely prevent herself from crying out impatiently, or even furiously. She longed to dash the cup down upon the floor. Her face contracted and the brows lowered over her eyes, which were sickly, like the eyes of a malicious invalid. But just as she was on the edge of her self-control, her husband lifted his hand from the divan, took the cigarette from his lips and said—

"What is it, Caryll? Why do you look vexed?"

Without answering she stared upon the sapphire. The exquisite clearness had gone from it with the intense glory of colour that had made it so rarely beautiful. A tiny cloud had surely floated upon it, and it had become almost black. She dropped the silver cup as she bent to gaze at it more closely.

"Caryll, what on earth is the matter?"

Sir Reuben moved with quick agility, and lifted the cup from the floor. She followed his hand with her eyes, completely fascinated. He put the cup down.

"Is there anything on my hand? Why do you stare at it like that? What do you see?"

"A black sapphire," she replied.

And she looked straight into his eyes as he stood opposite to her. He glanced at the ring.

"What extraordinary fancies you have about your jewels!" he exclaimed. "This sapphire is not black. How could it be?"

"It is black," she reiterated. "Now you wear it."

There was such a strange depth of meaning in her voice, that he was startled, as a man is startled by the apprehension of an impending tragedy.

"Now I wear it!" he said. "How could that affect it?"

Suddenly, and scarcely knowing why, he began to try to take the ring off. But, since it was really rather too small for his finger, this was difficult. The flesh had puffed up slightly along the golden band, and the effort to remove it was useless and caused him pain. The resistance offered to his instinctive desire showed him its absurdity.

"What nonsense!" he exclaimed. "Why should I take it off? But it is too small, as I said, and will be difficult to remove."

"Yes," she replied.

She was looking at him with the most fervent attention. He thought that a passion of expectation gazed out of her eyes. It was so definite, so vivid that he felt as if she had expressed it plainly in words. And he answered it—

"What are you waiting for?" he said uneasily.

He glanced round and behind him. He stood and listened, though he could not have said for what he listened—whether for a step in the hall, for the rustle of a curtain, or for the faint sound of a voice. She sent him some of her mind just then. She did not send him all; for he was perplexed and confused, and knew not what he anticipated. An echo is ignorant, as a voice is not. He turned round to her again—

"Caryll, what is it?" he said urgently. "Tell me—what is it you are waiting for?"

Now there was a sound of fear in his voice.

"It is for you to tell me," she said, almost in a whisper.

"For me?" he stammered. "For me?"

As he spoke the last word a sudden fury of life ran through his body. A sudden fury of thought flooded his brain. Light blazed before his eyes, and there came upon him an amazing sensation of being lifted up and swept on toward some tremendous experience. Caryll saw all this reflected in his appearance, which became totally unnatural in its abrupt and hideous energy. She saw him move forward upon her, and she thrust out her hands, mechanically, to keep him off. When she did so, and before her hands touched him, all the life, that was like light, in him went out swiftly, as when a lamp that stands at an open window is extinguished by a gust of night air. He stood before her, all dark it seemed, as the aperture in which the lamp flame has died. He swayed, and fell down at her feet with his face hidden.

She stood quite still, looking at the heap he made. Then a faint smile flickered over her face.

"My sapphire told me the truth," she whispered.

She was conscious of a thrill of pleasure. It passed; but it was not at first succeeded by any actual terror. She knelt down on the carpet, turned her husband over slowly, carefully, and looked into his face. His eyes were wide open and gazed at her. There was expression in them. He was not dead. All the jewels sparkled upon him. Only the sapphire was clouded and dim.

She thought of the curative properties of certain jewels. A new fervour of curiosity and of desire seized her.

. . . . . .

When, a few minutes later, the Arab servant entered the room, bringing the iced water that Sir Reuben always drank before going to bed, he found his master lying motionless upon the floor, with his head propped upon a cushion.

Lady Caryll was reading diligently in a small book. Its cover was dingy brown. Its label, on which was written in old lettering its name, was tattered.

The Arab bent down, looked closely at his master, then approached Lady Caryll and touched her arm softly. She started and glanced up. Then she made a sign to the Arab not to interrupt her. She pointed to Sir Reuben.

"I will cure him," she said. "I will cure him, D'oud. Have no fear."

The Arab made her get up and come with him to where Sir Reuben lay.

The expression had gone out of his eyes. He was dead.

Lady Caryll's book fell to the floor.

CHAPTER XXVIII

THE news of Sir Reuben's sudden death from paralysis greatly astonished those people who are always ready to be amazed by anything abrupt. But certain doctors and certain wise men of the world heard of it without wonder. And others—City men— believed that they had actually expected such a tragedy. The reason of their belief soon appeared. Sir Reuben had sunk to the grave in the midst of financial ruin. His frequent visitors from the City had been birds of ill-omen. All through the previous London season the hoarse voices of the whirlpool had been muttering predictions of a reckoning day, while the jewel merchants came daily to the door of Allabruth House, and Lady Caryll went into the world wearing the gifts of those far countries that made Sir Reuben's latest dream. That dream was dead with the so desirous pilgrim. And the men of the City, knowing of liabilities that could not be met, of immense loans raised and promises of fantastic interest, of feverish gambling with stocks and shares, talked of old age as an inevitable period of mania, and of paralysis as its natural close.

They thought of mental worry and shook their heads gravely. Certain doctors and men of the world thought of Lady Caryll. They shook their heads and smiled, as some will always smile at a mental vision of human nature bearing its burden to the abyss.

One class saw Sir Reuben dead in the arms of despair, the other saw him dead in the arms of pleasure.

His creditors merely saw him dead, and clamoured for their dues. The exact story of his ruin is not worth the telling. As his original success sprang from the fierceness of his nature, so did his eventual failure rise from the same source. The death of the Creole marked the dividing of the ways. Till her death he had won because he could believe in the worth of Life's gifts to men. After her death he lost because he could believe no more. His relation with Caryll was but an episode occurring at the mouth of the black valley. It could not stem the wild tide of his imprudence, because it could not make him believe rightly again. But after she came into his life he had one more reason for living.

And so he lived, and his vitality was like the artificial glory that pigments give to fading cheeks. At last Death grew weary of waiting for him, came upon him, showed him for one moment, dark, the pigments gone, to the woman by whom he had paused near the valley, then took him with no more ceremony than the butcher shows to the chased sheep pinned at last in a corner of its field.

How his death, if it had been succeeded by a normal period of peace, would have affected Caryll can never be known. Would she have grieved? Would she have shuddered under the shock? Would she have been grave and prayed—have been contumacious and blasphemed? Ruin would not grant her any moment to play the ordinary widow according to her nature. Ruin fell upon her at once; with ruin—tumult.

The *Emerald*, fitting out at Southampton, was become a sort of emblem of the dead man's recklessness. His last project was talked of as the mental exploit of one who was willing to cheat, or who was really astray in the mazes of a dream, drugged by old age and wandering blindly. The other emerald became Caryll's rock, the one thing left for her to cling to now that the great sea came upon her. For the engraved emerald was the only thing Sir Reuben had settled upon his wife.

And that settlement, too, had been one of his fantasies. The jewel was worth a fortune. In the dark garden at Epsom it had played its part in the comedy of life. Sir Reuben always thought of it as of some live and cynically smiling thing, standing alone. So he left it alone to her whom he had called a slave.

Was it not worth a fortune?

After his death, then, all his property was seized; the great house, the yacht, and all the other jewels. The horror of ruin is always great. It moves humanity. The horror of this ruin was peculiar, for it showed a woman struggling at first, vainly, against the approach of an infernal solitude. When Caryll was told, by lawyers, something of the truth of her situation, she did not appear surprised or appalled. They spoke to her of money losses, of the necessity of giving up a great house, of removal, of an altered way of life. They spoke sympathetically. She heard them calmly. In solicitor's offices she was talked of as a plucky woman. Later, in those offices, she was talked of differently, almost nervously, as men speak of ugly and mysterious things. For only when she knew that she no longer possessed any jewels, except the great emerald, did she allow herself to be partially understood. There was a moment then in which her legal advisers feared her, a moment that they could not easily forget. There is a white wrath that comes upon a human being as a white squall comes upon the sea,

Its pallor is more horrible than any darkness, the livid hue of destruction that makes men think of hell as white.

Aubrey was not near Caryll when she learnt her fate. He came afterwards, in the wake of Lady St. Ormyn chattering like a distressed pie, of Lord St. Ormyn—always at home in ruin,—of others who joined in the loud chorus of condolence. Caring so much more for her than others, he had not dared to thrust himself sooner into the sorrow he wondered about and attempted to realise. His own most deep and exact sensation he had not tried to analyse. That all the world seemed suddenly changed, he knew; in what manner changed he did not know. Confusion was in his life. His heart seemed all littered with strange odds and ends of feeling, of fear and something else. He did not know that it was hope.

The white squall passed upon the sea. He never saw it. He had written to Caryll that he would come when she wished it, when she sent for him. He received no summons till several weeks had passed. Then a note came from her. It was very brief, and was addressed from a hotel in a fashionable part of London. It named an hour as kept free for him on the following day. At that hour he followed a servant from the lift to the door of Lady Caryll's sitting-room. She was there when he came in, sitting by a window and gazing out to the open space before the hotel, in which stood a number of cabs. It was one of those slippery wet days of late autumn, when London glistens and yet looks ineffably dreary. The rain, very small and persistent, had not ceased since the grey morning. It was a patient rain, discreet but untiring, desirous apparently of remaining unnoticed and yet of producing an enormous effect upon the great city that was its victim. Those who were taken in by it and went without umbrellas, walked in the way of pneumonia. In the open space the cabmen, who had not taken refuge in their shelter, looked like mournful bundles as they sat hunched upon the perches of their hansoms. The horses were decorated with dark streaks, and held their heads down, as if examining the wet surface of the wooden pavement on which they were presently to slip and stagger. In the distance Caryll could see a policeman directing a very wet old lady from the country in the way that leadeth to Gunter's. As she gazed from the shiny hats of the cabmen to the shiny tops of the cabs, thence to the shiny pavement and to the shiny roofs of the houses opposite, she thought of the pilgrimage that would never be taken, and saw the white sails of the *Emerald* set in a warm wind that journeyed between the clasping blues of sea and sky. The servant spoke at the door. She turned and saw Aubrey standing among the chairs that seemed to murmur together of the shop from which they came. As she looked at him, while the servant shut the door, she saw an expression of almost shrill surprise slip across his face. She did not care. She came from the window slowly, as if her black gown weighed upon her, gave her hand to Aubrey, and asked him to sit down. He glanced at her furtively now that they were close together. The surprise that had left his face stayed in his heart. For to him she seemed so altered that, for a moment, he felt as if he were sitting with a stranger. She did not look older. She did not look actively unhappy. The exact impression he had of her first was that she was entirely dulled, like a window-pane just breathed upon. Of her eyes he must have said—had he spoken absolute truth—that they were persistently obstinate. Her lips were obstinate, too. Perhaps they had aged. Her whole person suggested resistance, a species of congealed activity—force held fast by ice, ineffable possibilities of outbreak partially smothered. Behind the dulness there was surely danger. When the mist faded from the pane there would be a blood-red gleam on it as of fire. There would be no droppings as of tears. He remembered that nothing can seem harder than hidden sorrow. When grief conceals itself, does it not lurk behind an iron door?

They spoke of one or two indifferent matters. The timbre of her voice was dull.

"Are you staying here long?" he asked presently.

"No. It is too expensive."

He started. She smiled.

"The charges here are horrible," she said. "And I am a pauper, as you know."

"But where will you go?" he asked.

"I have taken a small flat near Baker Street Station."

"Baker Street!" he repeated.

The idea of Caryll living in the named quarter seemed to him as ridiculous as the notion of a charwoman retiring from her peripatetic labours about other people's homes to spend the evening of her days in a palace on the Bosphorus.

"You are going to live there?"

"Yes."

"Alone?"

"Naturally. With whom should I live?"

He could suggest nobody, but he knew that such a solitude presented itself to him as the most inconceivable of events.

"I cannot imagine——" he began.

"What?" she asked, as he paused.

"I cannot think that you will be able to endure such a life."

"Why?"

"Because you have never been accustomed to it. You don't know what it is like."

"What would you advise me to do?"

He looked up at her. He was thinking of the emerald which she still possessed, and which must be worth an enormous sum of money.

"I have only a small allowance from my father," she said. "Some day, as you probably know, I shall inherit a fortune from Lord Verrender, my father's uncle. But he is neither very old nor very weak. I may die before he does—die in the neighbourhood of Baker Street. Why not?"

Aubrey had little to say. He was comparing her poverty with such a poverty as prevailed in Milk Court. The former seemed entirely horrible and hopeless, the latter, by comparison, quite natural, sanguine, and humane. From the former he revolted absolutely.

"I am sure," he said, "that you will find such an existence quite intolerable."

"I hope not. I have taken a basement flat. I get six rooms, two servants' rooms, and a kitchen for ninety-six pounds a year. It is marvellously cheap, and there is far more light in the rooms than you could expect. I only signed the agreement this afternoon."

"For how long?"

"Three years."

There was no self-pity in her voice. Aubrey found himself astonished by the strength of character she was showing. Yet he had always known that she was strong.

"You did not think of going—of staying for a time with Lady St. Ormyn?" he said tentatively.

He was longing to protect her from what seemed her own cruelty.

"My mother? Oh no!" she said.

An expression of irritation had come into her face.

"My mother does not understand me at all," she added. "We could never get on together."

As she spoke, the door of the room was opened and the servant announced Lady St. Ormyn. The expression of irritation deepened on Lady Caryll's face as her mother hurried in.

Lady St. Ormyn was one of those women who never look more worldly than when they are dressed in mourning. Black seems to emphasise their chattering impiety. Crape throws their disorganised vivacity into high relief. They walk in weeds as a circus horse might walk harnessed to a bier, and ostentatiously piebald in the midst of its sombre trappings.

As Caryll submitted to her mother's pecking kiss, Aubrey thought he saw grief as it appears at the Music Halls, a sniff, a grimace, and a pair of black thread gloves, too long in the fingers.

"Ah, Mr. Herrick," cried Lady St. Ormyn, "you here! I'm so thankful. Now I shall have an ally. You are such a friend of Caryll's, and so full of common-sense, that—I always say of men that they spend half their time in trying to hide their common-sense, for fear of being thought old-fashioned. But there are moments.—Caryll, I've got great news for you."

She had sat down on one of the hotel settees. Lady Caryll listened with apparent indifference, but two hard lines showed themselves on each side of her under lip.

"Prince Mirzoroff called on your father again to-day, and it will all be arranged quite charmingly and without any publicity. No going to the dealer's, or anything of that kind. Publicity is so horrible in grief—isn't it, Mr. Herrick? Grief should be sacred; but nothing's sacred in London, not even one's most holy emotions. I remember when I burst into tears once at the opera—Tristan's death, you know, when he tears open his wounds to that marvellous accompaniment—it got into all the evening papers. So cruel! 'A Countess cries,' they headed it. But one has to endure these things. Well, Caryll, the Prince will give whatever you choose to ask. It's so lucky. He wants it for the little Biondetti girl who made such a sensation at the Roman races last spring. It seems she saw you wearing it once at Prince's, and—what's the matter? Are you ill? What is it?"

Caryll's face was full of a cold indignation.

"I am not ill, mother," she answered. "What are you talking about? I don't understand."

"The emerald, of course. Your father will have it properly valued by Ritching, and then you will have enough to live upon in a quiet way. How much does thirty thousand pounds bring in a year, Mr. Herrick? You've been in the City, so you're sure to know. You mustn't let your father invest it, Caryll, because if you do, you'll never——"

"There will be nothing to invest."

"Nothing to—but the Prince——"

"Prince Mirzoroff will never possess my emerald."

"What? You've found somebody else? Really, Caryll, you might have spared me all this trouble. I've had the Prince to lunch twice. And he's the most—you know the kind of man, Mr. Herrick! He's been everywhere in the world, and can only talk about young women who dance. Nothing exists for him except dancing girls with over-developed muscles. He never heard of

Wagner, although he's spent months in Germany. Whom have you found, Caryll? Not that dreadful old African who——"

"I haven't found anybody."

"Then the Prince——"

"I am not going to sell the emerald, mother."

"But you must!"

Lady St. Ormyn grew rather shrill.

"You must. If you don't, you'll starve. Mr. Herrick, wasn't it shocking, poor Sir Reuben throwing away his money in the way he——"

"We won't discuss it, mother."

Aubrey got up to go. He felt that the atmosphere, though undoubtedly domestic, was becoming tragic. Caryll spoke quite calmly. But he divined an amazing depth of feeling behind her stillness. He remembered that the emerald was the only souvenir of her husband that she now possessed, and thought he understood her passion. He longed to still Lady St. Ormyn's clamour, to open her blind eyes to the refinement of a sorrow that was deeper, perhaps, than any she could understand. But he felt that he ought to go. He held out his hand to Caryll, but she said quickly—

"Please stay, Mr. Herrick."

She had looked into his face and had, perhaps, seen his thought. Lady St. Ormyn was rapidly becoming excited. Her forehead reddened in its frame of powdered hair.

"Caryll," she cried, "you are a pauper, and you must——"

"Live like a pauper! I am going to do so, mother. But I am not going to sell my husband's first gift to me."

She had caught Aubrey's thought. He believed he had caught hers. Lady St. Ormyn tried to interrupt her daughter, but Lady Caryll continued—

"I shall live quietly and I shall need very little money."

"Live quietly!" cried Lady St. Ormyn, with as much amazement as if her daughter had said that she was going to live in a balloon. "What do you mean, Caryll? Where are you going? To Boulogne? To Dieppe? To one of those places where one sees nothing but bankrupts listening to brass bands!"

"I have taken a little flat near Baker Street."

"Baker Street!" exclaimed her mother. "The place where the waxworks live, and there's an underground railway!"

For a moment she seemed benumbed. Then she turned to Aubrey and said—

"Did you ever hear of a more horrible notion, Mr. Herrick? Am I not justified in asserting my authority? If Caryll had been born a Tussaud——"

"Baker Street is a perfectly respectable neighbourhood, I believe," Aubrey said.

He could scarcely help smiling, and Caryll's face had become less grim.

"It may be respectable, but it really doesn't matter in the least what it is, because nobody lives there. No, Caryll, that's impossible. If you were a dentist's widow, or something absurd of that kind, it would be different. But as it is——"

"My dear mother, don't let us argue. Please tell the Prince that the emerald is not for sale."

"I can't. He will be furious. It seems that the little Biondetti is determined to——"

"A woman of that kind shall never possess my emerald," said Caryll.

Her calm, her obstinate self-possession suddenly deserted her, and she spoke with a fierce intensity that startled, even alarmed, her mother. Lady St. Ormyn sat for a moment staring at her daughter in silence. Then she tried to recover herself.

"Nowadays," she began, "all the finest jewels are in the hands of members of that class. Everybody knows it. Why——"

"I don't discuss such people," said Caryll. "And my emerald is not for sale."

As Lady St. Ormyn left she said to Aubrey, who put her into the lift——

"I'm really afraid the shock of poor Sir Reuben's sudden death has—you know, Mr. Herrick! Caryll in a Baker Street flat with that emerald! It's mania. Why, one might as well settle down at Southend—or one of those places where trippers eat shrimps and fall off donkeys—with the Crown jewels! One really might. Do use your influence. I always say that men——"

The lift sank with her, carrying her conversation to the ground floor.

Aubrey returned to Lady Caryll. She looked at him with an unusual kindness and gentleness which made his heart beat fast.

"You understand me," she said. "This afternoon I feel that."

"Yes," he said. "To-day I think perhaps I do. But——"

He paused. He was thinking of the many days when he had wondered about her, had almost feared her.

"But what?" she said.

"I was thinking that possibly I have often misunderstood you," he answered.

"Misjudged me too, perhaps," she said.

Never, since her marriage, had she spoken to him with quite so much intention. As Aubrey listened he felt, for the first time, that Sir Reuben's absence would be eternal, that he was speaking to a woman who had no husband.

"I daresay I have," he said, almost shyly.

And he thought of the episode of Alf's death, and resolved to forget it.

"You are very difficult to read," he continued. "And I daresay I am very stupid and blundering. Perhaps I shall blunder less from to-day though. I will try to be clever."

"He was clever," she answered slowly. "Clever even in the way he died."

As she said the last words she looked straight into Aubrey's eyes.

Suddenly there came upon him that same sensation of mystery and of oppression which had beset him long ago in the garden at Epsom. Caryll was apparently speaking to him. Yet her voice sounded like the voice of one who talks in loneliness, to develop thought, to trace the trail of surreptitious motive in a mind.

When Aubrey was alone he asked himself what Caryll had meant.

He did not know that a great sapphire was hidden in the darkness of the dead man's tomb.

CHAPTER XXIX

DESPITE the horror of Lady St. Ormyn, who spread on all sides voluble hints of the madness of her only child, despite the reproachful and pathetic appeals of Lord St. Ormyn, who had naturally intended to pocket a nice little commission when the famous emerald changed hands, despite the tears of a lady's-maid, and the pale and spectral despair of a faithful but distracted footman, despite all these, and many other lets and hindrances, Lady Caryll took up her abode in the Baker Street quarter. Her flat was, as she had said, in the basement of a big building containing a whole alphabet of flats. Even the letter Z was annexed as an address by a stout lady, of uncertain age, but certain vigour, who followed some peremptory profession, wore a shirt front, cooked her own supper, and smoked a strong cigar afterwards with her spats boldly displayed on the mantlepiece of her "den." Lady Caryll's letter was A, and the milkman could look down from the pavement on to her drawing-room chairs and sofas. In fact, all the world could look down on her if it liked to do so. Her windows in the front of the building opened on a narrow area, above which the usual railings lifted their mournful spikes towards heaven. Her windows at the back opened on a most dreary court, a small stretch of unrelieved asphalte, bounded by brick walls pierced by the windows of other flats.

Lest the unknown dwellers in the evidently prodigious basement should permit themselves the liberty of raking her humble abode, Lady Caryll dressed her back windows in those hanging strings of beads which let in light but exclude vision. All the windows were also fitted with shutters which were closed and barred at night.

She furnished the flat very simply, and spent most of her time in a small room at the back, which rather resembled a library than the boudoir of a pretty woman. This room contained the only effects of Sir Reuben that Caryll had bought in at the sale of the contents of Allabruth House—the collection of books about jewels. These were ranged in tall book-shelves round three sides of the room. Caryll often spent hours among them, reading steadily. When she read them she lived in the past, or was able to dream in the present. For she learnt the art of losing herself, of wandering down long avenues of thought, until the life around her faded, and all its weariness grew pale and died. These books led her once more into the cave from which she had been driven forth, a sad new Eve expelled from a garden of jewels. She trod again among the flickering fires. She met again the burning eyes of all the silent things she loved. Sometimes she sat and listened for voices that were vague, or lay back as one who rests on a gleaming bank in some magical grotto. Sometimes, too, she seemed as one who seeks, who stretches out a hand for some familiar hand, who gazes down dim ways for the flitting shadow of a friend. Was she not then a pale and woeful Esmeralda, searching for the geni who had led her long ago to the desired place? Did she not miss the small and shrunken figure that, like a kindly goblin, had once shuffled so solicitously at her side, gathering for her, with crooked brown hands, all the wonders she desired, all the charmed flowers that bloomed in this fiery under-world? He was no longer there. He lay still. The black sapphire that told the truth watched over him for ever. No longer could he smile upon the rapture of his slave.

Sometimes Caryll sighed, and laid down the book over which she had been dreaming, and stared before her in the little gloomy room. It seemed to her as if between floor and ceiling in the dusky twilight, hemmed in by the tall cases of the books, a faint shape hovered, a faint mouth smiled, bright eyes, old and mischievous, shone at her in a gleam of twinkling triumph, or again, in a gloom of tragic, cold despair. She listened, and fancied she could hear the distant murmur of a voice, that was husky and remote, telling her once more the strange histories of jewels, the histories of her jewels that were gone into other hands than hers. Then she felt that perhaps Sir Reuben, in his grave, knew of her loneliness, or could watch upon her deprivation, that he was angered at her present fate, that he stirred in the shroud of death and longed to come forth, like another Lazarus, to give her again the life for which she was surely meant, the beauty, the changefulness she loved.

The rain dripped on the asphalte pavement of the dreary court. The winter evening closed in. Darkness came and the hovering shade vanished, melting towards the silent ranks of the books. Then Caryll rose from her chair, went to her bedroom, sought in a secret place a hidden friend.

She passed long hours holding in her hand the great emerald. And when she held it she was happy.

Did not Sir Reuben, perhaps, regard her from the place of his penance or of his joy? And did not other eyes, too, dark and mysterious, gaze on her from some distant region of the air, the eyes of that Eastern man who, long ago, graved on the emerald the story of the soul? Had he not seen, through many years, faint shapes of women floating, as in ethereal dances, about the treasure that was, in a sense, his child? Did he not see now a shadowy woman, fair and pale and solitary, quiet in the darkness with the wonder he had made? And, thinking of the graven jewel and of this woman, could he not trace the path she was to tread, or perceive, far off, the vision of her eventual fate?

Lady Caryll presently began to go once more into the world. She was still a subject of much conversation, of much surmise in society. Even Baker Street had not power to deprive her personality of all importance so long as she possessed such a jewel as the emerald. Indeed, there were many people who found her more interesting now than in the days of her unquestioned triumph. Her situation was so delightfully peculiar. It is not every day that one can meet an aristocratic pauper, who lives in a basement, and has for companion in her rather dingy solitude a jewel whose sale could give her not merely a life on the ground floor, but a life in every respect airy and complete. Lady St. Ormyn continued to hint at mania. Lord St. Ormyn was quite overcome by the necessity of paying any one—even his only child —a fixed allowance. But the world was fascinated by Lady Caryll's queer situation and strangely selfish self-denial. It became known that Prince Mirzoroff had made an enormous bid for the emerald, and that the little Biondetti woman had torn his hair, as well as her own, in the fit of fury caused by Lady Caryll's refusal to give it into the greedy hands that were held out to take it.

So society still talked of Lady Caryll's passion for gems. And the imaginative, the young, and the odd inhabitants of London still set her in a place apart from the other women of the world.

When, after her time of mourning was over, she went once more to certain houses, men turned to look at her as she came in, plainly, inexpensively dressed and wearing her wonderful jewel. Women whispered about her and stared with envious eyes. She never passed unnoticed, or went away without leaving behind her a very definite and very unusual impression. Although she was less brilliant in appearance, less triumphant in manner, than when she had ruled at Allabruth House, she seemed neither discontented nor dismayed. There was change in her. Before Sir Reuben's death she had looked like a girl ignorant of failure or defeat. Now she looked like a woman aware of the cruel possibilities of life, a little hardened, a little contracted by knowledge. The dulled, the blurred expression once noticed by Aubrey—the breath upon the window-pane—had almost gone. But something of her former sparkling vitality had gone with it. She was tarnished. She was not effaced.

Lady Rangecliffe had been one of the first among the visitors to her basement, and one of the most sincerely sympathetic. It was impossible to Lady Rangecliffe to think ill of any one permanently, impossible to her to think ill of any one in trouble. After Sir Reuben's death she forgot the afternoon on which she had first seen the emerald, she forgot the night in which the sickly smell of lilies had seemed so to offend the pity in her heart. She forgot even those red roses she had bought, and remembered only the death of her friend and helper, of Lady Caryll's husband. But, despite her short memory and long charity, it was not ordained that she and Lady Caryll should get on together. Uneasiness prevailed between them, and a feeling of continual necessary effort that could not be overcome. Lady Rangecliffe was more aware of this than was Lady Caryll. Her humanity appreciated certain facts more quickly, and though she never recoiled before any difficulty because it was cruel or surprising, she had a sense that told her what obstacles could not be overleaped. A woman always knows when another woman shuns the best that is in her. Lady Caryll shunned the reality of Aubrey's mother, even when that reality was quick sympathy for her.

Lady Rangecliffe was obliged to know of her son's apparent success where she so entirely failed. Aubrey was Lady Caryll's most intimate visitor. Like so many of those who drift for a while in London, and are without a talent that marks their path in life, he had come at last to the threshold of the Stock Exchange. The roaring crowd took him, and his days were spent where money is set to hideous music. He no longer allowed himself to condemn the struggle in the street, or to sit down with his contempt for the aims of City lives. The necessity of work showed itself to him as worthy. He was able to fear more the tinted existence of the gay idler than the grey travail of labour, even the least congenial. Industry claimed him. It seemed that he might, in time, grow successful. His chance was good, and he developed perseverance. From what secret cause this perseverance sprang only one person knew. Lady Rangecliffe began to understand that Aubrey had once more an ambition. She thought of a conversation she had had with Sir Reuben in Eaton Square, and the rapid turning of the wheel of life made her blink her short-sighted eyes. But she was resolute in inaction before the steadfast sameness of her son.

Sometimes Aubrey called upon Lady Caryll late in the afternoon as he was returning from the City to Jermyn Street, where he was once again living. Sometimes he sat with her in the little room whose windows looked upon the dreary court. One day, when he was waiting for her, he pushed aside one of the hanging blinds, and glanced idly out across the asphalte, and up at the many windows opposite. He began to wonder about the innumerable dwellers in the other flats, living their enclosed lives behind the mysterious lettered doors. There was something strangely disagreeable to him in the fact of Lady Caryll's dwelling in the midst of such a human beehive. The great house in Park Lane, with its curious atmosphere of mystery, and of secret, silent places, its latticed windows, its heavy-curtained doors, and falling fountain, had been an ideal shelter for her and all her shining jewels. But this home was sordid and offensively public. Remembering the sedulous care Sir Reuben had always taken to protect himself and Caryll from all sights and sounds of the busy London world without, Aubrey found himself realising what would be Sir Reuben's horror if he could know where Caryll's present life was spent. Looking from window to window, while his mind compared the present with the past, Aubrey saw here and there some sign from which he gathered vague ideas of the personalities and lives of the various owners of the flats. From one window, high up, a servant-girl leaned out, holding in her arms, bare to the elbow, a tiny child. She pointed to the sky along which clouds were slowly drifting. The child gazed up and began to cry. Instantly a second figure appeared. Aubrey saw a pretty, fair head, arms that snatched at the child to comfort it. He felt that married life, new and eager and solicitous, pulsed in the flat behind that window. Lower down he saw a bit of an elderly man who was reading in a book, part of a tired face, a long beard, hands that held the book close to spectacled eyes. He thought of the student's life, remote and monotonous in the changeful London crowd. Presently his eyes, travelling along the ugly walls, sank down to the line of windows that, on a level with Lady Caryll's, looked close upon the asphalte of the court. Across an open window, almost exactly opposite, he saw the figure of a man pass, disappear, return, and pause motionless. He could not see clearly the man's face, but he felt as if its eyes were staring fixedly at Lady Caryll's windows. And he recollected afterwards the disagreeable sensation that came to him with the idea that she was overlooked, thought about, perhaps, by some stranger. He stood for three or four minutes watching the motionless figure. Then it abruptly disappeared. Aubrey was about to drop the blind when, at another window, on the left of the court and nearer, he saw a girl standing with her back to him. She had dark hair, and wore a straw hat with a black riband round it. There seemed to Aubrey something oddly familiar in her appearance or posture. As he was wondering why he found her friendly almost to his eyes, he heard Lady Caryll come in behind him. And he thought of the other flats and of their occupants no more.

But that day, as he left the big building and stepped into the street, he came face to face with Diamond. She did not start on seeing him, but two small spots of red glowed suddenly in her pale cheeks, and, for a moment, she looked as if in doubt whether to recognise him or not. Then, as he took off his hat, she gave a little nod, and walked on without stopping to speak to him. Aubrey knew in a moment that she was the girl he had seen at the window of the flat on the left of Lady Caryll's. He was walking just behind her. Now he considered what he should do.

Diamond did not look back, as she had looked back long ago, on the night of their first meeting. She went on steadily, neither hurrying nor walking with an elaborate slowness. It seemed she had no sort of desire to have him for companion. But Aubrey felt that even his promise to Alf did not bind him to deliberate avoidance of her in such a close, unpremeditated encounter. He hastened his steps and caught her up.

"Miss Diamond," he said, and he held out his hand.

He saw that she hesitated to take it. But she did take it at last without a word. They had paused on the pavement, and looked at each other now with questioning eyes. Aubrey felt unpleasantly embarrassed, almost guilty.

"I think I saw you just now," he began. "I was in one of those flats looking on to the court, in the basement, you know. Weren't you standing with your back to a window, talking to some one?"

"Yes," she said. "Quite well?"

"Quite. And you? I hope the children—all your people are——"

"They're all nicely, thank you. Well——" she began to move away.

"Diamond," he said quickly, "this is absurd. I'm going your way. I shall walk with you. You will let me?"

"I can't see why ever you want to," she said in the old simple way he remembered so well. "We ain't friends, so what's the good?"

"Not friends!" said Aubrey.

He felt deeply hurt.

"How can you say that?" he continued.

"Because it's true. I thought we was friends once. But I'm a silly and always thinkin' wrong."

She was not looking at him now. She had cast down her eyes, and, with the point of her umbrella, was making imaginary tracings on the pavement.

"Always thinkin' wrong," she repeated. "Except about——"
Her voice died away.

"What?" Aubrey asked.

He did not know what to say, how to explain his long avoidance of her.

"Mr. King," she said. "I'm—I'm goin' to get married to him!"

"Married to Mr. King! When?"

"Next week. We're goin' to live in that flat where you saw me to-day. He is good."

A load seemed suddenly to fall from Aubrey's shoulders. Alf's prophecy was about to be fulfilled, and Aubrey felt that now, perhaps, he could tell at least part of the truth. As they walked slowly down an almost empty street, he said—

"I'm so glad. Do you know, Diamond, Alf wanted this?"

"Alf!" she said, and her voice was sad. "Ah! we do miss him. It's been awful. Lill has had a time with poor Vaux. Everything's different now—everything. I'm glad I'm goin' to stop dancin'. Yes, I am. It's always the same now. When I see the lights and hear the music—them drums especial—I always see him fall. Poor Alf! He was fond of me."

"I want to tell you how fond he was," Aubrey said quickly.

"You tell me?" said Diamond, in plain surprise.

"Yes. Diamond, when Alf was dying, he spoke to me about you."

"What about?"

"About you and Mr. King. He wanted you to marry, and he thought——"

Aubrey hesitated. He scarcely knew how to put the suspicions of Alf in any form that would not hurt Diamond's sensitive delicacy or make his own position intolerable.

"Eh?" said Diamond.

"He thought that perhaps you and I saw each other too much."

"Why, though? Whatever for?"

There was genuine surprise in her voice.

"Well, Diamond, perhaps Alf was right, even if he didn't know much about it. You and I often talked of—well, of——"

"Bert, you mean?"

"And Alf wanted you to forget everything and marry a good man. Don't you see?"

"And he said it to you?"

She was looking at him now with her great eyes, which were always pathetic and full of a sort of shadowy sentiment.

"Yes, when he was in all that dreadful pain."

"It was awful that night," she murmured. "I shan't never forget it, never."

"Diamond, Alf wanted me to go right away from you. He asked me to. He didn't want us to talk any more. That's why I've never seen you since—since his funeral. He's dead, but he kept me away. D'you understand? I promised not to come."

All the time he spoke she looked at him steadily as a child. When he stopped, she said—

"I'm glad. Then you wasn't tired of seein' us?"

"No. I wanted to come, but I could not."

"It was funny of Alf," she said. "Because it didn't make a bit of difference—you not comin'."

"No?"

"Not a bit—about my thinkin' of Bert, I mean. Of course I was sorry. I cried about it oncest. I cried awful."

"Did you?" said Aubrey humbly.

"Yes. It was one night. I thought about Alf, and you and me that night in the Park, and the people under the trees, and the woman—you know as was fightin' the man, and the other woman cryin', and no money—and Bert, and all. Everything seemed in a muddle—worse than washin'-day or rehearsal—and dark, and callin' out, and strugglin'. I wanted to go that night."

"Go?"

"After Alf, and be done with it. Oh, I did cry. The pillow was in a state nex' mornin'."

"Poor Diamond," Aubrey said.

He felt a deep sense of relief at her evidently complete ignorance of Alf's suspicion, her absolute unconsciousness that her heart had, perhaps, taken some little steps on one more wandering journey with sorrow at its end.

"I was bad," she continued. "But we can't go—not when we want to. Can we? We have to off it, like Alf, just when we're thinkin' p'raps we're happy. It is odd. I can't never understand things. Mr. King says we ain't meant to."

"I expect he's right. And so you've got fond of him at last, Diamond?"

"Yes."

She was silent, thinking. Then she nodded her head, in answer to some thought, and added—

"Because I know he's good. That's why. But that's not why most girls care, nor not why I used to care for Bert."

"It's the best way."

"Is it?"

Her face was full of a sort of soft, half-puzzled interrogation.

"Is it silly to care for people just because you do?" she asked. "That's like most girls, like me oncest."

Aubrey thought it was very like him, too. But he considered that subject dangerous, and he talked resolutely of Mr. King. He learnt that the riding-master had just taken the large basement flat near to Lady Caryll's, and in the same building.

"Why Diamond," he said, "you'll be close to a friend of mine, close to——"

Suddenly he stopped, remembering the death of Alf, and Lady Caryll's connection with it.

"What friend?" she said. "Eh?"

"Why—well, Lady Caryll Allabruth."

Diamond's face flushed.

"You was in her flat when you saw me to-day?" she asked.

"Yes."

She said nothing, but her soft lips stuck out as she pressed them together, and her dark eyes became almost fierce. Aubrey understood what she was feeling. At first he thought he would change the subject. Then a desire to turn Diamond towards greater charity induced him to say—

"Diamond, I know what you are thinking. I want you to think differently."

"It ain't no use. I can't," she said. "She treated Alf bad, cruel bad."

Her low voice sounded obstinate, even bitter.

"She was grieved at his death. It was not her fault that he died."

"She wouldn't come. He wanted her, and she wouldn't come. She's no feelin's."

"She was afraid. She had never been accustomed to see people ill. Can't you understand how she felt?"

"No. She's no feelin's, and I don't like livin' near her," said Diamond. "Can I see her windows, then, acrost the court?"

"Yes."

"I shan't look at 'em, but I don't like it. I shall always think of her and Alf. She's no feelin's."

It was obvious that she was really disturbed by the idea of living so close to Lady Caryll. Aubrey saw that it would be useless at present to speak further of the matter. Her reiteration of her verdict on Lady Caryll showed the cult of the fixed idea. Yet Aubrey could not resist saying—

"Some day perhaps you'll know that she has feelings."

"Why?" said Diamond. "I shan't never see her—not to speak to, I mean."

"Perhaps not."

"Sure not. No, I couldn't never speak to her. I should feel I was lettin' Alf know as I'd forgot him, and after all he'd thought of me when he was goin'."

Tears now filled her eyes. She shook her head as she felt quietly at the back of her black skirt for her pocket-handkerchief.

"No," she said. "I don't like livin' near her, and I shan't never look at her windows. I'd better take a 'bus at the corner, please."

She wiped her eyes.

"The green 'bus, please," she said.

"May I come and see you when you are married?" Aubrey asked.

"Yes. Would you care to, then?"

Already she was brightening, though she wiped her eyes again.

"Very much."

"We'd like to see you. Mr. King always says how nice and quiet you was that night—at my birthday. He likes people quiet. He is good."

Aubrey pressed her thin hand.

"You'll be happy with him, I think—very happy."

Her eyes clouded again, but she answered—

"He is good. And we ought to care for people, because they're good. I'll get happy from tryin', p'r'aps."

She paused on the kerb, looking at him pathetically. Her dark eyes seemed to be always asking childish questions.

"Could you?" she said. "Get happy only from tryin', I mean."

Before Aubrey could answer the 'bus conductor said snappishly—

"Now, Miss, please!"

Diamond nodded to Aubrey and mounted, with her habitual light gracefulness, into the omnibus.

"So long!" she said, as she disappeared.

It seemed very strange to Aubrey that in a week she and Lady Caryll would be living their lives side by side. Would fate ever draw them together? That seemed impossible. These two women in his life were so different, so necessarily apart. One had brought him much pain, one a little comfort. For both he felt deep sympathy. Now he thought, as long ago, of the tales of enchantment and of the old street stories that make up the volume of the book of life. And a desire came to him to mingle the complicated with the simple, to draw the brilliant enigma towards the sincerity which was plain, to set mystery with revelation, the soul apart with the soul that was human, and that had spoken—but never sordidly— with the passers by the way.

In the gloomy street Aubrey stood still for just a moment,

and lost the sense of its hurrying crowds, of all its cries and shadows.

He saw two women at their windows; they watched each other strangely across a little court. The sunshine faded; twilight came; evening fell around them. Still they watched, but never spoke. Night entered the little court, and black darkness.

Sometimes, with the darkness, come the shining feet of Truth.

CHAPTER XXX

DIAMOND became Mrs. King, and was soon settled in her flat near Lady Caryll. But Aubrey's fancy of the street was not imitated by reality. Two women did not sit at their windows watching each other across the little court that divided them. Lady Caryll did not know of Diamond's proximity. If she had, the near presence of a girl, not of her own class, to whom she had never spoken, would doubtless have been a matter of most complete indifference to her. The knowledge of Diamond's close connection with the dead acrobat, had it come to her, would scarcely have stirred in her a clear memory of him. Once she had heard a boy was dying and she had sent him lilies. He had died. The lilies had faded. All that was long ago, and had happened on the other side of the gulf which divided her present from her past. She never thought about it, and when by chance she sat reading in her little room among her books, she was never attracted to look out and across to other windows, was never stirred by any uneasiness telling her that some mind near at hand, perhaps hostile, fixed its thoughts on her. Certainly Diamond played no part in her life.

In the life of Diamond, nevertheless, she was more than a shadow. The simple nature of this girl was extraordinarily tenacious. The quickness of her emotions did not spring from their weakness, nor did she float to forgetfulness upon her easy tears. Her heart held fast to those whom once it accepted, and gratitude in her was the same thing as love. She had loved Alf, his impudence, his tricks, his mischief, his manly thoughts for her. Perhaps more than all his relatives, except Vauxhall, she had mourned him. Her meeting with Aubrey, his explanation of his apparent coldness and curious neglect, again set Alf before her, protector of her future from the assaults of sorrow, even in the moment of his pain and preparation for death. She cried openly in the street at Aubrey's explanation, probably with no greater secrecy in the omnibus on her way home. But her tears sealed her to recollection, and recollection sealed her to a still more sensitive bitterness against the woman for whom Alf had called in vain.

It is no doubt very improbable that, had she been ignorant of the fact of Lady Caryll's nearness, she would ever have divined it. But, knowing of it, she was certainly affected by it. Gradually something began to play upon her nerves, which were more than normally sensitive at this early period of her married life. She had given up the stage in order to marry Mr. King. The persistent occupation of years was forsworn, and the abandonment let free her mind in unaccustomed idleness. A power of thought, long concentrated upon the great theatre, the autocratic ballet mistress, her position, her companions, and her dancing hopes must be now directed in some other channel. That channel soon stretched to the windows of Lady Caryll, who sat so indifferently beyond her hanging blinds. In her solitude Diamond began to believe that she actually felt the near presence of her unseen neighbour. She had said hastily to Aubrey that she disliked the thought of living within view of Lady Caryll, but she had never imagined that she would come to shrink, as at an unpleasant touch, from a fact that should surely have taken little hold on her, since she neither saw, heard, nor was materially affected by it. For at first she never looked out of her windows to Lady Caryll's. If she had, she could only have seen dimly the hanging beads, or sometimes perhaps a servant pushing a window up or down. But she felt at moments as if she knew that Lady Caryll had come into the room which looked upon the court, or was sitting so near to her that they might have spoken to each other. Then she grew restless, uneasy, and perturbed. Thoughts of Alf thronged about her, and of the influence to which he had, boyishly, thrown his life. Knowing the influence to be so close to her, she said to herself that now she felt it actually as wicked. Sometimes a sort of fear fell on her, at other times a kind of unnatural rage possessed her, despite her gentleness and the childlike softness of her character. She imagined Lady Caryll happy in her life, self-centred, unperturbed; a shining, cold inhabitant of a different world from hers. And then she remembered the horror of Alf's painful death, the almost greater horror of his denied request, made so pitiful by the reserved bravery with which he saw his latest hope so swiftly fade away. Diamond felt all this and much more without analysing what she felt. But she knew that she began to hold the little dreary court in a sort of horror. And she knew why.

She never said a word on the subject to her husband. He was infatuated, and was far too happy to observe subtleties or to search after things unseen. When he was at home he beamed upon his wife and spent his time in trying to give her pleasure. When he was away he thought about her, never doubting that she was gay in their cosy little flat. He meditated teaching her to ride, or, running towards the future, glowed with silent hopes.

THE SLAVE

As time went on, Diamond found herself thinking more and more persistently about her neighbour's windows. The furtive curiosity wakened by dislike had been strengthened by a visit paid to her by Aubrey. During this visit Diamond had made a discovery. Now that she was married, either she had stronger intuition or he a weaker power of reserve. Lady Caryll's widowhood, too, had revived a feeling long held in check by circumstance, given to Aubrey a sense of freedom that formerly he lacked, and so had given to Diamond an opportunity of observation and deduction. Suddenly her eyes were opened to the truth of his desires for the future, and she realised almost exactly how he thought of Lady Caryll. She felt the vital power over a man whom she admired and respected of this woman whom she had so long secretly condemned. And, from the day of Aubrey's first visit to her flat, she began to feel a curious inclination to go to her windows and to gaze out upon the court. She yielded to it, and she knew that when she did so she looked forth with a hope of catching a glimpse of Lady Caryll. By degrees she grew familiar with the life of this deep and dismal well, the walls of which were formed of the discoloured bricks of the great building in which she and so many others lived. She thought she could recognise the varied characters of the sparrows which chirped upon the asphalte, and differentiate them one from another. Like Aubrey, she glanced sometimes from window to window, letting her mind wander about the supposed lives of the usually invisible inhabitants. She saw the rare sunbeams enter the dark place, and the rain which made so complicated and plaintive a music sometimes upon the pavement. She knew the morning and the evening aspect of the court. But she never saw Lady Caryll. Often, while she stood by her window watching the black surface on which no one ever walked, she was seized with a longing to judge this woman for herself, to use the terrible penetration of another woman upon her. For even the simplest girl, in moments, knows her power, and feels herself more able than the most complex man. Thinking about this sister woman to whom Alf had flung his life, Sir Reuben his intellect and fortune, Aubrey, apparently, his heart, Diamond longed to be actually with her, if only for a short time, to hear her speak, to watch her while she spoke. Something almost irresistible often seemed to bid her step out across the court to those inexpressive windows behind which a mystery sat. There was a voice in the pale twilight urging her to undertake the little journey, and in the heavy London dusk surely sometimes a shadowy hand that called her with its gesture.

From a variety of causes, her new mode of life, her loneliness in her husband's absence, her now frequent contemplation of a small and dreary scene, Diamond fell into a condition of mental and physical unrest that was unnatural and that inclined her to secret exaggeration.

One afternoon, when she went to her window and looked out, she saw at a window opposite to Lady Caryll's the figure of a man. It was motionless, and was not close to the window, but slightly withdrawn in the shadow of the room beyond. Diamond could not see the face at all distinctly. But she felt that this man had been attracted to his window by a curiosity akin to hers, that he was watching the blinds upon which she so often fixed her eyes. She stood for two or three minutes looking towards the stranger, and then retreated to some woman's occupation of dressmaking in another room.

In the evening of that day she found herself often thinking about this unknown companion in curiosity. Her happy husband talked on to her, and she scarcely heard him.

On two other occasions when she looked into the court she saw this rather vaguely defined figure of a man in an attitude of contemplation, and on the second of these occasions a little incident occurred which stirred her to excitement. There was sunshine in the court, an unusual glowing brightness. The sparrows chirped with a heedless impudence here and there upon the asphalte, then flew up between the narrow walls and out over the roofs towards the spacious blue. Diamond stood quietly, looking at the quiet stranger whose face she could not see. She was thinking how strangely still he was, like a waxen figure in a solitary show, and had begun to rely upon his continued inactivity with a certainty of which perhaps she was hardly conscious, when —abruptly—he moved forward, bending as if to stare at something. The action startled her. It was so strongly suggestive of a new feature in the prospect that, without a pause to observe the stranger's face, Diamond turned to look where he was looking. She saw that one of Lady Caryll's blinds had been pulled aside to admit the full light of the sun, which fell upon the figure of a woman, with a pale face and shining hair, who stood close to the window looking down upon something which she held in her left hand. Diamond saw a flash of green light. Then the blind fell and hid the woman. Diamond turned to see the man. He was no longer at his window.

She thought of the green flash, and guessed that it issued from Lady Caryll's famous emerald. Then she thought of the vehement motion of the man. Her nerves tingled as if danger came near her. That night she was sleepless. She lay very still and heard the regular breathing of her husband. The faint noise at first perplexed, at last irritated her. She knew that she had sometimes lain awake on other nights, that then she had heard this breathing, and that it had not annoyed her. For a long while she did not know why it vexed her so keenly now. Its momentary alteration, then cessation, informed her. Something, some thought in a dream perhaps, disturbed her husband's tranquillity. He stirred, sighed, drew a long breath, then was silent for a moment. During that silence Diamond found herself listening with painful attention. For what? She did not know. But, when her husband's breathing once more became regular in sleep, she was aware that for a long while she had been wishing to listen for some other sound. The night wore on. Confused and violent thoughts seemed struggling together in her mind, striving simultaneously to engross her attention. She saw a green light that danced before her shut eyes, withdrew, faded—then many figures of men and women, all posed in the strangest attitudes at open windows; then only one man leaning out into a great space, and staring horribly at a thing she could not perceive. It seemed as if she saw and could not see him. For she could not tell what he was like. She could not have recognised him again. He leaned out farther and farther. It seemed that he must fall. But his violent interest in the distant thing that attracted him made him heedless of his danger. He cast himself out of the window and disappeared into the air—as Diamond at last fell asleep.

When, in the following week, Mr. King was obliged to leave London for a couple of days in order to visit a great horse-fair near Darlington, Diamond felt almost glad that she was to be left alone. He suggested that she should have Jenny to stay with her, but she refused.

She was fanciful, and longed for nights of complete silence.

CHAPTER XXXI

On the second night of Mr. King's absence it chanced that Lady Caryll had no evening engagement. In the afternoon she had received a visit from Aubrey. He had stayed late, and, in going, had hesitated near the door.

"What is it?" she asked him. "You have something still to say to me?"

"Yes, Caryll. I can't understand how you endure this life of yours so calmly. Are you not unhappy? Oh, forgive me for asking. There are always so many lives about which I wonder. We all wonder at the lives of others, I suppose, when we see people going on day after day doing the same dull things, seeing the same dull prospect. But often they seem created for their fate. Yet even then we wonder. So how can I help thinking that you—who should have everything—must feel——"

He paused. He had been speaking with emotion, full of the desire to give her, some day, a different life from this meagre, prisoned existence in which she seemed so out of place. But her calm face, her eyes, in which a faint inquiry flashed, daunted him. She claimed no pity, no sympathy.

"I am not unhappy," she said.

"No? But now—when I go—what will you do? There are hours to get through before you can sleep."

He glanced round the little room.

"You will be all alone. No one will come. If you were a man, you could go out, to a club, anywhere, to meet other men. What can women do with their lonely evenings?"

Perhaps for the first time he wondered.

"I have no idea what most women do," she said; "but it would give me no particular pleasure to go to a club, although I might even do that. For you know I belong to one."

"You don't mind loneliness at all, then?" he said.

He spoke almost with pleading. He longed at that moment to see her show some weakness, some sorrow even, a desire to lean on him, to claim his sympathy. In reply she said—

"A long while ago you asked me that question, or one like it. Do you remember?"

He called on his memory.

"Faintly," he said. "Wait—where was it? Ah, yes, I remember now. We were in the Park."

"And I told you I did not altogether fear loneliness. You said I had never known it. Well, I know it now. Look at me. Did I not understand myself even then, when I was almost a schoolgirl?"

She stood and smiled at him; and seeing her smile, he felt how impossible it was to pity her. In the small, dull room, she looked commanding, strong in an undoubted satisfaction. He went out wondering, and left her to her lonely dinner, to her lonely evening. It seemed as if such solitude, in such rooms, must be dreary. Yet he could not question her contentment in it. She was not acting. As he walked away down Baker Street, he said to himself that her spirit could never be broken; that she could never kneel in the dust, bent, destroyed beneath the chastisement of fate. There was something in her that was invincible. He feared that unconquerable spirit. It was like a sword stretched out between him and her. Yet, while he feared, he almost worshipped it. For he said to himself that Caryll possessed a strength, a force, that could not be found in other women. In the past he had thought that she feared to gaze on the ugliness of pain, the great stillness of death. Now he told himself that even then he had read her wrongly. A refusal that he still remembered could not have been prompted by so common-place a timidity. He sought for other reasons. He was always searching for a clue to the enigma of this woman.

Meanwhile she had already forgotten him and their conversation. She put on a tea-gown, ate her dinner, and heard the request of her only footman that he might go out for the rest of the evening. His family lived near. Some relative had joined the circle. A natural feeling summoned the footman to greet this new-comer, if her Ladyship did not want anything more. He was allowed to go, and, like Aubrey, was at once forgotten. Presently Lady Caryll rang for her maid and dismissed her also for the evening, to bed or whithersoever she pleased. It seemed as if far from fearing, she actually desired, and rejoiced in solitude. She shut herself up in the little room that looked upon the court. The footman, in his warmth of family feeling, had forgotten to close the shutters, which he barred every night at the falling of darkness. Lady Caryll did not notice his omission. She did not even glance towards the windows as she came into the room.

It is a habit of man to suppose that, so soon as a woman is left alone, she performs a solitary operation called dropping the mask. Lady Caryll dropped no mask now that night had fallen and she stood among her books. In the front of her grey gown, which was loose and long, the emerald was fastened. No one would see it to-night but its mistress. She wore it now, as always, to please herself. One electric light was turned on in the little room. As the shutters were not closed, a gleam shone out into the black court, giving a phantom air of pale gaiety to the dreary place. Diamond, looking from her window, noticed the unusual illumination, and wondered whether Lady Caryll " had company." One of the other neighbours also observed it, and remarked that the shutters were not drawn across the window and barred, as they had been on every other night since Lady Caryll had inhabited the flat.

Meanwhile, Lady Caryll, unaware that any unusual circumstance called attention to her modest window, confident of her complete solitude, stood for a moment in her little room and glanced round contentedly enough. It seemed that she had not lied to Aubrey, either by word or look. The loneliness that might have weighed on many women did not apparently weigh on her. For there was a slight smile on her lips and in her eyes. The utter silence, her freedom in it, pleased her. She looked down on the great jewel in the bosom of her gown. It shone to greet her shining eyes; and, as she gazed at it, her expression changed, becoming more definite, more vivid. In that moment she surely became younger. A ripple of golden youth ran over her. The faint shadow that dwelt upon her now, since the events that had followed the death of Sir Reuben, faded away. She forgot all the lost jewels in the jewel that still remained to her, and as she looked down upon it she seemed to be again the girl who once paused before the diamond shop, and lost herself in the white fire of the things she loved. As she stood there, motionless, her head slightly bent, she was surely the dreamer that Aubrey had called her when, in the dark garden, he made that vain effort to show her what he was in truth, and to win her by the difficult revelation. She was a dreamer as she gazed, but then something more, something different. The expression grew in her face till all the tender vagueness died away, carrying with it much of her beauty. Hard lines, like lines drawn by the eager fingers of sensuality, first flickered, then grew firm about her mouth. The soft fire that seemed to swim in her long eyes, as if diffused in some mysterious way through a mist of tears, concentrated itself in fierce and hungry sparks. Something of that strange and sudden ugliness long ago remarked in her by Aubrey, and attributed by him to the outside influence of environment, crept up in her and peered forth, as if her nature stirred deep down, then slowly, almost sluggishly, forced its way to the surface of her, to stare out unabashed upon a world it seldom faced so frankly. She had looked at the emerald as an imaginative woman looks at a thing that is beautiful, at a thing that stirs quick and furtive tenderness in her, and a delicate, not wholly understood desire. Now she began to gaze at it as a greedy woman gazes on the thing she has seized, on the thing that she will keep, ruthlessly, cruelly, passionately if need be, against man, devil, or another woman. In such an expression of love there is a tinge of something that is not far from hate. For the things that can hold us in so fierce a grip often seem monstrous, appalling to us, even while we watch them with lust, with worship in our eyes. They are the fearful pleasures that are the heaviest burdens upon our tottering lives. They persecute us when we desire to rest. They are like an everlasting clamour of the street, that will not let us, with a clear soul, work out the problem of conduct, or of thought, to which we began to apply ourselves long ago in some lost day of youth.

Lady Caryll looked on her jewel with this love, in which hate vaguely lurked. Then she sighed, lifting her eyes to the narrow walls of the mean little room in which she stood. She went to a book-shelf, took down a volume and carried it to a sofa, on which she slowly lay back. But at first she did not open the book; some thought pre-occupied her. She stared before her, opening her eyes widely. Perhaps she was thinking of Bond Street and of its morning dream; of the touch of Aubrey's hands, and of the strange stirring within her that for a moment had made her feel so horribly afraid. Perhaps she was thinking of her wedding-day, or of Aubrey's first evening in Park Lane, when Sir Reuben filled the night with magic. Perhaps she was thinking of the mysterious prophecy of the sapphire that was buried in the darkness of the grave. Or perhaps she heard a singing voice that was hard with discontent, or saw faded lilies lying on a dead boy's breast.

Her reverie was long.

The light gleamed from her window out upon the dreary little court. Diamond, in the flat close by, was doing some fancy work. She sat on a wicker chair that creaked whenever she moved, and held the work close to a lamp. On the table beside her lay a tangle of gold and bright green silk. She put in some threads slowly, drawing her brows over her big eyes. Then she paused, laid the work down almost furtively, got up from the complaining chair and stood for a moment, resting one hand, palm downwards, on the tangle of silk. The night was very silent here, though in the front rooms of the flat a distant sound of the traffic of Baker Street might be heard. Diamond seemed to be listening. Presently she walked softly to the window and looked out. She saw the steady radiance in Lady Caryll's room, and longed to steal across the asphalte, and to peep in upon this woman of whom she knew so much and so little.

She glanced at her watch. It was ten o'clock. The chair protested as she sat down again to go on with her work.

Lady Caryll opened the tattered book at last, and began to read. She joined the crowd of the lapidaries, followed their occupation with them, was excited by their difficulties, rejoiced in their achievements. She stood with them, weighing coloured gems in air and water, leaned over strange diamonds to examine the mystic clouds enclosed within their brightness—clouds mystic as those silver looming shadows that dream within the circle of the moon—followed, with a grave attention, the operations of the jewel-cutters, toiling to make more precious the precious material they handled with so much gentleness and shaped with such a crafty care.

When Diamond, having put away her work, looked out once more from her window before she went to bed, she perceived the light still shining steadily across the court. She watched it for some minutes, then turned out the lamp reluctantly, and left the room.

It was then nearly twelve o'clock. Half-an-hour later Lady Caryll closed her book, returned it to its place on the shelf, and put out the electric light. She crossed the passage to her bedroom, and undressed slowly, leaving her things about the room for her maid to put away in the morning. Her gown lay over an arm-chair like a grey and weary ghost. When she had unfastened the emerald she carried it to its case, opened the case and was about to put it in. But she hesitated, shut the case again, and presently got into bed, still holding the jewel in her hand. On a pedestal at the bed-head stood a small electric lamp covered with a dark green shade. By stretching out her hand Caryll could turn the light on or off at will. Often she read at night after she was in bed. To-night she did not read. She lay, propped up high on her pillows, opened her hand and looked at the emerald, upon which the light shone. She shut her hand, opened it again, and again shut it, performing the action with some of the whimsical softness and swiftness of a child. When her hand was open she smiled. When it was shut she became grave. Two ideas alternated in her mind just then. Two visions stood, by turns, before her fanciful imagination. She dreamed of herself, she saw herself, with, without her emerald. She looked into darkness and perceived presently two flashing panels of light. In one panel she stood, a radiant, powerful figure, with uplifted head and sparkling eyes. In the other she was like some haggard phantom, with bent head, drooping towards the dust.

She kept her hand open, resting it with the palm upturned towards her upon the white sheets of the bed. And at first she lay smiling. But presently the smile died, first from her eyes, then from her lips. A frown that was bitter wrinkled her forehead. Now and then she had horrible moments, when all her contentment vanished and fury surged abruptly into her heart. These moments came to her seldom. She never knew when they would come, whether in loneliness or when people surrounded her. In them she saw spectral processions of all the jewels she had lost. They went by slowly, and each of them was faded like a lovely woman on whom time has taken hold. Faint were now the colours that had been once so vivid, dulled was the silken lustre that had shed glory through her days. And she thought that every jewel looked upon her with a distant, yet a piercing despair, such as stares from the eyes of the dying when they gaze for the last time upon those rare beings who have been to them true friends. And Caryll knew that all the jewels were sad because they were separated from her, because they might stay no longer with the one who understood them. In these frail and haunted moments she felt the sickness of an immense sorrow creeping upon her, like some dreadful malady that will only fade in death. And she felt it not only in her mind, but in her body, as we feel our deepest and most inexorable griefs. It lay upon her flesh like snow, or burned in her blood like flame. Or she felt it like a hard hand, squeezing her heart which it contained. So insufferable was this agony when it came, that it often produced upon Caryll intense physical effects. Perspiration broke out upon her. She could not cry with her eyes, but her whole body seemed to weep, in every vein and sinew, in every shuddering nerve. This despair rummaged through all her being, as a violent and ruthless investigator rummages through a box, scattering, destroying, mingling, separating, till stark confusion—of horrible distance, equally horrible proximity—grows before the cruel will to seek.

These moments of iron pain had set the faint shadow upon Caryll's face, the hard lines by her lips. In them she was dispersed in a torture of weakness. But she came out of them hard as steel, as some natures come up out of their sorrows. She was never more mistress of herself and of fate than after one of these attacks, during which she stood in outer darkness, gazing into the Cave where once she had walked in triumph.

Now, as she lay still in the bed, she shut her eyes; her face became drawn and pinched, till every feature looked sharp as a witch's, old as a withered crone's; her teeth were set; her body became rigid under the white bed-covering, and she clenched the hand that held the emerald as if she would grind it into powder. Her breast heaved, and she breathed with a hissing swiftness; drops of perspiration ran down from her forehead upon her white cheeks; she turned and turned in the bed, burying her face in the pillows as if she would suffocate herself, stretching out her limbs as if in obedience to the summons of the rack.

Suddenly she thrust out her arm to the electric lamp, and wrapped herself and her torture in darkness.

Nearly half-an-hour passed, then light again filled the room. Caryll was sitting up in bed, the clothes were thrown back. All her hair fell round her, twisted and in an ugly disorder; but her face was calm and hard. She got up, poured some cold water into a basin, took a silver phial from the dressing-table, dropped some of its contents into the water, and bathed her face. Then she took out of a drawer a large white fan, got into bed again and lay there slowly fanning herself, while the hair fluttered up and fell again round her damp forehead. Over the fan she looked at the emerald in her hand till at last she could smile once more. The motion of the fan presently grew uncertain. It wavered and dropped upon the bed. Sleep was near. Once more Caryll turned out the light; soon she lay motionless, breathing regularly. In her relaxed hand she still held the emerald. It was the medicine she took to combat the malady of her despair.

Between one and two o'clock, when the night was deep and silent, it seemed that some one in the flat opposite to Lady Caryll's, being sleepless, wished to enjoy the air of the little court. A man stood in a room which contained no light, opened a window with precaution, and, looking into the court, saw that now it was enfolded in obscurity. No ray gleamed from any window of the big building whose walls towered up into the blackness. The man leaned on the sill of his window. There was a faint breeze rustling about in the dimness, pressing against the dirty bricks, stealing to and fro across the asphalte. The man drew it into his nostrils while he listened. He bent down to the floor of his room, picked up a tiny covered lantern, swung himself over the window-sill, and stood in the court. He waited a moment, and then moved across it towards the window of Lady Caryll's library. His feet made no noise as he walked. When he reached the window he paused again, and remained motionless for several minutes, holding himself very close to the wall. Then he put out his hand to the window and pushed it. Slowly it moved up, it was not even fastened, the bead blind shook slightly, and made a faint grating sound as the man held it aside and stepped into the room where Caryll so often sat reading the histories of jewels. He flashed a light upon the covers of the books. On the back of one was a large white label which caught his eye, and on the label, in big letters, was printed its title, "The History of the Emerald." Under the thin black mask which he wore the man smiled. He did not linger in the room, but opened the door and stepped, with infinite precaution, into the narrow passage of the flat, leaving the door and the window open behind him.

Although Diamond had gone to bed late that night, and had been tired when she put away her work, she did not fall asleep when she lay down. This was the second of her two lonely nights. On the first, too, she had been the prey of insomnia. But she had rather encouraged it than fought against it. She had chosen to think. She had chosen to allow her ears to be attentive to all the faint and stealthy sounds of night. She had even spent hours in keen listening, sitting up in her bed. Her reward had been a painful sensation of fatigue towards dawn, and a flooding feeling of vague, and yet large, apprehension which rolled around and upon her in speechless black waves. Overwhelmed by these waves, she had at last fallen into a heavy, crushing sleep just at sunrise. On this second night when she was alone, she had resolved to summon, instead of repelling, sleep. So she lay down and kept very quiet. Only one low pillow was beneath her head. She repeated some foolish rhymes over and over with dull reiteration, pressing her head again and again upon the pillow as a sort of monotonous accompaniment to the jingle of the whispered words. Yet, though she certainly began presently to feel dazed and bewildered, she did not begin to feel that sleep was near. A sudden heat ran over her and her forehead tingled. She felt as if she were being pricked by multitudes of tiny needles, and that the sheets had become almost intolerably rough and unpleasant to her skin. She had made the mistake of being too active, too determined, in her attempt to capture sleep. She ceased from repeating the foolish rhymes, pushed the pillow higher, turned over and rested her cheek on her hand. Recently she had been irritated by the sound of her husband's breathing; now she found herself desiring it. The complete silence weighed upon her, and she felt certain that some slight and regular noise would help her to fall into a more drowsy and less nervous condition. She still felt the tiny needles pricking her, and she thought that as each one pricked her, it seemed to emit a little spark, which burned her. She twisted from side to side till the bedclothes were all in disorder. Then she got up to make the bed. This action roused her so completely that she felt disinclined to get into bed again. She looked at her watch. It was a little past one. She put on a dressing-gown, sat down in a chair by the side of the bed, and began to read a book. It was called "His only Love," and was published in a series called—for its purity's sake, perhaps—"The Snowdrop Series." The plot was full of crime. Many of the characters were unbridled ruffians, and the book could not have done harm to a child. Diamond, whose tastes in all directions were very simple, found this bald narrative of unusual, if not of impossible, deeds quite interesting. She passed from one arson to another, through murder to sacrilege, thence to weddings, by way of forgery and theft, with a quiet and serene enjoyment. Gradually the soothing influence that dwells in such books began to get hold upon her, preparing her insidiously for sleep. She nodded over the book. It shook in her hand, and at last dropped into her lap. She was becoming deliciously drowsy. Realising this, she laid the volume down, got up from her chair and prepared to step into bed again. As she was standing up by the bedside, pulling back the clothes with one lax hand, she was startled by something. She scarcely knew what it was. It might have been some very distant sound, a call in the street perhaps. Her exact sensation was that, if she had not been so sleepy, she would have heard it quite distinctly, but that, being so sleepy, she heard it confusedly and faintly. Indeed, she could hardly have said that she had actually heard anything. Rather, she seemed to know that there was something to listen for in the night. That was all. But it was enough to drive sleep from her, to render her sharply alert. She stood perfectly still, straining her ears to listen. She heard nothing. She looked round, darted across the room to the door, opened it and again listened, standing in the doorway and looking into the dark passage. This time, after an instant of waiting, she heard distinctly a faint but, as it seemed to her, most horrible cry, short, sharp, full, she thought, of fury. It was like a distant imprecation uttered with supreme intensity. It chilled the blood of Diamond and filled her with fear. So terrified was she, that she suddenly shut her door, locked it, ran back to her bed, and fell upon it trembling, and stopping her ears with the bed-clothes. She felt as if she had heard some one cry out in hell. For an instant she really believed this. There had been in the cry a power of fury that seemed to her entirely unearthly. As she crouched trembling on the bed she kept repeating aloud, "Hush! Hush! Hush! Hush!"

She wanted to prevent a repetition of the appalling exclamation. She thought that if she heard it again she would lose her reason. But now, as silence continued around her, she began to recover from her panic. Presently she sat up, taking her hands from her ears. Her huge eyes were staring with fright, but a sort of ghastly curiosity began to wake in her, a feeling that if the cry were being repeated she must listen for it, must hear it again. This curiosity of terror at length governed her so utterly, that she stole back to the door, unlocked it, opened it, listened. She heard nothing. She looked into the darkness of the passage. Whence had come the cry? She could not tell. She stepped into the passage and crept softly into the room which looked upon the court. There she paused again. A belief had seized upon her. It came abruptly, for no imaginable reason, as if it were furiously thrust into her from outside—the belief that the horrible cry had been uttered by Lady Caryll in her rooms on the other side of the court. Diamond went to her window, opened it, and stared into the court. All was dark and silent there. No light gleamed. But the silence, the darkness, beckoned her forward. She could not resist the summons. She felt that she was being led by the hand and must go. She wrapped herself in a shawl, traversed the court, and arrived before that mysterious window at which she had so often looked. It was open. This discovery—why she hardly knew—again filled Diamond with panic, and she began to tremble. But she did not go back. She dared not. But she was obliged again to pause, leaning against the damp wall of the court. While she waited she looked into Lady Caryll's room through the open window. She could scarcely see anything in it, only the vague outlines of furniture, barely defined in the blackness by the very faint light which entered from the court. At last she took courage, stepped into the room, and felt her way to the door. That, too, was open. She passed out into a passage. And now an extraordinary vagueness came upon her. It was born of this strange action of hers in a strange hour, like a dream-action in a dream-hour. An odd sensation of swimming lightness invaded her brain; with it came an abrupt personal carelessness very characteristic of dreams. Fear left her, for she no longer felt entirely conscious of herself or of what she was doing or meant to do. She was wandering somewhere in darkness, somewhere far from home, feeling her way with her hands. She was heedless, inconsequent. Nothing mattered now. She had a sense of actually tripping, with an absurd sort of jaunty liveliness, towards the dream-goal that lay before her—far or near?—she could not tell. Never, in after days, was Diamond able to understand or to explain the hallucination that beset her at this time, an hallucination that came so swiftly, and that for the moment was so singularly powerful, so singularly complete. Doubtless it sprang from the confusion of a brain wearied by insomnia, which, on the very threshold of sleep, had been struck a blow by the shocking cry which had risen up in the night. Rendered furiously alert by this blow, terrified, curious, repelled, and desirous, the brain perhaps partially collapsed in its turmoil of confusion. It seemed to spin like a ball in the darkness, to whirr like machinery, to be at the same time recklessly active and oddly sluggish, vigorous and impotent, ardent and inert. The darkness of this unknown flat swallowed it in a nightmare influence.

Diamond, at this moment, resembled one of those somnambulists who, partially conscious while they feebly travel on some incoherent errand, surging with tattered purposes, grope their way towards they know not what, driven by desires they cannot fully apprehend. Such somnambulists often go aimlessly backward and forward. They reiterate their journeys, under the impression that they are travelling onward, or are turning to the right or left to pursue some unknown path. Within a very small space they will sometimes move incessantly for a long period of time, always strong in the belief that they are steadily advancing. So Diamond, beset by this vagueness of the night, wandered several times to and fro, feeling with her fingers along the passage walls. Gradually she grew more definite. She was seized by a sensation of being imprisoned. With a violent effort she partially recalled her scattered senses. She stood still, stretched forth her hands, and laid them on the handle of a door which, turning, made a slight but distinct sound in the night. Instantly an event occurred which drove all vagueness away and braced her once more to a terrified alertness. There came a violent knocking upon the door from the inside, a knocking so sudden, fierce, and sharp, that Diamond felt as if she were being beaten by the hail of blows. She took her hand from the door and stood still, scarcely breathing. No doubt the circumstance that this desperate assault was delivered inside a room instead of outside helped to terrify her. There is nothing very odd in the fact that somebody wishes to come into a room whose door is locked. But this passionate endeavour to break out of a locked room at this hour of night proved the existence of some strange event, of some nature roused to a grim determination of combat.

Diamond feared to set free the person who had knocked upon the door.

The blows ceased as suddenly as they had begun. Diamond stood perfectly still, listening. The knocking was not repeated and the intense silence was most horrible to her. Presently she bent down, and perceived a tiny gleam of light under the door. As she did so, she fancied that she heard the two faint sounds, continuously alternated, made by a person breathing close by.

For a moment she was divided between two keen desires, a longing to turn and escape from the mystery and the violence that were close to her, and a longing to stand her ground and to investigate them. She never knew how long her irresolution lasted, nor why she abruptly bent down—at its end—to search for the key of the door. But she did bend down. The key was outside the door, in the lock, but loosely, as if it had been nearly pulled out. Diamond hesitated no longer, but pushed the key home, turned it sharply and threw the door wide open.

Something white,—animal it seemed,—sprang instantly upon her and caught her by the throat in a grip as hard as steel.

Lady Caryll and Diamond met at last.

CHAPTER XXXII

The sleep into which Caryll fell, when the strange paroxysm which had seized her passed away, was profound as the sleep of a child; no dreams troubled it, no broken words came from her parted lips. Her relaxed limbs had fallen into a posture of most delicate abandonment in their repose. One arm lay outside the coverings, and in her half-shut hand the emerald rested. It seemed that she could dismiss the sorrow which had come upon her, that, having dismissed it, she knew how to forget it. No slumber could be more calm, more youthful, than the slumber that now was hers. When the man whose face was concealed by the thin black mask glided down the dark passage of the little flat and paused outside Caryll's bedroom door, no furtive anxiety, partially piercing her sweet unconsciousness, made her stir on her pillow or unclose her eyes. When, with rapid softness, he opened her door and slipped into her room, she still slept on. He waited in the dark, listening to her gentle breathing, until he had assured himself that, for the moment, there was no danger. Then he allowed the light from his lantern to gleam for an instant over the room, while, with a rapid glance he surveyed it. He perceived that Caryll's bed, which stood out from the wall on a level with the door, was hung with curtains, and that these curtains were not drawn. Shielding the flame of the lantern he pulled the curtain at the side next to him forward as far as it would go. He had noticed that Caryll was sleeping with her back turned to him. This was a fortunate circumstance. But he dared not run the risk of waking her by flashing his light near her eyes. On the other hand, he could not conduct the search which he was there to undertake in darkness. So, when the curtain was drawn, he allowed his lantern to shine out once more. He saw that the bedroom was narrow, long, rather crowded with furniture. Thick curtains of pale yellow stuff hung before the two windows, between which stood a satinwood dressing-table containing a number of drawers, above which there was a mirror. On this dressing-table stood a quantity of silver things, bottles, brushes, boxes for pins and other trifles. In the mirror hung a pale reflection of the bed and of Caryll lying in it. Another small table near the fireplace on the far side of the bed was covered with framed photographs. It contained a couple of drawers larger than those of the dressing-table. The man noticed all this in an instant. Then he glanced more searchingly about the room. He could not see either a dressing-case or a safe, only a sofa, a chair or two, a divan in an angle of the wall heaped with cushions, Caryll's clothes lying here and there; a pair of satin shoes, silk stockings, a wisp of black tulle like a butterfly, a tiny embroidered handkerchief.

He knelt down to examine the floor beneath the bed. Perhaps he had heard where Caryll kept her jewels at Allabruth House. He found nothing. As he got up from his knees, by accident he touched the grey gown that lay on an arm-chair. It rustled slightly. He held his breath, inwardly cursing himself for his awkwardness. Caryll's steady breathing continued, and the man smiled under his mask. There was nothing to fear and he gained in impudence. He moved behind the bed-curtain, set his lantern down on the floor, went to the dressing-table and opened all its drawers. They slipped easily to and fro. Only one stuck when he was trying to shut it. He left it gaping. With a deftness that was amazing he turned over the contents of the drawers, ransacking every corner. But he found only women's fripperies— laces, gloves, ribands, perfumed satchets, and a few trinkets of little value. He took none of these trinkets. He had come in the night to seek a gem that was worth a fortune, and he had no inclination to carry away anything else. His nature revolted against pettifogging theft. In his fashion he loved to play the large-minded man. So all the trinkets and the laces were put back for Lady Caryll to wear when she would. The other table was then exhaustively examined. Here the man was again at fault, for he found in the drawers only loose photographs, writing materials, two or three French novels, and a small despatch box. With silent dexterity he forced the lock of the box, and discovered a few receipted bills, some gold, and a paper. This paper he held to his lantern. It was a printed history of the great emerald for which he was seeking. He read a few words with keen interest, then dropped the paper into the box and proceeded to examine the whole room thoroughly, moving about with the silent quickness of a cat. At last he satisfied himself that either the emerald was not in the bedroom at all, or that it was concealed in some pocket of the bed, or beneath the pillow on which Lady Caryll was sleeping. The man thought this was not improbable. He knew the notorious passion of the sleeper for the only valuable jewel she still possessed. She might well guard it with her body while she slept. He crept to the bedside, and, for the first time, looked closely and long at Caryll. She was very lovely, but he did not allow himself to become romantic, although he noted the shining hair streaming over the pillow, the soft arm stretched along the sheet. While Caryll slept she had folded her fingers over the emerald and concealed it from view, but so softly, so naturally did her hand hold fast its treasure, that her visitor glanced at the pretty hand, and glanced away, without suspecting that the thing he sought lay there close to him. He scanned the bed, considering how he could examine it thoroughly without disturbing its occupant. This would be no easy matter he knew. For though he were as quiet, as ingenious, and as swift as possible, the mere fact of his close proximity to Caryll might very well awake her.

This man was not an occultist. Probably, like most of the members of his ingenious and exciting profession, he did not know the meaning of the term. Yet how many thieves could, if they related the histories of their lives, tell truths of the darkness, and of tragic nights, as strange, more interesting, than any narrative of prolonged and doleful séances, complicated by tambourines and psalm-singing of elderly voices. They could relate facts which prove the possibility of mysterious messages being sent by one body to another against the desire and intention of the will inhabiting the first body. They could describe, too, the curious rebellions of the body against the mind, rebellions sudden, bitter, and ruinous, which seem to spring, armed, from some secretly nourished enmity of the flesh against the spirit. But the people who work in gloom keep their counsel, they make no parade of their strange knowledge. Perhaps they are hardly aware that they possess it until they stand, as the man in the thin, black mask now stood, in a dim twilight beside some sleeper and prepare to put it to the test in action. To search is easy. To search in silence is not very difficult. Fingers can be trained to cleverness in theft as they can be trained to cleverness in conjuring. The body can be drilled into moving with swiftness and caution, without noise or dangerous awkwardness. A thousand things can be guarded against, a thousand things foreseen. But fate dwells in the unforeseen. The body and the mind, in crises, develop the most amazing and unexpected aptitudes, or crumble in failures that are as the twisted ruins heaped by earthquakes. The successful criminal is he who has drawn his mind and his body together into a perfect friendship, and even when he has done this he has something still to fear from the subtle and apparently irresistible communications that pass between body and body in darkness and in silence.

The man in the mask was not inexperienced, nor was he thoughtless. He lived by his hands, but he had a mind. Now he was on the verge of a difficult and dangerous adventure, and, while he stood silently by the bed where Caryll slept, he deliberately performed a mental action as preface to the physical actions he was about to undertake. Making a strong effort of will, he withdrew his mind almost entirely from Caryll. He thought of her no more as a sleeping woman who must not be awaked, but as a doll to whom he need pay no attention, who was nothing to him and could be nothing. Then he began to search for the jewel. And Caryll still slept, now enclosed within the circle of his quick activity. He examined every portion of the bed. He ran his hands up the curtains on each side of Caryll's head. Bending over her, he softly felt the pillows on which her cheek was resting. His fingers crept beneath them as delicately as insects creep in hidden places. He explored the framework of the bed from end to end, the mattress which rested on the woven wire, the sheets that enveloped Caryll, the coverlet on which the white fan still lay where it had fallen. She must have been completely wrapped in this man's atmosphere had he not, through all his search, avoided the thought of her. At length he paused. He was at a loss. He stood still in the shadow of the bed-curtain considering what he should do. For a moment he thought of searching the other rooms of the flat. Then he dismissed the idea. He felt positive that the emerald must be in this room. Lady Caryll would keep it near her. Of that he was certain. But where was it? He had examined everything. His clever hands had touched every surface, had dived into every secret place of the chamber. Looking round him, he asked himself if there was a corner that had not been explored, a drawer that had not been opened, a trifle of any kind that had not been submitted to his diligence. And, thus considering with an intensely active mind, by a process of exhaustion he at length arrived at the doll which lay upon the bed, at the one thing from which he had hitherto sedulously driven away his thought.

Only Caryll had been left untouched.

Now, standing by the back of the bed, the man lifted the curtain slightly, and peered cautiously upon her. She had not once moved since he entered the room. He saw the tangle of her hair on the pillows, the curve of a shoulder, the soft whiteness of a delicate cheek, the fringe of eyelash that looked so exquisitely sensitive above it, the half circle of a breast almost hidden beneath the loose night robe she wore. His eyes travelled on, down the arm that lay outside the bed-clothes, to the hand.

He noticed, for the first time, that the hand was shut.

This shut hand fascinated him, and he stared at it from his hiding-place. The nails of the curved fingers were concealed from him by the sheet on which they rested. The thumb was turned inward under the first and second fingers. Only the back of this motionless human box was visible. And the man gazed at it with the most concentrated attention, wondering if it contained the precious thing he sought. How improbable that seemed to him. Yet it was possible. He stole forward, softly drew back the clothes of the bed and looked at Caryll's other hand. That was open, relaxed in slumber. This fact renewed the man's fever of curiosity. Why should this exposed hand, on which he stared again, be so fast closed in sleep? There might be a reason. Do the passions always slumber in the body when the body slumbers? Is the will dead when the soul lies dreaming or lies beyond the gate of dreams? Or is there for ever in life something that cannot sleep in every man and woman, that secret tyrant, the ruling passion? Does avarice ever sleep in the sleeping miser, lust in the roué, love in the faithful woman, hate in the one who cherishes the thought of vengeance? Does not the mourner weep before she wakes? Does not the coward shiver in those dream alleys where he wanders? The thief's thoughts trooped about the delicate hand of Caryll; they could not leave it. He was accustomed to judge and to read the body. Yet to-night, either because he was unnaturally excited, or because the light in the room was very dim, he could not decide whether the hand he watched held, or did not hold, something. In an ordinary hour, in daylight, he could have known, or have been nearly certain that he knew. Now, when it was necessary for him to know, he felt doubtful. He leaned forward a little, bending his head nearer to the hand. He was forgetting to continue the mental action which had so far rendered him secure. No longer did he put the sleeper from him altogether, or before him as a thing without life or any power. How could he, since his whole soul was, for the moment, intent upon the consideration of the power of this live hand to plunge him in uncertainty. Every fibre of his being strove in a silent effort to compel it to give way to his desire for enlightenment. There are moments in which men forget that they are men, that they are living, thinking, feeling. Self-consciousness drops from them, and they become merely a red-hot desire, hanging like a fierce point of light in space. At this moment this man was such a desire; the desire to know—not for theft's sake just then, but for the sake of knowledge only—whether that hand of Caryll was closed upon anything but itself.

He leaned farther forward, protruding his masked face beyond the curtain till he almost touched the hand of the sleeper.

Suddenly Caryll turned her arm upon the bed, showing its inner surface and the pink finger-nails of her hand. The man trembled and drew back, startled by the knowledge that this hand was preparing to obey the irresistible desire of his will. Once more concealed by the curtain he gazed at the hand, and, while he gazed, the fingers gently unclosed and he saw the emerald resting in the cup made by the soft palm.

At this moment, for the first time, a sense of almost imaginative awe—strange to his nature—came upon him, hand in hand with the instinct of sex. He thought of Caryll as a beautiful woman, of all he had heard about her, whispered or loudly spoken, in many times and places. Hitherto his practical and criminal mind had ignored the shining mystery of her peculiar reputation. He had come into her bedroom as he would have come into a jeweller's shop, intent upon his own ends, heedful only of himself, his desire, his safe achievement and subsequent escape. Caryll had been to him, then, but the possessor of something he wanted and meant to take from her. Now, as he looked at her, and at the jewel which she grasped even in sleep, he was conscious of a new sensation. Wonder and admiration shot through him. He gazed at her with a man's—rather than with a thief's—eyes, and while he gazed he recalled many things he had heard about her in Paris and elsewhere. Lying there, asleep in the dim light, half-shrouded in her frosty yellow hair, she seemed very young and very calm. Who would have said that within that soft body, so gracious in its contours, there dwelt a voracious soul, eternally greedy, a soul that had ruined so clever a financier as the notorious Reuben Allabruth? The man in the mask admired cunning and worldly cleverness like most thieves. Such women as Lady Caryll seemed to him almost like adepts in his own profession. They drew to themselves all they wanted, drew it from the pockets of infatuated men. The men, being fools, let them take it, and so made their proceedings legal. But what of that? These lovely greedy women are at the top of the thieves' class. That is all. So the thief thought, looking down on Caryll, and on the soft hand that had received so much, and that now held unconsciously its last treasure. He knew that he was going to take away that treasure. Yet a certain sentimental pity came to him at the thought of the awakening which he would never see. What would that be like? He was beginning to wonder, when something roused him sharply to a sense of the necessity for instant action. Caryll's hand, as if mechanically, closed slightly over the emerald. In a moment all the man's business-like instinct and sordid intentness returned to him. He glanced swiftly at Caryll's face, saw that she was still asleep, bent down, and, with exquisite delicacy of touch, tried to slip the emerald out of her hand on to the bed. He nearly succeeded in his object, but just as the jewel seemed about to fall from Caryll's fingers, she shut her hand firmly and turned in the bed. The man did not draw back. He waited, keeping his eyes on her face. She was near to wakefulness. He knew that. The attention which he was now obliged to fix upon her penetrated into the heavy underworld of unconsciousness, vaguely disturbed her there. Her movement in the bed had been full of an odd, unfinished petulance. And she had opened her lips as if to utter some childish remonstrance. In her sleep she was becoming faintly aware that there was a project afoot against her happiness. Some strange stirring of instinct had caused her to close her hand ere it lost its possession.

The man drew back. He knew that he must again possess his soul in patience. Folly had made him lose one chance. He must wait for another which he would not miss. And, while waiting, he must withdraw from Caryll the attention which troubled her like a touch. He leaned against the wall behind the curtain, glancing round the room. In the faint light the furniture looked spectral and uneasy. The gown, hanging over a chair, had the distraught aspect of some thin, fainting woman, whose drooping head was hidden by the neighbouring sofa. The boxes and ornaments on the dressing-table, the vases and candlesticks, the photographs in their variously shaped frames were like a crowd of miserable sufferers from insomnia, forced, by their malady, to be alert in this empty hour of the deepest night. In the mirror the reflection of the bed seemed fading away from the man's eyes, fading in a mist, as if some one had gone up to the glass and had breathed upon it. He let his attention wander from one sad thing to another, while he remained absolutely motionless, carefully managing his breath, lest the slightest suggestion of any presence near to her should continue to increase the disturbance already set up in the sleeper. Not until this painful pause of inaction had lasted for several minutes, perhaps for ten, did he resolve once more to risk the trial of his will upon the closed hand. Then he moved the curtain gently aside, and glanced towards the enigma. His joy was great when he saw that the fingers had again unclosed, and that the emerald lay in the flat palm, gleaming gently in the light. He had only to take it softly and go, and this he meant to do without glancing again at his unconscious victim. He leaned cautiously forward, put out his hand and touched the emerald.

As he did so Caryll uttered the horrible cry which so shocked Diamond as she stood at her open door. Although the thief was unaware of it, Caryll's disturbed intelligence had not been lulled once more to rest by the deliberate withdrawal of his attention from her during his long and patient pause. The uneasiness in her had developed until sleep slipped from her, and, without movement or sigh, she opened her eyes to the dim light that shone from the hidden lantern. Although she was unaccustomed to sleep with a light in her room, she was not immediately astonished by the illumination. Absolutely full consciousness had not yet come to her, nor had she begun to realise where she was. But, being able to see, she looked instinctively at the hand that held the emerald, and, just before the thief leaned forward to take it, she opened her fingers and gazed with a quiet, half-drugged feeling of contentment upon it, neither asking herself how she could see thus in the night, nor forming any definite thought, serene or sad. She was possessed by a luxurious languor as she lazily contemplated the treasure her hand caressed. The thief's sudden movement struck her awake with a lashing sharpness which drew from her that terrible cry. In an instant fierce consciousness came upon her. Even as she cried out she closed her hand on the emerald, and, turning violently on her pillows, looked behind her with eyes that were full, not of fear, but of a passionate menace. With the emerald she had grasped two of the thief's fingers as they touched it. And, while she turned, she caught his wrist with her other hand in a grasp of iron. In the silence that followed her cry she faced this masked intruder, against whom the curtain swayed, and she felt that his wrist shook for an instant beneath her clutching fingers.

Her cry had startled him for the moment into an agony of surprise that was akin to an agony of fear. His confidence in her sleep had been so great that he was thrown into tragic confusion by her unforeseen wakefulness and the amazingly complete display of vital energy that accompanied it. Had Caryll released his hand then it is probable that he would have fled precipitately, guided out into the darkness by his quivering nerves. But she clung to him with the tenacity of an animal that has fastened its claws in its assailant. Her cry, her vice-like grasp, were purely instinctive. She had scarcely begun to realise what was happening. But she prevented the man from flight. She held him till his fear told him to remain inactive no longer. He looked down into her hideously expressive eyes, at her twisted figure half uplifted in the bed. In deadly silence he resolved to attack her.

Then all that there was in Caryll, all that Aubrey had faintly discerned and forgotten, that Monsieur Anneau had suspected, Sir Reuben partially known, certain lawyers trembled before—all that there was of tiger-like strength, of unnatural passion, of animal persistence and of ruthless resolution, all rose upon her to do battle for her jewel.

She had no more thought of fear than has one of the fierce beasts when brought to bay. She was too full of fury to think of personal danger. In the moment when the thief met her eyes and was prisoned by her grip, he knew that there was room for doubt as to the issue of the conflict. For he felt that he was going to fight with a being who had become utterly savage, and who had a force different from any he had known in the past. A sense of fear clung to him; such a fear as is roused in man by all intensity that seems entirely abnormal. But his fingers were crushed against the surface of the emerald. What could he do but set his teeth hard and attack the white fury who would not let him go?

During the combat that followed the thief was at a disadvantage, for his imagination was haunted by a terror from which Caryll's was free. He was fighting to seize what she possessed. He should have been moved by the eager daring that rises with the fierce activity of attack. But from the moment when her iron hand seized his wrist till the moment when the fight was over, he was ceaselessly beset by an impression that was novel to him and terrifying—an impression that he was defending himself against the cunning fury, the measureless hatred, of something that had no imagination to be moved by terror, no heart to be stirred by irresolution. He felt as if this woman's bedroom were a cage, as if he were shut up in it with the animal whose habitation it was, as if—could the animal have its will—he would not be allowed to escape from the cage alive. Could he succeed in reaching the door—leaving the emerald behind him—he felt convinced that Caryll would pursue him, that she would not cease from pursuit till she gained him or fell dead. He would have fled if he could till he understood the unyielding character of her rage, and that escape without struggle was impossible. Then, underneath his horror, his obstinacy stirred, though still the horror stayed. Since she would not let him go without the emerald, he would force her to let him go with it.

With his left hand, which was free, he caught the bed-curtain which impeded his full activity, tore it down, and threw it on the ground behind him. Then he grasped Caryll's arm, and strove brutally to tear her fingers from his wrist.

She bent down her head, and set her teeth hard in his hand.

For a moment he shut his eyes, more cruelly overcome by the sickening feeling that he was indeed fighting with an animal. Then the sharpness of the pain woke his spirit. He forced Caryll down and back upon the bed. She still clung to his hands with mouth and fingers of steel. Her hair streamed over his arms. He could no longer see her face, for her forehead was against his forearm. Nor could she see him. The veil of his limb blinded her eyes. She set her teeth harder—harder, till they were against bone. He forced her farther back among the pillows, but she curved her body rigidly till his hands were imprisoned between her knees and the mouth, which, like the mouth of a vampire, was red with his blood. And she bit, as if she strove to grind the bones of his fingers to powder between her teeth. Despite the thief's great muscular force, he could not get his hands free, though, since he was standing and was above Caryll, he was able to force her down in the bed till the wire mattress creaked as if about to break under the burden laid upon it. Leaning forward over the bed, squaring his elbows and using the full power of his strong arms, he shook her to and fro, trying to thrust her down on her back into a position in which she must be helpless. But she thwarted him. Her body seemed made of iron. She kept it curved like a serpent, and still the unyielding teeth—teeth of a trap surely—clung to his hand. The sheets of the bed were spotted with blood, all the framework of the bed jangled. The sticks of Caryll's white fan were splintered. The feathers were torn into shreds. Perspiration burst out under the mask the thief wore. The horrible sickness crept upon him. He began to fear that it would overcome him, that it would develop into a fainting fit. Gathering all his force, he drew himself violently up and back, raised his arms, and pulled Caryll with him till she was high out of the bed. He dashed her down.

But the teeth kept their vicious hold on him.

Then the vigour of despair came upon him. He rested one knee on the bed, stretched out his arms along it, and gradually pushed Caryll towards its farther edge. She could not see. Her hair was tangled about her eyes, and she had shut them fast, contracting all her face, striving to add to her tenacious force by making herself for the moment blind. Blindness assisted her. She did not want to see. She wanted only to feel, to send her soul into those clenched teeth. She never tasted his blood; she never knew that it was flowing. She felt as if she were suspended in the air in some deep and narrow pit, pressing a hated thing down to destruction. Dense was the darkness in the pit. The thing she held, but could not see, struggled with a frantic strength, dashed her to and fro, lifted her up and cast her down. Only the force of her hatred enabled her to keep her vice-like grip upon it. She hated more—to gain more power. Strength inhuman seemed to pour out of her mind into her body, making it a new body, the most powerful ever created. She ground her teeth on the man's fingers.

Suddenly she felt that she was falling, as if to the bottom of the pit. Leaning across the bed, the man had at last succeeded in thrusting her to the floor. But she dragged him forward with her, and now he was deprived of the advantage his upright posture had formerly given him. He lay across the bed. His face protruded over its edge above Caryll's, as she sank to the ground. He strove furiously to drag himself up and away from her. She resisted, trying to drag him down upon her. The sensation of mortal sickness gained upon him. He felt as if blood were surging into his eyes, but as if his heart were becoming bloodless, cold, and faint. He saw great spots of darkness leaping before him in the dim light. They formed devilish patterns, rushed together, separated, shooting out furiously in all directions like things escaping from some monster that gave chase. They vanished.

He felt now that his hands, to which the animal's teeth inexorably clung, were far away from him, at the end of arms stretched to so great a length that they might have bridged the distances between the spheres. Pain tortured him still, but it was pain gnawing him in some place that seemed miles away, where surely he had a second body, not the same as that now invaded by this loathsome sick feeling which was rendering him powerless. His head began to swim. Now he thought that he could see the teeth of the animal. At first they were small and vague; little things, white, inflexible and motionless. Then they grew. He saw them gleaming. They became gigantic. They were pointed as spears, teeth of a monster such as the world had never known. He saw his bleeding flesh compressed, tortured, shuddering between them.

The horror of this vision became so keen that it gave the man a new access of strength. He cast himself over the bed upon Caryll, and, with a supreme effort, tore his mutilated hand from her mouth. Then, catching her by the throat, he held her away from him and stared into her face, while the blood from his hand jerked down upon her breast. Her lips were red. Her teeth were red. With half-shut eyes, that had no humanity in them, she watched him steadily, and—he fancied—with a sort of malignant stupidity. Her mouth was set in a grimace that was like the grimace of a snarling animal, fended off for a moment but waiting an opportunity to rush upon its prey. Her cheeks and forehead were starred with bright red spots. The stiffness of her body, reared up at his arm's length, resembled the stiffness of some abominable puppet. Her arms hung down at her sides. Her right hand was still closed upon the emerald. She did not attempt to use her hands against him now, but he could feel the muscles of her throat contracting as she tried to bend down her head and set her teeth once more in his hands. He compressed her throat with his strong fingers. The blood surged into her face. He closed his fingers more firmly. Her veins swelled. Her cheeks puffed out. The whites of her eyes were bloodshot. The eyes themselves protruded. He thought they would come out of their sockets. He pressed upon her throat harder, harder, till her tongue lolled out of her gaping mouth. Then he heard a faint noise as if something had fallen to the floor. He looked down and saw the emerald, which had dropped from her nerveless fingers. Still keeping one hand upon her throat, he felt for the jewel with the other, grasped it, lifted it. As he did so he saw an appalling expression of hatred and despair rise, as if behind a veil, in the swelled face and blood-suffused eyes of his victim. With the hand that held the emerald he struck Caryll down to the floor. He leaped over the bed, opened the door, snatched the key from the keyhole, darted out. He heard behind him the rustle of her night-dress as she threw herself across the bed after him, and then a horrible cry as he escaped, locking the door of the cage upon the animal.

CHAPTER XXXIII

WHEN Caryll leaped upon her, Diamond was, for the moment, too utterly confused, even too terrified, to attempt either resistance or escape. She did not know what had seized her, why she was furiously attacked. In her first paroxysm of fear she had shut her eyes. The grip on her throat seemed to her wholly inhuman—no grip of a woman. Only when it was relaxed, only when she heard the backward movement of her assailant recoiling from her did she open her eyes to face the horror that was her companion, and that seemed to be her enemy. Then she saw, in the dim light which shone from the lantern left behind by the thief, something that in shape was human, something that had the outline of a woman, the flowing hair of a woman—but the eyes, the features, the expression—of what? Those stained lips drawn away from the discoloured teeth, that furrowed and bruised forehead, those cheeks, one dabbled with scarlet, one yellowish-white, those hands which moved incessantly as if trying to clutch something invisible in the air—did they belong to woman? For a moment Diamond scarcely knew.

Caryll had half fallen against the blood-stained and disordered bed. Her bare feet were entangled in the curtain that lay twisted on the floor. Under her tattered night-robe her breast shuddered as she drew her breath heavily, gasping, sometimes almost sobbing. Her eyes, nearly shut, squinted from exhaustion and had lost all their expression. She swayed her head feebly to and fro, and this rhythmical and unconscious movement, at the same time piteous and absurd, conveyed to Diamond's mind a most filthy suspicion. She thought the woman before her was suffering from some access of mania produced by drunkenness. Diamond knew the gutter, the wretched creatures who dwell there. The curse of drink had been laid upon more than one of her dancing companions, and she had seen the terrors that crowd about the victims of this most dreary and unaccomplished sin. She looked at the swaying figure and at the chamber in which it had been caged. Everything there cried aloud of violence and of ferocious brutality. The clothes were torn from the bed. A blood-stained pillow lay doubled up on the floor, protruding from its white slip, which had been rent by furious hands. One of the iron rods of the bedstead was bent, and the brass knob which had been at the top had fallen on to the curtain where Caryll's feet were set. A chair, thrown down by the thief as he escaped, lay near the door, and on the door panels there were spots of blood. The electric lamp at the bed-head was smashed. Splinters of broken glass covered the carpet, and the green cord which protected the electric wires curved like a thin snake about the feet of the bed. In the faint light the chamber looked like a chamber into which a dreamer might come in a nightmare to gaze upon some vision vague but terrible, to shudder among the furtive ruins heaped and tangled by a crime.

Diamond looked from this brutal room to the brutalised woman whom she had found shut up alone in it. She did not at first recognise this woman. She did not discern Lady Caryll in the disordered, shuddering, and blood-stained creature who lay back against the bed, feebly rocking herself to and fro. The horrible confusion and the loneliness of the chamber induced the street-bred girl to believe that its sole occupant, tormented by an hallucination, had been fighting with an imaginary enemy, struggling frantically against the darting shadows which, moving in activities like the activities of hell, beset the sodden brain, cringe and posture before the staring eyes of the drunkard in the deserted hours of night. And Diamond supposed that her abrupt entrance into the shadowy realm had turned this woman to a new and terrified violence, then struck her back to dazed stupidity that was nevertheless malignant in its lethargy.

She twined her hands in her hair, rocked herself to and fro, and gazed at Diamond with her fearfully inexpressive eyes.

Neither of the women spoke. Nor could Diamond conceive of coherent words issuing from the gaping mouth of the creature opposite to her. As well could she have imagined an animal talking, or a dreadful image of some vice or misery laying hold, for some mad purpose, upon the speech of man. In this crisis of Caryll's life her unreality, as a woman, beat upon the perception of Diamond, and turned her very cold. But behind that awful unreality there lay a reality more awful, more explicit, and more venomous. Vaguely, by others, had the unreality been divined. To Diamond it was already clearer than it had ever been to them. And, in the past, sometimes the reality had flitted for a moment before certain puzzled eyes. Now it moved not, but stood up like a sentinel half-hidden in the night—half-hidden because still there fell before it the veil of the unreality. Diamond felt as if she looked on distant horror through some heavy sombre mist.

She never knew how long the silence lasted, but there came a moment when it was intolerable, and she broke it with a word.

She said something—what she could not afterwards remember—
and, as she said it, she moved a step forward. The effect of the
sound of her voice and of her movement was startling. Caryll
ceased from her palsied gesture, so mechanical in its repetition,
started sideways against the wall, then rushed forward and gained
the doorway, through which she vanished into the black passage,
leaving Diamond alone in the disordered chamber. This abrupt
activity and display of purpose, succeeding the dull and almost
bestial reverie in which Caryll had seemed wrapped, startled
Diamond like the sound of a shot. She turned and looked towards the passage, down which the rustle of Caryll's night-dress
almost immediately died away. Her exit, and the quick fading of
the sound of her, left the room so lonely that Diamond shook with
fear, discovering that this removal of a living and dreadful thing
from its home increased, instead of diminishing, the tragedy of the
aspect of that home, the grim and ghastly eloquence of its silence
and its twilight. She had felt afraid with Caryll, but now felt
more afraid without her.

After waiting for a moment, till her situation seemed to her
unbearable, Diamond hurried to the door and down the passage,
turning presently into the little room that looked upon the court.
She found no one, and she ran to the open window and gazed out.
At first she saw nothing but the night leaning against the towering
brick walls from which no light shone to give her courage. The
blackness in this deserted funnel confused her eyes because they
had just been used with so much intensity. She gazed forth,
indeed, like a blind woman. Then the plaintive wind of the night
pressed gently against her cheek, and she thought that scales fell
from her eyes. In the court she saw Caryll searching along the
walls, searching swiftly like one in a frenzy. Her bare feet
pattered on the asphalte. The loose sleeves of her robe fell back
from her arms as she raised them, feeling the lower windows of
the building with her hands. Diamond stayed where she was
and watched the white and ghostly figure as it circled round
feverishly. She dared not interrupt this search which she could
not comprehend, though she supposed it to be the fantastic quest
of a creature impelled by mania to seek things non-existent. The
uselessness of such a quest appalled her. Why should it ever have
an end ? She imagined it continuing through all eternity without
result or pause ; the arms for ever raised, the fingers clutching at
the closed and slippery windows, the bare feet reiterating their
naked note upon the pavement, the torn robe fluttering out from
the thin and eager body. To watch this body was like watching a
creature in a circus, that could never cease from a performance
in which it suffered pain. The violent monotony of its action

fatigued Diamond's brain and eyes. As she gazed out of the window she began to feel stupid, and as if she would be forced to see for ever the eternal progress of this crazy pilgrim of the night. This sensation was killed in her by a circumstance that informed her with a new excitement. In her tour round the court, Caryll came to the window of Diamond's flat, found it open, stopped before it, then sprang in and disappeared.

The two women had exchanged their homes.

Caryll's last action destroyed in Diamond the vagueness that had come to her out of the night, swept away her confusion and her abnormal fears, and let in upon her another fear, very natural, even very bourgeois—the discreet anxiety of a newly-married woman who perceives a frantic stranger invading the sacred precincts of "the home." In such a newly-married woman awe fades before such great intrusion. Not for a moment did Diamond hesitate. She sprang across the court in the wake of Caryll, and came upon her in the bedroom to which her dreadful cry had penetrated so short a time before.

She was standing near the bed, in the midst of a confusion caused by the continuance of her impassioned search. The window curtains were pulled back, and one, caught by the edge of the dressing-table, protruded into the room. The door of a large cupboard, in which Diamond hung clothes, stood open, and the gowns within it were disarranged, one of them being thrown upon the floor. Chairs had been moved from their places and the bed had been pulled out from its station against the wall. Diamond reddened at the sight of so much anarchy. She opened her lips to utter chiding words, to proclaim her ownership and the intruder's impertinence, but, before she could speak, Caryll, hearing her enter, started, angrily not nervously, and turned sharply round as if she were disposed to attack any one who should dare to interrupt her in her mysterious and apparently crazy purpose. When she saw Diamond clearly, however, she stood still. Her eyes were wide open and were no longer inexpressive. In them burned the fires of an immeasurable despair. As Diamond looked into them she understood that her first impression on entering Caryll's flat had been entirely wrong. The woman who stood here was the victim of some tragedy, but she was sane. For the first time Diamond began to feel that the struggle which must have taken place in the dreadful chamber she had left had been a struggle with no shadow. She recognised that her companion was Lady Caryll and divined some dreadful incident as the cause of her despair.

"Whatever is it?" she asked. "Whatever's the matter, eh?"

The sound of her voice seemed to frighten Caryll, for she

moved back feebly, fell against the bed, and sank down on it. Her expression became suddenly as weak and helpless as that of a child who has been beaten till it can stand no longer. Her head drooped and her hands, and her teeth chattered as if she were very cold. Diamond's anger disappeared. She was filled with deep pity for this child in agony. Caryll looked down on the floor. She trembled, till the bed creaked and the dark blue stuff that bordered its edge shook uneasily to and fro. Diamond pulled the shawl from her shoulders quickly, came up to the bed and wrapped the shawl round Caryll, who did not glance up, and who seemed unconscious that anything was being done for her and that she was not entirely alone. Her silence and her shuddering stupor of despair began to unnerve Diamond. She pushed Caryll gently and exclaimed—

"Why ever 've you come in here? What was you lookin' for? What's the matter? Can't you say?"

Caryll made no reply.

Then, after another long look at Caryll's bending figure, Diamond sat down beside her on the bed and seized her hands. There was dried blood upon them, and they were very cold and damp. Their message to Diamond was poignant and deepened her wondering pity.

"Why ever was you locked in?" she continued, speaking in a very distinct voice as if to a small and confused child. "Who did it?"

At the final question Caryll looked up for the first time. Her discoloured face was transformed by an expression of intense hatred. She glanced slowly round the room and then at Diamond.

"He came from here," she said in a whisper. Her hand stiffened in Diamond's.

"He came from here," she repeated, still whispering. "He must have come from here."

The expression of fury grew in her face, her strength seemed to be returning, and she began to move restlessly on the bed. Diamond was utterly puzzled.

"From here?" she exclaimed. "Whatever can you mean? Why, I live here."

Caryll grasped her wrist.

"You!" she said fiercely. "Then tell me where he is!"

She stared threateningly on Diamond.

"I dunno' who you mean," Diamond answered, holding Caryll fast, and trying to speak firmly and to show no fear. "Whoever is it, and what's he done?"

Caryll wrenched herself away from Diamond, sprang up, and stood over her as she sat back on the bed looking upward. The direct interrogation gave to the victim a clear sense of her condition, of her present fate, set before her, in a white and cruel radiance, the impotence that she bore like a crushing burden. She perceived her solitude standing by her, a towering spectre, fleshless and immovable. She looked back over her past, and the glance was like an immense journey taken with incredible swiftness. As a train flashes along vast plains, under bridges, through the darkness of tunnels, above the flitting silver of running rivers in the twilight, between the whispering armies of the woods, she flashed along the vanished days, and saw their gifts and heard their voices. Their lights gleamed upon her as gleam the flying lights of retreating cities upon the roaring train that heeds them not. The smoke of their sacrifices shook round her like a veil. Their wisdom and their folly and the stillness of their joy rushed before her like the landscape that hurries to its end. In the dusk she saw their jewels, in the shadowy dawn their fading stars, and with the moonlight came their awful magic, and with the clouds fled fast their transient loans.

For had she ever a gift, or has any one that lives?

Diamond grew terrified as she sat looking up at Caryll and watching the expressions that swept across her face.

"Whatever is it?" Diamond said at last in an unsteady voice. "Whatever is it? What's he done?"

Till she had finished her journey Caryll could not speak. But then the thin veil of her unreality fell from her. The naked reality stood before Diamond. Caryll put forth her hands, grasped Diamond's shoulders and leaned heavily upon them. She began to speak, at first in a mechanical voice, and, while she spoke, she looked away towards the wall at the far side of the bed. The words came rapidly from her lips, as if she had said them often to herself in hours of solitude, as if she said them now very familiarly, with a hard certainty of all they meant to her if not to her auditor.

"You want to know what he has done," she said. "Well, then, what do women want in their lives? What are they always crying out for? You ought to know, I suppose. You're a woman. Aren't you like all the rest? What do you all want? He told me once—Aubrey Herrick told me."

Diamond started at this name. Caryll glanced at her for an instant with indifferent eyes and continued rapidly.

"Love, he said, of course—the gift of a heart, of a thing that's subject to disease, failure, change—isn't it? For what is it exactly? I don't know. But that's what they all say women want, and so I suppose it's true. If they all say it, mustn't it be true of all of them? I don't mind if it is. I never did mind. All you women don't mean much to me. I don't understand you, perhaps. I don't know that I want to. But you go about, directly you're old enough, searching for what you wish for—somebody's love or something of the kind—very likely somebody's pretence of love. Does it matter? If you get it, you're in a state of bliss, and if you don't get it, you put on a starved look. You must know that look—hungry and sour. Lots of unmarried women have it here in London. It's the look men hate most in women's faces—because they've put it there, I suppose. They've made it, and men hate most of the things they've made, in the end—especially the things they've made of women. But, suppose you've been lucky and got the first thing women want—you begin to want something else directly. For none of you are ever satisfied, so far as I can see. Are you? No; you want to have a child. If you're denied that, another sort of hungry expression comes into your faces, and you surround yourself with things that are what is called alive—birds, or horrible little dogs, that get illnesses, and have changeable tempers, and are always worrying you to do something for them, and horses that you have to go into the stable to visit, and wretched things that twirl in cages. You don't care whether they want to get out of their cages or not. But perhaps you do have a child. Then you want to have another. For if it's a girl, you can't be happy till you have a boy, and if it's a boy, of course you need a girl too. And then your health breaks down. You become ugly, and the kind man who's made you so is angry or contemptuous. And he's faithless and you're jealous. Or else the children are delicate, and, for years, you think of nothing but their illnesses. You read medical books and have the doctor for ever in the house. If you're not that sort of motherly woman, your children soon begin to bore you, and you wish you'd never had any. You see them growing up, and you're angry. If you have a girl, and she's good-looking, she reminds you of all the attractions you're losing. She keeps showing you your exact age in the mirror of her youth. You hate her. Lots of mothers in London wish their pretty daughters dead whenever they look at them. If you have a boy, you're always in misery because he won't tell you anything about his affairs, or the people he knows whom you don't know, and he doesn't intend you ever shall know. You fancy he's being dissipated, and you can't bear the idea that he's getting to understand all about life, far more about it than you ever will. You expect him to trust you, and of course he won't. Why should he when your mind is as different from his as mine is from yours and from other women's?"

She paused and pressed her lips tightly together.

"So different," she said, with much more emphasis, grasping Diamond's shoulders more firmly. "I see the horror, the disgustingness, of all these things you women seek for, of these human relations. It is always these human relations with others that make lives abominable when they're entered into for the usual reasons. Only once, for a moment, did I think that I could ever long for them—for a usual reason—and why d'you think that was? Because I was out in a garden after dinner, and somebody touched me with well-shaped hands, and it was night."

She burst into a laugh that made Diamond shiver.

"After dinner!" she repeated with bitter emphasis, "that's how you are all made—to be played upon by all the miserable, second-rate things that crowd up life, by food—actually food!—and by flesh touching your flesh, and by eyes staring into yours, and by shapes that can be altered entirely by gluttony, or illness, or a fall, and by the noise of voices, and by smells—the smells of plants, or perfumes that you buy in shops—and by—Ah! I needn't say them all. Well, I didn't want the things you women all want. You hear? I didn't want them. But I did want something. I——"

She hesitated, and, for the first time, looked hard at Diamond, trying to read her.

"But you won't understand," she cried fiercely. "You won't—but I found some one who did understand me. He was old and ugly, and nearly tired out. Some people thought him mad, and some ridiculous. But he understood me. And, because of that, I gave myself to him. And he gave me in return all I cared for. What was that, d'you say?"

Diamond had not spoken. She sat upon the bed quite still, never shifting under the hands that grasped her, or shrinking from the glittering eyes that were now fixed upon hers. She looked up, puzzled, horrified, fascinated. Caryll's eyes drew her. She had a sensation of being pulled up towards this extraordinary being whom she had seen shaken by hysteria but a few minutes before, but who now displayed a growing force that was like the force of some contemptuous and inhuman fury. As Caryll asked the question her face changed. An ugly and cunning look transformed it.

"Shall I tell you?" she said.

She paused. Diamond moved her head in a sort of vehement nod. The ugly look died in Caryll's face.

"I cared," she said, speaking with an excitement that continually increased, "I cared for things that were silent and beautiful, that came from far away, from hidden places, from mountains, and from the depths of mines and from the depths of the sea. They can do no harm to those who understand them and who love them rightly, for themselves. Lots of women think they love them—vain women, egoists, creatures who live to startle other women and to capture men. I love them differently. They gave me dreams. They took me into fairyland."

Her manner became impregnated with mystery, and imagination flowed into her eyes, which were now luminous and curiously vague, and which seemed no longer to see Diamond.

"With them I was happy. He knew that. He took me into the cave. That was what he called it. I was there with him and I wanted nothing else—nothing, nothing that other women want. The things in the cave had no connection with the loathsomeness of life—and if he had, well, I forgave him. I accepted his manhood because he did so much for me. And then he had to accept change. They hadn't. They were freed from the necessity of undergoing that transformation which comes to the vilest animal as well as to the human being—to a rat, or a jackal, or a pariah dog that lives on offal—to every ugly, greedy, dangerous, degraded live thing—live in the way you think of, you and the other women. A boy once asked me—sent for me in the night—to come and see him go through that filthy change, to leave my fairyland and come." (Diamond shuddered.) "I wouldn't. Why should we go into the mud of life? Why should we pursue its curse? Why should I have come out of my true life, my own land, to watch a hideous change in one I scarcely knew? They thought ill of me perhaps. What did that matter? My beautiful things couldn't die. For that I loved them. They could only be destroyed by violence—or taken. But they were helpless, horribly helpless."

The passion in her face was mingled again with the terrible despair which Diamond had already noticed.

"Yes, they were helpless," she said again, and her voice became thick and hoarse. "He went through that filthy change. The one who gave them to me died—as that boy died. And then——" her voice diminished, "then there were men who came and took them from me, took them all——"

The horror on her face turned Diamond to answering horror. Never before, not even when standing by the death-bed of Alf, or when striving to comfort Vauxhall after his brother's funeral, had she understood so absolutely the ultimate tragedy of loss.

"All but one," Caryll continued, almost murmuring. "But that one was nearest to me, was most mine. Mine! It was more than that. It was part of me. He said so and he knew. I gave myself to it and I drew it into me. It was of me and I of it. Sometimes he said that I lived in it—like some one long ago, like a goddess whom men worshipped. Perhaps she has never died."

Caryll's voice sank and ceased. She had forgotten Diamond. She had forgotten where she was. She stared before her in deep meditation.

"Long ago she lived in the thing she loved," Caryll continued presently, speaking slowly like one who is puzzling out some elaborate problem. "The priests knew it, the priests who worshipped her, who made her their religion. And he thought—one night he said so—that perhaps she has come again upon the earth, although now no one could ever know her, no one except—except the one thing that she loved."

She fixed her eyes again upon Diamond questioningly.

"That would know her," she said. "That would miss her. What is an empty home? What is it? Do you know? Isn't it desolate? Isn't it terrible? Isn't it—isn't it?"

Her voice rose in a cry.

"You come here and ask me what has been done to me tonight," she exclaimed. "What he has done? He has stolen the home of a goddess. He has stolen the thing she loved. He has stolen part of her—part of her very soul."

She dropped her hands from Diamond's shoulders and stood listening intently.

"Hark!" she whispered. "Hark!"

Her face was grey and drawn. She held up her right hand and moved a step towards the door.

"Hark!" she whispered again, looking back over her shoulder to Diamond, who stayed where she was, almost paralysed by fear. "Can't you hear them? Can't you hear the hoarse voices of the priests? They're waking, I tell you—they're waking in their tombs out there—out there in that far country—they know—they know—they're waking from their sleep—they're rising up—they're coming. Hush! Listen now! Don't you hear their footsteps—and all their voices cursing—cursing in the dark—cursing him who has profaned the temple of their goddess! I hear them—they're nearer now—they're nearer—they're marching—marching like an army in the night—they shall fight for me—let me go to meet them—let me go!"

She made a tottering movement, turning towards the door and thrusting out her hands. Her face was full of awe and of shuddering expectation.

"The priests!" she muttered. "The priests of the goddess Esmeralda!"

She caught her breath, choked, fought for air. She strove to cry out, to rush forward, but her voice was strangled in her throat, and she stood where she was, swaying to and fro. Then a long wailing sob tore her, and she fell down, striking her head against the post of the door.

Diamond watched her from the bed, not daring to go near her.

For all the black night seemed full of the hoarse voices and of the tramplings of men.

CHAPTER XXXIV

In crowds the individual qualities of men and women seem to faint and grow pale, as travellers grow pale in long journeys. Even pure merriment, hustled by a thousand differing gaieties, loses some of the liveliness of its meaning. Even sheer despair may often pass —if it will—unrecognised, unfeared. Nevertheless, in the gigantic human masses that surge through modern cities, there are sometimes figures that claim notice as definitely almost as a man seen in a lonely landscape to which he gives, ignorantly, the atmosphere of life. The watcher of such a landscape starts at the man's unanticipated entry upon the scene, of which he creates the loneliness when he gives to it his presence. Far away he may be, but a pigmy black and forbidding among the wide ploughlands to which the sun declines, yet his vague and scarce perceptible movements fascinate the eyes that have been fixed on Nature, his weary, creeping progress grips the attention that has been drawn elsewhere. A tired labourer, moving against a sunset, speaks to the watcher as the sunset never can. The sunset may contain all the mystery of heaven; the dark shadow contains all the mystery of life. In such a moment and scene the exact species and amount of life which the shadow contains matter not at all. The watcher is conscious only of a fact, of a naked sincerity, illuminated and thrown into prominence by a tinted, dream-like pageant. The pageant fades, and the watcher feels that because he can no longer see it the existence it had is ended. Nor can he see the shadow any more. Yet he is conscious of its continuing presence, however far away.

Sometimes in a great city, against the background of its turmoil, there stands such a shadow, so full of meaning because of its naked sincerity. It draws the attention. The crowd assists, instead of destroying, the strange influence it has in the scene where it abides. It may be tired in a circle of voluble activities, yet it has more power than they. Its calm has more significance than their movement. Its silence wakes long echoes that their voices cannot stir.

There was a period when Caryll was such a shadow, standing out against London like a figure against the sunset.

. . . .

The notoriety of her disaster was naturally great. When the emerald went, there was a very definite splash in the whirlpool. A great jewel with a history and a satire, worn by a beautiful woman and greatly loved by her, stirs quickly the attention of the mob and plays upon its passions. It quickens the pulse of avarice and whips the rage of envy. Vulgarity turns to it as a dog turns to a smell in the gutter. Poverty creeps about it as a beggar creeps about a lighted house. The world talked of the loss of Caryll's emerald. The world was engrossed by the efforts of the police to discover the identity of the thief. And this was natural enough. What was less natural was the peculiar impression created by Caryll upon the minds of many persons when the police authorities at last acknowledged that they were at fault, and she was obliged to consider her loss as permanent and to resign herself to the decree of a fate that was inflexibly cruel.

The newspapers had rung with her story. The public had battened on descriptions of her struggle with the masked robber. Pictures of her bedroom, before his entrance and after his departure, had appeared in the journals that are read on Sunday mornings by tired men in shirt-sleeves, and by women whose hair seems to be in process of arrangement for the Last Day. Caryll's heroism had been praised and her subsequent collapse had been duly recorded. Diamond had been interviewed, and had said very little to the importunate journalist who beset her with his desire. There had been the usual fictions and reports that the thief had been found here or there, that he was a peer or a noted cracksman, that he had been watching Lady Caryll's flat for months before he entered it, that he had only entered it casually to steal the silver spoons, and had carried off the emerald without being aware of its value. Both Diamond and Aubrey had mentioned their observation of a man's attentive figure in an opposite flat. But inquiries there had only led to the discovery of an apparently most respectable and peaceful old Frenchman, who was utterly shocked at any misfortune overtaking *une belle Anglaise.*

This sort of sensation lasted a long while, but at length inevitably died away. Not till it died away did the strange figure rise up and come upon the scene to make its sensation, so different and so new. Only one or two people who were intimate with Caryll thought dimly, from the beginning, that she would interpret her rôle unusually, that she would play the part of victim as few have ever played it. These noted in her a double peculiarity, a profound mental indifference linked with an extraordinary bodily activity. Caryll never repeated the outburst of which Diamond had been a witness. She never spoke of it to Diamond, whom she afterwards ignored. Diamond grew to believe that Caryll was unaware of the words she had uttered in her wild moment, and that she would never again listen for the voices of the priests, or dream of the vengeance of the dead. She woke from the trance that succeeded her passion to a calm that was pertinacious, to some people alarming. She showed no interest in the proceedings of the police. She answered their questions without irritation, but with the vague carelessness we give to children who interrupt us when we are reading some interesting book.

She scarcely glanced at the theories put forward by the newspapers as to the thief's identity. When, after a time, it was acknowledged by police and press that every clue had failed, she made no comment. Nor did she offer any reward for the discovery of the thief. This avoidance of a natural act was at first attributed to her poverty. But fate speedily proved such a surmise to be false by taking away her great-uncle, Lord Verrender, and giving her his fortune. He succumbed to an attack of apoplexy, and she was once more rich. Now the world thought that she would make some definite move, that a huge reward would be offered and the emerald perhaps returned to its owner. Caryll did nothing. She did not even bid farewell to the scene of her tragedy. She still slept each night in the bedroom that was haunted by its memories, and sat each day in the little room that looked upon the court.

There came upon her then a white stillness that, despite the activity of her body, seemed to many people akin to the stillness of death. And this abnormal calm set her against the sunset to strike wonder through the world, and a mysterious pity, like that mysterious pity some feel at times for life, through the hearts of one or two who thought they understood her. These regarded her indeed as the shadow is regarded, as emblem and as truth. They saw tears in her eyes that were so dry and fixed, despair in the face that was so pallidly serene. The tide of natural vigour that flows in a healthy body had ebbed from hers. Her expression, her voice, her movements, her attitudes, were so lifeless as to be terrible. Yet in her deadness she conveyed an impression similar to the impression conveyed by the life against the sky; for there was something within her, something distant, that sat for ever gazing, tireless as the Arab in his tower gazing across the desert sands.

Had Caryll become a recluse, people would have talked of her far less than they did. The wretched beings who hide their misery by hiding themselves are unheeded by London. They can live or die as they please. But Caryll still went into the world. This moving corpse of a human being was seen at parties, drove perpetually in the Park, visited the playhouses, went to race meetings, sent a cold chill through the ardent mobs that stare at private views. Her youth, her activity, and her ghastly indifference to all the things and people whom she continually sought made her now more famous than she had ever been before. The new arrivals in society always desired an introduction to her. The crowd about the Park railings whispered her name as she drove by, turning her half-shut eyes upon the scene that was so instinct with life, and that she observed as a mummy might observe its tomb. Hostesses desired her presence at their parties; men thronged around her like schoolboys round a show. She gave nothing in return for all that was given to her. If she spoke, it was without animation, in a voice that had lost the ringing note of life. Her rare smile was like that first light of the dawn which makes the watcher sadly realise the tenderness of night. Nothing pleased or displeased her. There was something shocking in her incapacity for anger. One day, as she was passing through a side-street of London, a half-tipsy man caught up a cat that was purring before an area railing, and dashed out its brains against a wall. Caryll watched the action from her carriage without moving a muscle. A friend who was with her was overcome by nausea, caused less by the cruelty than by the woman who observed it.

Caryll never became more animated in her more private life. She preserved always the same unchanging calm. Her servants feared her; children shrank from her. Nothing that was very young, and so instinctive, could bear to be long with her. Her atmosphere to them was like the atmosphere of death. In it they felt as if they could no longer breathe.

Many people asked wondering why she still chose to go incessantly into the world. There is always in London a brigade of women who may be seen everywhere, carrying their despair from one party to another, bearing their hopelessness along the public ways. Their hands are full of cards, their hearts of lost illusions. About their tattered mouths crawl the wrinkles that seek the unrepentant. The gold dust in their hair is as the dust of the ages to the man who sees them rightly, and the dim fire in their eyes as the first flashing of the purgatorial fires. But they are old. It is their age, and their vain battle against it, that gives to them their horror. Caryll's horror lay in her youth, even in her abiding freshness; for her body was not tarnished. Even as the spectral brigade carries the terror of its age and deep despair through the grinning faces of the show, Caryll carried the terror of her youth and its calm hopelessness. Why? People asked the question, recognising that the world could give this girl nothing on which she set a value.

Aubrey, too, asked himself the question.

At first, when Lord Verrender died, expectation waited on Caryll's steps, seeing them in fancy already set towards the jewel shops. She bought no jewels. A man who admired her greatly ventured to send her a strange Persian necklace that he had found in Bagdad, making the excuse that it was unique, a curiosity that was absurd in the possession of a man. She sent the necklace back with a cold line of refusal.

Had the love for jewels, then, died out in her strange nature? Aubrey was led to think so.

The change in Caryll was terrible to him. At first he tried to combat it, and believed that it would be transitory; that it was perhaps a mental illness due to the nervous exhaustion that had followed her struggle with the thief. He questioned Diamond closely on the events of the tragic night, but he found her less frank than usual, and he could get little from her. Once he surprised a strange look of pity in her eyes, and he remembered that he had seen such a look in the eyes of his mother.

"What is the matter?" he asked quickly. "Why do you look at me like that?"

Diamond flushed.

"Don't ask me any more," she said; "don't ask me any more, then."

"Then there is something you have not told me?" Aubrey cried with quick suspicion; "something about her?"

Diamond looked obstinate. She did not answer. If she had received a revelation, it was one she could not rightly understand, could not rightly explain to another.

"What is it?" Aubrey said, speaking with unusual sharpness. "Tell me, Diamond."

"I dunno," she replied. "There ain't nothin' to tell—any more than you know. But—but——"

She hesitated.

"Well! What is it?"

Again the look of pity came into her eyes.

"Look here!" she said. "We're pals, aren't we now? Pals for always?"

"Yes," he answered. "You know we are."

"And pals ought to stand by each other."

"Stand by me then, Diamond, and tell me all you know."

"I know as you'd better give it up," she replied, looking down on the carpet.

They were sitting in her flat. It was afternoon.

"Give up what?" Aubrey asked.

His voice had become cold, full of suspicion and reserve.

"You know. It ain't no good. She's—she's—not like any of em."

"What do you mean?"

"Girls—other women. She's by herself. She don't want anything they do. She's not nat'ral." She looked down on some tiny clothes that she was sewing.

She would say no more. She never described to Aubrey the fierce outburst of Caryll, her wild hallucination in the night. And he ceased from questioning Diamond. Her blunt and simple summing up of Caryll in the sentence—"She's not nat'ral," had moved him more than all the gossip of the world. He strove again to break through Caryll's impenetrable indifference, but in vain.

He said to himself that she must be ill. Her mother told him so. For Lady St. Ormyn honestly believed that her daughter was mentally affected.

"Shock!" she cried. "Shock! Sir Reuben shouldn't have died as he did. He must have known it was coming on, and he ought to have gone to bed. Death is much more natural when a person's in bed. One sees them like that, and one is prepared. But to die dressed, on a carpet, and when one is in the act of packing a box, is really—I always shall say that poor Caryll has never recovered from it. If she has, why should she live in Baker Street?"

Aubrey secretly consulted a great brain specialist, not mentioning Caryll's name, but describing the tragic circumstances of her life rather vaguely—so he thought—and her present perpetual condition of utter indifference to all things, people, joys, and sorrows.

"You are speaking to me of a very-well known woman," the specialist replied, looking keenly at Aubrey.

Aubrey reddened.

"We need not mention her name," continued the doctor, "but I know the lady you mean. I have met her in society. You have alluded to the sad circumstances of her life, to her losses, to her present apparent lethargy of mind. Her circumstances have been strange. Her present condition is abnormal. She is, to my thinking, the most extraordinary figure now in London society. But you haven't touched upon her most peculiar characteristic."

He paused. Aubrey looked at him eagerly.

"Why is she for ever in society? Why does she hurry from one party to another? Why does she travel to race meetings? Did she race formerly?"

"No," Aubrey answered, wondering.

"Why does she spend hours at private views, and try to be wherever there is a crowd of people? Do you know that last week, when there was that Sportsman's fête at the Crystal Palace, she drove down to it?"

Aubrey was amazed.

"Alone?" he asked.

"Quite alone. Since you have consulted me I will tell you that, if you want to discover the truth of this enigma, you must seek for the cause of this perpetual activity—an activity existing in one who apparently cares for nothing, looks at nothing with any interest. The strangeness of this lady arises not from one reason alone, but from two in combination. There is something almost appalling in such a union of inactivity with activity—inactivity of the soul, activity of the body. It is not natural, and so it both distresses and fascinates people. They are accustomed to see the desires of the mind being accomplished in and by the body. In this lady they see a body acting with vehemence on its own account, and apparently quite irrespective of the commands or desires of the mind."

"Apparently?" Aubrey said.

"Apparently," the specialist replied with a slight smile.

And there the interview ended.

From this time Aubrey observed Caryll more closely than ever, but he could find no clue to her strange conduct. Once he asked her why she went about so incessantly, and whether doing so did not tire her.

"No," she said, in her dry, dull voice. "One must do something."

"But you don't enjoy these things."

"And does any one enjoy them?" she asked.

Her remark, and the way in which it was made, seemed to take all the colour out of life. Aubrey remembered that, long ago, he had told Caryll she was a dreamer. But that dream of hers had been beautiful. This was terrible.

He felt hopeless about it as the days went by. Things prospered with him in the City. He was making money. Soon he would be in a position to support a wife. But Caryll always seemed far away from him now. How could he ever draw near to her again? He was tortured at this time by his consciousness of one of the most painful mysteries that complicate human relations, and make them often sad—the terrible power of the soul to remove itself when it chooses, and apparently without effort, to some vast distance, beyond the reach, beyond the vision of its friends and those who love it. When he sat with Caryll, and could have touched her hand, he was conscious that she—the real Caryll—was not with him, did not choose to be with him. Where she was he knew not. And sometimes he sickened with despair, with the hungry desire of such knowledge that comes to those who love and that cannot be gratified. But he never now made any of those useless efforts that men and women are for ever making to compass the impossible. He never sought to pursue the soul to its remote lair, to surprise it in the hidden place, and see it turn to bay. There was something tremendously powerful in the white stupor of Caryll that acted both upon him and upon the world, holding the most tender as well as the most idle curiosity in check.

Lady Rangecliffe felt it, and was weary for her son and for his long delusion. She never spoke of it, either to him or to any one else. But she began to think that Aubrey had in his nature a feminine obstinacy of love that is rarely found in men. And at last she even ceased to pray that his faithfulness might die. For she recognised the grandeur of its folly, and felt that without it her son would be something less than he was. Perhaps, secretly, she was one of that company of big-hearted and brave beings who see in the shadowy face of sorrow most clearly the Divine expression—God in the pallor and the tears.

CHAPTER XXXV

SPRING dawned in London. The *Morning Post* announced each day the return of fashionable pilgrims from their Continental wanderings. Many people were staying at hotels in order to search at their ease for furnished houses for the season. The theatres and smart restaurants were crowded every night. A good many small dinners were being given, and all the gossip was of the future. Would the season be a gay one? Who would entertain? What great houses would be thrown open, and what new hostesses would rise to the surface? Who would be the new lion, and who the new beauty? Would there be a wit, and would there be a salon? Most important thing of all, would there be a sensation—a great scandal, a great tragedy, or a great triumph—something to set the world talking, something to stamp this season, to set it apart from all its forerunners? Nobody knew. Everybody gossiped.

People flowed upon London from the four quarters of the globe. Thither came, from South Africa and all places honeycombed with mines, gay millionaires anxious to play the part of the Calf of Gold in the eternal cotillon. The painters flocked to their studios, welcomed their friends, and stood in knots, if they were elderly, praising the Royal Academy; in knots, if they were young, abusing it. Musicians swarmed across the Channel like locusts; authors flew to town like returning swallows to their English eaves. Explorers turned up from hideous wilds and melancholy deserts, hairy, debilitated, but still pertinacious. Actresses arrived from foreign tours, and beauties from now deserted capitals. Heiresses superintended the packing of gigantic trunks and thought of titled husbands. Handsome male paupers dreamed of such heiresses, and sent up the prices of lodgings in St. James's. On the Atlantic rolled mighty vessels full of the Americans who despise England but cannot keep away from London. The dressmakers prayed fervently against the sudden death of any Royalty, and the hotel-keepers against any war scare. The shutters slipped away from many a window, and flowers bloomed in many a hitherto empty window-box. Bond Street was packed with women every morning, and the Park was gay with carriages every afternoon.

The great town stirred, shook itself, awoke, and lifted its heavy head to greet the summer.

At the Opera-House, in Covent Garden, there was a wild bustle of preparation for the musical season. Some of the principal singers had already arrived. Among them was Monsieur Anneau. He had been re-engaged, despite his previous failure. Mr. Wilson had chanced to hear him sing a few weeks before in Paris, and found that he had almost recovered his former strenuous power. His voice had regained much of its mellow beauty. The curious malaise which had destroyed his value for a time seemed to have passed away.

He had seen Lady Caryll.

She did not know it. She never knew of his secret journey from Paris, of the surreptitious watch he kept, until, one day, he saw a white image pass by him in the soft dusk of a damp winter's afternoon. He stood under the skeleton of a great tree, and his fierce eyes were ablaze with anticipation. She sat alone in an open carriage, staring straight before her into the growing gloom. Her horses trotted fast. In a moment she was gone. But the singer had been rewarded for his journey. He had looked upon the white beauty of despair.

Now he could sing again, for now he could forget. He could sing again—less well, perhaps, than formerly; for trust, once it has been tarnished, can never more be quite the radiant thing it was. But he could sing. And he knew well that few would ever divine that his faith in the power of a great art had once grown sick, had faltered, had fallen in the dust. His glory would return. His triumphs were not over. His sin had still its servitor, if its sweet slave had sought for, and had won, the sacred boon of freedom.

Lady St. Ormyn was enchanted. Mrs. Luffa Parkinson wept in the confessional with joy, and asked Father Grimble if such ecstasy were sinful. Monsieur and Madame Villet besieged Monsieur Anneau with invitations to lunch, and as for Albert Sprigg—well, he quite forgot that Paris had ever forgotten its great high priest.

A few weeks before the opening of the opera season a certain society of young painters sent out cards for a private view. Their exhibition was a protest against accepted things, and more especially against those things which are accepted by the foolish nonentities who sit in judgment each spring at Burlington House, to "pass" pictures of puppy-dogs and canvases displaying the wooden cattle grazing upon a thousand oily hills. Protest has become popular in London, where pugnacious infants are worshipped. The cards of the young painters drew a mighty crowd to their surprising gallery. All the fifth-rate people who were bidden came, as a matter of course. They never refuse an invitation. All the bilious gentlemen who think dyspeptic thoughts and express them in dyspeptic articles were there. All the conceit that dwells apart in honoured suburbs, all the contempt of the gods the mob has crowned, walked in to see the show. But this year the young painters scored an exceptional triumph. The noise of their shrill cackling against that shameful thing, Success, pierced through the malady of the deaf monster whom all desire to move. The smart world rose up and clamoured for a card. The card was promptly sent. The smart world presented it at the turnstile, and was politely ushered in, and shown by the young painters the way to be intelligent. Fashion walked, gaping, round the amazing walls, and, towards five o'clock, the throng was become so dense that many Philistines, overtaken by confusion and the nervous hallucinations begotten of stewed tea, wondered whether they were not at the Royal Academy, and stared vaguely about them, trying to discover how many of their own disgraceful failures the Academicians had dared to hang upon the line. Celebrities were still flocking in, amid the buzz of comment they excite on such occasions, when there was an abrupt and very general movement towards the door. A whisper ran through the long room. The few people who were sitting down took courage and stood up. Even the contemptuous suburban nonentities deigned to display a certain amount of frigid interest in one who knew nothing of their sacred wilds.

Lady Caryll had come in. She was alone, and looked more cruelly indifferent even than usual. Her eyes were bent down under their drooping lids, and she seemed to see no one as she moved very slowly towards the middle of the gallery. She was evidently quite unconscious of the mob that pressed upon her. She did not seem desirous of glancing at the pictures. Her beauty, her intense pallor, and her wholly unnatural abstraction elevated her into a really terrible figure in the midst of such an assembly. To certain strangers who had never seen her before she gave a sensation that was akin to fear, for some contrasts are horrible merely from their sharpness. The chattering and busy throng made Caryll's grim silence and motionless features seem dreadful as the silence and insensibility of a corpse standing, by some artificial means, upright among the living. And, on the other hand, the contradiction of her inflexible appearance gave to the gaiety around her a hideous and unnatural aspect, transforming even most excusable liveliness into the palsied or epileptic travesty of a temper too hectic, too grimacing almost for long endurance. By the force of her presence Caryll made the crowd about her assume a new and most disagreeable aspect, like the aspect of a crowd in a nightmare, in which every feature, every motion is distorted, crept upon by the disease of exaggeration. By the force of its presence the crowd made Caryll appear dangerous and abnormal in her pallor, in her speechless and merciless contempt of all its merriment, of all the music of its words and its desires.

Having gained the middle of the gallery, she paused for a moment, and, for the first time, looked up. Some of those near her shrank instinctively from the still glance of her inexpressive eyes, and more than one tumultuous conversation died before her deadly silence.

Then an intrepid young man, who had painted a huge picture of Dieppe by night, with early Victorian ladies eating oranges on a lawn before a small pavilion, and ogling the Great Bear, came up to her, greeted her, and tried to convoy her round the room.

He struggled to make a way for her. She followed him like a woman in a dream. He shrieked information at her. She bent her head and seemed to listen. He pointed out Dieppe, and explained, in a crying voice, the significance of the oranges, the symbolism of the Bear. She smiled slightly in reply, and examined the early Victorian ladies with her unmeaning eyes. Then Aubrey spoke to her, and the young painter was engulfed.

"How can you stand these crushes?" Aubrey asked her.

"You endure them," she said.

"I knew I should meet you here," he replied.

He looked at her white and impassive face, thought of what the specialist had said to him, and was filled anew with wonder at her curious and obstinate activity.

"Why do you go about so incessantly?" he said in a low voice. "You care for nothing. Tell me why you go."

The crush was so great that he was pressed forward till his body touched hers, and as he uttered the last words his body felt hers start violently, so violently and abruptly that his nerves quivered.

"What is the matter?" he asked quickly, looking down at her.

She put her hand on his arm and closed her fingers tightly. He gazed at her, and saw that her face had changed. The death that had been in it was replaced by life. A veil had surely dropped from her, passion stood in the place of indifference, her eyes shone with excitement, and she bent her head to him and said hurriedly—

"Tell me who that is—that man who has just come in."

Aubrey glanced round.

"Which one?"

"Not there—not there!" she exclaimed impatiently; "on the left. Look where I am looking."

Aubrey did so, and saw, not far off, a tall man, perhaps forty years old, who was slowly making his way in their direction. His hair was mouse-coloured and was cut very short. His face was long, clean-shaven, with lantern jaws, high cheek-bones, and a resolute and coarse mouth, from the corners of which two deep lines spread away obliquely. Aubrey could not see well what his eyes were like, but one stared through a glass with a black rim. He was elaborately dressed, and wore a silk hat, whose brim was perfectly straight and unusually large. As he drew slowly nearer, Aubrey noticed that his face was exceptionally mobile, and that his eyes were very small, and very pale and furtive. He carried himself well, and had indeed the sort of ostentatiously upright bearing and allure that very common and unobservant people are apt to call distinguished. His figure was thin. His coat was made with a distinctly defined waist. His cane had a gold top in which a turquoise was set. He was self-consciously self-possessed. He seemed to have no acquaintance, for he spoke to no one, greeted no one with a bow or with a smile. Yet he looked at every one as he slowly moved along, walking, Aubrey thought, with a curious ingenuity that was almost cat-like in its ease and softness.

"That man!" Aubrey said, and there was contempt in his voice. "I don't know him, but I think he looks like——"

"Yes, yes!" she interrupted quickly. "Like what? Tell me what you think he looks like. I want to know."

Aubrey gazed at her with growing amazement. Her excitement was inexplicable.

"Like a cad, I was going to say," he answered.

"That is hardly a clever description," Caryll said, with a touch of sarcasm. "It is far too indefinite for that man."

"Why?"

"Don't you think he's the most definite personality in this gallery?"

Aubrey stared again at the new-comer, who was nearer to them now. Whether Caryll's remark, which was uttered with intense conviction, governed him, Aubrey scarcely knew, but he did know that, after it, the stranger meant much more to him than before, seemed to stand out clearly from every other man in the crowded room.

"Definite!" Aubrey said. "Yes, he is that. But why?"

"Definitely hateful," she answered. "Everybody must feel enmity against such a man."

There was violence in her low voice. Her excitement increased as the man drew nearer.

"It is very strange," she continued. "I have certainly never seen his face before, and yet I feel as if I had met him, as if I had had some intercourse with him, and loathed him in the past."

"Caryll!" Aubrey said.

His amazement at her passion increased. The man was now close to them, staring about him with his furtive light eyes. He had not seen them. Caryll began to tremble.

"What horrible hands he has!" she whispered.

Aubrey looked at the man's hands. They were encased in very tight-fitting lavender gloves sewn with black.

"What's the matter with them?" Aubrey said. "You are really unreasonable."

"They are horrible, horrible!" she repeated. "He is the most hateful human being I have ever seen. How can he have got in here?"

"But this sort of function is always a frightful mixture. You should not have come."

The man stood by them now. He was very tall. He glanced down, met Caryll's eyes, and immediately looked away. Aubrey thought that he started very slightly, and that an uneasy expression flashed across his face. He moved on slowly in the crowd. She turned to look after him, and seemed inclined to follow him, but she hesitated.

"Go," she said to Aubrey. "Go at once and find out for me who that man is. I must know before I leave. I must."

"I will see if any one can tell us. But it is——"

"Go, please go, Mr. Herrick. Don't waste time."

Her manner was terribly irritable. She frowned as she spoke. Aubrey left her wondering, and soon lost her in the throng.

He made the inquiry she desired, and pointed the man out to several acquaintances, but could not gain any information about him. One painter said, "I've seen him somewhere in Paris." But no one knew his name, and at last Aubrey was obliged to give up the effort to discover who he was. Meanwhile he had vanished in the crowd.

It was now late in the afternoon. Aubrey turned to regain Caryll, but she was not where he had left her. People were beginning to leave, and, still looking for her, he was drawn by the impulse of the crowd towards the door of the gallery. He resolved to stand there and to meet her as she came out. People streamed by, exchanging loud comments on the pictures, bidding each other good-bye or making arrangements for future gaieties. Aubrey felt dazed by the uproar, and by the vision of open mouths, flushed cheeks, and animated eyes. He began to wonder whether Caryll had already gone, and, turning, stared into the now half-empty gallery. His astonishment was great when he perceived her coming towards the door escorted by the stranger of whom she had expressed so unfavourable an opinion but a short time before. She was talking to him eagerly, and, while she talked, she stared intently into his face. She passed Aubrey without noticing him, and he was almost petrified by the contrast between her words—the few words that he heard in the hubbub—and her face as she looked incessantly at her companion.

For she spoke with a pressure of animation, with an odd and nervous cordiality to this stranger.

But she gazed at him with hatred in her eyes.

This union of two contrasts, her manner and appearance, seemed to set treachery before Aubrey, treachery endeavouring to conciliate that which it intended presently, and under favouring circumstances, to attack.

He followed Caryll and her companion slowly. When he gained the street he saw the man putting Caryll into her carriage. He took her hand, leaning familiarly on the carriage door to say good-bye. Horror crept into her face as he held her hand.

"Come to see me," she said.

She withdrew her hand hastily, sought for her card-case, and presently gave the stranger her card.

"You will come?" she said, with a pressure of obvious anxiety.

The man bowed, and took off his hat with a certain vulgar elaboration of manner.

As the carriage drove away he looked at the card, and a faint smile flickered across his face, deepening the two lines that stretched away obliquely from the corners of his coarse mouth. Then he drew from the breast-pocket of his coat a small green and gold case, put the card carefully into it, slipped the case into his pocket, buttoned up his coat, lit a large cigar, and sauntered gently away into the dusk that brooded over Piccadilly.

Aubrey stood and watched him go. When the shadows took him, Aubrey still remained upon the pavement gazing into the gloom that shrouded the humming city. Two or three people, coming from the gallery, spoke to him, but he did not hear them. He was suffering, and he was fighting a battle against the enemy that was ever with him in all the ways of his life. Presently he clenched his right hand with a fierce gesture, raised it, and hailed a hansom. He sprang in and ordered the man in a loud voice to drive to Caryll's flat, and to go fast. The man drove towards the unfashionable north. When he reached Baker Street, Aubrey got out quickly, paid him, entered the big building in which Caryll lived, and rang at her door. Her man answered the summons, and said that her Ladyship had just come in.

"Ask if I can see her," Aubrey said.

The man looked doubtful. He hesitated for a moment, glanced furtively at Aubrey, and seemed almost confused. At length he cleared his throat and became respectfully confidential. He had been with Lady Caryll for some years, having originally been in the service of Sir Reuben.

"To tell the truth, sir," he murmured, "I don't know that her Ladyship can see anybody just at the moment. She—she——"

"She's alone?"

"Oh yes, sir; quite, quite alone. But—well, sir, her Ladyship don't seem quite herself this evening."

"She's not ill? Why, I was with her a moment ago."

"Oh no, sir, not to say ill. But, in fact, sir, I thought her Ladyship looked upset when she came in—very much upset, I might say."

"Please take her my message, Charles; say I specially wish to see her."

The servant retired and returned almost immediately.

"Her Ladyship asks if you can send in a message, sir."

"I can't," Aubrey replied, with a ringing decision that amazed the footman, who again retreated, and was away for a longer time.

"Will you come this way, sir, please?" he said, appearing once more.

He showed Aubrey to the drawing-room. About five minutes passed, then the slow rustle of a gown announced the approach of Lady Caryll. Aubrey had become very pale. He turned towards the door, fixing his eyes upon it. Caryll came in, walking languidly. He had expected to see the strange excitement that she had shown in the gallery still in her face; but it had gone, and she looked as weary, inexpressive, and remote as usual. She shut the door gently and came to him.

"What is it?" she asked. "Forgive me for saying that I am tired and must rest. The gallery was hot and noisy. I was just going to lie down. What is it that you wish to say to me?"

She paused. They stood together on the hearth. She did not look at him. Aubrey felt the chill of her presence, but he struggled against it.

"There is something I want to say—something I must say," he answered.

She looked a little surprised at the firm and unusually resonant sound of his voice.

"What is it?" she repeated.

"Please sit down," he replied; "I will tell you."

She obeyed him, and sat down on a low sofa. He stood looking down on her.

"Caryll," he began, "I want you to grant me the greatest favour a woman can grant to a man."

"And that is——"

Her voice was cold and full of indifference.

"The right to protect her."

She moved slightly on the sofa, clasped her hands one over the other, unclasped them, and said, still in the same level voice—

"You want to protect me! From what?"

"If I said, from yourself!"

"From myself! If you said so, well?"

She never looked at him.

"Would you call me intrusive, impertinent? You couldn't, Caryll, and you know the reason why you couldn't."

"Tell it me."

"The reason is that I love you, and that you are alone. I stand nearer to you than any other man."

"Why?"

"Because of my love."

"That isn't necessarily true. A man's nearness to a woman does not depend merely on his feeling for her."

"On what, then?"

"It depends also on her feeling for him. And that need not be love, but it must be a strong feeling if she and the man are to draw close together."

"But what could it be, then?"

"It might be the reverse of love."

"Dislike!"

"Hatred!"

The word came from her lips like a stone. Aubrey was silent.

"We can draw very near to others in our hatred of them," she continued.

"You're speaking of—of that blackguard we met this afternoon," Aubrey exclaimed abruptly.

He flushed with anger, and was conscious of an extraordinary sensation rising up in his heart—jealousy of Caryll's hatred of this man. She moved again quickly as if she were startled, and laid her hand on a cushion, which she squeezed with her fingers as she replied with a forced carelessness—

"That man—a total stranger! How absurd!"

"But you know him!" Aubrey exclaimed.

As he spoke he sat down beside her, so that he might see her face better.

"You know him!" he repeated roughly, staring hard at her.

Never before had he been so carried away by passion. He forgot himself and his reserve. Self-consciousness utterly forsook him.

"Do you deny it?" he added almost fiercely.

She shot a swift glance of ugly inquiry at him and looked away again.

"So you saw us coming out together?" she said.

"Yes."

"Very well. Yes, I know him. What then?"

"Who introduced him? Who dared to present such a blackguard to you?"

"I see no reason why I should tell you."

Aubrey suddenly returned to self-consciousness. He saw a deadly obstinacy waking in her.

"Forgive me," he said, "and tell me. I ask in your interest."

"If that is so, the question is unnecessary, and I don't answer it."

"Then—then I ask because I love you, because I am—am jealous, Caryll—jealous even of your hatred."

She looked unmoved, even absent-minded. He resolved to tear her from her hideous reveries. He seized her hands—as once he had seized them in the night—and held them fast in his while he continued—

"I love you, I have loved you all this time, and you could love me if you would. I knew it long ago in the night we both remember. I lost you once. I lost you then. But time has given you your freedom again. And I—I too am free."

"Do you know what freedom means?" she said bitterly. "No, or you would never say that now I am free. I—now! This—freedom!"

Her indifference was dying. She drew her hands away from his.

"If this is freedom," she exclaimed, "I was born to be a slave."

She looked up at him.

"He said that," she continued, staring fixedly at him, "and he knew me. Very well; if it is so I must fulfil my destiny."

"Caryll! No, you must be guarded from rushing upon that which is not your destiny."

"I need no guard," she said.

"You need one more than other women."

"Because I am weaker than they are?"

"Because you are stronger. Danger dwells in strength. Don't you know it?"

She said nothing.

"Don't you know it, Caryll?" he repeated. "Weakness walks in the paths of convention. Weakness fears the world, fate, a thousand things; and so it keeps in the safe and familiar ways.

The greatest ruin comes upon those who are strongest, upon the fearless who defy."

She glanced at him with a furtive cunning that, in his excitement, he did not notice.

"Caryll," he said, "to-day I am afraid for you—horribly afraid."

"Why?" she said sharply.

"You go deliberately into danger."

"How?"

"You draw near to—to what you hate—to that man."

He paused. She was silent.

"That shows strength," he went on. "The kind of strength that is dangerous, that I dread in you, that I dread unspeakably. It is my dread that has brought me here. I can't explain it. I don't try to excuse it. I love you. You must accept my love. The time has come when you shall accept it, as a protection, if nothing more."

He spoke resolutely. She glanced at him with amazement.

"You are a stranger to me to-night," she said.

The words set Aubrey's past before him in a pale light, wavering and weak. He felt, perhaps for the first time with complete fulness, that man fashions circumstance and guides the chariot of life. He was stricken almost to the dust by a quick vision of his own nature, at work in the past on the destruction of the happiness that might have been his.

"Give me the right to protect you," he said in a low voice. "Don't let us be strangers any more."

In saying the words he made a mistake of manner. His decision shrank into pleading. The stranger was no longer there, and she felt at once that she sat with a too familiar friend.

"I need no protection," she said quietly, "and I will not accept it. One's fate is not a would-be assassin that can be 'run in' by one's next-door neighbour, or by the acquaintance of one's childhood."

"You are a fatalist?" he said.

Against his will his voice shook.

"I do what I must," she answered. "I go where I must."

"And where are you going? What are you about to do?"

He spoke with a sort of terror of earnestness, looking close into her eyes. His manner, his inquiry, filled her with a repugnance that she herself could not understand. She could only act in accordance with it, and this she did.

"It is useless to continue this discussion," she said. "You make the mistake of a kind and loyal friend. You want to manage my life for me—that is to say, you are anxious to trip up my fate.

Will you never know that you might as well strive to alter the courses of the stars as strive to prevent me from being what I was created to be?"

"And what is that? Oh, Caryll!"

"He said—a slave," she answered slowly.

"A slave! To what? To whom?"

"Perhaps to myself," she said dreamily. "To myself, to my own nature."

And then she fell into a deep and heavy reverie.

He waited for a moment. All his confidence had faded. He felt that she had gone away and left him, had left him almost as the dead leave us when they die.

He stooped to bid her good-bye.

She gave him her hand, but did not look at him.

At the door he turned, and saw her leaning back on the sofa and gazing straight before her with fixed and steady eyes.

As he went out he wondered where she was, and with whom.

CHAPTER XXXVI

On a warm and delicious May night the innumerable clocks of London sang, in straggling chorus, the hour of eight. Upon the pavement of Bow Street a crowd of more or less dirty loungers was gathered to stare upon the carriages that passed slowly down the little hill to the Opera House in Covent Garden. It was the first night of the new season, and the line of vehicles was long. Above the wooden aprons of hansoms stiff men gazed out upon the beggars, the match-boys, the disordered old women in black bonnets selling unauthorised libretti to the ignorant, the round-eyed, murmuring shop-girls, the market porters smoking filthy pipes, the flower maidens—who had never heard of their operatic and Wagnerian sisters—the cheeky children from the Drury Lane Alleys, and the calm police constables from the station over the way. Women leaned back in their sedate night broughams and talked of the coming season. Americans, just arrived from their great country, to conquer the little Island where abide the meet husbands for democracy and dollars, glanced sharply through the windows of smart hired coupés, and gave themselves up to a rather nasal turmoil of comparison. Critics fluttered towards the ugly portico, holding fast their scores, and looking cheerfully important, like men created to support upon magnificently bowed shoulders the big round world of music. Country cousins, rather unnecessarily crimped and too promiscuously beflowered, showed their flushed and excited faces above the creaking doors of four-wheelers. Tiaras gleamed from the elaborate heads of wrinkled dowagers, enthroned in enormous equipages that danced on quivering springs. Here and there an auto-mobile conveyed a self-conscious burden rather uneasily poised above the hidden tank. The moving and pausing procession seemed endless in the night. The horses champed their bits, sending the white foam flying from their nervous lips. From the boxes of the carriages the stern, contemptuous servants surveyed the gaping people on the pavement with cold and repellent eyes. Two large landaus drove up a side street to a private entrance, and some slim ladies, wearing their hair in heavy fringes and gazing straight before them, were escorted over a red carpet by bowing gentlemen, who looked like depressed bulwarks of the State.

The chorus of clocks joined in an uneven statement of the fact that it was a quarter past eight. And still the stream flowed on. From the winter garden above the mighty porch the electric light gleamed out upon the carriage roofs, and the attendants who stood among the palms prophesied that the house would soon be crowded to the doors. In the vestibule a certain number of men who were weary, perhaps, of listening to Italian renderings of the English National Anthem, stood together talking of the musical and social prospects of the season, and examining the people who rustled in looking rather furtively about them, touching their hair, shaking out their gowns and blinking in the light. When a beautiful woman went by, these men hushed their chatter and became instantly observant effigies. When a celebrity passed, they whispered of his fame. When they saw a millionaire, they looked deeply religious, and named his income as a Catholic names her saint. When a popular man drew near, they smiled as if they knew him. Insignificance alone found them distrait, a little blind, a little stolid, and went on its way meekly, too sensible or too well trained to murmur. The crowd grew thicker as people stopped in the vestibule to greet their acquaintance, and to exchange those disjointed scraps of geographical information that make the opening conversations of the season so like the child's guide to knowledge. People just arrived from Naples talked of Mascagni's last opera and of D'Annunzio's latest play to friends who had been among the Kaffirs, and who knew all the latest gossip of Buluwayo and of Cape Town. An ancient Egyptologist, who had recently dug up a temple not a thousand miles from Thebes, spoke enthusiastically of the exquisite colours of the figures on its walls to a venerable friend who had been excavating in Greece, and who could scarcely restrain a sneer at the musty memory of Ti. Singers from all parts of Europe, who had not been engaged by the Syndicate, forgathered to condemn the unfortunate stars who had. A noted German conductor, with blue spectacles and a blonde beard, expressed his indignant grief that the Ring was not to be given to an Italian confrère, who was hand and glove with Mr. Wilson, and who secretly thought Wagner the most pernicious maniac that ever gave his madness to the world. Some stern Englishmen, with prominent noses and straight figures, spoke coldly together about grouse prospects, the future of China, a new Spanish dancer, and a new "pick-me-up" called "Amber Swizzle." They dropped their G's, clipped their sentences more viciously than a gardener clips a too vivacious yew hedge, and adjourned wearily to an omnibus box full of opera-glasses to spy out the nakedness of the land of fashion.

Presently Paul Villet and his wife stepped out of a neat coupé with bright yellow wheels, and swept into the lobby with all the plump assurance of success. Villet was now so much the reverse of starved in appearance that unkind persons called him distressingly obese. He walked like a pouter pigeon sunning itself on a roof, wore his hair crimped and his moustache waxed, spoke languidly, but with an air of brutal authority, and never mentioned the name of any one who was not perfectly well known. His wife grew daily more deliberately eccentric. Her elongated gaiety mind was now applauded as the mind of a genius. Her freaks were chronicled by those unfortunate ladies who earn a precarious living by writing about people whom they will never know, and houses that they will never enter. She waxed offensive, and her flippancies were not seldom unworthy of the bar. But did that matter? She had been "accepted." She had even been to Court. Tolerated by the right set, she was worshipped by the wrong. Young men found it did them no harm to think her handsome, and old men liked her because she knew how to tell smoking-room stories with an innocent air, and could appreciate the peculiar brazen wit that is the delight of the old campaigner and doting citizen of the world. Her coffee parties after the theatre had become the rage, and a Russian Grand-Duke had condescended to join her in her favourite diversion of building card houses for the accommodation of living beans.

In the lobby the Villets were joined by Albert Sprigg, who had just arrived from Paris with a stronger French accent, a more elaborate manner, a more seductive voice, and a more tripping acquaintance with titles than ever. His round and rosy face shone with self-satisfaction as he distributed bows—most carefully and conspicuously foreign—to those happy aristocrats whom he knew, screwing up his small eyes in a fascinating manner at every woman with money, and laying his plump hand familiarly on the shoulders of those enviable beings whom he called "useful men." When he perceived the Villets he hastened forward, took the left hand of Madame Villet in his left hand, and held her gently clasped while he murmured, in French, sly compliments upon her appearance, and upon her strangely done hair which made her look like a dissipated Esquimaux.

"So good of you to take me into your box," he said presently, making a grimace, like an amorous butcher-boy, at Madame Villet. "Before we go to it, I want to show you both something."

He looked archly secretive. Madame Villet, who was the most inquisitive woman in London, was immediately on the alert.

"What is it, Boo-boo?" she said. "Now don't be tiresome, but tell me quick."

"What is it, mon cher?" asked Villet, arranging his buttonhole and staring through his eyeglass. "Has the little princess followed you from Paris?"

"Ah! give me a day's respite! She will be here to-morrow! Come, and I will show you!"

He led them to the curved passage that runs behind the boxes on the ground floor of the opera-house. Upon the white doors of these boxes are printed the names of their owners. Passing rapidly by many of these doors, he stopped at length before one next to the steps down which the stall-holders make their way to their seats. On the door was printed:

"Vernon Demetrius, Esquire."

Mr. Sprigg waved his plump hand towards this name.

"There!" he said.

Madame Villet read the name and uttered an exclamation. Paul Villet threw up his hands, which were encased in very tight lavender gloves.

"Mon Dieu!" he ejaculated. "They will be here to-night! All London is talking of that tragedy! All London is asking me questions! Am I Providence that I should know every secret of such a woman? It is true that——"

"But who do you think is exactly opposite?" interrupted Mr. Sprigg, glistening with vulgar satisfaction at his power of revelation: "Guess!"

"Aubrey Herrick!" cried Madame Villet.

"Fifi St. Ormyn! She said at first she wouldn't come. But she can't keep away. They're not on speaking terms, of course. She's simply furious!"

He was walking now with the Villets towards their box.

"Has she discovered who this Demetrius really is, Boo-boo?" said Madame Villet. "A cad, of course. One knows that—and a beggar. So, quite impossible! But what else? Is it true—a shocking thing I've heard—that he's quite well known to the Paris police? Surely——"

She entered her box, followed by the two men.

The Opera House was already very full. Most of the boxes contained occupants—women who sat well forward to show their gowns and their jewels, men hidden in the shadow and whispering gently of a thousand things unconnected with music. Many of these men were speaking of Mr. Demetrius, and the women, too, murmured his name, asking if it were not perhaps assumed, taken by an adventurer for the purpose of making an impression upon the credulous persons who are susceptible to sound, and who are easily won to worship by any hint of the unusual. Almost everybody in the boxes knows almost everybody else on the first night of an opera season at Covent Garden. The attention of more than half this intimate world was certainly concentrated upon the box of Mr. Demetrius during the performance of the first act. And many people in the stalls turned perpetually to level their opera-glasses at his red curtains and his empty chairs.

Seven days before, the following announcement had appeared in the *Morning Post* :—

"We are informed that the Lady Caryll Allabruth, widow of the late Sir Reuben Allabruth, Bart., was married yesterday to Vernon Demetrius, Esq."

The wedding had taken place at a registrar's office.

As nobody in Lady Caryll's world had ever heard of Mr. Demetrius, the amazement caused by this paragraph was intense. Curiosity was roused. Scandal desired to be busy. But scandal had literally nothing to feed upon, for the ignorance of the smart set concerning Lady Caryll's new husband was singularly complete. His name and his personality were both unfamiliar.

Lady St. Ormyn, who was besieged with questions, was scarcely wiser than the rest of society. She had seen Mr. Demetrius, but only after the marriage had taken place. Her account of him was deplorable. She could not say where Caryll had picked him up. She could get no information about him from her daughter or from any one else. She could not conceive why Caryll had married him. She could only affirm hysterically that he was impossible, totally impossible, and that she and Lord St. Ormyn had resolved to have nothing to do with him. And she reiterated her firm conviction that Caryll had never properly recovered from the shock of Sir Reuben's death, and ought not to be considered responsible for her actions.

This view of the case was not generally adopted. Those who knew Caryll were all impressed with her strength rather than with her weakness. The men were specially disinclined to believe her capable of hysterical folly in giving herself to an "outsider" merely because he had a handsome face or an attractive manner.

"Lady Caryll doesn't care tuppence for men," they said. "She never did. There must be some other reason."

What could it be? Both men and women asked that question, turning their opera-glasses towards the empty box of Mr. Demetrius.

Lady St. Ormyn was in her box next the stage with Mrs. Luffa Parkinson and Mr. Fraser, to whom she was tearfully recounting her woes in a voice that distracted the singers and drove the conductor almost to despair.

Towards the middle of the act Monsieur Anneau had come into the house. He was not singing to-night, and had a stall in one of the back rows. But he did not go to it immediately. He stood for a time in the vestibule, glancing fiercely about him and talking to one or two friends. Then he strode to the passage behind the boxes on the ground tier, and began to pace up and down restlessly. He seemed to be on the watch, and the attendants were surprised by the strangeness of his demeanour. When he met any one whom he knew, he smiled and bowed with his habitual magnificence; but when he was for a moment alone his face contracted, his eyes gleamed with anger, and once or twice he muttered some words to himself, as if the impulse to express his emotion audibly had become uncontrollable and he had forgotten that he was not isolated, beyond the reach of curious eyes and ears. More than once he paused before the box of Mr. Demetrius, stared at the name printed on the white door and surrounded by narrow gilt bars, then resumed his walk with increasing agitation.

Lady Rangecliffe did not often go to the opera, but it chanced that she had been lent a box for the opening night by a friend, and presently, as Monsieur Anneau turned from his contemplation of the name that was on so many tongues, she passed him, accompanied by Aubrey. Lady Rangecliffe, who knew Monsieur Anneau very slightly, bowed and went on. Aubrey, who was pale, and who looked older than usual, and weary like a man recovering from an illness, nodded and was following his mother when Monsieur Anneau stopped him.

"So you have come!" he said, staring into Aubrey's face as if he sought to feed his fury on the sorrow of another. "You have come too! Ah! my friend, you have lived in ignorance so long. I know! I have watched you. Well, to-night you will understand. To-night your eyes of the blind will be opened at last. Your dream—your foolish dream will die. Do you hear?"

Aubrey drew back haughtily. His lips stiffened. His face became hard and inexpressive as he turned to follow his mother, who was now at the foot of the staircase which leads to the Grand Tier. But Monsieur Anneau stepped forward, caught him by the shoulder, and held him for a moment forcibly.

"No one understands this crazy marriage," the singer said. "Do you? No—not yet! But look—look close when your white dream lady comes, when she comes forward into the light. Look close, and you will understand it, and at last you will know her, as I knew her long ago, as he knew her—he, that dead man."

While he spoke Aubrey's face changed. Interest woke in it, excitement, a piercing fervour of interrogation. But he said nothing, and when Monsieur Anneau's great hand dropped from his shoulder, he followed his mother quickly. He found her seating herself in the box.

"Anneau wanted to speak to me, Mater," he said, shutting the door.

His brain was on fire, but his voice was calm.

"What a full house!" he added.

He came to the front of the box, sat down by his mother and glanced round coolly, nodding to some of his friends. But his hands were shaking. He could not keep them still. He laid them on the arms of his chair, which he grasped tightly. He gazed down upon the brilliant house and a cloud seemed to float before his eyes. It was heavy and black. It rolled away, and then the lights, the flashing of the jewels worn by the women, the colours of their gowns and of the decorations of the Theatre mingled together, and shrank into a tiny circle of fierce yellow whose ragged edge was bordered by vivid violet. He shut his eyes for a moment. He heard a noise of music; of violins, of a trembling horn, of some one singing with a clear soprano voice. This noise sounded faint and far away, and seemed to be enclosed within the yellow and violet circle which he could still see very distinctly. It vibrated, quivered violently, flashed like a firework and disappeared. And as it disappeared the music suddenly grew terrifically loud and menacing.

"Aubrey, you are ill?" said his mother's voice anxiously.

"No, Mater," he answered. "Who is singing?"

He took up the programme that lay on the edge of the box and looked at it carefully. And now his hand was steady. He was master of himself. He fixed his eyes on the empty box of Mr. Demetrius. Every other box that he could see was occupied.

"It's a tremendous house," he said.

Lady Rangecliffe nodded. Her black gown rustled as she moved incessantly. To-night she was suffering from a more definite return of the malady of her childhood than she had endured for many years. She looked away from her son unnaturally, not even glancing at him when she spoke to him.

"Very full," she said. "What is the opera?"

Aubrey told her.

"It's very odd," she said. "I know it quite well, but it seems unfamiliar to-night, I think——"

She checked herself abruptly, recognising that the travail of her heart rendered all things strange to her just then. Putting her opera-glasses to her short-sighted eyes she glanced round the Theatre.

"Only one box empty," she said nervously. "I wonder whose it is."

"That box belongs to Mr. Demetrius, Mater," Aubrey said calmly.

Lady Rangecliffe nearly let her glasses fall. She looked at her son, opened her lips to speak, then closed them without saying anything, and looked away.

Aubrey remained motionless, keeping his eyes intently fixed upon the empty box. There were two arm-chairs in it, with red damask seats and white and gold arms. He stared at them until he saw two figures seated in them, a woman and a man—Lady Caryll and the tall stranger whom she had met at the private view, whom she had trembled before, whom she had hated, whom she had married.

Why? What did the singer mean by his strange words? And how could Lady Caryll, in silence, tell Aubrey the reason of her mad act, of her new and horrible departure?

The woman and the man faded. Aubrey saw again the red damask seats of the chairs, their white and gold arms.

Then the music grew louder, travelling towards a climax. Instruments that had been silent began to speak with their various and almost human voices, and Aubrey, being in an unnatural condition of excitement, sorrow, anticipation, wonder, heard the orchestra unnaturally. He felt that he was listening no longer to the voices of lifeless instruments, but to the voices of live and hidden commentators upon the mysteries of destiny. Some of these commentators spoke of him, some of Lady Caryll. They recounted pitilessly, made deductions, from facts drew inferences, and founded statements upon a broad basis of unanswerable truth. He heard them clearly, and some of them he hated more than others. There was a certain flute, which was to him like the thin but pellucid voice of conscience penetrating with consummate ease through the turmoil of the more fierce and louder voices which strove in vain to overwhelm it. This flute worked upon him as a file works upon iron. It was at the same time a voice and a weapon, whispering and plying its way through a resisting substance. He heard it distinctly telling him of his weakness, and laying bare to him present reality as a result of his reserve. And it laid this bare like a penetrating intellect that lays bare truth, and like a scalpel that lays bare some hidden portion of a quivering body. His nerves shrieked under it and his soul cried out. Nevertheless he had to endure. Sometimes this flute, this voice of conscience, this deadly trickling stream of truth was lost in the chorus of the voices of the other commentators. They became importunate as the sea when a black storm expands within it, and seems to enlarge it. And they led Aubrey fiercely from one scene to another of his past. They seemed, then, to give themselves up to curious fantasies, and to become imitative.

One instrument, or set of instruments, resembled the voice of Monsieur Anneau singing " Crépuscule " to the sunset long ago in the garden at Epsom. And the sound—as sound can, or as scent —called up not only an earthly scene full of details, but also simultaneously the exact mental condition of the hearer set in that scene. Aubrey saw the red gold-fish moving blandly around their artificial home, gleaming and growing dim as they vanished in the opaque shadows. He saw the long locks of the wisteria rustling gently in the cool breeze of evening. He saw the melting primrose of the imaginative sky and the soft darkness of the suggestive trees. He saw a girl's frosty yellow hair and long grey eyes. Colour and music flowed together. Song became the divinity of colour, and colour the inmost secrecy of song. And, born of them, and of all the wonder of the evening atmosphere, that something strange which dwells far down in the deep recesses of each human being seemed suddenly to live again in Aubrey and to be restless in its life. Again the voices called to it, and it listened to them with pain. Again, in its remote place, it felt the touch of magic and longed for the wonder that it could never see. Again it aspired, and, flying beyond the realm of reason, knew what it could not prove, loved what it could not know.

Another instrument stole in. That scene was shattered. Now he saw the blood-red stars, like eyes, looking out among the leaves of the chestnut trees and the green glow-worms crawling along the dusky garden paths. The fountain played, leaping towards the crescent of the little moon, and on the grass the sacred dew lay like the tears of God. And there was a white robe in the distance, like the robe of a ghost that treads a sorrowful round on the dark nights of the year. Aubrey followed that robe. He heard the voices of horns, those misty human voices that have talked with all the fairies on all the midsummer eves. They set the trees before him, and the white and gliding ghost. And he followed. But the wood was very dark and far larger, far more impenetrable than the little wood at Epsom. And the white robe fluttered on as if its phantom wearer sought ever deeper recesses, and more sad and sombre paths. Where could it be going, and what could be its quest? Now, for a moment, in the towering blackness of the wood that had become a forest, the white-robed ghost was like a white butterfly fluttering forward with trembling, outstretched wings, and Aubrey heard among the trees a deep and muffled murmur, like the murmur of a weary city hidden somewhere in the gloom. The forest became a jungle full of amazing undergrowths and inextricable mysteries of intertwining plants. Terrible flowers, with gigantic folded petals, slept all around him. Among them were dying lilies. He heard the beating of the wings of monstrous bats. A trumpet in the orchestra typified the flowers. They woke as he passed through them, yawning with brazen mouths. The butterfly was far before him, a white shadow in the gloom. Now all the flowers were gone. He had passed beyond the regions of any flowers. All around he saw but one sort of plant, growing rankly in pestilent abundance, a sickly and haggard plant, with flaccid leaves, round the edges of which crept a horrible decay. The air was full of the odour of death. Dense and noisome mists rose from the yielding swamp beneath his feet, and the white butterfly vanished in the dark.

The little flute spoke again in its pitilessly clear voice, telling him that he might have rescued the butterfly if he had not delayed, if he had had more courage, more reliance on his manhood.

Then other voices arose. Again he seemed to be following the dolorous progress of the ghost. And now he could see what led it forward—the chimera, or the Will-o'-the-wisp, it eternally pursued. Far before it in its path there shone a flitting light, green, mysterious, and delusive, moving for ever towards some hidden place. Sometimes this light was high up, as if mounting into heaven to take its place among the stars. Sometimes it was low, as if sinking into the earth. Sometimes it shone more fiercely a few feet above the earth. And then, as in a vision, Aubrey saw beneath and around it the shadow of a hand that held it, saw above it the shadow of a dim and whimsical face. Some goblin grasped it, and ran onward with it in the eternal mazes of the wood. He longed to see the goblin's face more clearly, and he bent his mind upon it, commanding the goblin to show itself to him plainly. Then the green light flashed, and he saw a Mandarin sitting cross-legged and with a heathen smile upon its flexible lips; and the mandarin had Sir Reuben's face. The green light flashed again. Now Aubrey saw no face, but only something dark, black and forbidding like a mask. While he looked on it the white ghost rushed forward, lifted eager lips, and kissed the ugly thing. Then the green light shone with an abnormal brilliance, and Aubrey saw that it was an emerald, and that it lay upon Caryll's breast. He gazed upon it. The noise of the orchestra rose in a roar and ceased. The curtain fell. Upon the red damask of the chairs in the empty box of Demetrius there floated again two figures of a woman and a man. On the white and gold arms of the chairs rested human arms. The figures stayed in silence. They grew more clear. Aubrey started. He heard all around him the hum of conversation. He heard the rustle of his mother's gown as she moved. But still he seemed to see Lady Caryll, with the great emerald glowing on her breast. Yes, it was she, and she was dressed in white like the ghost. Beside her was the tall man whom Aubrey had seen at the Private View. She spoke to him and smiled happily. Then she sat forward in the box, as if she wished to be more plainly seen by the crowded house. Aubrey said to his mother quietly—

"Can I have the glasses, Mater, please?"

"Yes, Aubrey," said Lady Rangecliffe.

She handed them to him, and, turning away from him, pretended to glance about the house. It seemed to her as if many hours passed before she heard Aubrey move again. At length he laid the glasses down carefully upon the ledge of the box.

"Mater," he said, "Lady Caryll has found the emerald that was stolen from her. She is wearing it to-night."

His voice was perfectly calm. He got up and went out of the box without another word.

Meanwhile the entrance of Lady Caryll and Mr. Demetrius had caused a sensation in the crowded house. In all directions men and women were putting up their opera-glasses to gaze at her and at her companion. Lady St. Ormyn, half-hidden behind a curtain, examined her daughter with round and agitated eyes, then whispered eagerly to Mrs. Luffa Parkinson and Mr. Fraser, whose pantomime of astonishment and deprecation was most expressive. A prince, who had once resolved to know more of Lady Caryll, stared at her from an omnibus box, and recalled a certain ball to the recollection of a gentleman of his suite. As to the Villets and Albert Sprigg, they were really in a turmoil.

"How utterly changed she looks!" exclaimed Madame Villet. "Why, she's perfectly radiant. Is she in love with the man?"

"She looks as she did that night—that night when I saw her first," ejaculated Paul Villet, screwing his eyeglass into his eye to glare at the woman who had drawn him from the fangs of poverty and laid upon him the curse of his fame. "A goddess, ma foi!"

He smacked his sensual lips.

Albert Sprigg protruded his fat face between his host and hostess and half shut his eyes.

"Delicious!" he murmured. "The little princess would be jealous of her—jealous to salt tears."

"But," cried Madame Villet suddenly, "what's she staring at? What's she touching? Has she some ornament? But she never wears jewels now. She has none—since the emerald was stolen."

"Mon Dieu!" exclaimed Paul Villet, bringing his hand down violently on the shoulder of Albert Sprigg, who started effeminately and looked elaborately disgusted. "Mon Dieu! It cannot —it cannot be!"

"Mon cher Paul," began Mr. Sprigg, "you really——"

But Villet, who was leaning forward excitedly, took no notice of his friend's injury.

"What is it, Paul?" twittered Madame Villet. "Are you going to have a fit?"

"It is—it is the emerald!" he cried. "Mon Dieu! She wears it on her breast!"

"The emerald!" exclaimed his wife. "Impossible! You are mad, Paul!"

"You must be mad, mon cher," cried Albert Sprigg, getting up from his seat in great haste. "Give me the glasses."

He snatched them rudely from Madame Villet, who was taking them, stared for a moment at Lady Caryll, and then said, with no French accent—

"By Jove! I believe you're right! I'll find out for certain."

He hurried out of the box. In an instant they saw him standing in the stalls just under the box of Demetrius. He returned to them greatly excited.

"You're right, Paul," he said. "It is the emerald. Every one's talking of it. But what a miracle! Has it fallen from the skies?"

"Was it ever stolen?" cried Madame Villet sarcastically. "Who knows? Women——"

She checked herself, glancing narrowly at Albert Sprigg. He smiled disagreeably.

"Women—exactly!" he said.

Madame Villet gazed at Lady Caryll with bitter eyes, and then at her companion.

"He's a handsome man, rather," she said. "But abominable looking. Where can she have picked him up? Why can she have married him?"

At this moment Monsieur Anneau entered the box. His eyes were flashing and he looked tremendously excited. Madame Villet turned upon him.

"You know of the miracle?" she said.

"The miracle!"

"Of the emerald—of the emerald's return!"

"Is it a miracle?" he said.

An evil smile ran over his dark face.

"Perhaps it is," he said. "Every one talks as if it were!"

"Well, but you—was it ever stolen?" began Madame Villet. "What do you think?"

"I?" said Monsieur Anneau. "I?"

He shrugged his great shoulders.

"I never think seriously. I am a citizen of the world. But—if I thought——"

He paused, and looked with almost ferocious significance at the three faces that were turned to his.

"Yes, yes!" cried Madame Villet, restlessly tapping the ledge of the box with her hand. "Tell me—tell me!"

"I might perhaps be led to fancy — we artists, you know, madame, are full of fancies — that Miladi had had a stroke of strange good fortune."

"How? How?" cried Madame Villet.

"How, mon cher?" ejaculated Villet.

"How the deuce——?" exclaimed Albert Sprigg—nearing Greenwich, and leaving Paris in the distance.

"In marrying the man who—well, let us say, who has been taking care of her treasure, of the only thing she loves, for so many months. And perhaps I might be led to fancy, further, that having won a rich bride, he has been moved to generosity, and has given back her jewel to her as his wedding gift."

His hearers were silent for a moment. Astonishment deprived them of the powers of speech. At length Madame Villet said—

"Demetrius, the thief who robbed her! But she would have recognised him!"

"Did he not wear a mask?" said Monsieur Anneau.

"But—but why should she have been drawn to him, why should she have married him?"

"Did not her jewel call her from its hiding-place, draw her to it whether she would or no? Piff! I only hazard a theory, an absurd and childish theory, at which I am the first to laugh."

As he spoke he burst into a great laugh that was like the laugh of Mephistopheles at the end of the garden-scene in *Faust*, but his eyes were full of anger and his hearers were petrified. There was a moment of uneasy silence. Then Albert Sprigg dashed out of the box to spread abroad the theory of Monsieur Anneau.

He did his work so well—like a good conversationalist, allowing theory to develop into fact—that before the third act was over all Lady Caryll's world agreed that she had linked her fate with a thief, in order to get back the treasure she had lost; though how she had discovered that Demetrius was the thief, or how, having discovered it, she had wedded, instead of denouncing him, nobody could explain.

Aubrey heard the rumour, and, as the opera was nearing its end, he said to Lady Rangecliffe—

"Mater!"

"Yes, Aubrey," she answered.

"Will you do something for me?"

"Yes, Aubrey. What is it?"

"I must tell you something first. I believe Mr. Demetrius to be a backguard. Now I'll ask you—will you call on his wife to-morrow and let everybody know you've done it?"

"All right, Aubrey," Lady Rangecliffe said, in a very low voice.

The orchestra played the last chord. The curtain fell, and the crowd surged into the vestibule, where grooms with staring eyes stood in eager rows to claim the notice of their employers. People gathered together in mobs, waiting for their carriages, and discussing the great scandal of the evening with animated voices.

Suddenly an attendant outside shouted :

" Mr. Demetrius' carriage ! Mr. Demetrius' carriage ! "

A hundred pretty heads turned towards the glass doors. Men moved quickly forward, and innumerable conversations died away.

" Mr. Demetrius' carriage ! " shouted the attendant more fiercely.

There was an agitation at the back of the crowd. An elaborately refined and over-polite man's voice said several times, and each time with an increasing and more intolerable sweetness—

" Will you have the great kindness to permit this lady to pass ? Thank you ! Thank you ! Will you courteously permit—Thank you ! I am obliged ! "

And Lady Caryll, with one hand on her new husband's arm, passed slowly through the staring throng. There was a defiant smile on her face, but she looked straight before her.

No one spoke to her. Lady Rangecliffe had already gone.

No one bowed to her. She did not pass by Aubrey.

Every one gazed at her white face and shining eyes, then turned to stare at her solicitous companion, who smiled meretriciously as he continued to repeat,—with a damning crescendo of gentlemanliness, as a wit said afterwards at White's—

" If you will most courteously permit me—one moment—allow this lady to reach her carriage, I beg of you. Thank you—thank you—I am indeed greatly obliged."

As Lady Caryll got into her carriage, a detective who was standing outside with a companion, smiled, jerked his thumb at Mr. Demetrius, and remarked—

" Paris Jack's in luck ! "

The other man laughed as the carriage drove away.

Aubrey had seen his mother off. He meant to walk to Jermyn Street. As he was coming from the cloak-room to the door he chanced to meet Adela Reckitt, the white-haired American poetess whom he had taken into dinner at Lady St. Ormyn's on the night of the festivities at Epsom. She stopped him, looked at him with a curious gentleness of compassion that he could not resent— it was so sincere, so humane, so incurious—and said to him softly—

" Is it not true that on the famous emerald there are engraved three figures ? "

" Yes," he said, wondering.

"The Soul, and two Pleasures?"

"Yes."

"Only two," she said. "Remember that. Pleasures die—but the Soul lives on."

She vanished in the crowd, but her words remained with Aubrey. He seemed to hold Caryll again in his arms, to feel again that she was still a dreamer, and that he alone had the power to wake her at last from her dream to true understanding, to true and beautiful life.

One Pleasure had passed into the shades.

As Aubrey walked home under the stars he, the true, the eternal dreamer, gave himself to his dreams once more. He saw the light of a tender sunset struggling in the arms of a cruel, wintry sky. He listened for the inner voice which he still believed to be murmuring in the Soul that was borne away by Pleasures.

. . . .

And surely, far away among the roses of his Eastern Paradise, the cunning artificer, who had graven his irony upon a jewel long ago, smiled as he looked down and saw the dreamer wandering in the night among the voices of the City—smiled, thinking of the generations that had vanished, and of all the dreamers who had died, since he drew forth his tiny tools in a shadowy bazaar, and leaned above his shining scroll in a strange country of the Sun.

THE END

Printed by BALLANTYNE, HANSON & Co.
Edinburgh & London

www.ingramcontent.com/pod-product-compliance
Lightning Source LLC
Chambersburg PA
CBHW022119290426
44112CB00008B/731